THE ARTS AND CRAFTS MOVEMENT IN CALIFORNIA

LIVING THE GOOD LIFE

THE ARTS AND CRAFTS

Kenneth R. Trapp

WITH ESSAYS BY *Leslie Greene Bowman,*
Bruce Kamerling, Cheryl Robertson,
Joseph A. Taylor, David C. Streatfield,
Karen J. Weitze, Richard Guy Wilson

THE OAKLAND MUSEUM   OAKLAND, CALIFORNIA

MOVEMENT IN CALIFORNIA

LIVING THE GOOD LIFE

ABBEVILLE PRESS PUBLISHERS   New York London Paris

∾ "The Arts and Crafts Movement in California: Living the Good Life" is produced by The Oakland Museum with major support from the Lila Wallace–Reader's Digest Fund.

∾ Initial support for the exhibition and book was provided by The Henry Luce Foundation, Inc.

∾ Additional support was received from the National Endowment for the Arts, a federal agency; The Oakland Museum Women's Board; the National Endowment for the Humanities, a federal agency; The L. J. Skaggs and Mary C. Skaggs Foundation; and The Kahn Foundation.

EXHIBITION ITINERARY

The Oakland Museum: February 27–August 15, 1993
Renwick Gallery of the National Museum of American Art, Smithsonian Institution, Washington, D.C.: October 8, 1993–January 9, 1994
Cincinnati Art Museum: February 18–April 17, 1994

Front cover: Detail of Claycraft Potteries, *Tile,* c. 1926. See plate 56.
Back cover: Arequipa Pottery (Frederick Hürten Rhead?), *Vase,* c. 1912–13. See plate 108.
Frontispiece: Detail of Frederick H. W. Leuders, *Electrical Lamp,* c. 1910. See plate 20.

EDITORS: NANCY GRUBB AND FRONIA SIMPSON
DESIGNER: JOEL AVIROM
PRODUCTION EDITOR: SARAH KEY
PRODUCTION SUPERVISOR: DANA COLE
PICTURE EDITORS: VICTORIA CARLSON AND KENNETH R. TRAPP

First edition

Library of Congress Cataloging-in-Publication Data

The arts and crafts movement in California : living the good life /
    [edited by] Kenneth R. Trapp ; with essays by Leslie Greene Bowman . . . et al.].
        p.   cm.
    Includes bibliographical references and index.
    ISBN 1-55859-393-4   1-55859-493-0 (pbk)
    1. Arts and crafts movement—California—History—19th century. 2. Arts and crafts movement—California—History—20th century. I. Trapp, Kenneth R. II. Bowman, Leslie Greene. III. Oakland Museum.
NK1141.A78   1993
745'.09794' 09034—dc20   92-28352
                                                                        CIP

CONTENTS

FOREWORD

In keeping with its commitment to collect, preserve, study, and interpret the visual arts of California, The Oakland Museum proudly presents *The Arts and Crafts Movement in California: Living the Good Life.* We hope that this book and exhibition will stimulate further research into a fascinating chapter of California's—indeed, America's—history.

A project of this scope succeeds by the efforts and the goodwill of many people. The Oakland Museum gratefully acknowledges the generous support of those who have funded this book and the exhibition it accompanies. Major support came from the Lila Wallace–Reader's Digest Fund. Initial support for the book was provided by The Henry Luce Foundation, Inc. The National Endowment for the Arts and the National Endowment for the Humanities, both federal agencies, awarded grants for this project. Additional support was provided by The Oakland Museum Women's Board. Early support for the project came from The Kahn Foundation and The L. J. Skaggs and Mary C. Skaggs Foundation.

The eight authors who wrote the essays for this book deserve our deepest gratitude for their contributions. Without their tireless commitment, and that of Abbeville Press, this book would never have been realized. We are also profoundly grateful to the lenders who have generously shared their collections with the public. Their willingness to part with treasured works of art for an extended period of time has made the success of the exhibition possible.

I am pleased to acknowledge the tireless work of the volunteers of The Oakland Museum Women's Board and its Collectors Gallery and of the Art Guild, all of whom contributed to the success of this undertaking. The unwavering commitment to the museum and its programs made by the members of these vital organizations is greatly appreciated.

Although many people have been involved in the planning and implementation of *The Arts and Crafts Movement in California,* no one has been more committed to the project than Kenneth R. Trapp, curator of decorative arts. He provided the vision and the direction for this demanding project, and he saw it through with exemplary patience and perseverance. I am most grateful to him.

Philip E. Linhares
Chief Curator of Art

1. Ernest A. Batchelder. *Firescreen,* 1904. Painted repoussé tin in oak frame, 36 x 29⁵⁄₁₆ x 8¾ in. Christy and Scott Kendrick.

7

INTRODUCTION

Kenneth R. Trapp

alifornians welcomed the Arts and Crafts movement with an enthusiasm that rivaled its only slightly earlier reception in highly industrialized Massachusetts, New York, and Illinois. The ideals of the movement were energetically propagated in California by advocates and practitioners who came from elsewhere—usually the East, but surprisingly often from Great Britain and Northern Europe. California's reception of the Arts and Crafts movement was, however, more than merely a cordial adoption of an eastern gospel. Inspired by California's Mediterranean climate and paradisiacal landscape, by its colorful Spanish-Mexican past, by its flora and fauna that offered rich sources of subjects and decorative designs, artists and craftspeople in California created a unique regional variant of the Arts and Crafts movement, from the mid-1890s to the 1930s. That they created designs equally as brilliant in conception and execution as any made elsewhere in the United States is evident in the movement's architecture, art pottery, ceramic tiles, metalwork, stained glass, leatherwork, furniture, needlework, and bookmaking.

The transmission of the Arts and Crafts movement to California and its evolution on the Pacific Coast paralleled the development of the movement elsewhere in the United States. One important similarity is that the movement in California was rooted in Arts and Crafts guilds and other organizations that fostered both the ideology of the movement and the creativity of individual practitioners. Further, California public schools were strongly committed to manual-arts education, which taught students the principal tenets of the movement—in particular, the belief that the union of hand, head, and heart in handicraft yielded therapeutic value. Another similarity is that artists often used the local landscape as a wellspring of inspiration. In California this meant that artists were challenged by the wealth of natural subjects as close as their windows. Whether depicting the golden poppy, the Torrey pine, the redwood, or the sublime majesties of Yosemite, California's artists extolled the state's natural beauty and bounty.

2. Furniture Shop (Lucia K. Mathews). *Folding Screen,* c. 1910–15. Framed plywood panels with oil, gilding, and oil-resin glaze, 72 x 80 in. The Oakland Museum; Gift of Concours d'Antiques, Art Guild.

Like its counterparts elsewhere in the United States, the Arts and Crafts movement in California was fundamentally a white, middle-class phenomenon. At a time when American and European artists were searching the world for designs and inspiration, especially from the decorative vocabularies of the Far East, it is ironic that the Chinese and Japanese inhabitants of California, whose artistic traditions were so eagerly appropriated, were themselves ignored as an aesthetic resource. One scans the roster of practitioners of the Arts and Crafts in California in vain for Asian participants—or for Native Americans, Mexicans, and African-Americans.

However much the movement in California resembled its counterparts in other regions, there were also noteworthy differences. For example, although the state was a lucrative market for Arts and Crafts goods created elsewhere in the United States, very few California Arts and Crafts producers sent objects to eastern markets. And the sources of most Arts and Crafts goods in California were small workshops that operated too briefly to assert artistic identities strong enough to influence the larger movement, either inside or outside the state.

Another feature that distinguished California's Arts and Crafts movement was its embrace of elements from its Catholic Spanish-Mexican heritage, which remained most visible in the twenty-one Franciscan missions from San Diego to Sonoma. Reminders of California's colonial era, the missions offered subjects rich with nostalgic allusions to a romanticized past. For newcomer Californians eager to anchor themselves in tradition, whatever their political and religious views, the missions were convenient symbols of a special history, inspiring a West Coast equivalent of the Colonial Revival in the Northeast.

What most distinguishes the Arts and Crafts movement in California from the movement elsewhere in the United States is the special bond that Californians had with nature. Whether they lived in the deserts of the far south, along the coast, in the fertile Central Valley, or in the rugged, mountainous north, Californians were never far from the wild. Builders, architects, and garden designers often took the land into account by incorporating nature into the daily living experience. It is no accident that the detached bungalow became the domestic architectural form most identified with California during the Arts and Crafts period. In addition to its spectacular scenery, California is blessed with an equally important advantage: mild climates that encourage outdoor living in all seasons. That California was extolled as an Eden resulted as much from the restored health many newcomers enjoyed as from the state's magnificent scenery and delightful climate.

The Arts and Crafts Movement in California: Living the Good Life presents nine essays by eight authors exploring the major manifestations of the Arts and Crafts in the Golden State. It takes as its starting point the movement's ideal of "the good life," in which the virtues of simple living and high thinking were complemented by material well-being.

3. California China Products Company. *Four-Tile Mural,* c. 1913. Machine-pressed fired clay with slip-trailed design and multicolored glaze, 6 x 24 in. San Diego Historical Society; Gift of Kathleen Suros.

Previous books on the Arts and Crafts movement have largely shied away from attempts to define it, presenting instead a chronological narrative with little interpretation. Accordingly, it seemed essential to include here introductory and concluding essays that explain some of the issues important to the movement, both in general and in California, thus providing a context for the other essays. Such important elements of the movement in California as garden design, domestic interiors and rustic resorts, and the ceramic-tile industries—all ignored or slighted in earlier publications—are addressed here. The three essays that are most focused on Arts and Crafts objects—particularly pottery, furniture, and metalwork—have been organized according to where those objects were created, in the three major urban centers of the state at the turn of the century: the San Francisco Bay Area; the Southland, from Santa Barbara to Los Angeles and Pasadena and east to the Inland Empire of Redlands and Riverside; and San Diego.

Several considerations guided the choice of objects for the exhibition. In an effort to expand knowledge of the Arts and Crafts movement in California, we have included as many pieces as possible that have not previously been published, along with some well-known and well-loved "icons." Several critical questions were asked in determining the suitability of an object for inclusion: In what context and under what circumstances was it made? To what extent does it embody the Arts and Crafts ideal of design appropriate to its intended use? Was hand craftsmanship an important factor in its creation?

Finally, we confess to finding some comfort in regarding the Arts and Crafts movement as a kind of dynamic organism that grew and adapted and mutated into forms that confound any attempt at taxonomy. Indeed, that splendid diversity is what most fascinates us as we seek to understand the vital forces that energized the Arts and Crafts movement in California.

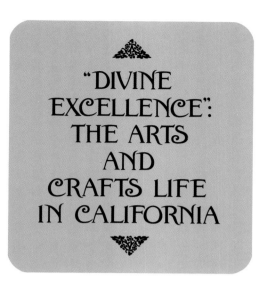

"DIVINE EXCELLENCE": THE ARTS AND CRAFTS LIFE IN CALIFORNIA

Richard Guy Wilson

4. A. Page Brown, designer, and Alexander J. Forbes, maker. *Chair,* from the Swedenborgian Church of the New Jerusalem, San Francisco, c. 1894. Maple with rush seat, 36½ x 20⅞ x 19¾ in. Swedenborgian Church; Courtesy of Dr. James F. Lawrence. *The eighty chairs in the sanctuary of the Swedenborgian Church are described in* House Beautiful, *February 1901, as "beautifully modeled, suggestive of the primitive old mission furnishings, but with a certain indescribable variation from the straight line that eliminates every suggestion of awkwardness."*

The San Francisco Examiner *of September 30, 1895, reported that an unnamed "old Scotchman" wove the rush seats for all eighty chairs, using California marsh tule. Adrienne Kopa in her chronicle "The Garden Church of San Francisco: A History" identifies Alexander J. Forbes as the old Scotsman. A. Page Brown's simply designed square-framed chair was used by Joseph P. McHugh and Co., New York, as the prototype for a chair that popularized the term "Mission furniture."*

urious it is that the best work in Arts and Crafts in America is already being produced on the Pacific Coast," wrote Charles R. Ashbee, a leading English designer and polemicist, during a visit to the Bay Area in early 1909.[1] Ashbee knew the American Arts and Crafts scene, having traveled in the East and Midwest in 1896 and 1900–1901. Another trip in 1908–9 took him to California, where he observed a consummation of William Morris's ideas. Ashbee admired the "architectural unity" of Stanford University and gave a talk there entitled "The Arts and Crafts and the Spirit of Socialism," which a local reporter described as "ethical and altruistic."[2] In Southern California he discovered the old Spanish ruins and raved about the landscape. He met "dreamy" Charles Sumner Greene and viewed the houses and caressed the furniture of Charles and his brother Henry. He found himself at home in their workshops; they exuded the "spell of Japan." Drinking tea while watching the snow-covered San Gabriel Mountains turn a "rose red" caused him to exclaim, "California speaks. . . . Here things were really alive—and the 'Arts and Crafts' that all the others were screaming about, are here actually being produced."

Other observers going west echoed Ashbee's enthusiasm. Gustav Stickley—who as editor of the magazine the *Craftsman* (1901–16) became "the American William Morris," according to the writer George Wharton James of Pasadena—journeyed west in the spring of 1904.[3] He found the beauty of California equaled only by that of the Italian Riviera, and he mused, "The Golden Age of the poets then becomes . . . a realized dream." The thick and finely kept orange groves with their "lantern-like globes of gold" surrounding Riverside reminded him of the suburbs of Genoa, and Frank Miller's Mission Inn overwhelmed him. (Miller had paid Stickley the compliment of using his United Crafts furniture for the inn at first and then producing a variation.) Beginning with a small adobe structure, Miller and his architect, William Benton, had created what Stickley perceived as an "atmosphere of historical romance," with bell towers, round-arched arcades, exposed beams, red-tile roofs, and rough, plain plaster walls. The plantings of eucalyptus and palms, the campanile, and its "simplicity" were all "Californian" to Stickley. The intensity of the Mission Inn with its recall of the exotic mystery of Catholicism and the Franciscan padres—especially poignant to a Presbyterian like Stickley—induced a reverie. A host of associations poured forth: the chapter house at Salisbury Cathedral, Venetian palaces, and ultimately a deep spiritualism, for, as he concluded, "*Aves* and *Pater Nosters,* . . . the vows of Poverty, Chastity and Obedience[,] . . . the light of St. Francis, like a new sun[,] streamed out upon the world."[4]

Continuing up the coast to Santa Barbara, Stickley remarked on people living out-of-doors, on the "bewildering scene of color," on the landscaping by Charles Frederick Eaton and the leather and shell crafts of Elizabeth Eaton Burton (plates 5, 144, 145).[5] For Stickley, California became the golden land, and articles on it in the *Craftsman* outnumber those on any other region. California offered a lesson, since it was separated by land and sea from the "demoralizing influence of the classic formula of the art successes of other nations." The Pacific Coast offered the hope of a "truer democracy than anything in the Middle or Eastern part of America." The separation between thought and labor—between thinkers and workers—that John Ruskin identified as the root of modern failure did not appear in California; the still-alive pioneer spirit provided a foundation for a "progressive democracy."[6]

For Liberty Hyde Bailey, the founder of the Country Life movement in America and editor of a magazine with the same name, California's isolation made it "a promised land." Standing next to a palm-thatched garden hut on Smiley Heights in Redlands and looking out across the neat citrus groves dotted with houses to the snowcapped San Bernardinos in the background (plate 49), Bailey let his imagination run free. California offered no basis of comparison with the rest of the United States; it was a "wonderland," he exclaimed, for it was winter and yet warm. He listed the tremendous range of climates and landscapes, from the southern deserts and the giant yuccas of the Mojave, the Matilija poppy, and the "Grizzly Giant" redwoods of Mariposa Grove to the cypresses of Monterey, the shaggy Washington palms, and the tall peak of Mount Shasta. California life was "out of doors, . . . [it was a] Land of action and dreams!"[7]

California's appeal included the variety of vegetation, some native, other imported, and the special light and atmosphere that gave a greater range and intensity to color. A garden room in a house by Irving Gill near San Diego was cataloged as having shining-foliaged rhus, heliotrope, rows of lavender stock and sweet peas, borders of nemophila, spangling dwarf verbena, wisteria, clematis, plumbago, pansies, violets, asters, purple- and violet-tinted foxgloves, larkspurs, mariposas, and more, all "so ethereally lovely" against the white wall of the house.[8]

5. Elizabeth Eaton Burton. *Electrical Lamp,* c. 1905–10. Hammered copper and copper tubing with black abalone–shell shades, 15½ x 15⅝ x 20⅝ in. Isak Lindenauer.

The climate was mild, the air different. Here on January first, with snow on the mountains a few miles distant, one could stand in an eighty-degree sun for a Tournament of Roses (established in 1890) that recalled Greco-Roman and Mediterranean festivals. The atmosphere and landscape brought forth not just a Latin heritage but a flavor so exotic that descriptive analysis failed. Ralph Adams Cram, the Boston-based architect and critic, sensed a "defiant originality," a "California style" emerging from the architecture of individuals such as the brothers Greene and Louis Christian Mullgardt. "Heaven alone knows," puzzled Cram, the origins of this "real and revolutionary thing," and he suggested Japan, Scandinavia, Sikkim, Bhutan, and Tibet.[9] Other writers claimed Swiss chalets, barns, Bavaria, and the Mediterranean as possible sources.[10]

For many people involved in the Arts and Crafts movement, California meant the bungalow and Mission furniture. The bungalow was the major American middle-class housing innovation of those years, and the Golden State, "Bungalow-land," was said to be its birthplace.[11] Odes were written to the California bungalow, characters in novels portrayed it as close to Nirvana: "Mama and me are planning to go out to Pasadena and buy a bungalow."[12] California also gave the movement one of its most identifiable labels, the Mission style. The name came from a chair designed in 1894 for the Swedenborgian Church of the New Jerusalem in San Francisco and manufactured in New York (plate 4). Its over-scaled and simple solid maple (later changed to oak) structure and tule-rush seat were thought to have originated with the California padres.[13] The term "Mission" came to mean more than just a furniture or building style; it became allied with home reform, based on the precept that a "missionary" intent should underlie both physical and spiritual life.[14]

From a longer perspective, this apotheosis of California is part of the oneiric hold that this "rim of the western world" has exerted on the American imagination since the mid-nineteenth century.[15] California was the natural conclusion—at least on the continent—of America's manifest or, as some would claim, divine destiny. Always a place where life appeared to be easy, California had evolved in its reputation from a place where gold could be picked off the ground, in 1850, to a Garden of Eden by 1900. In this land of health, with the possibility of regeneration, a new life could be made, free of the physical and spiritual confinements so common to the Midwest, the East, and Europe. Here the shackles could be broken, and life could be lived as one wanted—primitive and free, urban and bohemian, or safely suburban and domesticated. The vast and ever-changing landscape gave people the opportunity to try almost anything, and many did. California was more than a dream; it offered to many committed Arts and Crafters a higher life, a mysticism, or, as Bernard Maybeck claimed, a "Divine Excellence."[16]

The Arts and Crafts movement, whether in America or Europe, was expressed not in a specific style but as a mood, an attitude, a sensibility. At its core, the Arts and Crafts movement advocated a search for a way of life that was true, contemplative, and filled with essences rather than superficialities. Certain elements appear frequently—motifs derived from nature, a concern with simple form and complex details, a glorification of medieval art and society, and the exaltation of the vernacular—but the visual forms and social concerns differed. Like any movement that persists over many years, in this case from the 1870s through the 1920s, the Arts and Crafts comprised a loose confederation of individuals, both true believers and those only peripherally involved. Most members subscribed to beliefs in design reform, in a revised relationship between production and consumption, and in the ultimate issue of how that new relationship would manifest itself in daily life. Process, or how a thing was made, and its contribution to life were as important as the appearance of the object. The catalyst for this effort to remake the appearance of the world was the English poet, essayist, socialist, and designer William Morris. All the various branches of the Arts and Crafts movement—in Scandinavia, Vienna, Berlin, Nancy, Brussels, Paris, Boston, Chicago, and Pasadena—paid homage to its English origins and polemicists: John Ruskin, Thomas Carlyle, Augustus Welby Pugin, and, foremost of all, William Morris.

Morris's initial focus was to create alternatives to the low-grade, poorly designed, machine-produced objects for the home. Morris emphasized the "real" over the imitation and devised a maxim: "Have nothing in your houses that you do not know to be useful, or believe to be beautiful."[17] Beginning in the late 1850s a network developed of designers' and artisans' guilds, organizations, and clubs that supported a reform in the arts. The concern was not just a replacement of machines with handicraft but a revolt against an entire system of academic art and what was seen as a false distinction between the elite arts, sculpture and painting, and the so-called lesser arts, the applied and decorative arts. The entire method of art education and the arbitrarily imposed, classically based method needed to be revamped. In the most ideal of all worlds—and the Arts and Crafts was built on idealism—the designer and maker should be one and the same person, and the arts, whether pottery or architecture, should be rooted in the vernacular and not in some imported style. The initial stages of the movement in England were known by a number of rubrics, of which "the Aesthetic movement" and "Queen Anne" were the most common. The term "Arts and Crafts" had floated around for a number of years but was not formally tied to the cause until 1888, with the formation of the Arts and Crafts Exhibition Society.

The origins of the American branch of the Arts and Crafts go back to the 1870s, when the ideas and products of Morris and other English Aesthetic movement followers were introduced to this country. The line separating the Aesthetic and the Arts and Crafts movements is thin, almost imperceptible, but by the mid-1890s the nomenclature changed as Arts and Crafts clubs and societies were established throughout the country. The prime years of the American Arts and

Crafts movement were 1895 to 1918. The first California organization, the San Francisco Guild of Arts and Crafts, was established in 1895; it held an exhibition of bookbinding and graphic materials in 1896.[18] This event preceded the first major East Coast exhibition, which was held in Boston in April 1897; the Boston Society of Arts and Crafts was founded in June of that year.

Americans continued to import, exhibit, and imitate English products. Englishmen like Ashbee were a frequent presence in the United States, and a number of important American and Californian figures came from Britain: Frederick Hürten Rhead, the potter, went from Staffordshire first to St. Louis and then to Marin County and Santa Barbara; Ernest Coxhead, the architect, studied and worked in London before going to Los Angeles and then San Francisco; and George Wharton James, the writer, had been born in Lincolnshire and worked in Nevada before settling in Pasadena. Americans drew substance from England: Charles Sumner Greene visited in 1901 and 1909, and Ernest A. Batchelder traveled there in 1905. This tie with the English movement meant that Americans frequently identified the Gothic or medieval as the basis of design. To Batchelder, a Gothic cathedral "is no mere mass of stone; it is a veritable organism, alive with energy, pushing, straining"; it was not inert like Roman architecture but had "spiritual life."[19]

The American movement was also fertilized by other cultures and their design sources, such as the French Beaux-Arts and the Dutch, German, Austrian, and Italian traditions. Exotic and native cultures such as the Japanese and the Native American were viewed as uniting symbolism, belief, and the material world, and thus being more integrated than European systems. Added to this mix was an intensified quest for an American idiom in the arts. The vast scale and distances of the continent, the diverse heritages of Americans, the presence of foreign-trained designers (both immigrant and native-born), along with ingrained American individuality, resulted in an intense regionalism. Artists were to draw sustenance from the local soil, flora and fauna, and vernacular design, whether embodied in Indian pottery, mission furniture, or cabins. The state of California itself was divided into regions; needing the stimulus of cosmopolitan centers, individuals clustered around San Diego, Los Angeles, Santa Barbara, the San Francisco Bay Area, and even in the smaller cities of Redlands, Riverside, Pasadena, and Stockton. Although claiming roots in the vernacular, the people connected with the Arts and Crafts in California were anything but naive, and they created sophisticated objects.

The American and the English Arts and Crafts philosophies diverged on the issue of technology. Morris and his followers argued that art should not come from or be made for the elite but should be the work of ordinary people. The work itself should be not toil but joy. Handicraft was praised as being the product of an involved, "thinking" worker. Batchelder explained: "Workmen knew the joy of work, because the whole man—mind, eye, hand, heart and soul—

6. Arequipa Pottery (Frederick Hürten Rhead?). *Plate,* 1912. Earthenware with multicolored glaze and traces of luster, diameter: 10½ in. The Oakland Museum; Gift of the estate of Phoebe H. Brown.

entered."[20] Designers most often rejected the machine, feeling that the factory was inhuman and took all pleasure and creativity out of work. Many Arts and Crafts products show conspicuous handwork, such as hammer marks on copper, protruding pegs, and irregularity and roughness. Handicraft meant a greater cost in labor, and one of the conundrums of the Arts and Crafts movement was how to provide quality designs to those of limited means. For Morris the solution was political, and from the late 1870s to his death in 1896 he argued that not only the machine but the entire capitalist system needed to be dismantled before any

change in art could be effected. Only a few members of the English Arts and Crafts community followed Morris to the far left, but all agreed that the ultimate concern was not a perfectly designed and handmade bowl, but how that bowl could contribute to a proper life.

In the United States the technocratic and commercial spirit ruled, and the issue for the American Arts and Crafts movement became the wise use of the machine rather than its rejection. Many Arts and Crafts enterprises developed into substantial businesses, and objects were mass produced by Stickley, his brothers, the Dedham Pottery, the Shop of the Crafters in Cincinnati, and Roseville Pottery in Zanesville, Ohio. The bungalow was a staple of builders' guides and magazines and was available prefabricated, or ready cut, from a host of manufacturers. In a sense, the Arts and Crafts became a style that anybody could use, and schools such as William Lees Judson's School of Fine Arts near Pasadena and Frederick H. Meyer's California School of Arts and Crafts in Berkeley and Oakland were established to spread further the ideals of the movement and to educate new designers and craftspeople. Implicit in all these activities was the belief in design reform, establishing a new basis of composition that would replace the reliance on historical models and classicism; Morris had written much on the necessity for design reform.[21]

Following Morris, most American Arts and Crafters had political interests, but they lacked a consolidated agenda. Although party affiliations differed, the reformist impulse within the movement prompted most people to subscribe to progressive politics and the replacement of party machines, bosses, and graft with trained experts. Most Arts and Crafters considered large businesses and especially corporations to be bad; preferable were small enterprises where profits were shared. More radical members espoused Henry George's idea of a single tax on all

7. Shreve & Co., *Smoking Set*, c. 1910. Hammered copper with silver trim and attached projectile points. Tray, 15 x 12¼ in. The Oakland Museum; Gift in memory of Karl E. Schevill. Pipe tray, 6⁹⁄₁₆ x 3³⁄₁₆ in.; ashtray and matchholder, 2¹¹⁄₁₆ x 5⅝ in. Don Ritchie.

8. Ye Olde Copper Shop (Hans Jauchen) *Desk Set,* c. 1923–24. Hammered and patinated copper with cast green-pigmented eucalyptus leaf. Double inkwells and tray, 3¹⁄₁₆ x 16¾ x 5 in.; letter holder, 5³⁄₁₆ x 6¼ x 2½ in.; letter opener, 9¾ x 1½ in.; blotter, 2¼ x 5⅛ x 2½ in. The Oakland Museum; Kahn Collection.

increments in the value of land and agreed with Thorstein Veblen's critique of conspicuous consumption, both of which reinforced the ideal of the simple life.[22] The dilemma of being both anticonsumption and yet depending on consumption for a livelihood was resolved with a pretentious simplicity. Gaudy and heavily ornate objects traditionally had implied great expenditure of labor, which imputed wealth on the part of their owner, whereas simple objects cost less and indicated a reduced standard of living. The Arts and Crafts movement reversed this distinction, and simple became not just more noble but, ironically, more expensive.

Nature and the connection to landscape stands out as one of the key features of Arts and Crafts design in California. The diversity of nature—the native materials and colors, the different woods, the clays, the rocks—found its way into the products of various craftspeople, from lizards on the Theosophist-oriented Halcyon Art Pottery to poppies used by the San Francisco art printers Henry H. Taylor and Edward DeWitt. The particular color of the clay in Redlands inspired Wesley H. Trippett to take up pottery, and he threw and molded the red earth into forms ornamented with frogs.[23] Earlier, in the 1870s, Walt Whitman's "Song of the Redwood Tree" had recognized the spiritual possibilities of the two-hundred-foot-high sequoias:

> Out of its stalwart trunk and limbs, out of its foot-thick bark,
> That Chant of the seasons and time, chant not of the past only
> but the future.[24]

Redwood became identified with California, and for such people as Charles Keeler of Berkeley, this seemingly decay-resistant wood exuded an almost mystic quality.[25]

ARTS AND CRAFTS LIFE

For Keeler and many others, including Charles Sumner Greene, fitting the house into the landscape through the use of native materials became a dogma.[26] There was, however, no codified approach to using native materials. In Pasadena the brothers Greene, Myron Hunt and Elmer Grey, Charles Fletcher Lummis, and the Arroyo Guild operated within a few blocks of each other. Hunt and Grey were suave and could design houses in every style but with little conviction. The Greenes gloried in sophisticated and intricate details designed for contemplation. The Arroyo Guild and Lummis admired roughness. Clustered on the rim of the semiarid and semiwild canyon, the guild had a clubhouse and published the *Arroyo Craftsman,* which lasted only one issue. George Wharton James, the leader and editor, wrote several of the articles and explained that a "Spiritual Era" had

9. Bernard Maybeck. *Untitled* (design for *Circe,* by Isaac Flagg), undated. Tempera drawing, 17⅞ x 22¾ in. University Art Museum, University of California at Berkeley Bequest of Mabel H. Dillinger.

dawned, in which the objects made in the guild workshops "are by type, shadows of the beautiful real things themselves."[27] The two great egotists James and Lummis detested each other, even though they both promoted the idea of a new culture's rising from the rough-hewn missions and Native Americans, from boulders and chaparral. "The lands of the sun expand the soul," wrote Lummis, who titled himself "Don Carlos" and wore corduroy with a Mexican sash and sombrero.[28] Lummis built his house, El Alisal, out of arroyo boulders (plates 29, 57): a tough building aspiring to a primitive state in purposeful coarseness, it was decorated with Lummis's own photographic glass plates in the windows, Maynard Dixon's ironwork, and Gutzon Borglum's sculpture. On the interior Lummis displayed his collection of Indian artifacts, which would later become the core of the Southwest Museum, which he founded (plate 58).

California also suggested to some artists the classical landscape of the Mediterranean. The San Francisco painters Arthur F. Mathews and Lucia K. Mathews became entranced by the soft, rolling hills and the great oaks and cypresses of Monterey. They populated their painted landscapes with colorfully garbed figures recalling the classical past. Their brilliantly gowned figures swirl, dance, celebrate, or muse, with the Monterey hills or the Pacific surf as a backdrop. The landscape spills onto their lovingly carved and high-gloss furniture; poppies, larks, vines, lemons, and gowned figures overwhelm boxes, chests, and desks. In California the classics could reign, Greek and Latin poetry and drama could be performed in the open air. Charles Keeler replaced his customary corduroys with a toga (plate 10), and Bernard Maybeck, who described himself as "an artist that paints pictures in stone and concrete," designed the setting for the play *Circe* by his friend Isaac Flagg (plate 9).[29] Foliage, hanging vines, and gargoyles of serpents cover primitive masses and columns of variously tinted stone, and at center stage is a dragon-shaped fountain. Maybeck's classicism is a sensuous world of myth and exoticism.[30]

Another part of California's identity came from outdoor living derived from the Spanish heritage. Already in 1884 Helen Hunt Jackson had foretold this possibility in her best-selling romance *Ramona*. In Jackson's book the Franciscan padres in their adobe missions were beneficent overlords, and the houses of the landowning families were described as low-lying, "half barbaric, half elegant," surrounded by an outdoor room, a wide veranda where the "greater part of family life went on. . . . Nobody stayed inside the walls, except when it was necessary."[31] Down in the arroyo Lummis took note of these features, while up north in the Berkeley hills the Hillside Club claimed, "Hillside Architecture is Landscape Gardening around a few rooms for use in case of rain."[32]

Against these accomplishments, another side of the Californian Arts and Crafts movement must be recognized—the state's dark side. Ashbee was not a complete Pollyanna; he knew his talk on Arts and Crafts socialism at Stanford would mean little to "reactionary" financiers who already ran most American universities "as machines." Indeed, at Stanford, Henry Winchester Rolfe, an old Arts

10. Charles Keeler in a toga. From Charles Keeler, *The Simple Home,* 1904.

and Crafts comrade and a professor of classics who arranged for Ashbee's lecture, was fired within a year of the talk for opposing the autocratic president David Starr Jordan. And life close to nature was not always so pleasant: Janet Ashbee recorded an uncomfortable week at Rolfe's bungalow, "where every wind of Heaven beats upon it & where consequently the rain drives into his precious library . . . all in a state of confusion & Bohemianism very pleasant when you are feeling quite on top & simply awful when you get up wrong foot first." Down south, Los Angeles was a center of "hucksterism," and Ashbee noted, "the whole thing stamped with all that is worst and most transient in American Civilization."

Having been presented to the world through poetic phrases and atmospheric pictures, California in actuality was sometimes disappointing. Charles Sumner Greene's mother warned him that the missions "look much prettier in a Picture, than [they] really do to see them." She complained that the Mexican and Indian inhabitants "are very dark," thereby revealing an ingrained American racial prejudice.[33] On his trip west in 1904 Stickley was prepared to admire the natives, but he found the Yuma people "motley." He did protest, however, that the Yuma's "primitive simplicity" would be better than "our own too artificial life."[34] Helen Hunt Jackson had intended *Ramona* as an exposé of governmental policy; instead, it helped hasten the disappearance of Native Americans under a morass of tourist trinkets.

The Arts and Crafts sympathy for the common man is nowhere better illustrated than in Edwin Markham's phenomenally successful poem "The Man with the Hoe" (1899). Markham, who taught in Oakland, was a Swedenborgian socialist. His poems had been accepted by William Morris for publication in the Socialist magazine *Commonweal*. Inspired by Jean-François Millet's painting of a French peasant, Markham emoted:

> Through this dread shape the suffering ages look;
> Time's tragedy is in that aching stoop;
> Through this dread shape humanity betrayed,
> Plundered, profaned and disinherited,
> Cries protest to the Judges of the World.[35]

But this picturesque protest did not transfer to the migrant workers of the California fields nor to any of the urban poor. The concern of East Coast designers with poor immigrants did not appear in California, where most of the population was solidly middle class. California's poor seemed not to exist, for they were primarily Mexicans who remained invisible to most Anglos, or Portuguese and Italians on small farms, or Chinese and Japanese caught in ghettos and deemed so picturesque that they were beyond the scope of social concern.

The Arts and Crafts stood for a freeing of traditional restraints, yet as Charles Keeler, the cosmic "One Ideal" philosopher of the Hillside Club, explained, the home was "a temple consecrated to love," and the woman's role was raising children and "duty of service toward her helper." He claimed: "The idea of woman's rights becomes insignificant in the face of this great privilege of service."[36]

The sentiments expressed by many of the California Arts and Crafters were both profound and commercial; they strove to find meaning in life and at the same time were unabashed real-estate promoters. Both Keeler and Lummis wrote extensively for landholding interests.[37] Charles Sumner Greene penned paeans such as "All art loving people love nature first" and "Once the soul awakes to the spell one cannot come away without a pang," yet in the same article, written for a Tournament of Roses celebration, he pleads: "God send us the people! Not that we havn't [sic] any but we want more."[38] This is the cry of promoters everywhere. The Arts and Crafts movement in California had ties to large-scale land speculation; to the buying, selling, subdividing, and exploiting of the landscape; to the bringing in and controlling of the life-giving substance, water. The motifs of the Arts and Crafts were readily reproducible to serve many different ends: they could signify intense spiritual devotion, evoke the romantic California past, and cloak houses, hotels, and railroad stations.

Within the Arts and Crafts celebration of nature lurked a primitivism, which, in the case of the novelist Jack London, became the ultimate darkness. London's own Wolf House, in Sonoma's Valley of the Moon, was a prime example of Arts and Crafts domestic architecture: redwood, timber with the bark left on, huge halls, giant fireplaces. Wolf House, designed by Albert Farr, burned on the eve of its completion in 1913. In London's writings men are superior, women should strive to match male strength and exploits, wolf and coyote skins cover the native-wood floors, and raw meat is devoured. He hoped for a superior race to save the West from recent immigrants and dark-skinned people. London's message had been clear for years—either Nietzschean supermen dominate or, as Buck demonstrates in *The Call of the Wild* (1903), a return to the tooth and claw is inevitable.[39] Three years after Wolf House burned, Jack London—lost in alcohol and a physical wreck—committed suicide.

This dark side of the Arts and Crafts indicates not failure but rather the disappointment that many people felt when confronted with reality instead of a new culture arising on the shores of the Pacific. Speaking at the University of California in 1911, George Santayana, the Harvard philosophy professor, provided a program for this new culture. He defined a "genteel" America, inhabiting a neat reproduction of a colonial cottage, too bound to tradition. Bemused by "your forest and your sierras," whose "non-human beauty and peace . . . stir the subhuman depths and the superhuman possibilities of your own spirit," he bemoaned the Calvinist-agonized conscience and enervated sweetness that had become Transcendentalism. Walt Whitman was the one American writer who had left the genteel tradition behind. Invoking William James, who had spoken at the university in 1898, Santayana called for directness of experience, for opening the mind to action as well as to contemplation, for openness to a new spirit with

25

"no predetermined goal." James, he claimed, "gave a sincerely respectful hearing to sentimentalists, mystics, spiritualists, wizards, cranks, quacks and impostors." If philosophers had lived in the California mountains, "their systems would have been different from what they are." Santayana's—and James's—new spirit used the past "as a stepping-stone, or rather as a diving board, but it has an absolutely fresh will at each moment to plunge this way or that into the unknown." Intensely romantic, Santayana suggested the open-ended possibilities of California and what the Arts and Crafts movement might achieve.[40]

The search for the meaning of life, for an essence beyond material reality, for a defining cosmology and metaphysics emerged as a mystical-spiritualist current among many Arts and Crafts leaders.[41] Mysticism appears to have been deeply rooted in America, though certainly there were English and foreign manifestations and exponents ranging from Art Nouveau to Edward Carpenter and William R. Lethaby.[42] The link in America between the Arts and Crafts and mysticism is apparent in the careers of many individuals, such as Claude Bragdon, Bertram Goodhue, Charles Sumner Greene, Bernard Maybeck, Louis Sullivan, Louis Comfort Tiffany, and Frank Lloyd Wright. In their writings frequently appear telling words—"higher truth," "unity," "beauty," "spiritual," and "symbolism." Mysticism had many versions, ranging from Christian-based groups— such as Christian Science, Swedenborgianism, Anglo-Catholicism (or High Episcopalianism), and High Catholicism—to more esoteric theories of correspondences, "new thought," "cosmic consciousness," Theosophy, and Eastern religions. An eclectic assemblage of Kantian-Hegelian notions of progress and world spirit and Neoplatonism underlay most mystical thought. On the West Coast metaphysical concerns reached a peak of intensity. In California two of the more important formally organized groups were the Swedenborgians and the Theosophists, the best-known manifestations being Joseph Worcester's Swedenborgian Church of the New Jerusalem in San Francisco and the Theosophist-oriented Point Loma Art School north of San Diego.[43]

The problem was (and is), as one writer noted, "very few can define mysticism."[44] Oscar Wilde observed that mysticism has a "marvelous power of making common things strange to us" and that there is an inherent obfuscation (or "shadows and twilight") about it.[45] But the new, turn-of-the-century American mysticism had a bright light; observers described it as "optimistic" and "positive." Experience and intuition were more important than doctrine in Arts and Crafts mysticism, in which organic perceptions dominated purely rational thought, and a unity of all things was seen to exist. A few critics identified American mysticism as a revulsion from the modern age, a product of "physical and mental ill-health."[46] But Michael Williams, a San Francisco writer and promoter of the arts, defended American mysticism as a belief in the goodness of the human race and its destiny.[47] Williams wrote with reference to California and the Panama-Pacific International Exposition of 1915: "Art" should be a "vision of the soul." It "concerns itself with the inner essence of reality and less and less with merely its outer

forms. . . . The new spirit in art is psychic and spiritual."[48] Bernard Maybeck explained the meaning of the Palace of Fine Arts (plate 15): "There is something bigger and better and more worth while than the things we see about us, the things we live by and strive for. There is an Undiscovered Beauty, a Divine Excellence just beyond us. Let us stand on tiptoe, forgetting the meaner things, and grasp of it what we may."[49] Maybeck believed that material things were symbols of higher truths, and as such, objects or buildings or landscapes could expand the human mind.

The Pure Design movement was one attempt to discover essences or underlying unity. The axis of the Pure Design movement ran from Boston, with Arthur Wesley Dow and Denman W. Ross, to Chicago, with Frank Lloyd Wright and the Prairie School, to end in Pasadena, with Ernest A. Batchelder. Suffused with Eastern, particularly Japanese, art and Hegelian cosmology, Pure Design attempted to forge a basis of art creation unrelated to European styles. Dow's goal was to express "Beauty," not "Representation."[50] Batchelder had studied under Ross at Harvard University. Ross, who vied with Dow as the founder of the theory of Pure Design in America, equated design with music and claimed the designer should seek a "worship of the Ideal" and "Order and Beauty."[51] Batchelder in turn claimed that the fact that "we have no tradition . . . is our best hope," and he advocated fundamentals that underlay all styles.[52] Batchelder's articles and books exhibit a disarming simplicity: they appear to be a set of progressive exercises, but their purpose was to synthesize the visual arts into a unity.

Another method of discovering inner essence came through intuition, as in the case of the coppersmith Dirk van Erp, who, when heating and hammering the copper into a red, warty surface (plates 11, 12, 103), found that his motions became spontaneous: he "had it in his head and in his hands. . . . It came out a

ABOVE

11. Copper Shop (?) (Dirk van Erp). *Vase,* c. 1908–10. Hammered and patinated copper, 15¾ x 8¾ in. The Oakland Museum; Gift of Mr. and Mrs. William van Erp.

RIGHT

12. Dirk van Erp Studio (Dirk van Erp and D'Arcy Gaw, designers). *Monumental Jardiniere,* 1910. Hammered copper patinated deep red, 10½ x 16¾ in. Don Ritchie.

very nice piece, [or] it never got finished."[53] In a similar way, the painter William Keith, a Swedenborgian who had studied under George Inness, claimed that his work resulted from moods striking him, at which times he was "a mere instrument," and the final form was a revelation to him.[54]

A potent example of the search for a higher meaning appears in the Church of the New Jerusalem, San Francisco, designed in 1894 for the Reverend Joseph Worcester, who came from a long line of New England Swedenborgian Transcendentalists. As a Swedenborgian, Worcester subscribed to the theory of correspondences, in which every physical object—nature, plants, redwood—could induce spiritual reverie.[55]

His Church of the New Jerusalem, located near the top of Russian Hill in San Francisco, has a complicated design history, for while the architect of record is A. Page Brown, who recently had gone west from the New York office of McKim, Mead & White, the hands of A. C. Schweinfurth and even Bernard Maybeck are evident. Its exterior form contains a variety of references: the red-tiled and arcaded entry recalls California missions; the campanile and red brick are Italian; and the long horizontal form resembles Mexican ranch houses. The specifics are not so important as the general effect of calmness and meditation (plates 13, 35). The entry boasts no sign, and the visitor enters a walled garden that contains "tones of the orient," as a later minister claimed, with a Shinto bell and Japanese plantings. Also in the garden is a simple iron cross taken from one of the Spanish missions, a locomotive bell, and plantings such as a Cedar of Lebanon, indicative of wisdom.[56] The nave suggests both a grove of trees and a residential interior, and there was a "primitive quality about everything,"[57] with the roof supported by madrone tree trunks with the bark left on. Worcester personally selected them in the Santa Cruz Mountains and so inspired the forester that he not only gave them to the church but delivered them as well. Against the madrones and the leather thongs that held them in place and the redwood wainscoting and altar along one wall, were four bright spots of color—landscape paintings of the California seasons by William Keith (plate 14). They give the effect of windows that have opened to a world beyond this life. Bruce Porter, a painter, writer, landscape designer, and secretary of the San Francisco Guild of Arts and Crafts, contributed two stained-glass window designs: on the east wall over the altar a circular window shows a dove resting on a fountain shaded by apple blossoms; and on the south wall is a depiction of Saint Christopher carrying the Christ Child over an angry river. Worcester disapproved of symmetry and probably determined that the altar would be placed off-center at the east end; the large brick fireplace at the west is also asymmetrical. Even the wrought-iron chandelier hung not from the center line but to the side. Instead of pews, large wooden chairs (the origin of the Mission myth) could be moved about as needed. Woven Japanese grass mats covered portions of the natural-wood floor. Photographs and descriptions of the interior during Worcester's day indicate the decoration—a bonsai tree, stalks of Indian corn in the corners, oak or eucalyptus

ABOVE

13. A. Page Brown, architect, with contributions by A. C. Schweinfurth and Bernard Maybeck, Swedenborgian Church of the New Jerusalem, San Francisco, 1894. View toward the altar.

OPPOSITE

14. William Keith. *Dark November,* undated. Oil on canvas, 22 x 32 in. The Oakland Museum; Gift of the Keith Art Association.

limbs around the reading desk, and Spanish moss hanging from the ceiling or flowing over the altar.[58]

The Palace of Fine Arts at the 1915 Panama-Pacific International Exposition in San Francisco marked the most public attempt to create what Bernard Maybeck explained as the "ideas and sentiments" of "spiritual significance" (plate 15).[59] A complicated decorative program of architecture, sculpture, and murals was enhanced by a color scheme of nine hues derived by Jules Guerin, the Director of Color, from the atmosphere, climate, and landscape of the region. These colors, ranging across the spectrum and enhanced by plantings, created a phantom kingdom. Louis Christian Mullgardt, the designer of the Court of Ages, claimed that the architecture nestled "like flamingoes with fine feathers unfurled within a green setting."[60] The entire composition, Maybeck explained, was to produce a "succession of impressions," as the visitor passed through the different courts, with the Court of Ages suggesting medieval idealism in conflict with physical reality, the Court of the Universe portraying a placid Rome, and the Court of Four Seasons as the land of beauty, grace, and peace, where the souls of poets and philosophers dwell.

At the end of the journey was the lagoon, the "crux" of the composition, whose irregular form suggested "romantic . . . Gothic ideals"; on the far side of it lay the Rotunda, the peristyle, and the enclosed structure for the art exhibition. Maybeck explained that the role of the architect was to find historic forms and to see if they could produce the desired effect, akin to a poet who searches for words. The experience of art was a spiritual endeavor, resulting in a sense of sadness, a melancholy at the transitory nature of beauty, of sentiment that cannot last. Maybeck cited as an example Arnold Böcklin's *Isle of the Dead,* a painting he had seen in Munich in which a boat carrying the dead approaches an island of tall black trees enclosing a white marble columbarium. But, as he noted, this was too sad, and a tempering effect was needed, which took the form of the extensive decorative program of sculpture, both applied and freestanding, and the range of colors. The architectural sculptural figures are all posed in attitudes of contemplation, not action; on the peristyle they turn inward, away from the viewer. Spread around the grounds were individual pieces of freestanding sculpture. Off to one side and dwarfed by the giant peristyle was a small statue under an acacia tree, *The Muse Finding the Head of Orpheus,* by Edward Berge, symbolizing sadness modified by the soothing influence of beauty. The intended purpose of the ensemble was to invoke the "artist's dreams" before they are executed, to transmit "the spiritual meaning of things," to expose that "secret to the layman." The effect of the ensemble was to be felt as much as perceived, for the divine quality of art is indescribable in mere words.[61]

If Maybeck's scheme for the 1915 exposition was the most public expression of the unity of art and life, Irving Gill's solution to the same challenge was very different. His white box houses, devoid of most trim, were designed to reveal the "source of all architectural strength—the straight line, the arch, the cube and the

15. Bernard Maybeck, *The Palace of Fine Arts and Lagoon, A Foggy Night.* From Bernard Maybeck, *The Palace of Fine Arts and Lagoon,* 1915.

31

16. Irving Gill, *Drawing for Miss Marion Olmsted House,* San Diego. From *Craftsman,* May 1916.

circle—and . . . these fountains of Art that gave life to the great men of old" (plate 16). He assigned meanings to these elemental shapes: the horizontal line is greatness and grandeur; the arch, patterned from the dome of the heavens, is exultation, reverence, and aspiration; the cube is the symbol of power, justice, and honesty; and the circle represents completeness, motion, and progression. These ideas are similar to some of Louis Sullivan's, for whom Gill had worked, and also to tenets of Theosophy. Unlike Sullivan, however, Gill found he could dispense with an overlay of organic ornament and concentrate on purity, simplicity, and honesty, which had the additional attributes of being sanitary, laborsaving, and (supposedly) inexpensive. The artistic effect came from the creamy walls rising boldly into the crystal blue skies, unrelieved by extrusions and unornamented

17. Charles Sumner Greene and Henry Mather Greene, entry hall of the David B. Gamble House, Pasadena, 1908.

save for vines that softened a line, creepers that wreathed a column, and flowers that "inlay color more sentiently that any tile could do."[62] The houses were hymns of an intense reverence for the California landscape.

The emphasis on mysticism is also found in the work of Charles Sumner Greene and his brother Henry, where an intensity of contemplation, a reverence for creating beautiful objects, inspires higher thoughts. Charles was the "dreamy" one; his unpublished novel, "Thais Thayer," reveals his belief that formal academic systems of design were worn out and devoid of life. He felt that inspired design comes from intense contemplation of art, music, or even an old Chinese bronze urn: "I didn't draw a line or form a contour but my mentor stood before me, bathed in the still morning light where it always met my gaze."[63] In the Greenes' work, each part is recognized as part of a higher unity, from the joints and beams of the house to the surrounding plantings and gardens. Charles liked to use "lichen-covered field stones" for the foundation, "laid in nature's own color and form."[64] He filled the David B. Gamble House with symbolic content. The front porch is an abstraction of a Japanese temple gate, or a torii, which both shelters the inhabitants and frames the landscape. In the front door a great California oak is portrayed in Tiffany glass by Emile Lange (plate 17). In the interior a transcendental experience greets the occupant or visitor: the window glows with a magical light. In the living room a sixteen-and-one-half-inch-high frieze of California redwood surrounds the space; carved in the Japanese *ramma* manner, the frieze's mountains, trees, and vegetation relate to the landscape of Japan as well as to the various features outside the house. The interiors are dark, inducing a hushed, transcendental tone appropriate for contemplation.[65]

The Arts and Crafts movement in California exhibited a number of tendencies, which ranged from prosaic bungalows to several works—such as the Greenes' Gamble House, Maybeck's Palace of Fine Arts, Gill's Dodge House, and Joseph Worcester's Church of the New Jerusalem—that would rank as great creations in any age or place. They are landmarks in the history of America. Infusing them, and indeed animating much of the Arts and Crafts movement in California, was a mystical content, an attempt to create objects and buildings that would induce a transcendence from the material to the spiritual. The attempt had an enigmatic quality, but it appears to have been successful. Yet problems remained, for if one could make the quest in one's head, was the physical object necessary? And if one could not mentally make the trip, could any object induce the transcendence? Californians thought that the landscape and the houses, the furniture and the crafts could assist with the journey. For the period between about 1900 and 1915, they succeeded in making California the culmination of the Arts and Crafts movement in America.

THE ARTS
AND CRAFTS
GARDEN
IN CALIFORNIA

David C. Streatfield

The garden was one of the most important contributions of the Arts and Crafts movement to creating natural, unpretentious, and harmonious environments. English theorists fashioned the basis of an approach to garden making, extolling the virtues of nature and the independence of the artist-craftsman. Gardens were intended to express regional character, to be built from local materials and simple plants according to color theories. They were meant to be used as outdoor rooms and places for growing productive plants. The influence of these ideas in America was considerable, with regional variations appearing in the eastern and midwestern states as well as California. Because of the extraordinary variety of the physical landscape, California garden makers achieved a diversity of gardens that explored Arts and Crafts themes, exemplified by the hillside garden in the San Francisco Bay Area and San Diego; by the open-landscape garden, primarily in the Los Angeles Basin; and by the patio garden, throughout the Southland. In addition, the open-landscape and patio gardens influenced some popular bungalow gardens.

The Arts and Crafts garden emerged in the first decade of the twentieth century as part of a strong reaction against nineteenth-century gardens, which had embraced a wide variety of styles and a heterogeneous array of plants; these collectively represented a set of cultural ideals that had little to do with the landscape itself. Such floristic and stylistic diversity thrived in California, where it was possible to create any kind of garden. The benign climate, the long growing season, and the apparent abundance of water for irrigation led to the importation of plants from many other regions. In this way the landscape had already been substantially changed before the introduction of Arts and Crafts ideals.

When the prodigality of this floral abundance came into question at the turn of the century, Arts and Crafts gardens provided a new set of choices for regional

18. Claycraft Potteries. *Four Tiles in a Square,* c. 1926. Press-molded fired clay colored with pigmented slip, 17⅝ x 17¹¹/₁₆ in. Gary Breitweiser.

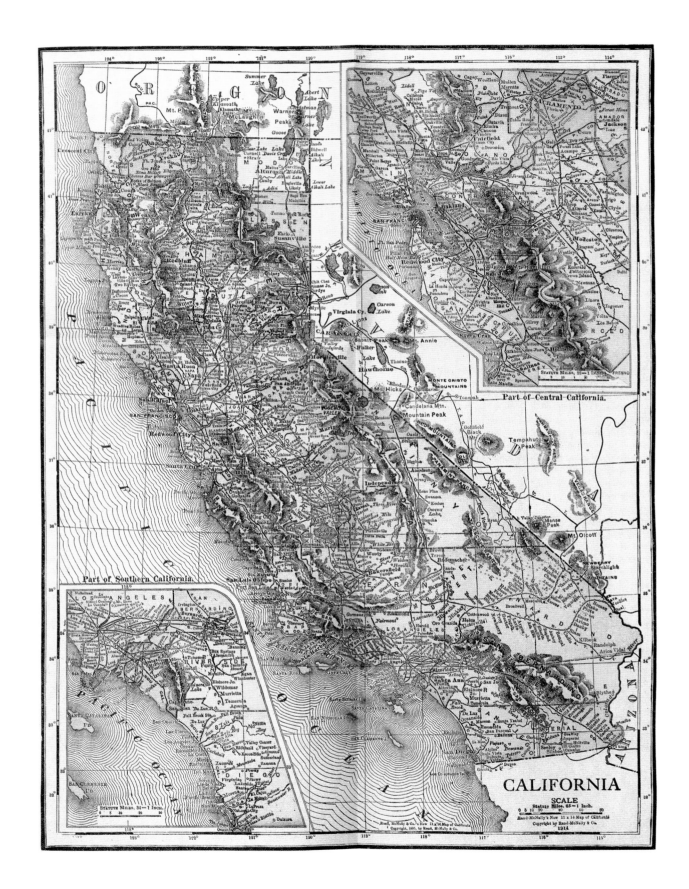

Part of Central California.

Part of Southern California.

CALIFORNIA

SCALE
Statute Miles, 65=1 Inch.
0 5 10 20   40   60   80

Rand-McNally's New 11 x 14 Map of California
Copyright by Rand McNally & Co.
1914

appropriateness. Outwardly oriented to frame views of the landscape, the various garden types provided places in which a domestic space could be settled into the outer landscape. The garden thus became an important transitional space in a continuum of experience from the interior of the house through the garden and out into the landscape. California's mild climate made it possible to spend more time out-of-doors, in the outdoor room, than in England or other parts of America.

California's visually dramatic physical setting is defined by a series of mountain ranges. The Coastal Mountains rise directly from the waters of the Pacific Ocean on a north-south axis from the Oregon border to the Tehachapi Mountains, south of which lies Southern California, known colloquially as the Southland. Below the Tehachapi Mountains is the Transverse Range, running on an east-west axis and including the Santa Ynez Mountains, the San Gabriel Mountains, and the San Bernardino Mountains. To the south of them is a lower plateau known as the Peninsular Range, the western edge of which follows the crescent-shaped shoreline south to the Mexican border. The Los Angeles Basin is a roughly triangular plain lying between these ranges and open to the ocean.

This rugged yet fragile topography has been and still is being created by earthquakes; in addition, wildfires have a recurring impact on native plants and human settlements. These dynamic processes were largely ignored by settlers, who were preoccupied with the admirable climate. California enjoys a climate that is generally similar to that of the Mediterranean Basin: very mild, wet winters; hot, dry summers; and warm springs and autumns. Since the difference in temperature between winter and summer is only ten degrees, it is the presence or absence of water that defines the seasons. In coastal California the rainfall decreases from north to south, but the entire coastal region experiences morning fog in the summer. This is caused by a large mass of moisture-laden air flowing landward over extremely cold, deep water lying just offshore (deep because there is no extensive coastal shelf). Enough condensation occurs to produce fog, which provides a form of natural air conditioning by reducing the temperature at the shore. Away from its influence, temperatures in inland California are very high during the summer.

In the second half of the nineteenth century the climate was used to define the character of the state. Every county history contained a copious array of climatic statistics to prove that it had the finest weather in the state. Popular writers enticed potential immigrants by comparing the state favorably with Italy. Major Ben Truman, promoting California for the Southern Pacific Railroad Company, called the Southland's climate "semi-tropical."[1] In fact, the Southland is really a desert facing the ocean.[2] The moisture from the ocean transmutes the harsh white desert light into a beautiful softness, which not only has been celebrated by many painters[3] but also has attracted many settlers to the Southland.

19. Map of California from George Wharton James, *California Romantic and Beautiful,* 1914.

The landscape of each of the major settled coastal regions is distinct. San Francisco Bay is a large, enclosed body of water protected to the west by the Santa Cruz Mountains, which rise to heights of fifteen hundred to two thousand feet. The eastern sides of these mountains are clothed with forests of redwood and Douglas fir. The softly rounded foothills and the plains at the edge of the bay are covered with grass and open groves of round-headed oak trees. The landscape of the east side of the bay is similar, although there are fewer oak trees on the plain. The softly sculptured, grass-covered hills are bisected by small valleys filled with trees. These vegetative patterns reflect differences in the amount of available

STREATFIELD

water: redwoods require more moisture, whereas the thick leaves of the native oaks are well adapted to long periods of drought.

Water, or the lack of it, is a more important factor than geography in shaping the landscape in the Southland. The Los Angeles Basin is a desertlike prairie. The Transverse Range, still geologically young, has been produced by frequent earthquakes. It rises to 11,400 feet and 10,064 feet, respectively, at San Gorgonio Mountain and San Jacinto Peak and has deeply carved, rugged slopes whose ridges are capped with snow in the winter. The soils of the Los Angeles Basin are extremely poor and were originally covered with grass and scrub vegetation. Before irrigation, trees grew only on the banks of rivers and in a large open grove of oaks in the foothills at Pasadena and San Marino. The eastern end of the basin is a true desert, becoming progressively drier as it continues through the narrow pass into Palm Springs. At the turn of the century, the foothills of the basin were covered with great masses of kaleidoscopically colored wildflowers. Their vibrant color led many writers to refer to this landscape as "a garden of flowers." Ecologists now believe that their appearance was due to intense disturbances of the soil caused by heavy fires and rains.[4]

The landscape of Santa Barbara County is quite different. This is the only part of the California coast that faces south rather than west. The Santa Ynez Mountains and the Channel Islands create a protected microclimate for the long, narrow coastal plain, which was recognized as early as 1878 as the finest of the coastal subregions for settlement. At the base of the mountains is a thin band of open southern-oak woodland, which covers the undulating plain and rises into chaparral, a group of drought- and fire-tolerant plants.

The landscape in and around San Diego is completely different from that of the other southern coastal areas. Mesalike formations rise from the ocean and form a continuous fringe to the Peninsular Range. They once were clothed with the coastal sage community—a mixture of shrubby plants, mesembryanthemums (ice plants), and the yellow, blue, and purple bush lupines.

Prior to 1870, California gardeners attempted to replicate either the forms of gardens that were typical wherever the settlers had come from or garden styles that were popular elsewhere at the time. Such cultural imposition was made possible by the unusually extensive range of plants available from other regions in the United States, Europe, and Australia, plus an unlimited supply of irrigation water: exotic plants were imported to Northern California starting in the early 1850s, to Southern California in the 1870s; artificial irrigation began in the early 1850s and gradually became more sophisticated as the technology developed. Many of the plants cultivated in California could be grown in the rest of the country only under glass. Formal gardens and beds of mosaiculture (a European technique for growing closely cropped succulents in mosaiclike designs) jostled with broad lawns fringed by groves of an extraordinarily large range of trees and shrubs. In 1874 a writer suggested that the ideal mood for California was the "tropical."[5] In practice this involved the lavish use of palms and many subtropical species that had to be imported into the state.

Victorian gardens were largely plant collections, and they had a markedly introverted, self-contained character; only later did gardens begin to take full advantage of outward views.[6] The writer Grace Ellery Channing criticized the typical California garden for being no more than a collection of eucalyptus, pepper, dracena, fan and date palm, calla lily, bamboo, and the India rubber tree.[7] Although such gardens displayed floral luxuriance, they lacked a coherent spatial order. Nonetheless, they continued to be created into the twentieth century. In the San Francisco Bay Area, designers such as John McLaren created parks with large, irregular lawns and groves of native and exotic trees, following English picturesque theory of the eighteenth and early nineteenth centuries, as is evident in his Golden Gate Park (designed 1888–1910s).[8]

Many writers were concerned about the appropriate character of the California garden. Architects and architectural writers approached the issue in terms of historical style. Herbert Croly, editor of the *Architectural Record,* argued in 1913 that since much of the landscape of the coastal region was "classical" in character, the Italian villa was a logical appropriation for both building and garden.[9] Another architectonic approach adopted, though with far less frequency, was the French Baroque style of the seventeenth century.[10] As Arts and Crafts theory and practice became an alternative to these styles, in the early twentieth century, it was taken up by communities such as Berkeley and Pasadena, which had active civic-improvement societies, as well as by individual designers who sought to achieve regional appropriateness.

The concepts of Arts and Crafts gardens in the United States were loosely derived from English theorists' ideas, most notably John Ruskin's insistence on looking to nature for the development of aesthetic principles and on handcraftsmanship in which the artisan-craftsman had autonomy.[11] Other English writers also extolled the virtues of the independent artist-gardener. The important English contributions to garden design were the woodland garden, developed by William

Beautiful as these trees and flowers undoubtedly are, it will be noticed by an observant visitor that most of them are exotics, which thrive not only on account of the comparatively high temperature in which they, as settlers have, but that their existence is equally dependent upon supplied moisture and the gardener's care. Look beyond the confines of these cities into the valleys and plains of California, and you will find that they are for three seasons of the year, sunburned deserts. But they respond spontaneously to the application of water. It is the liberal use of the hose pipe and garden sprinkler which are turned on with such lavish generosity in the gardens and parks, that has been the main factor in making the wilderness blossom as the rose. Indeed, the quantity of water which is used upon the ornamental gardens, not to mention the streets of Pasadena, would appear to be more than that consumed for all other purposes.

Arthur T. Johnson, *California: An Englishman's Impressions of the Golden State* (London: Staley Paul & Co., 1913), pp. 26–27.

Robinson as a natural-seeming collection of hardy trees and shrubs; the revival of old-fashioned flower gardens according to systematic color theory by Gertrude Jekyll; and the revival of vernacular traditions.[12]

Americans quickly absorbed these ideas, published in new magazines such as *House and Garden, House Beautiful, Country Life in America,* and especially the *Craftsman,* the main organ of the Arts and Crafts movement. Regional differences developed. In the eastern states the revival of colonial garden traditions was associated with Jekyll's color theories for flower gardens. In the Midwest, designers such as Jens Jensen and Ossian Simonds practiced the prairie school of gardening, a regional version of William Robinson's woodland gardening.

In California there was a general fidelity to Ruskinian principles, but the influence of English writers and designers was not particularly strong. In the San Francisco Bay Area, the Swedenborgian minister Joseph Worcester's reverence for the holiness of nature was close to Ruskin's, and both strongly influenced the architect Bernard Maybeck and Charles Keeler, the Berkeley poet.[13] (Worcester also appears to have been attracted by Japanese gardens and their symbolism.) The absence of a strong English tradition, the existence of a competing Hispanic tradition, and a majestic landscape so very different from the gentle pastoral nature of England provided new challenges to the designers of California's gardens. The Hispanic tradition was strongest in the southern part of the state, where the ruined mission churches and remains of adobe houses remained a palpable presence. In 1888 Frederick Law Olmsted, working on a plan for Stanford

22. Muresque Tiles, Inc. *Two-Tile Mural,* 1927. Press-molded fired clay colored with pigmented slip, 8¼ x 16⅛ in. Frances Butler.

University, also proposed a set of design principles appropriate for a new Californian design tradition, which he based on the Spanish missions and on Mediterranean courtyard gardens using little water.[14] His principles, unfortunately, were not followed. But Helen Hunt Jackson's essays and her popular novel *Ramona,* first published in 1884, focused attention on the Mexican adobe house with its enclosed patio garden. These were very simple derivations from Moorish gardens in Spain. Laid out on a four-fold plan around a central fountain and using a mixture of decorative and productive plants, they represented an appropriate alternative to Victorian floral gardening that paralleled the English revival of vernacular traditions.

The physical scale and dryness of the California landscape and the mix of multiple, generally recent cultural traditions produced different forms of regionalism within the state. The simple dignity of the California ranch house—such as Rancho Camulos, near Piru, and Rancho Guajome, near Vista, with their outdoor living spaces—was invoked by many writers as an appropriate source for a new garden mode, as were the surviving mission gardens. The architect Myron Hunt noted that the Moorish, Roman, and Mesopotamian sources of the Spanish garden suggested that "paradise was a welled garden. . . . The real California garden is on the border of the desert. . . . [We] must accept the wilderness and use it as a background for our picture, the setting for our jewel."[15]

The Japanese garden at the California Midwinter Fair, held in Golden Gate Park in 1894, did much to promote the broad popularity of Japanese gardens.[16] Charles Keeler called for gardens that would combine aspects of the mission and the Japanese garden to create places for repose, study, and domestic leisure. Both traditions emphasized order and the control of nature, and both could be brought together so that "the charm of the wilderness [would be] tamed and diversified for convenience and accessibility."[17] Each of these design modes was practiced singly and in combination, with Japanese gardens more generally evoked and more literally copied. One writer suggested that the Japanese garden had much to offer to the owner of a small garden since it was perfectly adapted to small spaces.[18]

Alfred D. Robinson, nurseryman and editor of the *California Garden* (published in San Diego), voiced yet another opinion. Believing that the mixture of European and Japanese garden traditions would produce only a patchwork-quilt effect, he concluded that the courtyard gardens of North Africa would provide a more suitable model.[19] These varying points of view confirm the fact that in California the Arts and Crafts movement embraced diverse forms that were not limited to any one style. This range reflected social differences among the garden owners and specific design responses to the distinct physical regions. The one element shared by all of these approaches, with the conspicuous exception of Kate O. Sessions's work in San Diego (plate 32), was dependence on profligate use of water.

A coordinated set of principles for private gardens and the entire landscape of the Berkeley hills was developed by the Hillside Club, an improvement society founded in 1898 by Keeler and Bernard Maybeck.[20] Under the guidance of this organization, members completely transformed the existing landscape into a wooded hillside of mixed, exotic trees, within which a variety of carefully sited shingled houses commanded sweeping views of San Francisco Bay. This landscape was experienced as a continuous public garden as well as a series of private gardens. Roads were treated as country lanes, following the contours of the hills and avoiding existing trees and rock outcrops. The blocks of houses were irregular in shape, with individual houses stepped back into the slope to minimize disturbance of the site. Terraces were built over garages and as extensions from rooms at several different levels.

The plan resulted in an irregular path system through the landscape. Sidewalks did not parallel the roads. Instead, staircases and paths threaded through the center of the blocks, providing a means of traversing the hills and giving access to individual gardens. Many of the stairs expanded at landings into broad platforms with seats where one could rest and enjoy the view. This pattern of movement was also used in the gardens to which the paths led. The routes created effects of intimacy and mystery and made each garden seem larger than it actually was. Paths were paved with the local stone, which was also used for low retaining walls. Even these minor structural features of the garden seemed like creations of nature. The colors of materials were carefully selected to make each house appear to be an organic element of the landscape, with the brown of the hills determining the color of the house. "A house should not stand out in a landscape, but should fit in with it. This is the first principle that should govern the design of every house."[21]

This thinking was not, however, extended to plants. Believing that indigenous plants might appear "dull in color and lacking in character," Keeler advocated creating a natural-looking landscape by using redwood trees underplanted with small native trees and shrubs; he also recommended that the California garden should have "a massy bloom at all periods of the year."[22] The Hillside Club suggested that individual owners cooperate to turn the visible parts of their gardens into large masses of color. "Here a roadside of grey olive, topped with purple plum, there a line of trailing willows, dipped in a frame of ivy-covered walls. Long avenues of trees with houses far back from the roads, hidden behind foregrounds of shrubbery. Never grass on a hill. The same expenditure of time and money on bushes will be more effective."[23] Individual gardens consisted of informal open areas above and below the house defined by trees and by the house itself. A sketch by Maybeck poetically conveys the fluid, integrated character of the linked, naturalistic garden spaces advocated by the Hillside Club (plate 23).

Santa Barbara was the only part of coastal California that had extensive, open groves of indigenous oak trees. Charles Frederick Eaton—a landscape gardener, architect, and craftsman—embellished his estate in the foothills there over a period of twenty years using a highly painterly approach. He called this system "Nature under Control." Recognizing that the landscape was basically "golden

23. Bernard Maybeck, *Sketch for Hillside House*. From the *Hillside Club Yearbook,* 1908.

bronze" in color, he selected a broad range of plants to complement and display this color. Ocean views were broken up so that one never saw too much at once, and the views up the slope of the hills were punctuated by "sky-trees" (Eaton's term for trees taller than the surrounding canopy of trees). Eaton planted groves of trees to be seen in easterly views, with the sun's afternoon rays highlighting the forms of the trees and the color of their foliage. He also carefully pruned his trees to emphasize their sculptural qualities and asymmetrical foliage.[24]

A most successful form of natural hillside gardening was practiced in the Ojai Valley by the architects Myron Hunt and Elmer Grey in their gardens for C. W. Robertson and E. D. Libbey. In both, there was little disturbance of the natural landscape of rough grass, rugged boulders, and scattered oak trees. The simple, almost shacklike houses, based on wooden Swiss chalets, were carefully sited among the trees. Grace Tabor used a photograph (plate 24) of the Robertson bungalow (1906) as the frontispiece to her *Landscape Gardening Book* (1911), in which she drew attention to the remarkable similarity between the silhouettes of the house and of the mountains. The rough wall along the road, built of local stone, also served to relate the structure to its setting.

A completely different form of hillside garden was created in San Diego by the horticulturist Kate O. Sessions, working with such architects as Irving Gill, Frank Mead, and Richard S. Requa. San Diego's mesalike landscape with its steep-sided canyons lacked native trees and, despite the extensive planting of trees in Balboa Park and on Point Loma, the city never developed a forested character like Berkeley's. The barrenness reflected both the hardpan and the small size of the lots, which Sessions believed "will never make San Diego the Italy of America."[25]

24. Garden of the C. W. Robertson House (Felsengarten), Nordhoff (now Ojai), 1906, by Myron Hunt and Elmer Grey. From Grace Tabor, *The Landscape Gardening Book,* 1911.

25. Irving Gill, cottages for Alice Lee and Katherine Teats, San Diego, 1912.
❧ *These cottages were sited on the side of a narrow canyon. Each house was planted with vines to provide a delicate tracery, breaking up the plain surfaces of the walls. The houses were united by common gardens stepping down the hillside, which featured a formal system of paths, cobble retaining walls, and robust trees and shrubs.*

This group of San Diego designers established a garden type using drought-tolerant plants and low cobblestone terrace walls. A typical example is the garden that Sessions created for the Alice Lee and Katherine Teats cottages, designed by Irving Gill in 1912. This group of houses rose from the steep slope of a canyon that was terraced with a series of retaining walls made of the local red Camp Kearney stone. Italian cypresses, banana trees, and eucalyptus trees were used as specimens to provide vertical contrast to the predominantly horizontal shrubs on the terraced slope (plate 25). Sessions's planting sought to establish a new ecological order derived more from a sense of what would grow in the specific climatic conditions than from a predetermined set of visual ordering principles. In this respect her work is important more as an example of horticultural than of design technique.

The only similarity between the open-landscape garden of the Arts and Crafts movement and the English landscape garden of the eighteenth century was the use of an irregular, fluid pattern of movement through space. This Arts and Crafts garden type was used frequently in the Southland. Houses were placed in the center or on the edge of large lawns, looking out toward the mountains or a nearby arroyo, and the garden spaces were completely open to the street. The

garden space functioned as both a foreground to the views of the distant land-scape and an extension of the house. The color palette used in most of these gardens was restricted to a range of greens. Although there is no documentary evidence to support this supposition, this tendency may well reflect the function of the garden as a visual foreground to rich, strongly colored natural landscapes outside the garden.

The most important exponents of this garden type were Charles Sumner Greene and Henry Mather Greene of Pasadena. Despite their apparent formality, each of their designs employs irregular ways of moving through space. Charles Sumner Greene became particularly fascinated by the aesthetic qualities of Japanese gardens after Mrs. John Bentz, one of his clients, gave him a book on Japanese temple and domestic architecture. The Greene brothers' use of Japanese garden forms was evocative and not derivative. Indeed, like many other architects, they frequently conflated elements from several sources.

Despite a number of Italian flourishes, the David B. Gamble House in Pasadena (1908; plate 26) is one of the best examples of the Greenes' use of Japanese themes. The design of the service-yard fence, the use of stepping-stone paths across the lawn, the specific forms of the grading, and the battered retaining wall of the living-room terrace all make specific references to features of Japanese gardens and castles. Pairs of Italian cypress trees flank the semioval, brick-paved entrance drive. The house is lifted up on a terrace that surrounds the bulk of the house and extends the space of the living rooms out toward the garden (plate 42). The lawns were graded into softly flowing mounds so that from the street the drive was completely invisible and the house appeared to rise from the soft forms

26. Charles Sumner Greene and Henry Mather Greene, David B. Gamble House, Pasadena, 1908; photographed c. 1911.
∿ *The shingled house is lifted above the sensually graded lawns on a retaining wall made of boulders from the nearby arroyo and clinker brick, planted with creeping fig. The terrace is the principal out-door living space, providing panoramic views of the mountains and a range of open and partially shaded sitting areas.*

... an arbor leading at one side to a secluded spot, sheltered but not gloomy, where one may leave one's work or book and take it up again at will, where one could look out into the bright sunlight on groups of flowers, and where one may hear the tinkle of water and see the birds drink, where the shapely branches of tree or bush cast their lacy shadows fitly around a winding path.

Charles Sumner Greene, "California Home Making," *Pasadena Daily News,* Tournament of Roses edition, January 1905, pp. 26–27.

of the landscape. Seen from the house, the drive forms an abstract pattern complemented by the random lines of stepping stones that cross the grass.

Three alternative designs were produced for the Gamble House; in each, the house was oriented to take full advantage of the cooling prevailing winds and placed to benefit from three large eucalyptus trees already on the site. These trees served to integrate the house visually into the landscape and reduce its apparent size. The terrace walls were created with boulders from the nearby arroyo and with clinker bricks—slightly distorted, over-burned bricks whose dark colors and fluid forms harmonized well with the rounded forms of the boulders. These walls, which established a sense of the region, were further integrated into the landscape by a fluid layout that curved outward near the main group of trees to encompass a small pond and by being partially covered with a small creeping vine, the *Ficus repens*.[26]

Arts and Crafts designers favored patio gardens because of their associations with Spanish California and Italy. Helen Hunt Jackson's writings, together with essays by writers such as George Wharton James, drew attention to the old ranch houses and the missions, whose gardens comprised formally planted courtyards with a central fountain.[27] These houses were not truly Spanish or Mexican but a compromise between the Hispanic garden tradition and the formal gardens familiar to Yankee traders. Little attempt was made to revive the Spanish gardens, since almost nothing was known about the original planting. Charles Francis Saunders, a popular garden writer, was a lone figure who attempted to determine that information by corresponding with the descendants of old Spanish families.

The patio provided space that could be used for a variety of purposes: some patios were covered with a retractable glazed roof or removable canvas panels to become an additional enclosed room, others housed swimming pools.[28] Patios were designed in two ways. In one type, two or at most three colonnades of the house would enclose a small formal garden or panel of lawn—a feature of several houses by Myron Hunt and Elmer Grey. These gardens established a transitional zone, integrating interior and exterior spaces.[29] In the second type, the patio was enclosed and paved, becoming another room within the house. A number of Irving Gill's houses were designed around a patio defined on three sides by colonnades and on the fourth by a wall with glazed openings to a walled garden beyond. These paved patios, furnished with vines, a banana tree or small palm, and wicker furniture and rugs, were used as rooms. In the Homer Laughlin garden in Los Angeles (1908), a door in the outer wall opened onto a columned pergola in the center of a large walled garden (plate 27). In larger gardens a detached wooden pergola would provide a shady place where one could sew, read, converse, or enjoy the view of the garden and the mountains.[30] This created a spatial transition from full enclosure in the patio to partial shade to full sunlight in the garden.[31]

Gill's houses represent a form of regional appropriateness derived from Spanish-Mexican precedents. But they were also progressive. His concrete houses

27. Irving Gill, Homer Laughlin garden, Los Angeles, 1908.

‿ *This view was taken from the pergola in the middle of the principal garden, looking back into the patio. Each spatial element of the house and garden is a clearly defined entity, related visually to each other along axial lines. The sequence of spaces provides a transition from the coolness of the interior to the bright sunlight of the garden.*

28. Frank Mead and Richard S. Requa, Theosophical Society Building, Krotona Court, Hollywood, 1914. From *Western Architect*, October 1914.

‿ *The central court with its lavishly planted pool provides a tropical flourish and contrast to the abstract masses of the wall planes. The pool is planted with water lilies and papyrus and in spirit comes close to the ideal patio garden described by Alfred D. Robinson (opposite).*

united advanced building technology with simplified and abstracted references to mission buildings and a romantic delight in the color and wildness of the land-scape. The abstract forms were anchored to their settings by pergolas—sometimes open and sometimes covered with creepers and vines that created a delicate tracery on the walls. Color was an important aspect of these designs. Gill achieved a "second blooming" on the walls of his garden rooms by placing red geraniums close to the walls, which were colored by a mixture of primary colors with white paint. Ceramic tiles arranged in geometric patterns were also used to provide minor concentrations of color.[32]

29. Charles Fletcher Lummis, wildflower meadow at El Alisal, Los Angeles, photographed 1901.

∾ *On my own little place there are, today, at least forty million wild blossoms, by calculation. Short of the wandering and unconventioned foot-paths, which are almost choked with the urgent plant-life beside them, you cannot step anywhere without trampling flowers—maybe ten to a step, as a minimum. One bred to climes where God counts flowers as Easterners do their copper cents, may not prefer to walk on them; but out here God and we can afford the carpet.*

Charles Fletcher Lummis, "The Carpet of God's Country," *Out West* 22 (1905): 306–17.

Let us treat it as an oasis in our desert of too much of everything. Let us get a tall palm for the court so that its crown shall rise well above the walls. . . . In the court, lilies in the pool, papyrus in one corner, two pomegranates or oranges in tubs and a grape arbor on one side. That is all.

Alfred D. Robinson, "The Fitness of Things," *California Garden* 4 (1913): 4.

North Africa also influenced the design of patios. In Mead and Requa's design for Krotona Court (1914), the Theosophical Society building in Hollywood, the central court contains a pool surrounded by colonnades. The pool, planted with water lilies and papyrus, provides a note of tropical lushness, in stark contrast to the abstract wall planes, and captures the spirit of the ideal California garden (plate 28).[33]

Meadow gardening was an unusual garden type, the earliest recorded example of which is Charles Fletcher Lummis's own garden, of 1898, at his house El Alisal in the Highland Park section of Los Angeles. Lummis created one of the most compelling Arts and Crafts images in California by building his house with boulders taken from the nearby arroyo, close to the grove of sycamore trees from which the house takes its name. The house overlooked a large wildflower meadow (plate 29)[34]—an uncontrived garden that was the quintessence of that harmonious naturalness sought by Arts and Crafts advocates. The usable area of the garden was confined to the paved patio around which the house was built and an orchard of citrus and fruit trees. The result unmistakably expressed a regional character.

Anita Baldwin McClaughry's estate Anoakia, in Arcadia, contained extensive planted meadows of California poppies. The orange of the poppies and the red of the climbing roses on the surrounding walls were a peculiarly Californian combination of colors.[35] But the Lummis and McClaughry gardens were isolated examples of wildflower use. Despite the very popular weekend expeditions by many Southland residents to view native wildflower meadows and despite the ardent advocacy of their use by the nurseryman Theodore Payne, they had to be restricted to large gardens, since it is very difficult to establish and maintain wildflower meadows in small spaces. Several estates in Montecito contained extensive areas of wildflowers, native shrubs, and trees outside the elaborate formal gardens surrounding the house. A number of very large wildflower preserves were created by rich patrons in the mountains above Santa Barbara and Santa Monica.

Many features from professionally designed gardens reappeared in vernacular bungalow gardens. Bungalows were the most popular type of house, not just in California but throughout the West Coast region. The novelist Mary Austin regarded them as indigenous manifestations of the desert because of their natural color and materials. In large bungalow tracts the relation of the bungalow's ridge line to the street or the position of dormer windows on the roof plane was often changed, giving otherwise identical houses a measure of individuality. Gardens provided similar opportunities for personal expression. In his book *California Gardens* (1914), Eugene O. Murmann advocated a plethora of different styles, which included the Tudor and Jacobean styles, formal gardens, and a variety of oriental forms.[36] Design number 17 shows a Japanese Hill Garden (*Tsukiyama-niva*) (plate 30), in which A, B, C, and D are small hills, and a small lake is fed by a waterfall. Despite these demonstrably Japanese features, the overall organization of the garden is virtually identical to Murmann's other designs.

Ernest Braunton, a writer for the *Los Angeles Times,* believed that "natural" or "landscape" gardening was the ideal form for any garden, no matter what its size. The central feature of such plantings was a lawn defined by curving, massed plants carefully arranged so as not to appear artificial. He strove for a garden in which "no scene is twice seen," since a repetition of plants would provide neither stimulus nor incentive to walk through a garden. Braunton and Murmann disagreed over garden style, but they both thought that the back garden should have what Braunton called a "homelike character."[37]

Whatever the style of a bungalow garden, the narrow width of a typical lot did not permit much planting at its sides. Functional features such as a garage and a small area for vegetables were invariably placed at the back of the garden for access from a rear alley. Edward J. Wickson, a popular writer on gardens and the dean of agriculture at the University of California, Berkeley, exhorted commercial California farmers to grow vegetables for their own table, believing that they would be superior to their competitors' in Southern Europe, China, and Japan. Saunders also wrote about the decorative value of vegetables in the garden, but he admitted that his own garden was merely a form of play and not a serious attempt to provide food for his table (plate 31). Vegetables and other productive plants were invariably hidden by vines and shrubs, suggesting that they were considered too utilitarian or ugly to be a part of the principal garden view.[38]

Despite Saunders's declaration of the desirability of making as little distinction as possible between internal and external spaces, this was normally achieved only on the front porch, which frequently spanned the entire width of the bungalow. Views were thus toward the street rather than into the private back garden. Visually, a typical bungalow was tied to the ground plane by a planting of shrubs

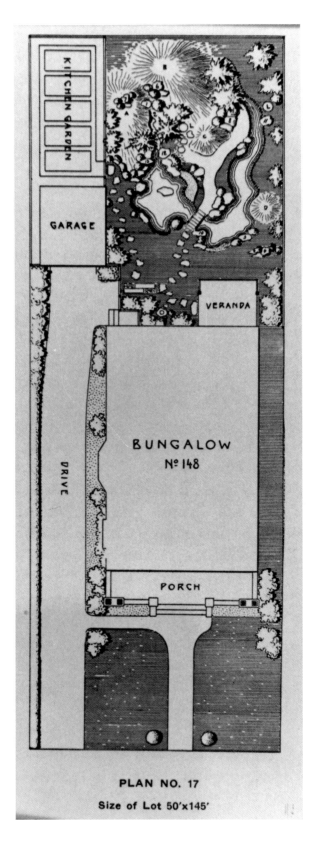

PLAN NO. 17

Size of Lot 50'x145'

and small trees placed against the house to hide its foundations. The ideal growing conditions of the Southland frequently ensured that such planting, especially vines, so embowered the structure that it almost disappeared.

On most bungalow streets the open front lawns formed collective parklike spaces, as advocated by Wickson.[39] J. E. Gould, a Seattle landscape architect, suggested that privacy and restfulness could be obtained by using well-planted curving paths, but his alternative was rarely followed.[40] Braunton believed that the enclosure of the front garden was essentially a matter of taste. He suggested that the side boundaries could be masked by walls that were low where they met the street and rose in easy tiers to a high wall at the rear.[41] Front gardens either had no walls at all or low walls of clinker brick and boulders against the sidewalk. Planting along the property line was very unusual. The customary practice of having outdoor living space facing the street confirms both the continuity of the American fondness for sitting on the front stoop and Grace Ellery Channing's belief that Americans needed instruction on how to live out-of-doors.[42]

This practice contrasted markedly with the advocates of the Spanish patio, who insisted that placing a porch on the street side was a "folly to sacrifice for outward show and living."[43] Although the traditional Hispanic patio house offered many lessons that could have been successfully applied to the small house, such explorations remained firmly in the realm of professional designers. Irving Gill's design for the Mrs. George D. Ruddy bungalow patio house (1912) in Los Angeles demonstrated that a small house on a small lot could incorporate a front porch, an internal patio, and a secluded rear garden approached directly from the living room. Gill's double houses in San Diego (1902–8) offer unusual examples of houses developed without front gardens, the houses being placed directly on the line of the sidewalk. His design for Bellavista Terrace (1911) in Sierra Madre was an even more potent demonstration of the alternative to the typical street landscape. Attached houses were placed on the perimeter of the block, with their outer walls against the sidewalk. The inner space was occupied by private gardens for each house and a communal garden at the center, with a large pergola for shared meals and conversation. This design represented an outline of a regionally appropriate form of communal living, which also acknowledged the need for individual privacy.[44]

Size clearly determined the character of most gardens. Saunders's own garden in Pasadena demonstrated how a medium-size lot, ninety by sixty feet, could provide a variety of the features associated with larger gardens (plate 31). On the street side a generous porch provided a place from which the residents could look out. Shrubs, including vines such as the Rêve d'or rose, visually anchored the house to the level front lawn. The rear garden had to take up a cross fall of some six feet. This was accomplished by a series of terrace walls, one to two feet high, constructed of cobblestones from the arroyo. The rear-porch steps led down to a

32. Kate O. Sessions, Mrs. Robert's garden, Coronado, c. 1916. From Mrs. Francis King, *Pages from a Garden Notebook,* 1921.

rectangular lawn of lippia grass, surrounded by decomposed-granite paths that gave access to a series of rectangular beds. These contained a variety of plants, including a collection of native California plants, vegetables, gaillardias, sweet alyssum, verbenas, mignonette, and foxgloves, with begonias and ferns on the shaded north side. The native plant collection included cacti, yuccas, cotyledons, California poppies, Indian paintbrush, shooting star, penstemons, gilias, phacelias, and cream cups. These plants represented themes or concepts that held meaning for Saunders and his wife. In its simple and unpretentious layout, its range of plants, and its provision of a variety of places to sit, this garden was an excellent and modest demonstration of Arts and Crafts ideals.[45]

The small garden designed by Kate O. Sessions for Mrs. Robert in Coronado demonstrated that colorful and drought-tolerant plants could be used as a carpet around the house, which was designed by William Templeton Johnson (plate 32). The ocher walls of the adobelike house had dark cobalt blue trim at the windows and doors, which complemented plantings in which the bold foliage of cacti and aloes was set off by masses of plants with yellow and orange flowers and other plants with gray foliage.[46] Mrs. Francis King, a popular garden writer of the 1920s, provided a detailed description of the garden in 1921, noting that one of its most striking features was the restrained use of creepers against the house. King believed, probably correctly, that quick-growing vines would often suffocate a house.

As the Arts and Crafts movement lost popularity, the design types described here were supplanted in private gardens by an increasing use of conservative, historicizing designs. Some of these gardens of the late 1910s and 1920s were created with a level of craftsmanship that extended the best standards of the Arts and Crafts period. The D. L. James House at Carmel Highlands (1919–23) and the water garden at Green Gables in Woodside (1926–29), both designed by Charles Sumner Greene, represent a belated apogee of Arts and Crafts style.[47] The ideal of creating designed garden spaces in complete harmony with the regional setting was also taken up by a major federal agency. The National Park Service was founded in 1916 with the idea that the landscape of each national park should be maintained as it had been prior to the advent of white culture. From 1916 until 1942 park structures and their associated landscaping were designed with an Arts and Crafts sensibility.[48]

The Arts and Crafts garden in California shared the general ideals of garden design elsewhere in the country in creating unpretentious designs out of local materials, in relating buildings to the broader landscape, and in treating garden space as an outdoor room. But it was unique in a number of ways, including the distinctive use of color, the value placed on views, the range of sources and styles, and the actual use of the garden as an outdoor room. In these various ways the Arts and Crafts garden in California established a memorable regional identity. However, like all other attempts to settle this volatile and fragile landscape, it depended on the imposition of both imported cultures and imported water.

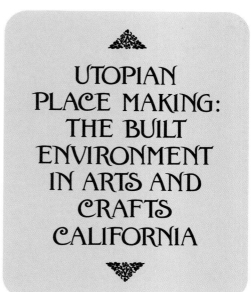

UTOPIAN PLACE MAKING: THE BUILT ENVIRONMENT IN ARTS AND CRAFTS CALIFORNIA

Karen J. Weitze

33. Detail of *Presentation Rendering for the Dr. Malcolm Goddard House,* 1914. See plate 40.

The Arts and Crafts movement achieved architectural excellence in California between 1906 and 1914—years bracketed by noteworthy early experimentation and memorable modern design. The rise of the movement found a parallel in a regional political intensity, a progressivism that, along with the socialist ideals of the upper Midwest, led America into widespread reform. In art and politics California had much in common with Chicago, for just as Chicago represented the larger region of Illinois, Wisconsin, Michigan, and Minnesota, so California included Oregon and Washington in a single political and architectural unit. California was also similar to the upper Midwest in that it offered an agrarian landscape with lively pinpoints of urban life. The state's geography and climate, however, distinguished the western region from the country at large. Its seeming isolation, exotic terrain, and extremely mild seasons caused California to develop a distinct Arts and Crafts imagery without losing elements that were essentially midwestern in motivation, spirit, and—often—in form.

As early as the 1880s the writer Helen Hunt Jackson described California as an "island on the land," as indeed the rest of the country perceived the state from the vantage point of east of the Mississippi River.[1] California offered a nearly perfect setting for the creation of the "middle landscape." A term coined by the historian Leo Marx for a concept embodied in Western literature for centuries, the middle landscape refers to a place of escape, of hope, of utopian endeavor.[2] Typically separated from the real world by oceans and deserts, it could be reached only via futuristic travel. Inhabitants of the middle landscape always sought out nature, wanting it to be both wild and domestically supportive.[3] Generally speaking, the British and the American Arts and Crafts movements wanted the middle landscape to be a halfway house between an idealized pastoral life and the improved convenience of the dawning Machine Age. California, like nowhere else, offered the Arts and Crafts movement a blank slate, a place to try out its philosophies. Clusters of manipulated microenvironments in different parts of the state embraced new technologies and simultaneously kept a partially tamed nature at their doors. Patrons and architects alike were often caught up with images drawn from utopian fiction, avant-garde building science, and premodern cultures and handicraft.

California did not present a uniform stage set but rather challenged proponents of the Arts and Crafts through its extreme richness and diversity to find appropriate forms of expression. In both Northern and Southern California, Arts and Crafts patrons found themselves caught up in political issues of social change, sometimes arguing from opposed vantage points but nonetheless consumed with the same issues. Social change—reform—demanded that people live together, and thus California's Arts and Crafts architecture and politics went forward intertwined. The architecture built in California during this period is intimately associated with the outdoors, reflecting the land on which it was built—ruggedly woodsy in the north and pastorally agrarian in the south. Full-scale farming, as well as thoughtful community planning efforts, typified only Southern California—where repeated days of sunshine and model irrigation encouraged such utopian activities. A few innovative architects settled in each region and experimented with both style and technology, in wood and concrete. Whether sited in the north or south, many, if not most, California Arts and Crafts residences had elevated, and often magnificent, views of bordering arroyos, canyons, desert mountains, wooded hills, cultivated orange groves, or coastal bays. Frequently, those dwellings without full views had upper-story glimpses and were within several blocks of an extended walk into nature.

In Northern California the Arts and Crafts activity was concentrated in the San Francisco Bay Area. Design theory was exchanged among members of the Bay Area architectural group, and the younger architectural draftsmen and draftswomen were active in the Arts and Crafts movement as a whole, planting hillsides in eucalyptus and keeping ties to urban San Francisco. To the south efforts were rural in the larger sense, with sufficient physical space and initial isolation from both the rest of the state and the nation to permit widespread experimentation. Design theory was far less cohesive in Southern California, yet Hispanic adobe traditions provided a model much stronger than any vernacular, handicraft building tradition in the north. International Arts and Crafts journals, too, captured the uniqueness of the adobe precedents in Southern California, and when featuring American building innovation in the movement they often turned to activities in this part of the state.

The central San Joaquin Valley surrounding Fresno near Yosemite, the coast near Atascadero–Santa Barbara, Pasadena–Los Angeles, Riverside–Redlands, and San Diego all showcased Arts and Crafts built environments. In every instance, human intervention substantially changed the natural landscape, forcing it to bloom exotically and prolifically, making it like no other region in the United States. Climate made the region healthful, while irrigation—well developed during the 1880s—made the living profitable, attracting substantial wealth to the region. Those areas of California truly of desert and mountainous character, inland to the east at the foot of the Sierra Nevada and the entire northern third of the state, witnessed almost no Arts and Crafts architectural effort.

California's architectural entrance into the Arts and Crafts movement began with the San Francisco–based competitions for the California Building planned for the World's Columbian Exposition at Chicago in 1893 (plate 34). Two competitions, in 1891 and 1892, formally introduced a group of about thirty architectural firms to the notion of a Mission style, although for more than a decade architects and romanticists alike had been exploring the idea of a regional architecture based on Hispanic traditions. The architect John Galen Howard had sketched Southern California vernacular adobes, as well as the somewhat more formal (although deteriorated) missions, during the late 1880s. Bernard Maybeck, who would become an Arts and Crafts design leader in Northern California, had worked as a draftsman for Carrère and Hastings on the St. Augustine, Florida, commissions for the Ponce de León and Alcazar hotels of 1886–88. These hotels are generally acknowledged to be the first nineteenth-century American buildings to express what was termed "Spanish Renaissance" imagery. These structures are also acknowledged as among the earliest to respond to ideas of indigenous structural form and materials. The central tower of the Ponce de León, a Maybeck feature, appeared again in the California Building of 1893.

Other designers explored the precedents of the Spanish Romanesque, building on the stylistic approach used by Henry Hobson Richardson in his treat-

34. A. Page Brown. *California Building, World's Columbian Exposition, Chicago*, 1893. Lithograph mounted on canvas, 28⅛ x 43⅞ in. (paper size). California State Library Collections, Sacramento.

ment of the medieval idiom.[4] Most significant was Shepley, Rutan, and Coolidge's design (1886–87) of a mission-inspired quadrangle for Stanford University, in Palo Alto.[5] (The university community as a whole would become active in living out the ideals of the simple life, emphasizing the benefits of the healthy out-of-doors, paralleling those bohemian lifeways of Berkeley.)

The thousands of visitors who saw A. Page Brown's California Building in Chicago gained their first introduction to the connections between the ideologies of handicraft and the imagery of the California missions.[6] The prominence of mission imagery in the California Building also introduced the American public to a new idea of medieval life. Typically based on a Hispanic medievalism seen through the lens of several centuries, cultures, and building traditions, Arts and Crafts medievalism in the West expanded almost immediately after the fair to include the more readily understood Northern European architectural rustic precedent. In 1894 the San Francisco Bay Area witnessed two key commissions of a Northern European model tied to the Arts and Crafts: A. C. Schweinfurth's Swedenborgian Church of the New Jerusalem, which commanded a view of San Francisco Bay from atop Russian Hill (plates 13, 35), and Maybeck's hilltop dwelling for Charles Keeler in Berkeley (plates 36, 59). (Both Schweinfurth and Maybeck had worked as draftsmen for Brown on the California Building.) Built for the Reverend Joseph Worcester, the Church of the New Jerusalem featured a visual and tactile interplay of eclectic, exotic themes—from Hispanic arcades and tile to rusticated wood and rush to Asian accent pieces, artificial and real. Like many later Arts and Crafts commissions, that of the Swedenborgian meetinghouse drew on the efforts of contributing artists, in this case William Keith and Bruce Porter.[7]

35. A. Page Brown, architect, with contributions by A. C. Schweinfurth and Bernard Maybeck, sanctuary of the Swedenborgian Church of the New Jerusalem, San Francisco, 1894; photographed 1991.

36. Bernard Maybeck, the Davis, Keeler, Rieger, and Hall houses, Berkeley, c. 1900. The Keeler House is second from the left.

On the east side of the bay, perched high on a steep hillside at Ridge Road and Highland Place, Maybeck's 1894–95 dwelling for the poet and naturalist Charles Keeler embodied another aspect of California Arts and Crafts. With its steep roofs, tightly massed spaces, and wooden construction, the Keeler residence reflected a more traditional Northern European medieval imagery that bespoke Maybeck's German heritage. Maybeck referred to his design as "Gothic," which was accurate only in the sense of the revived and abstracted Gothic of the earlier nineteenth century, exemplified by the highly intellectualized Gothic of the French theorist and architect Eugène Viollet-le-Duc, with its rational placement of structural members.[8] For the Berkeley perch with its dramatic bay panorama, Maybeck abruptly juxtaposed artificially heightened small interior spaces, creating allusions to cramped medieval quarters—allusions tinted with modern notions of delight and surprise.[9] By 1899 a nucleus of Maybeck houses graced the ridge, and their Gothicized Arts and Crafts wooden structures established an initial design that would evolve toward the Bay Area bungalow and shingle house. A commune of sorts developed on the ridge, with like-minded residents whose active involvement in Berkeley's politically and environmentally sensitive Hillside Club set the neighborhood tone.[10]

From the beginning, a fictional utopian vision infused such real-life communal enclaves in Berkeley and the Oakland hills. Joaquin Miller, a California poet, in his 1894 novel *The Building of the City Beautiful* juxtaposed an unsuccessful attempt at a City Beautiful in the Oakland hills with a gleaming model city in the deserts of Egypt. A cooperative society prevailed in the novel, where noisome workshops were banned, partial workdays were established, and a natural site was isolated from the greater world and enhanced through irrigated agriculture. "Pleasant porches" accented wooded lanes. High-speed rail transportation dominated the many machines presented to make everyday life easier. Miller intended his society on the Nile, a fictional middle landscape, to come to life in the Oakland hills through the efforts of the Arts and Crafts movement. In reality, Miller built a secluded house high above Oakland and planted groves of eucalyptus.[11]

At this same time Charles Keeler, too, spoke to sophisticated members of California's educated, and often intellectual, middle class in *The Simple Home* of 1904. His idea of hillside architecture as "Landscape Gardening around a few rooms for use in case of rain" captured the physical character of the clusters of early twentieth-century Maybeck-designed dwellings set at several sites in Berkeley.[12] These neighborhood nuclei followed the pattern of the original group at Ridge Road and Highland Place and, like the original, offered delightful and complex views of San Francisco Bay, as well as accessible walks into the wilderness at the edge of Berkeley.

Although Maybeck was by no means the only Arts and Crafts architect in the San Francisco Bay Area, his work has come to epitomize a thoughtful approach to the land itself and to represent a sociopolitical mind-set shared by Arts and Crafts architects and clients. Annie Maybeck, Bernard's wife, led the women of the Hillside Club in their fights to preserve Berkeley's maturing trees and ungraded hills. Hillside Club members, typically Unitarians and neighbors, campaigned for a shared public landscape, with Bernard Maybeck designing simple houses appropriate to preexisting nature. The most provocative of his hillside groups was the one rambling out from the corner of Buena Vista Way and La Loma Avenue in northeastern Berkeley. In 1907 the architect designed a house there for the University of California geology professor Andrew C. Lawson (plate 37). Lawson had been among Maybeck's first clients, with an 1896 dwelling like those of the Keeler group.

The Lawson residence on La Loma sits down the hillside toward Berkeley with a southwestern vista of the bay. Axial doors in the living spaces provide views to the west and east, with further vistas leading into the gardens and outward to the bay. Balconies, loggias, and sleeping porches highlight the second story. Diverging from Maybeck's wood-frame, rustic houses, Lawson's house showcases a simple design in reinforced concrete—dictated by Lawson's professional interests as well as by a raised consciousness following the San Francisco earthquake and fire of 1906. Designing for inexpensive construction through the experimental use of concrete and machine-tooled technologies became another interest for Maybeck, whose design theory, related to ideas of rationally expressed structure, pointed clearly to the modern era. His First Church of Christ, Scientist (1910), exemplifies the Bay Area Arts and Crafts movement through its reinforced-concrete construction, slab foundation, industrial-steel sash-paneled windows, and partial asbestos-tile sheathing (plate 38).

Mrs. Keith revived the Berkeley club, which soon doubled its membership and with the Oakland and Alameda clubs became a strong influence. There were three clubs in San Francisco and an active organization in Santa Clara county, made up of San Jose, Palo Alto and other clubs. . . .

The annual convention met October 24, 1902, in Century Hall, San Francisco, with a large attendance and many excellent speakers, among them Dr. David Starr Jordan, president of Stanford University. . . . An interesting event reported was a suffrage meeting of the Sierra Club of mountain lovers one summer evening in King's River Canyon, where it was encamped. In the audience of over two hundred prominent men and women were Professor Joseph Le Conte, John Muir, William Keith, Dr. C. Hart Merriam, head of U.S. biological department and Dr. Gannett, of the geological department. . . .

While in San Francisco [in 1905 following the annual convention of the National Suffrage Association in Portland, Oregon] Miss Anthony found time to give one sitting for a large oil portrait by William Keith, which was completed after her death in the spring of 1906 and looked down upon the audience from the chancel of the Unitarian church in San Francisco at the memorial services for her on Palm Sunday, April 8.

National American Woman Suffrage Association, *History of Woman Suffrage* 6 (1922): 28–29, 32.

37. Bernard Maybeck, Andrew C. Lawson House, Berkeley, 1907; photographed 1991.

38. Bernard Maybeck, First Church of Christ, Scientist, Berkeley, 1910.

When not designing structures of the shingled type, Maybeck frequently made allusions to classical Greece and Italy. Both the Lawson residence and the Christian Science church offer early Roman associations in detail and symbol. The plastered pink-and-buff walls with small inset tiles make the Lawson house scintillate with color. (The Bay Area Arts and Crafts artist community generally disavowed themselves of the publicly accepted and influential notion that ancient Mediterranean architecture had been white, instead displaying an archeologically correct understanding of classical polychroming.) For the Christian Science church Maybeck employed deep red, blue, green, black, and gilt in interior stencilwork, symbolic of the early Roman Christianity to which the Christian Scientists looked for an understanding of miraculous healing. Again the architect demonstrated a mastery of linked, indoor axial spaces and outdoor portico, trellises, and gardens. Cast-concrete piers with low-relief figured capitals and Gothicized tracery reflect Maybeck's fascination with eleventh- and twelfth-century medieval designs.[13]

After finishing the Lawson residence, Bernard Maybeck—along with Annie—purchased an entire tract of land adjacent to Lawson's, to the north and east. Buena Vista Way meandered eastward into the hills through the property. The Maybecks focused on careful hillside development; they intended to subdivide the land into lots and offer them for sale, accompanied by preliminary architect's drawings for appropriate housing. Maybeck's designs stressed the connection to a healthy outdoor life, and California's pastoral setting and Hispanic past were alluded to in the street names Buena Vista (Beautiful View) and La Loma (The Hill).

The architect actually designed several projects and houses for the Buena Vista streetscape from 1909 to 1916, including his own second residence in Berkeley. But closeness to nature ultimately had its drawback: in 1923 a devastating fire burned half of the Buena Vista dwellings. Nevertheless, during the 1920s and 1930s seven more Maybeck houses went up along the street. Maybeck's own third house (replacing his second on the same site in 1924) was of Bubblestone, an experimental material meant for simple, inexpensive, fireproof dwellings. Burlap sacks soaked in a concrete mixture hung like shingles on a standard wood-frame structure. A one-room residence without dining room or kitchen, it opened through industrial-sash glass doors onto the garden. Sleeping took place in the open air, and architecture did indeed seem to be "in case of rain."[14]

In addition to proximity to the outdoors in terms of siting and landscaping, Arts and Crafts houses in California feature a deliberate blurring of interior and exterior space. The modest California bungalow, one story and wood-frame, hid itself in its surroundings. In Palo Alto about 1896–1900, the head of the Stanford University art department designed and built a shingled bungalow with a mature oak tree growing through the front-porch roof; a ladder was set in place so that the artist could climb up and relax under the overhanging branches (plate 39). There were fireplaces in all rooms except the kitchen, with unstained redwood boards sheathing the walls. Carefully contrived play on nature's colors and textures accented the understatement of the built environment. Indeed, the retreat-to-nature quality of the bungalow characterized California—paralleling and possibly even contributing to the maturing of rustic design for the Victorian camps in the Adirondack and Catskill mountains in New York State. The bungalow in Palo Alto is among the earliest designs to establish a clear connection between Arts and Crafts centers on the East and West coasts, with influences flowing in both directions.[15]

An extension of the retreatlike quality of the bungalow was the bungalow tent—a simple one- to three-room structure built on a platform with clapboarded base, usually erected to the rear of the main house. Bungalow tents erased the distinction between indoors and out. Canvas wall flaps could be rolled up, allowing

39. Arthur Bridgman Clark, Bolton Coit Brown House, Palo Alto, c. 1896–1900. From *House Beautiful,* April 1907.

6 2

sleepers or sitters an open-air life with a shingled (or sometimes canvas) roof, canvas or burlap interior walls, wood floor, and typically informal furniture. Treehouses or platforms built between grouped trees carried the tent idea to its extreme.[16] To further their ties to the great outdoors, in about 1911 the professorial communities of both Stanford and the University of California at Berkeley established summer camps of rustic cabins in the El Dorado National Forest: Arthur Martin Cathcart, a Stanford law professor and graduate of 1896, pioneered the Fallen Leaf Camp near Lake Tahoe.[17]

Architectural as well as politically progressive activity clubs contributed heavily to the Arts and Crafts life in California—with a variety of such study groups in the San Francisco Bay Area. Notable examples included the Ruskin Club, the Hillside Club, the Lincoln-Roosevelt Republican League, and a wide range of women's clubs, all with their socialist components—albeit few definitively radical in their world view. Although the architectural-art clubs were a national phenomenon, they also made specific statements about the West Coast's architectural Arts and Crafts. Membership in the sketch clubs did not usually overlap with that of the American Institute of Architects' (AIA) clubs. Most often, established architects represented the status quo (and participated in the mainstream clubs of the national institute), whereas draftsmen and draftswomen more freely experimented with new ideas and more frequently participated in the Arts and Crafts movement (with its attendant sketch clubs). Official clubs connoted a certain exclusive success; the Arts and Crafts sketch clubs were a much more fluid environment, with some clubs being very short-lived and specific geographic areas almost over-represented by multiple groups. (As an example, on the eastern shore of San Francisco Bay alone, Oakland had its Ruskin Club, its founding Lincoln-Roosevelt Republican League group, and three chapters of the American Woman's League; Berkeley, its Hillside Club; and Alameda County, three architectural sketch clubs at one time.)

Sketch clubs educated young architects through their encouragement of learning: guest lectures, informal classes, jointly compiled libraries, sketching trips, and exhibitions all characterized the phenomenon as it swept the United States. Between 1908 and 1916 architectural sketch clubs and allied arts groups published annual exhibition catalogs illustrating their members' works, sponsored by a range of Arts and Crafts small businesses. In the West these publications reveal the circulation of architectural ideas between California, Oregon, Washington, and Hawaii, areas that all seemed isolated from the rest of the country. California and Hawaii, in particular, served as sources for new architectural ideas based on climate, terrain, and Asian or Hispanic cultures. The San Francisco Bay Area had the most active relationship with Honolulu: several architects, such as Charles W. Dickey, maintained offices in both places and brought ideas to club meetings in both the Hawaiian Islands and the Berkeley-Oakland hills.[18]

The collaborative Architectural League of the Pacific Coast, organized in Portland, Oregon, in March 1909, was the most provocative of the architectural clubs in the West, extending its interests beyond architecture to the crafted arts associated with the design of buildings. Through about 1915 the league drew the more experimental members of the established San Francisco, Southern California, and Washington State AIA chapters together with the draftsmen and draftswomen of the San Francisco, Los Angeles, Portland, and Seattle sketch clubs. Smaller sketch clubs from other parts of the Pacific Coast were represented in the league as well. The effort was geared toward the junior architect and a kind of craft-guild education. Clubs in the league were to be formed in cities without club representation and thus without a formal mechanism for the exchange of art and architectural ideas. Affiliations with the AIA and professional solidarity west of Denver were to be enhanced; scholarships for study abroad, improved. Annual exhibitions were scheduled throughout Pacific Coast cities: for the 1909 exhibition 132 craftsmen and craftswomen exhibited architectural drawings, landscapes, furniture, pottery, tile, friezes, sculpture, and art glass in 814 exhibits.[19] In 1910 the league published catalogs of exhibitions in Los Angeles, Seattle, and Portland.[20]

The most intriguing approach to architectural rendering offered in these West Coast catalogs was the use of dark, tonal watercolor sketches for house designs. Reminiscent of landscapes by William Keith (who had studied with George Inness), the abstracted style also employed framing devices such as attenuated eucalyptus and cypress trees. Published renderings by the English and Scottish turn-of-the-century architects and furniture designers M. H. Baillie Scott and Charles Rennie Mackintosh undoubtedly influenced these tonal watercolors with their high-keyed color accents. The watercolors also strongly exhibited the American aesthetic that Wanda Corn has labeled Tonalism, "the color of mood."[21] Through his renderings for the *Craftsman,*[22] the architect Harvey Ellis had introduced the American art community to abstracted, tonal presentation drawings during the final six months of 1903, but with his death in January 1904 that style had largely disappeared. For the West the approach had no real impact until about 1909 with the founding of the sketch clubs—and then it distinguished itself from the English precedent through its emphasis on the features of the western landscape.[23]

Indeed, a way of seeing that was Californian in both color and form likely motivated the western Arts and Crafts tonal presentation. Una Nixson Hopkins wrote for *Keith's* in 1914: "Color is more of a problem in the West. . . . East of the Rockies . . . the landscape and trees are not of so many tones . . . in the West there is a great range of shades . . . to be reckoned with when the exterior coloring of a house is at stake."[24] Such a consideration was particularly true in reference to the imported Australian eucalyptus that thrived in California, where the hazy, filtered sunlight augmented the tonal qualities of the tree's gray-green leaves. The sinuous eucalyptus, with its tightly clustered, spare, draped foliage, also lent itself to two-dimensional abstraction.

The stress placed on abstracted color and form by California's Arts and Crafts designers influenced the architectural profession as a whole, contributing

SIDENCE FOR DR. MALCOLM GODDARD·WALNUT CREEK, CAL·IRVING F. MORROW·ARCHITEC

40. *Presentation Rendering for the Dr. Malcolm Goddard House,* Irving F. Morrow, architect, Walnut Creek, California, 1914. Watercolor on paper, 14 x 24 in. College of Environmental Design, Documents Collection, University of California, Berkeley.

to the growing body of associated design theory. Traditional architectural renderings, crisp of line and with little or no color, dominated American presentation styles as late as 1910.[25] By 1914 architectural critics commented that color was a positive virtue, and by mid-1916 *American Architect* editorialized that lively color, coming from California, marked a shift in the accepted aesthetics for American buildings at large.[26] The shift likely began with the change to tonal watercolor rendering, which was primarily dark but had highlights of bright color. California muralists, most especially Arthur F. Mathews, further affected the architectural rendering style as it matured.[27] The presentation watercolor by Irving F. Morrow for Dr. Malcolm Goddard's Walnut Creek residence of 1914 represents the contribution of California Arts and Crafts to two-dimensional visual design theory (plate 40). The Architectural League of the Pacific Coast published the Morrow watercolor in its San Francisco yearbook of 1915.[28]

Southern California, too, developed an Arts and Crafts persona, attracting a group of artists and writers much published as a literati distinct from the individuals associated with the northern section of the state. Squeezed between the austere desert to the east and the ocean to the west, Southern California Arts and Crafts designers often played on imagery borrowed from the Hispanic, the Native American, and the Japanese. The writer-impresarios Charles Fletcher Lummis and George Wharton James adopted personas that amalgamated the Southwest and the Orient. In his costuming and name change, Lummis (who called himself Don Carlos) complemented New York's flamboyant Arts and Crafts advocate Elbert Hubbard (who called himself Fra Elbertus).

California south of the Tehachapi Mountains offered as inspiration the land itself. Arthur J. Burdick's 1904 book *The Mystic Mid-Region* used photographs to underscore the barren emptiness of then little-populated Southern California.[29] Mary Austin's 1903 book *The Land of Little Rain* referred to the region as the "Country of Lost Borders." Austin wrote about color—*tonal* color—commenting, for instance, on multiple shades of a particular green, orange, or yellow.[30] Focusing on the color qualities of the desert landscape appears to have fostered a regional Arts and Crafts interest in coordinating nature's vistas with vast, exotic constructed parks and estate gardens. The southern landscape provided a magnitude of viewshed that could be manipulated in ways impossible in the more densely featured Northern California terrain. Irrigation expanded the ways that views could be constructed and made possible the heightening of color accents.

All these distinctive regional attributes—a vocal literati; Hispanic, Native American, and Japanese aesthetics; the breathtaking beauty of the empty desert; and the startling color accenting indigenous and created landscapes—set the stage

41. Charles Sumner Greene and Henry Mather Greene, Arturo Bandini House (El Hogar), Pasadena, 1903.

for the commission that introduced the Arts and Crafts to an architectural form appropriate to Southern California. In 1903 Greene and Greene designed El Hogar (The Hearth) for Mr. and Mrs. Arturo Bandini of Pasadena (plate 41). Asked to design an informal dwelling evocative of the Hispanic adobes, Greene and Greene gave their clients a one-story, redwood board-and-batten-sheathed frame house, turned inward in a U-plan. El Hogar actually had a fourth wall screening its courtyard: a pergola covered in vining flowers. (During construction of the Temple of the Wings, Maybeck designed a two-pergola camp as temporary housing for the C. C. Boyntons and their six children in Berkeley in 1911, with the pergola becoming an outdoor room, or summer encampment.) All six of El Hogar's bedrooms opened onto the patio from the side wings; the elongated living and dining rooms also opened out, their interiors focused on massive cobblestone fireplaces. Boulders from the nearby Arroyo Seco acted as base supports for the veranda posts. Interiors were finished in the same redwood board-and-batten sheathing, with wood trusses exposed.[31]

Arturo Bandini, who came from the California Spanish elite and was the youngest son of Juan Bandini's ten children by two marriages, personified the Mexican tradition so fascinating to the new upper classes.[32] Wealthy Californians accepted socially the centuries-old Mexican aristocracy—often encouraging their inclusion in the Caucasian circles of wealth and education (Bandini had four prominent Caucasian brothers-in-law)—but the everyday Mexican was classed below the Native American. For the Arts and Crafts, clients like the Bandinis presented further ironies. Mrs. Arturo Bandini, although not permitted to become a member of the influential Los Angeles or Pasadena women's clubs, did receive invitations to speak and participate at certain club functions. During the first decade of the century she spoke several times on Native American craft and education to the Redlands Indian Association.[33] Primarily a woman's club, the Redlands group also included honorary male members during its first years.

For the Bandinis, Greene and Greene transformed a vernacular adobe architectural form into a wood-frame structure, a departure from their previous eclectic yet traditional designs. This shift in design philosophy was most likely prompted by clusters of adobe buildings they had seen—like Warner's Ranch at Agua Caliente in northeastern San Diego County—and by the Bandinis' Hispanic heritage. Warner's Ranch, an 1840s adobe outpost constructed for the Connecticut Yankee Jonathan Trumbull Warner, had functioned as a Native American *ranchería* and, as late as 1905, had been illustrated in George Wharton James's *In and Out of the Old Missions of California*. Near the Warner hacienda rambling roadside adobes sheltered Indian basket makers.[34]

Greene and Greene continued exploring the U-plan wood-frame dwelling in 1904 with the Charles W. Hollister and the Adelaide M. Tichenor houses (plate 120) at elevated sites in Hollywood and Long Beach.[35] The "patio house"—the name given to a one-story Southern California dwelling built with three or four sides around a rectangular court—was never as popular as the generic wood-frame

California bungalow, but bungalows with rear and center patios were prominent among the designs by the Pasadenans Louis B. Easton, Elmer Grey, Alfred Heineman, Myron Hunt, Robert H. Orr, and Frederick L. Roehrig, among others. Hunt and Grey apparently coined and defined the term "patio house" for a discussion of their work in the *Craftsman* of October 1907. Roehrig's patio house for the Chicago lawyer Arthur Jerome Eddy (Pasadena, 1905; plate 68), like the work of the Greenes, undoubtedly influenced the thinking of Hunt and Grey.[36] Walls were typically board and batten, with the dwellings' haciendalike forms retained after the translation from adobe. Often the fourth enclosing patio wall became a landscaped screen of vines or mature trees.[37] A *Craftsman* article in 1910 featured a bungalow with a rear U-shaped patio exiting from a "back doorway . . . [that was] . . . nothing more than a comfortable arch between a large orange and a large lemon tree."[38] Several years earlier the *Craftsman* had described the Pasadena bungalow and its interrelated setting: "The house, the garden, the terrace, the patio, the open porch are all one domain, one shelter from the outside world. It is home in that big, fine sense of the word that leaves the horizon, not four walls, for the boundary lines."[39]

As was the case with Maybeck's Berkeley dwellings in these same years, Greene and Greene's residences most often occupied sites at the accessible perimeter of nature. Many of the Greene and Greene houses, both modest and elaborate, bordered the Arroyo Seco, Pasadena's wandering dry riverbed with canyon walls. The valleylike Arroyo Seco offered a setting much different from the steep hills of Berkeley, yet both environments fostered an arcadian Arts and Crafts built landscape. Physically and ideologically, Pasadena accentuated its distinctly southern qualities. The climate gave residents predictable sequences of warm-to-hot days year-round, with a diffused light. With irrigation the soil produced in abundance, and the land was transformed with wide vistas of orange and lemon groves. Arts and Crafts neighborhoods along the Arroyo Seco, including the enclaves of Greene and Greene–designed dwellings, occupied the mid-region between the drop-off into the arroyo and the cultivated expanse beyond Orange Grove Avenue.

The contrast between the design philosophies of Pasadena and Berkeley reflected differences not only in the climate but also in the architects' patrons. In Berkeley, Maybeck's clients were often associated with the university, representing an intellectual elite but financial middle class. Socialism, new religion, and reform were active issues in their daily lives.[40] Many Bay Area architects lived in the Berkeley and Oakland hills—even those commuting by ferry across the bay to San Francisco. In Pasadena, by contrast, retirees from the Midwest or capitalists making their second fortunes commanded the scene, and they often resided in Southern California only during the winter months. Other patrons included the artists, craftspeople, writers, and musicians who constituted a kind of year-round art colony along the arroyo.[41]

Santa Barbara, on the coast a hundred miles north, paralleled Pasadena in its stratified collection of patrons. Bohemian middle-class intellectuals and artists, who lived along steeply climbing Mission Canyon—a place of wild grandeur focused on its imposing Franciscan mission—encouraged the founding of a Manual Arts and Domestic Science Normal School (1913) and a Woman's Club. The Mission Ridge, or Heights (a place of more secluded wealth similar to the Orange Grove Avenue enclaves in Pasadena) also stressed its ties to canyon life. The landscape painter Elmer Wachtel owned property on the ridge and embodied an Arts and Crafts gentility, albeit still bohemian, like that represented in Northern California by the painter William Keith. Wachtel painted exclusively in watercolor, vividly portraying the myriad tones dominating the Southern California landscape. The potter Frederick Hürten Rhead built his 1913–17 studio at the juncture of the canyon and the ridge. Rhead's artistry resembled the more straightforward Craftsman approach prevalent along the Arroyo Seco in Pasadena.[42] Philosophically, Wachtel and Rhead both appear to have been socialists, living in enclaves of clearly socialist bent.

The primary political affiliation in both Pasadena and Santa Barbara was to neither the Socialist nor the Progressive party but rather the mainstream Republican party. Pasadena's newspaper *Town Talk* did not support woman suffrage.[43] Yet in Pasadena and in Santa Barbara there were prominent female expositors of philanthropic Fabianism—a mild, peace-oriented British socialism of the late nineteenth century. Pasadena's Mrs. Thaddeus Lowe, Beatrice Goddard Gates, and Kate Crane Gartz (an extremely active socialist Chicago heiress who helped to support Jane Addams's Hull House and public parks in Chicago with her father's millions earned from iron and steel) all contributed to a phenomenon that Reyner Banham described as "the extraordinary spectacle of a whole class of remarkably nice people determined, world-wide, to promote policies that would destroy their own way of life."[44] Nearby Los Angeles was a hotbed of liberalism, frustrating Republican stalwarts like the *Los Angeles Times* publisher Harrison Gray Otis. Not surprisingly, Pasadena became known for its large-scale, elaborate bungalows and Santa Barbara for its mansions—although both communities also had their artist-writer bungalow-cottages. In Los Angeles, acre upon acre of low-cost builder bungalows sited on cramped lots became the typical housing form.

The Greene brothers considered the Bandini commission of 1903 a turning point in their design philosophy, an idea with which *International Studio* and the *Craftsman* both agreed, in 1906 and 1908, respectively.[45] From 1900 through 1906 Greene and Greene moved toward creating an exploded-box dwelling—opening up the center and creating rear U-shaped patios and asymmetrical wings with decking, pergolas, and porches. Most of their houses following this model lined Grand Avenue and Arroyo View Drive (now Arroyo Terrace) in Pasadena, an adjacent street east of the Arroyo Seco. During this early period Greene and Greene often incorporated well-worn arroyo rocks and boulders into their retaining walls, porches, pergolas, and chimneys. As early as 1902 the architects had also introduced expanses of clinker brick, whose warm tones they found attractive. Initially discarded by manufacturers, clinker brick was an irregularly textured red brick that was partially exploded, burned, and vitrified, with the final hues ranging from brown to purple—sometimes described by the contemporary trade as "blue brick," and by *International Studio* as "soft colored lava-bricks."[46]

Greene and Greene designed approximately fifteen houses adjacent to the arroyo, including a dwelling for Charles Sumner Greene himself. As Bernard Maybeck did in the Berkeley hills, Greene and Greene combined speculative land development with created rusticity. Three sequential commissions of 1903–5 for the real-estate entrepreneur Josephine van Rossem allowed the Greenes to explore their ideas of simplicity in nature through uniform siding, banded windows, and wide, overhanging eaves. In the final experiment, for van Rossem herself (see plate 67), they pulled the box horizontally in multiple directions, then added a screened porch, a cantilevered deck, and an elongated terrace to accentuate the effect. Huge cobblestone walls tie the dwelling to the ground. As early as 1906 the Greenes undertook the full renovation of two of the van Rossem houses that had just been built, creating complex, multilevel, large-scale bungalows with even more emphatically accented horizontal lines.

In the Greenes' work true sleeping porches were relatively rare; instead the architects favored open decks, cantilevered decks, and balcony roof decks. These outside rooms extended the exploding box. Clinker and cobblestone retaining walls fanned out along the streets and were themselves multilevel forms with gigantic sculptural corner masses. The horizontal architectural forms paralleled those by Frank Lloyd Wright and the Prairie School. Like many Wrightian architects, the Greenes had a keen interest in the actual crafting of an object, an interest focused early on by their first training in the manual arts at Washington University in St. Louis.[47]

Wood became the Greenes' favorite medium, inside and out. Joinery, sinuous line, craftsmanship, and patinated surfaces were the hallmarks of their dwellings built between 1907 and 1909. From 1905 on, the Swedish-born contractor-craftsmen Peter and John Hall further intensified the Greenes' efforts toward excellence through their complementary wood work for the architects. In 1907 the *Craftsman* first published Greene and Greene designs; in 1909 Gustav Stickley included two of their 1906 renovations in his book *Craftsman Homes*. These publications were instrumental in bringing the Greenes to the attention of wealthy patrons, whose "bungalows" were, in reality, estates. Such was the residence they built in 1908 for the Cincinnatian David B. Gamble (plates 26, 42). Greene and Greene monitored every detail, designing all the light fixtures and furniture.[48] Constructed around two mature eucalyptus trees, the dwelling responded sensitively to its site. The Greenes and the Gambles all appreciated Japanese design. In 1908, the year the U.S. Navy's Great White Fleet returned home after sailing to

42. Charles Sumner Greene and Henry Mather Greene, David B. Gamble House, Pasadena, 1908.

ease tensions in the Far East, the Gambles left for Japan and the Greenes enhanced their residence-to-be with refined Asian aesthetics.

Greene and Greene left a heritage not only of brilliant craft design but also of thoughtful interpretation for the civic as well as the residential site. They added numerous pieces of street furniture to Pasadena—gateways, pedestrian shelters, and retaining walls—and such civic embellishments became a hallmark of their architecture. All Greene and Greene bungalows have an expanse of lawn in front and gardens (often directed arroyo-ward) in the back. Other individuals, of course, also built near the arroyo, and they created an eclectic mix of revival-based bungalows more intimate in scale than the Greene and Greene bungalow-estates. Artists, for example, most often sited their homes right at the arroyo's edge. The artists Ernest A. Batchelder and Jean Mannheim designed houses for themselves in 1909 that faced the wild nature of the arroyo immediately and represented a counterpoint to the designs of the Greenes.[49]

Women from the Arroyo Seco wrote about the Pasadena bungalows in most of the major American Arts and Crafts periodicals. Transplanted midwesterners such as the artist and writer Olive Percival, the writer and photographer Helen Lukens [Jones] Gaut, and the writer and bungalow designer Una Nixson Hopkins documented the evolution of the Pasadena bungalow through articles in *House Beautiful, Craftsman, Country Life in America, Keith's, Ladies' Home Journal, Good Housekeeping,* and *House and Garden.* All three were active Pasadena and Los Angeles club women working for progressive change. Gaut illustrated her articles with her own architectural photography, while Hopkins designed bungalows and their interiors from at least 1911 (plate 43).[50] In many articles these women made the influential argument that the Southern California bungalow—a modestly built, inexpensive structure, well crafted and provided with some conveniences, yet rustic—could be transformed into a permanent dwelling in the American East, noting that the bungalow need not be interpreted as just a "summer camp or vacation home."[51]

Yet another enclave of Arts and Crafts architecture existed in extreme Southern California, bordering Mexico. Before the turn of the century, San Diego primarily attracted health seekers who needed a sunny, arid climate, including those who were recovering from tuberculosis. Hispanic traditions and desert life pervaded everyday activities in the region and provoked a fascination with indigenous plants and animals. Native American *rancherías* and reservations, as well as several Franciscan missions, were prominent local features.[52] Mainstream Republican politics satisfied most of the new inhabitants, but several liberal counterstrains also found adherents. By 1900 San Diego's milieu openly encouraged experimental communities: the Christian Scientists, the Theosophists at Point Loma, the Rosicrucians at Oceanside, the Little Landers at San Ysidro, and the art colonies in San Diego and La Jolla. The writer and water-rights activist

43. Una Nixson Hopkins, *Design for a Pasadena Bungalow,* 1911. From *Ladies' Home Journal,* February 15, 1911.

William E. Smythe, founder of the Little Lander colony, represented the most radical political fringe. These utopian enterprises, along with multiple art associations, gave an artistic aura to outlying San Diego similar in many respects to the one Berkeley gave to San Francisco. San Diego's socialism coupled the vibrant Socialist party organization and blue-collar unionism of Los Angeles with an idealism reminiscent of Berkeley's.[53]

The terrain and the ocean-cooled temperate climate encouraged the siting of Arts and Crafts dwellings overlooking the many steep-sided arroyos running toward San Diego Bay. Most houses featured views of the Pacific, offered walks down into an arroyo, and sometimes afforded more sweeping vistas across the eastern desert valleys. William E. Smythe commented in 1905 that his San Diego library featured a "seaward gable commanding a view of . . . a wide landscape of bay, ocean, mountains, islands, and the bold promontory of Point Loma."[54]

The architect Irving Gill—along with Emmor Brooke Weaver and Hazel Wood Waterman, both of whom first worked as draftsmen and draftswomen in Gill's office early in their careers—designed a number of Arts and Crafts houses in San Diego. The horticulturist Kate O. Sessions designed residence gardens for Gill and Weaver, while Waterman, whose interest and skill in landscape gardening paralleled her talents in built design, directly undertook landscape efforts for her clients. Gill experimented with severe, unornamented concrete architectural forms that highlighted the latest technology available in 1904–10 and became the basis for a popular arid-climate building type. Gill, like Maybeck, was clearly aware of German design innovations,[55] and the German-American concrete industries offered the most up-to-date design and technology. Possibly both Gill and Maybeck could explore their keen interest in low-cost concrete housing because, like Frank Lloyd Wright, they both designed for liberal-minded patrons who lived in communities that tolerated experimentation. In San Diego, as in Berkeley, the nucleus of Arts and Crafts residences also represented a nucleus of clients.

Perhaps the most evocative example of Arts and Crafts architecture in San Diego is the dwelling commissioned by George W. Marston at the northern terminus of an arroyo extending above Balboa Park (plate 44). Marston, who had come to San Diego with his health-seeking father in 1870, was of Congregationalist-Unitarian background and one of four Progressives from San Diego and Imperial counties attending the founding meeting of the Lincoln-Roosevelt Republican League, in Oakland in August 1907. He functioned primarily as a civic Progressive, contributing heavily to the development of Balboa Park, serving as local chairman of the Landmarks Club of Southern California, and selling Stickley furniture in his downtown department store (see plate 167).[56] Marston commissioned William S. Hebbard and Gill to design his Seventh Avenue dwelling in 1904, at a time when the elevated arroyo site still accumulated city trash on its slopes. Marston asked for an "English"-style residence for the fourteen-acre site and improved the north and east arroyos with trees and shrubbery. Sessions, who maintained a thirty-acre nursery on parklands adjacent to the Marston site, con-

tributed some remnants of landscaping to the view when she moved away in 1905.[57] Balboa Park (unnamed until October 1910) still lay fallow to the south.[58]

The Marston residence, with its terrace and bracketing loggias, faces south. A first design featured second-story half-timbering, but as executed, the Marston House reflects Prairie School aesthetics and bespeaks Gill's own tendencies toward the removal of ornament. Gill had trained with Dankmar Adler and Louis Sullivan in Chicago and had participated in Sullivan's design for the Transportation Building at the World's Columbian Exposition of 1893. Hebbard had also worked in Chicago, in the firm of Daniel Burnham and John Wellborn Root. Chicago played an influential role in the Californian interpretation of Arts and Crafts architecture, not only in San Diego but throughout the state: many of the architects had worked there, and many of the patrons maintained homes in both the Midwest and California.

From 1905 to 1913 ten additional dwellings were constructed along the block of Seventh Avenue first improved by Marston; most are in an unadorned brick Prairie style or are cubic, stucco-surfaced boxes. Three of the dwellings were built for relatives of Marston, and five more for speculation. In the latter category were three lower-cost houses for Alice Lee and Katherine Teats, which shared a U-shaped pergola and a communal garden. Later, in 1912–13, Lee and Teats commissioned Gill to design eight residences along the arroyo at Albatross and Front streets, with another joint garden and paths into the canyon (plate 25).[59]

Hazel Wood Waterman, who trained in Gill's office, clearly exemplified an Arts and Crafts approach to education and professional life. Slowly building a career for herself, almost as one would develop a craft, she also sustained a multilayered civic life that intertwined itself with her architectural endeavors.[60] (Greene and Greene had also trained a talented female designer, Mary L. Ranney.[61] In both cases, the architects first encountered the draftswomen as

ABOVE
44. William Hebbard and Irving Gill, George W. Marston House, San Diego, 1904.

OPPOSITE
45. Hazel W. Waterman, Wednesday Club, San Diego, 1910–11. From *Western Architect,* March 1913.
∾ *Waterman's design contrasts vividly with the homelike bungalows designed for women's clubs in Berkeley by Julia Morgan.*

clients who had participated in the design of their own houses.) Waterman's activities in San Diego's civic circles brought her into contact with Anna Gunn Marston (Mrs. George W. Marston), Alice Lee, and others. Waterman presented papers to the Wednesday Club on Christian Socialism (1900), the English Arts and Crafts (1902), contemporary social problems (1903), and Japanese prints (1905). After completing her own house in 1900—a simple, granite English cottage—Waterman began writing about architecture for *House Beautiful,* illustrating her pieces with her own watercolors and photographs.

One of her most noted projects was the restoration of the 1827–29 Estudillo family adobe with its interior courtyard garden. Among California's earliest families, the Estudillos had established themselves in San Diego as members of the Mexican aristocracy and as immediate neighbors to the Bandinis. For her work on the Estudillo site, Waterman studied adobes throughout Southern California, utilized appropriate building materials and techniques, and employed Mexican craftsmen. As in a restoration today, she photographed all stages of the project. Her watercolor plan for the dwelling detailed how all the cacti, citrus, vegetable, and flower gardens were to be replanted. The Estudillo adobe had captured popular imagination as Ramona's Marriage Place, and the behind-the-scenes client, John D. Spreckels, built a rail line out to "old town" San Diego from downtown—employing the restored adobe as a tourist attraction from his Hotel del Coronado on the peninsula across the bay.[62]

Waterman's most outstanding design, the Wednesday Club, 1910–11 (plate 45), followed the Estudillo adobe almost immediately. In March 1913, *Western Architect* published photographs of the stuccoed cube, which faces south, at the edge of Balboa Park. The clubhouse incorporates etched door hardware and an art-glass lantern by Anna Valentien as well as tiles by Ernest A. Batchelder; Waterman herself also designed some of the tile work.

46. Irving Gill and Frank Mead, Wheeler J. Bailey House, La Jolla, California, 1907.

47. Irving Gill and Frank Mead, Wheeler J. Bailey House, La Jolla, California, 1907.

Like Gill and other Arts and Crafts architects and patrons south of Los Angeles, Waterman was perhaps most noteworthy for the way she combined modernism with an appreciation of the indigenous vernacular past. Gill and Frank Mead's Wheeler J. Bailey House (1907) in La Jolla stunningly illustrates this particular San Diego contribution to the Arts and Crafts (plates 46, 47, 178). Mead also had first worked as a draftsman for Gill. As a designer, he used images gathered from his studies in North Africa and New Mexico—continuing to explore his distinct approach to the Arts and Crafts in subsequent years as a partner with Richard S. Requa.

Redlands, Riverside, and Atascadero, all to the north of San Diego, each illustrate a final aspect of the built environment in Arts and Crafts California: full-scale utopian town planning. The twins Alfred and Albert Smiley (Quakers born in Maine in 1828) became the patrons of Redlands, the earliest of these places. Well educated at Haverford College near Philadelphia, the Smileys came from modest farming stock and had attained their wealth through the development of the Mohonk (1869) and Minnewaska (1887) resorts in New York's Catskill Mountains. By 1889 the Smileys had purchased land in the Redlands area for a winter residence, which they named Cañon Crest (also called Smiley Heights). They brought in water from several miles away and hired the nurseryman Franz Hosp to orchestrate lushly exotic plantings. Indeed, it was through such intensive landscaping that the physical character of Redlands as an Arts and Crafts environment evolved. Eventually the Smiley estate also contained numbers of open-sided rustic huts, called summer houses, that offered shady retreats for the passerby (plate 48). During the winters the Smileys brought their carpenters out from Mohonk to build Catskill-type park benches and chairs.[63]

48. Garden designed by Franz Hosp for Cañon Crest Park, Redlands, 1906, with a roadside retreat made by carpenters from the Smileys' Mohonk resort in the Catskill Mountains, New York.

The park grounds in Redlands attracted thousands of visitors, offering one of the earliest models for an Arts and Crafts townscape in the mild West—albeit one based on what was really an older nineteenth-century landscape tradition. By 1902 interconnected drives guided travelers between pocketed parks, orange groves, and raw nature, "winding in and out like the 'lightning' pattern of a Navajo blanket."[64] In 1910 a trainload of hotel men from Chicago converged on Redlands with George Wharton James, who had been hired to lecture on the Southwest's breathtaking vistas, from the Grand Canyon to Southern California. The proprietors toured Cañon Crest and the other late nineteenth-century Redlands park improvements (including the Carnegie library grounds) landscaped by Hosp.[65] Outlying resorts also lured Redlanders to hideaways located in the San Bernardino Mountains, twenty to twenty-five miles from Redlands, where clusters of canvas tents or cabins sheltered seekers of the simple life.[66]

In 1891 Charles Dudley Warner had described in his book *Our Italy* the land stretching from Redlands to Los Angeles as "a continuous fruit garden."[67] Imagery of the land as garden captivated the public[68] and helped to make Redlands not only the site of a real attempt at utopia but also the setting for one utopian novel and two satires—all of which reflected the conflicting dynamics of a California Arts and Crafts idealization of both nature and the machine.[69] Just after the turn of the century, Charles William Wooldridge's *Perfecting the Earth* projected Redlands (New Utopia) into 1913 as "a landscape garden. Electric railways . . . thread the country in all directions, while paved parkways . . . thread the groves." Despite this futuristic vision, the real January 1913 brought a hard freeze to paradise, causing major crop losses and reversals of fortune.[70] In the satires, Harold Bell Wright's *The Eyes of the World* (1914) and Sidney H. Burchell's *Jacob Peek* (1915), Redlands (called Fairlands and Escalona, respectively) was portrayed through the insights of the embittered small farmer. Still, the view from the road along Escalona Heights (Cañon Crest) remained unforgettable: "On one side . . . a broad expanse of valley, fertile with the deep green of countless orange groves, interspersed with the red, grey, or white, roofs of imposing mansions. To the south, there was . . . a desert of mountain . . . given over to the browns and purples and yellows of sage brush and cactus and greasewood and parched prairie grass and rocky headlands" (plate 49).[71]

In March 1894 a group of women founded the Redlands Indian Association, a branch of the Woman's National Indian Association and the single most provocative Arts and Crafts endeavor in the community. With membership fluctuating between thirty and sixty women, the club met at private homes; initial issues were Indian rights, education, music, and basketry. From the beginning, Redlands women not only took an interest in Native American craft but also set out to encourage Caucasian crafts among Indian women, as a way to avoid "poverty from idleness."[72] Their first efforts focused on quilt making, with Redlanders providing squares for the Native Americans to quilt.[73] By 1899 Albert Smiley had spoken on the teaching of lace making to the Indian women. In 1910

The year 1913 found the United States at peace and in no danger of war, but nevertheless possessing an army of 553,000 men. . . . The world was treated to a novelty in the following general order:

To the army of the United States. Soldiers: you are now in the happy condition of having no human enemy, nor any probability of an enemy. Nevertheless, conditions are such that to disband you could not fail to produce intolerable evils both to yourselves and to the people among whom you would be scattered. In view of this situation the administration had determined to utilize your energies in the conquest of nature, so far as nature remains unfriendly to man.

In pursuit of this object, you are to be employed in the construction of works, greater than anything hitherto attempted by man, for the purpose of turning deserts into gardens. . . . Hitherto the work of armies has been destruction, henceforth your work will be construction, and with this change of purpose it is confidently believed that a better era for mankind has dawned.

Charles William Wooldridge, *Perfecting the Earth* (Cleveland: Utopia Publishing Company, 1902), pp. 23, 27.

49. Postcard of the Alfred C. Burrage House (by Charles Brigham), Redlands, 1901–2. *The estate of the copper millionaire Burrage abutted one owned by Edward Canfield Sterling, and together the two created a breathtaking landscape. Brigham was best known for the Brigham, Coveney and Bisbee design for the mother church of the First Church of Christ, Scientist, in Boston, of 1905–9. In 1910 Das amerikanische Haus reproduced an illustration of the Burrage residence, bracketed by two illustrations of Frank Lloyd Wright houses in suburban Chicago.*

the association women attempted to secure a lace teacher from the East to teach at Pala—the *asistencia,* or outpost settlement, for Mission San Luis Rey. Ultimately they hired a western teacher, supported through funding by the Sybil Carter Lace Association of New York and Pasadena's Mrs. Arturo Bandini. By 1912 Mrs. Edward Canfield Sterling, the wife of a relocated St. Louis millionaire, had convinced the federal government to support the lace teacher, and the women discussed extending lace making to eighteen reservations; activities were already taking place in Native American settlements at Banning, Cahuilla, La Jolla, Mesa Grande, Pala, Pauma, Rincon, Saboda, and Warner's Ranch. The next year the association attempted to market the Indian lace through department stores in Los Angeles, exhibiting pieces at a meeting of the Los Angeles Ruskin Club. The effort apparently failed.[74]

The Redlands Indian Association not only continued its involvement with lace making but also served as an intermediary for the selling of Southwestern baskets and rugs. The association contributed funds for building and furnishing a reading room at Pala and encouraged gardening there as well. Prizes for landscape improvement efforts were established for La Jolla, Pauma, and Rincon after

successful plantings of eucalyptus and roses at Pala.[75] Other philanthropic, progressive art-craft endeavors characterized Redlands between 1890 and 1915. Carolyn and Olivia Phelps-Stokes, sisters from New York, wintered in Redlands from 1899. When Carolyn died in 1909, Olivia (who continued her winter visits until 1927) founded the Phelps-Stokes Fund, which today still aids blacks and Native Americans.[76] Mrs. Sterling obtained the start-up funds from Andrew Carnegie in 1910 for a collection of Native American books and journals to be housed at the Smiley Library.[77] Redlands was also the site of Wesley H. Trippett's Redlands Pottery, the earliest known art pottery in Southern California.[78] And from the turn of the century until 1925, the socialist photographer Elias F. Everitt recorded magnificent panoramas of the area.

Riverside, near Redlands, was also caught up in the philanthropic Arts and Crafts drive to create a utopia in the desert. Founded in 1870 as a colony of orange growers dependent on irrigation, Riverside, like Redlands, initiated its Arts and Crafts self-image through landscape design. White Park featured one of California's largest early cacti collections (over four hundred varieties by 1902), while developers created the middle landscape of Fairmount Park from the bottomland adjacent to a hill quarried for street-paving rock. Riverside became known for its tree- and flower-lined avenues among the orange groves. By 1907 Magnolia Avenue stretched for ten miles, with quadruple rows of pepper trees, eucalyptus, grevillas, palms, and magnolias. Another drive, Victoria, paralleled Magnolia—with both avenues running to Arlington, a sector of the community settled by British colonists. Victoria Avenue, which featured center and side strips of Ragged Robin rose hedges propagated by Franz Hosp, led Riversiders to the Victoria Club—an airy two-story bungalow on a bluff.[79] The retired Minneapolis millionaire Charles M. Loring contributed thousands of dollars to a street-tree program before 1922, overseeing the appointment of a tree warden for the town. The father of the Minneapolis park system, Loring had actively participated in the design and funding for Minneapolis–St. Paul's interconnected lakes, creeks, ponds, parks, and boulevards.[80]

50. Arthur B. Benton, architect, and William A. Sharp, renderer. *Presentation Drawing for the Expansion of the Glenwood Mission Inn,* 1908. Watercolor rendering. Mission Inn Foundation, Riverside, California.

51. Mount Rubidoux, c. 1910.

Riverside differed from Redlands in its concern with constructed vistas, most notably that of Seventh Street between Vine Street and the Santa Ana River wash. Along this street and its immediately adjacent cross streets there unfolded a Beaux-Arts plan with Arts and Crafts buildings, making it unlike the downtown in any other California community. Composed primarily of dynamic variations on the Mission and Spanish Colonial revivals, the area featured the work of Arthur B. Benton, Myron Hunt, Elmer Grey, and Julia Morgan. Coordinated vistas culminated in the Mission Inn, which filled an entire city block (plate 50). Adirondack pergolas, with tree forms cast in concrete, bracketed the street (a late contribution, of 1929). Indian raintree-cross streetlights from about 1910, designed to evoke Native American motifs, accented about fifty miles of Riverside's streets.[81] Adjacent areas evolved into bungalow districts, with houses along Indian Hill Road dramatically surmounting their steep hillside landscaping. Natural landmarks defined the termini of the vistas: to the southeast was the bluff setting of the Victoria Club, and to the west lay Mount Rubidoux, a boulder-strewn granite outcropping at the edge of the Santa Ana wash (plate 51).

The Hispanicized Beaux-Arts environment that was Seventh Street led to a magnificent, quite rugged park. An arched bridge crossed Seventh at the foot of Mount Rubidoux, with a secondary one-way road ascending into Huntington Park—a hundred-acre development of 1906 jointly planned by Frank Miller (owner of the Mission Inn) and Yellowstone Park's engineer, Colonel H. M. Chittenden. Miller had first wanted a park like that of Cañon Crest in Redlands, but Chittenden advised him to forgo the lush vegetation and work with desert plantings. Mount Rubidoux had long been associated with Native American sunworship rituals. In its second life associated with Huntington Park it became a scenic Arts and Crafts retreat, with a winding drive up the steep grades, a mountain-top cross (a memorial to Father Junipero Serra), Easter sunrise services, Armistice Day sunset services, a Peace Tower, Japanese gardens at the base, and foot trails from Seventh, Eighth, and Tenth streets. For Easter 1915 the cross was strung with colored cut glass and floodlit. Seventh Street, renamed Mission Boulevard, continued past the turn up Mount Rubidoux to climax in a four-towered Mission Revival bridge across the Santa Ana wash. The second bridge, quite large and ornate, punctuated the single-direction descent on the opposite side of the mountain outcropping, completing the park and alternately serving as formal entry and exit to Riverside itself.[82]

Frank Miller was the man who orchestrated the creation of Seventh Street. His parents had operated a two-story clapboarded adobe boardinghouse, called the Glenwood Cottages, in the mid-1870s. By 1882 the boardinghouse consisted of two such structures set at right angles to each other. At the turn of the century Miller hired Arthur B. Benton to transform the hotel into a Mission Revival extravaganza, the Mission Inn. The original adobe boardinghouse was knocked down to a single story, converted to a rustic tearoom, and reroofed with tiles from the Pala *asistencia*.[83] In 1910 Benton expanded the Mission Inn (also known as the Glenwood) with a cloisters wing, and four years later Myron Hunt designed a Spanish Colonial Revival patio, dining room, and art gallery.[84] Miller continued to add to the inn during the 1920s, hiring G. Stanley Wilson for a notable wing in 1929.[85]

The Mission Inn became not only a highly successful resort hotel but also a museumlike center for art and the sale of Native American rugs and baskets. Ironically, the stagey atmosphere also encouraged a sincere involvement in the Arts and Crafts movement. Miller had purchased various pieces of furniture for his hotel through the renowned trade mart in Grand Rapids, Michigan. Remnants of bedroom suites custom-made by the Charles P. Limbert Company for the 1910 cloisters wing still remain at the inn. After building this addition, Miller also had some furniture manufactured at the inn, with several pieces thought to have been designed by the carpenter August Breckman.[86] Miller later bought Arts and Crafts Mission-style furniture from Gustav Stickley's manufactory in Syracuse, New York. The irony of importing Mission furniture from the East—*the* brand of Mission Arts and Crafts furniture recognized internationally—for a desert hotel in the West perhaps epitomized the ever-present mix there of the artificial and the genuine.

Elbert Hubbard visited the Mission Inn and lectured there at least once, in April 1909—at which time he announced that he was "contemplating the location of another Roycroft Shop somewhere in California."[87] Hubbard began referring to Miller as a "Royal Roycrofter," praising the Mission Inn and contributing to the myth that a mission (rather than the adobe boardinghouse) had "once stood on the same spot." Hubbard, who had long called himself by a medievalized title, Fra Elbertus, addressed Frank Miller as Fra Frank or sometimes even Fra Junipero Frank. He also likened Fra Junipero Serra to John Ruskin and William Morris.[88] Hubbard's Roycroft community in East Aurora, outside Buffalo, New York, featured a rustic Tudor Revival hotel, with community craftsmen making and selling Arts and Crafts books, furniture, leather goods, and metalwork. Implications of his announcement are provocative: if Hubbard had established a Roycroft Shop at the Mission Inn, then the New York and the Californian Arts and Crafts, East and West, would have been solidly connected.

Even though the Mission Inn never became a Roycroft center, the hotel did continue to sell crafted goods and to embellish its atmosphere of rusticity. After 1910 the inn featured the stained glass of William Alexander Sharp, and from 1912 to 1929 the inn maintained an art curator on its staff. Benton and Sharp shared office space in Los Angeles, working together frequently. Sharp made a watercolor promoting the inn in 1908, and his drawings often figured in Arts and Crafts books advertising the hotel and Riverside.[89] Benton's lengthy poem on the Mission Inn, published with Sharp's drawings by Senogram of Los Angeles in 1907–8, is a key piece.[90] The Cloister Print Shop in Riverside printed other Arts and Crafts books in the mid-1910s.[91] Elbert Hubbard, too, contributed to this type of Mission Inn art book with his *Days of Peace and Rest at the Glenwood by*

Those Who Know (1907) and *Music at Meals* (1912)—both Roycroft publications.[92] Finally, Miller offered to place Redlands Indian Association lace on sale at the inn in 1913,[93] and in 1919 he contemplated establishing a small pottery on the grounds of the hotel, to be run in conjunction with the Alberhill Coal and Clay Company.[94]

A second Arts and Crafts focus in Riverside developed at the Sherman Institute, a federal Native American manual-arts boarding school located south of downtown. By 1912 the school occupied forty acres of landscaped grounds with thirty-five Mission Revival buildings. Chemawa Park adjoined the school, and four miles away the institute ran a hundred-acre farm. In 1909 forty-three tribes from California, the Pacific Northwest, the Southwest, and the Plains were represented, with an enrollment of over five hundred. Growth continued until the mid-1920s, when the student body peaked at one thousand. Education, which ran through the eighth grade, concentrated on industrial training. Courses included carpentry, painting, cabinetmaking, blacksmithing, wagon making, tailoring, printing, agriculture, home economics, and nursing. For young women, home economics specifically included lace making, which was also incorporated at the six other Indian institutes across the country by 1916. For the young men, cabinetmaking notably included the making of Mission-style furniture; photographic evidence (plate 52) indicates that the Sherman Institute made Mission furniture from its opening in 1901.[95]

The transmission of ideas about simple furniture between California and New York deserves closer inspection. The Smileys were actively involved in the Riverside Native American school, and Elbert Hubbard, too, visited the Sherman Institute. Despite the shared knowledge, the proportions and slat details for armchairs and settles designed by Stickley and Roycroft, in particular, did not achieve until about 1910 the extremely regular simplicity found in the Sherman Institute furniture of 1901.[96] How the Sherman Institute furniture was used is not known: it probably furnished the school and was placed at reservations with which the

INDIAN CONFERENCE PROVES A SUCCESS PROMINENT FRIENDS OF THE RED MAN ARE SPEAKERS AT SESSIONS, WHICH ARE EXPECTED TO RESULT IN GOOD

The Indian conference at Riverside, which is being attended by several Redlands persons, is proving an interesting gathering. President David Starr Jordan of Stanford University, is presiding, and several of the friends of the California Indian are taking part in the discussions.

Two sessions were held Monday, one in the afternoon and one in the evening. The most inspiring feature of the conference is the number of Indians in attendance, who number about forty. They are from almost every part of the state. Frank Miller, with characteristic generosity, is giving them the best, and they are his guests at the Glenwood. There are four chiefs in the delegation from Mendocino county, four from Lake county, two from Chico and one each from Calaveras, Madera, the Tule river and Needles tribes. Southern California is represented by delegations from Banning, Palm Springs, Needles, Temecula, Cahuilla, San Jacinto and Mission Creek.

Monday evening the Sherman Institute band rendered several selections from the roof garden of the adobe. These performances will be given each evening during the conference.

52. Furniture making at the Sherman Institute, Riverside, 1901. From Frank Miller's promotional scrapbook for the Sherman Institute, c. 1902.

Redlands Indian Association had connections. Possibly some of the furniture appeared in the Mission Inn. Native Americans in New York also made Arts and Crafts furniture, notably at the Onondaga Reservation near Syracuse, which featured bentwood chairs.[97]

The fascination in Riverside with an idealized Spanish past, with medieval labor and handicraft, and—even in the desert—with Asian culture shaped both the physical appearance and the behavior of the community. The collectors Harwood Hall and Cornelius Earl Rumsey (see plate 53) each lived in Craftsman bungalows with "Indian rooms" full of baskets and rugs. Hall ran the Sherman Institute; Rumsey was a retired vice president of Nabisco, who arrived from Chicago about 1905 and started a second life as an Arts and Crafts orange-grove farmer.[98] The experimental Sherman Institute farm for young men also foreshadowed the published plans for Stickley's Craftsman Farms and Craftsman Farm School of 1908–13. Finally, Miller's made-over adobe tearoom at the inn mixed a variety of simple furniture (as yet unidentified) and Indian artifacts from as early as 1902, while at the Sherman Institute adolescent Native Americans absorbed Arts and Crafts aesthetics not only by handcrafting Mission furniture and making lace but also by performing a Japanese operetta, in 1914.[99] Miller, predictably, was a self-professed Japanophile, well known and honored in both the Japanese section of Riverside and in Japan.[100]

A third agrarian community in California—Atascadero—continued the evolution of Arts and Crafts utopian place making, epitomizing in many ways the crafted western setting sought for an idyllic daily life. Founded by Edward Gardner Lewis in February 1913, Atascadero shifted California Arts and Crafts

53. Mission Inn Native American Conference, April 1908.

∾ *Standing among the tribal representatives are (left to right) Cornelius Earl Rumsey, Frank Miller, Harwood Hall, David Starr Jordan, Charles Fletcher Lummis, and Albert K. Smiley.*

town planning from philanthropy and progressive politics toward a model environment based on a socialist vision and ideas garnered from Bolton Hall's *Three Acres and Liberty* (1907) and *A Little Land and a Living* (1908).[101] A precedent existed in another community planned by Lewis—University City near St. Louis. There Lewis had sponsored the American Woman's League and, through the league, a women's art pottery and education center. Woman suffrage issues also dominated the scene and were given publicity through Lewis's various newspapers and magazines. When his publishing empire unraveled due to financial overextension, Lewis moved west to establish the next phase of the American Woman's League, the American Woman's Republic. The republic sought to found agricultural colonies, first in California, then in Florida and on the Gulf Coast.[102] In early 1913 Lewis bought the land that was to become Atascadero—23,000 acres located 120 miles north of Santa Barbara, inland from Morro Bay.

University City's contribution to the American Arts and Crafts movement had focused on women's art pottery, but in addition, Prairie-style bungalows furnished with Mission furniture were erected across the country as satellite clubhouses for the rural members of the American Woman's League. Many league members were amateur potters. Lewis's distinguished art faculty included Taxile Doat, Adelaide and Samuel Robineau, and Frederick Hürten Rhead. Rhead wrote a pottery text for the league and ran mail-order courses, establishing early contact with the Theosophist Halcyon Art Pottery near Atascadero. Ultimately Rhead would arrive in California ahead of Lewis. The first plan for Atascadero also included the reestablishment of an art pottery like the one at University City, with Taxile Doat in charge. Doat inspected the Atascadero site in August 1913 (plate 54), and while construction was underway he prepared over four hundred pieces of University City pottery for exhibition in San Francisco in 1915. The pottery was never shown in the West, and Doat returned to France after the onset of World War I.[103]

54. Taxile Doat, Atascadero, August 22–25, 1913.

As it evolved, Atascadero represented a rustic futurism. Fully half the population of the surrounding county voted for reform, whether Socialist, Progressive, or Democratic, in 1914, and a Socialist concentration existed in the nearby hot-springs resort of Paso Robles.[104] The American Woman's Republic was to be a colony for single women and their dependent children, emphasizing self-government patterned after that of the country as a whole. (California women had achieved the state vote in the autumn of 1911.) The republic itself existed only through about 1914, but during its brief life it achieved significant recognition. In mid-1913 the International Woman Suffrage Alliance seated a representative from the republic at its seventh congress in Budapest—among such American luminaries as Jane Addams and Charlotte Perkins Gilman.[105]

During each successive planning stage for Atascadero, Lewis maintained ties between his California and St. Louis utopias. On the planning commission were Walter D. Bliss of San Francisco and Edward J. Wickson of Berkeley.[106] Bliss, with his partner William B. Faville, designed the Beaux-Arts core of structures for Atascadero. Only a small proportion of those planned civic buildings were actually constructed, but numbers of modest wood-frame and tilt-slab concrete bungalows were built. Bliss served as a design regulator for housing and offered predesigned bungalows for purchase. The colony restricted signage, forbidding both billboards and barn-side advertising. An art academy with pottery works remained under discussion until 1919, but was never erected.[107] Atascadero's orchards and farms spread across many hills and it quickly became a back-to-the-land colony for people interested in modest farming; the colony came to have the reputation of attracting retired couples. Wickson, a premier Arts and Crafts horticulturist, had written *California Fruits and How to Grow Them, California Vegetables in Garden and Field,* and *California Garden . . . Suggestions for Working Amateurs,* all appropriate for Atascadero. It was Wickson's small, productive Arts and Crafts garden, as the set-

55. E. S. Willis Bungalow, showing tilt-slab construction, Atascadero, 1915–16.

ting for the inexpensive—and sometimes prefabricated—bungalow, that character-ized Atascadero as it was actually constructed (plate 55).[108]

A significant factor in the shaping of California's built environment, and perhaps the most telling one, was the generational split between the two main groups of patrons and architects. Perhaps half were born between 1820 and 1860, into pre–Civil War America. The remainder nearly all came into life between the onset of the war and 1870. Most of the elder group could be characterized as philanthropists, naturalists, and visionaries; as a group, they enjoyed the region's perceived Hispanic past and participated heavily in civic landscaping for California's young communities. These people were split politically—from main-stream capitalist Republican to Fabian Socialist. Among these elder statesmen and stateswomen of the California Arts and Crafts architectural community were George Wharton James, Charles M. Loring, Charles Fletcher Lummis, George W Marston, Frank Miller, Alfred and Albert Smiley, and Edward J. Wickson. Politically intertwined with the architectural group were Andrew Carnegie, David Starr Jordan, Caroline Severance, and others. Many of the younger set designed the buildings or, as patrons, were leading lawyers and politicians of the Progressive party—including Helen Lukens Gaut, Irving Gill, Charles and Henry Greene, Una Nixson Hopkins, Charles Keeler, Edward Gardner Lewis, Bernard Maybeck, Chester H. Rowell, and Hazel Wood Waterman. The contrast in world views held by the Smileys and Maybeck, by Jordan and Rowell, symbolizes the wrestlings with reform in that time and place and how those wrestlings took physical shape.

For California nearly all the place-making efforts offered by architects affili-ated with the Arts and Crafts movement combined utopian idealism, a concern for environmental siting, futuristic expression coupled with deliberate Pacific Rim rusticity (Hispanic, Native American, and Asian), and free thinking—particularly with respect to religion, international peace, woman suffrage, and active political involvement. Experimentation with varied building materials, especially wood and concrete, preoccupied several of the major figures. Much of California's Arts and Crafts movement also favored agrarianism: a strong nineteenth-century tradition of the irrigated colony set the stage, a beneficent climate attracted those interested in finding a simpler life, with ties to the land. Connections between Arts and Crafts groups in California and New York, as well as between those in the West and Midwest, appear to be much stronger than previously thought, with exchanges traveling in both directions. With the emergence of a dominant rural aesthetic intimately dependent on vibrant urban centers, California offered the quintessential place for mature experimentation with Arts and Crafts ideas of house and home, of city and country. Today, despite the concerns and yearnings of yet another age, California is still the place created by the Arts and Crafts.

THE RESORT TO THE RUSTIC: SIMPLE LIVING AND THE CALIFORNIA BUNGALOW

Cheryl Robertson

Even as the turn of the next century approaches, Americans remain deeply committed to an Edenic myth of purity combined with plenty and prosperity. The "Californian/American dream" is a secular version of the "land of milk and honey," which recapitulates the biblical narrative of man's unity with—yet dominion over—the garden, his temptation and fall from grace, followed ultimately by redemption and reinstatement as divine deputy in the promised land. Puritan immigrants went to Massachusetts during the Great Migration of the 1630s to establish a settlement that would be "as a beacon upon a hill," broadcasting virtue to all mankind through the moral example set by its wholesome, industrious, frugal yeoman citizenry.[1] Although the Puritans viewed themselves as an elite, or "elect," they saw the practice of their religion as a daily struggle to subordinate material pursuits and rewards to spiritual endeavors and salvation of the soul. A remarkably similar scenario was again played out in the early twentieth century, when a "great migration" of white, anglicized freeholders from the eastern and midwestern United States flocked to California, especially the Southland, to complete the conquest of the continent through not only cultivation of the land but also practice of the "high thinking" and "plain living" of the Puritans, now recast as key precepts of the reformist catechism of the Arts and Crafts movement.[2]

Just as Puritanism was an international movement of dissenters, so too the Arts and Crafts movement was a multinational critique of conspicuous consumption, dehumanizing labor, and self-aggrandizement that reached its full flowering in the relatively unbesmirched soil of California. By putting matters of the soul, spirit, and mind at the forefront, California pilgrims might avoid the deleterious effects of avaricious capitalism, of competitive spending and accumulation of worldly goods, which made the home not a family hearth but an overstuffed fur-

56. Claycraft Potteries. *Tile,* c. 1926. Press-molded fired clay colored with pigmented slips. 12 x 15¾ in. The Oakland Museum; Timken Fund.

niture warehouse. California's colonial heritage, like that of New England, was deemed a usable past pointing the way to a righteous, salutary future—not ascetic but aesthetic, not quantitatively rich but spiritually and intellectually rewarding. Said the New-Englander-cum-Californian Charles Fletcher Lummis, "Plymouth Rock was a state of mind. So were the California Missions."[3]

Lummis was a Harvard-trained archeologist and journalist who became a staunch supporter of Native Americans and of conservation of the missions. Arriving in Los Angeles in 1885, he turned his energies to popularizing the preindustrial aboriginal and Spanish cultures of the Southwest. He founded the Landmarks Club in 1897 to restore the Franciscan missions; in 1907 he established the Southwest Museum to house his extensive collections of tribal and colonial artifacts.[4] Lummis's efforts to preserve the physical remnants and folkways of Indians, padres, and ranchers alike were not motivated by a merely objective, academic interest in collecting and cataloguing relics. He edited and synthesized the contested, exploitative history of California into a model of simple, rustic living, which incorporated contemporary Arts and Crafts ideals about rural wholesomeness, soulful labor, handicraft, and designs derived from vernacular antecedents.

Lummis was the preeminent spokesman at the turn of the century for the relevance of Spanish Colonial precedents to the conduct of modern life. In *The Spanish Pioneers* (1893), for which he was knighted by the king of Spain, he described the Hispanic colonizing of North, Central, and South America as the longest, most grandiose historical demonstration of manhood. Manliness was of pressing social concern since a national nervousness and physical lassitude threatened to undermine America's achievement of its manifest destiny.[5] This was the view of Lummis's Harvard classmate and longtime friend the Rough Rider Theodore Roosevelt, who urged citizens to exercise strenuously and to adopt a less complex way of life. For his part, Lummis championed the manly, rigorous simplicity of frontier culture through articles for the *Los Angeles Times,* editorials in the Southland's intellectual journal *Land of Sunshine* (later *Out West*), and personal example. He himself had trekked across the continent from Chillicothe, Ohio, to Los Angeles in 1884–85, and one senses his self-identification with mission founder Father Junipero Serra—"a barefoot enthusiast who was crank enough to walk from Vera Cruz to Mexico, from Mexico to Lower California, from Lower California to where San Francisco now is, and back and forth several times."[6]

In the construction of his home El Alisal (The Place of the Sycamores), begun in 1898 on two-and-one-half rock-covered acres along the Arroyo Seco, Lummis re-created aspects of the old mission days. In fact, original mission timbers purportedly were enshrined in the structure, which was built of concrete— the modern equivalent of adobe.[7] He recruited visitors as hod carriers for the concrete; his children and the boys he hired each year from Isleta Pueblo, in New Mexico, tamped mortar and helped transport local boulders to face the facade and the bell tower, copied after the one at the San Gabriel Mission (plate 57).[8]

The patriarchal epoch [of California], from about 1800 to 1860, was still more potent [than the mission era] in shaping our later destinies. It was human, of course, and not perfect; yet it came as near Arcadia as this country has ever seen. The old rancho life was not "progressive"; it might be called indolent. But it was very happy. Life was good not only to the home, but to the stranger within the gates. It was nearer the life of Abraham than we shall ever see again—and with no more faults or shortcomings, and with a finer hospitality and altruism. It did not breed a race of effeminates, despite its indolence. The Californians were the finest horsemen in the world. Their virtues were sterling, their faults petty. Their morals were clean—far cleaner than we can say of the California of today. The family ties were almost invariably beautiful, and the social life full of generosity and charm. The occupations were those of cattle-growers everywhere—even Americans—obviously not so slavish as those of the farmer or the money-maker. These people were not what we call "business." Money was nothing to them, except for what it could buy; and they cultivated to the highest degree those best things which money will not buy.

Charles Fletcher Lummis, "The Making of Los Angeles," *Out West* 30 (April 1909): 242, 244.

90

ABOVE

57. Charles Fletcher Lummis, *El Alisal as It Was Begun in Los Angeles in 1898.* From *Harper's Weekly,* September 1–7, 1900.

RIGHT

58. El Museo (The Museum) at El Alisal, photographed by Lummis on May 14, 1902. ∾ *El Museo demonstrated Lummis's belief that the creation of a home must be "personally conducted." Lummis himself hewed and chiseled the woodwork, and prominent features like the mantel received a charred "fire finish" to accentuate the wood grain. El Alisal was a composite of architectural ideas and artifacts inspired by aboriginal and Spanish-colonial sites in Central and South America, Mexico, and the American Southwest.*

"Strange? Not at all," said Lummis. "All these folk built sincerely and for use—not to show off. That is why you can add them all together and divide by your personal desire without getting a vulgar fraction."

The manual-training component of mission education inspired Lummis's plans for roof tiles fabricated on site and for furniture hand built by himself or by artist friends such as the painter Maynard Dixon, who crafted a pyro-engraved clothes-press during one visit.[9] The theme of handiwork was carried through in the principal interior space, called El Museo (The Museum), with extensive displays of Native American baskets, rugs, pottery, and other archeological bric-a-brac (plate 58). Although the profusion of objects in El Museo might appear to contradict the spare aesthetic of both the Arts and Crafts movement and the eighteenth-century missions, such clutter was not the result of conspicuous consumption. Instead, the plethora of objects was autobiographical testimony to Lummis's self-actualization through the labor of recording and resuscitating extinct or vanishing cultures.[10]

A typical day at home for Lummis consisted of carpentry, stone laying, gardening (see plate 29), making preserves, editing, writing letters, photographing, and crusading for historic preservation or other causes.[11] His reception room was the patio, where he conversed with a succession of illustrious guests while wielding plane and chisel at the workbench. Although he did not explicitly label himself an Arts and Crafter, Lummis consistently practiced an ideology of heart, head, and hands united in the joyful realization of an individualistic, enduring house:

> It should be good architecture, honest construction, comfortable, convenient, fire-proof, burglar-proof, time-proof. . . . The more of himself he [the owner] can put into it, the better for it and for him. . . . Everyone knows that the thing he has made is more genuinely his than the thing he has bought. The creative thrill is so fine and keen, it is sheer pitiful to see a man get a home off the bargain counter.[12]

During the twenty-plus years he invested in completing the thirteen-room El Alisal, Lummis never lost sight of the traditional rancho conviviality that was the essential reason for erecting what he called "the big Spanish house of stone."[13] On his much-publicized westward tramp from Ohio, he had been entertained at the San Mateo, New Mexico, hacienda of the Chaves family, headed by the aged frontiersman "Little Lion" Don Miguel Antonio.[14] The Chaveses' fun-loving hospitality had caused Lummis to rethink his views about the rigorous, "manly" simple life. Perhaps clean, uncomplicated, vital living was less a product of rugged combat against natural and human obstacles than a result of pastoral work *and* leisure.[15] Following the Chaveses' lead, Lummis initiated Saturday galas at El Alisal, dubbed "noises," replete with Mexican food, Spanish folk songs, poetry readings, and spirited high jinks. The house itself warmly embraced friends and family in the mottoes inscribed above the fireplaces:

> Gather about me! Who can weld iron—or friends without me?
> A casual savage cracked two stones together—a spark—
> and Man was armed against the Weather.
> Love and Fire they're easily lit; but to keep either—wood to it![16]

59. Bernard Maybeck, library in the Charles Keeler House, Berkeley, 1895–1907. From Charles Keeler, *The Simple Home*, 1904.
∾ *For his Berkeley library, Keeler chose straight-lined furniture in natural finish. The vernacular rush-bottomed chair symbolized not only traditional rural craftsmanship but also the Arts and Crafts principle of fitness for use. The seat and posts sloped backward to facilitate an informal, relaxed posture. Taste, rather than expense, was the guide in selecting such accessories as linen crash curtains and Japanese paper lanterns for electric-light shades.*

Keeler's favorite authors were Keats and Shelley; home life, he concluded, should radiate the lyrical spirit. But his quantities of literary and learned tomes served a decorative as well as an intellectual purpose: "Masses of books have an ornamental value which is heightened by the idea of culture of which they are the embodiment."

The conventions of art, when given a dominating influence, are sure to paralyze the true realization of the art ideal. It is only the good Earth Mother who can be invoked without let or hindrance by the artist, for she holds in her hand the cup of life with its unfailing inspiration to the flagging soul. . . . The great masters of all time have sought their models in nature while their petty rivals have merely echoed the inspiration which their teachers had derived at the fountain head.

Charles Keeler, "The Impress of Nature on Art in California," *Impressions* 1 (November 1900): 171.

Lummis's counterpart in the San Francisco Bay Area was the Berkeleyite Charles Keeler—equally sociable, idiosyncratic in dress and architectural tastes, and a man of letters who attracted like-minded intellectuals in the clubs and community organizations he headed. A friend and admirer of Lummis, he publicly praised the individualism shown equally in Lummis's feisty editorials and hand-built house.[17] Keeler himself was a "flamboyant California dreamer," who sported a black broadcloth cape and gold-tipped cane, but loved to don Greek robes and other costumes for the masques he wrote or directed (see plate 10).[18] He was not only a leader in the Dramatic Brotherhood but also an annual participant in Bohemian Grove encampments, president of the Studio Club of Berkeley, and founder of a neighborhood Ruskin study group as well as a Morrisian press christened Sign of the Live Oak.[19] He resided in one of Berkeley's first "freak" wooden houses, which eschewed decorative pediments, machine-made bracketwork, and even paint in favor of the organic ornament of climbing vines and hanging fern baskets (plate 36).[20]

Keeler believed in "The One Ideal" whence flowed all the arts capable of elevating man; he identified architecture as the most fundamental expression, especially in its domestic guise as the family shelter, which "shaped and sized" its occupants.[21] Sham buildings and tawdry furnishings reflected, and created, vulgar people. By contrast, simplified, open-plan houses with exposed rafters and board walls, lightly waxed to heighten inherent grain pattern and subtle color gradations, bred open-hearted offspring who sought riches in the structure of loving family life and the adornment of genuine friendship.[22]

Such sincere amity and a kindred home-building philosophy infused the relationship between Keeler and Bernard Maybeck—the architect son of a German wood-carver, who had a mission to restore handicraft to its rightful place alongside the mother craft of architecture. In 1895 Maybeck, Keeler, and Keeler's wife, Louise, "went off for a quiet rest in the Redwoods," during which they planned the couple's "house of redwood within and without" (plate 59).[23] Outlined by steeply pitched roofs and peaked ceilings, the domestic atmosphere was chapel-like: the vertical lines, Keeler rhapsodized, "pointed heavenward toward spiritual things unrealized."[24] Communion with the out-of-doors was effected in a sleeping porch, purportedly the first seen in Berkeley.[25] The house was missionary, since it led to the founding in 1898 of the Hillside Club to promote, as a community-wide aesthetic, Maybeck's architectural vision for wedding landscape, facade, and interior. While president of the organization (1903–5), Keeler wrote the book *The Simple Home* (1904) in order to spread "the gospel of the simple life"; he dedicated it to Maybeck.

As committed to handicraft as to environmentally sensitive architecture, Keeler is credited with designing his family's wooden beds and collaborating with Maybeck on the details of wrought-iron hinges for the front door.[26] In 1898 he formed a local Handicraft Guild, and as late as 1921 he tried to recruit Maybeck to create shelters and shops for an artisan colony conceived along the lines of

Pasadena's Arroyo Guild.[27] During some thirty years after the death of his wife in 1907, Keeler followed in Lummis's footsteps by toiling over a hand-built, organic house (plate 60). It was an open-beamed, neutral-toned stucco retreat in Berkeley, incorporating a rock outcropping in the floor plan.[28] Functioning as murals were the Claremont hills themselves; music consisted of the splashing of a neighboring stream and the chorus of frogs assembled at a nearby mountain spring.

Keeler's secluded aerie externalized his intuition that direct experience of California's soul-expanding scenery was more effective than the preachings codified in Hillside Club leaflets and *The Simple Home* for converting the general citizenry to unostentatious, naturally artful living. Indeed, tourist forays and camping expeditions in the Golden State's early national parks, forest preserves, beaches, and, especially, alpine resorts did prompt many people to aspire to a more habitual simplicity and rusticity at home. Coincidentally, Keeler himself commenced the Claremont "den" after spending a summer as a grieving widower in residence in Yosemite Valley.[29]

Yosemite was the first national park in the United States, set aside by congressional legislation adopted in 1864 but operated under state auspices until

60. Charles Keeler, studio, Claremont Hills, Berkeley, c. 1909.

∽ *"Simplicity, significance, utility, harmony—these are the watchwords!" Keeler implemented his own advice in his Claremont studio. The curvilinear shaping of the rafter, which provided delight to the eye, was "simple" in that it was executed in the solid structural members rather than merely applied as embellishment.*

Elaborately pierced, sawn, or turned oriental and Italianate furniture illustrated Keeler's dictum that things "may be as richly ornamented as taste suggests, provided the work be handwrought." Keeler's reductivist aesthetic was by no means spartan: "Italian chairs carved of black walnut have a grace and elegance that give a touch of luxury to the most unpretentious home."

OPPOSITE

61. Claycraft Potteries. *Tile—El Capitan, Yosemite,* c. 1926. Press-molded fired clay colored with pigmented slip, 11⅝ x 11½ in. Tile Heritage Foundation; Gift of Bart Huffman, Healdsburg, California.

BELOW

62. Claycraft Potteries. *Tile—Bridal Veil Falls, Yosemite,* c. 1926. Press-molded fired clay colored with pigmented slip, 11⅞ x 7⅞ in. Tile Heritage Foundation; Gift of Bart Huffman, Healdsburg, California.

1890. Unlike the other early national preserves—notably, Yellowstone, the Grand Canyon, and Glacier—Yosemite was not accessible by railroad in the initial decades of its development. Indeed, not until 1907 (the year Keeler made his pilgrimage to the High Sierra) did the Yosemite Valley Railroad reach the outskirts of the public park. The modest lodgings frequented by visitors set a standard for simplified domesticity amid nature. Spared the commercialism of railway promoters' log palaces for tourists—luxurious Gilded Age hotels that hid behind a thin rustic veneer—Yosemite had spartan accommodations and service buildings that enhanced visitors' appreciation of the simple life as participation in what John Ruskin called the "naked purity" of God-given alpine landscape art.[30]

Ruskin, the sage to whom English Arts and Crafters, and their American disciples, perennially paid homage, wrote that the Alps and other mountains "seem to have been built for the human race, as at once their schools and cathedrals; full of treasures of illuminated manuscripts for the scholar, kindly in simple lessons to the worker, quiet in pale cloisters for the thinker, glorious in holiness for the worshipper."[31] John Muir applied to the American Alps of Yosemite a Ruskinian interpretation, widely disseminated through articles and books, such as

9 5

The Mountains of California (1894), *Our National Parks* (1901), and *The Yosemite* (1912), and through the Sierra Club he founded in 1892. Keeler was one of the charter members of the San Francisco–based group, which financed construction in 1903 of Le Conte Memorial Lodge, a clubhouse and tourist-information center on the valley floor. Built from locally quarried granite, rough-hewn to preserve the weathered surface, the Sierra clubhouse was designed by Mark White, construction supervisor and brother-in-law to Bernard Maybeck.[32] An exaggerated Gothic roofline crowns the substantial blue-gray masonry walls, and the generous living room–library, which reveals the rough-finished roof beams, is dominated by a floor-to-ceiling granite fireplace. Rustic furniture included a "very unique table . . . [with] a heavy top, 9 x 5 feet, supported by two sections of the unbarked trunk of a large yellow pine."[33] Soon after the completion of Le Conte Lodge, the *Sierra Club Bulletin* (January 1904) reported "great interest" and praise "in the highest terms" from those who had seen it, and as late as 1926 it was given a full-page illustration—along with the Mariposa Grove, Cathedral Spires, Yosemite Falls, and other scenic attractions—in the promotional brochure "Motoring through the Yosemite."

The mass production and distribution of automobiles, first admitted to Yosemite in 1913, brought a significant increase in tourism and in the popularity of camping as a family recreation. Enthusiasm for sleeping under the stars had been fueled by the Boy Scout movement; in the first American handbook Ernest Thompson Seton identified camping as "the simple life reduced to actual practice."[34] *Country Life* magazine, founded in 1901, included advice from a female perspective on "Campkeeping as a Fine Art," in the California redwoods—with a Chinese cook.[35] By 1901 the Sierra Club was sponsoring more rigorous annual outings, including women as well as men, to the higher wilderness reaches of Yosemite. The park had a designated public campground as early as 1878, and by 1897 the promotional brochure for the Yosemite Stage and Turnpike Company was addressing campers' specific needs for equipment and transportation.

Yosemite's hotel owners during the Victorian era had helped make campers of genteel Americans, for money could buy only the "sorriest lodging and simplest fare," according to one disgruntled Pullman traveler.[36] In the 1860s and 1870s sightseers could stay at Clarke's—"a little log house and canvas tent on a meadow in the wilderness"—or at the shantylike Lower Hotel.[37] A British clergyman rented a chamber there that consisted of split-plank walls, a rough, gaping floor, and a ceiling admitting starlight; its door (with hair-covered cowhide hinges) opened directly into the forest. The Lower Hotel's major competitor was the Upper Hotel, taken over by the San Francisco journalist and editor James Mason Hutchings in 1864. Assisted by John Muir, he replaced the makeshift muslin doors and partitions with wooden dividers sawn from pines and cedars felled by a winter gale.[38] Verandas were added around the hotel; new outbuildings included guest sleeping rooms in The Cottage by the River and The Cottage in the Rocks.

Muir's genius was behind the Big Tree Room, which enveloped a 175-foot living cedar and served as a combined kitchen–sitting room.

The Big Tree Room was still intact at the turn of the century, although the original Hutchings House had been superseded on the same site by the more conventionally equipped Sentinel Hotel. Still, there lingered a legacy of roughing it in accommodations with coarse pine floors and thin walls covered in unbleached cotton. These were recorded with some relish by the author Helen Hunt Jackson, who lodged in the riverside cottage of the "artistic," "visionary" Mr. Hutchings in 1872.[39] The Sentinel's proprietor, J. B. Cook, operated the subsidiary Camp Yosemite (later called Lost Arrow)—a permanent tent village of various-sized habitations uniformly outfitted with canvas roofs and walls, wooden-platform floors, and metal cots accompanied by functional chairs, washstands, and mirrors.[40]

It was not Cook, however, but David Curry who had the personality and promotional skills to make tent cities a trademark of Yosemite (plate 63). Starting with seven tents and 290 guests in 1899, Curry pursued the goals of making "every guest feel at home" and of bringing wholesome outdoor living within the reach of all, however briefly.[41] His success was quantitative as well as qualitative: 540 tents in 1915 and 10,164 registered visitors in 1916.[42] A commentator of the 1950s enthused, "Camp Curry down through the years has not been just another resort but rather an American institution that has evolved into a Yosemite tradition."[43]

An argument can be made for the converse, insofar as the Golden State's "tent houses" were a variant of the "California bungalow" exported to the Midwest and the East, and constituting an "American institution" in homebuilding by the 1920s. The tent bungalow of California—which gave quick and thorough ventilation through side walls of coarse hemp, cotton, or linen adhered to hinged frames—was one of ten classifications devised by Henry Saylor, who wrote an encyclopedic volume on the bungalow house type in 1911. The bungalow was generally defined in the first decade of the twentieth century as a one-story informal vacation retreat

63. Camp Curry tent, Yosemite, 1917.

blending with its alpine, forest, or seaside site. "Simply built" and "simply furnished" in the stalwart Mission style, complemented by rag rugs or grass matting and heavy but distinctive fabrics with uneven warps, it was well "adapted to the simple life" in the out-of-doors.[44] Whether built of canvas or of more durable materials like shingles, stone, or stucco, the bungalow was uniquely suited to the gentle climate and magnificent scenery that made California a year-round outdoor playground. Charles Keeler declared of California: "Nowhere else on the American Continent is the out-of-door world so inviting. Its charm is intangible, but compelling. In large measure it is due, no doubt, to the near approach of the mountains to the ocean, so that the people of the State come into intimate and habitual contact with these two commanding phenomena of nature."[45]

Publicists for the Mount Wilson Toll Road Company also commented on the proximity of surf and snow in Southern California. The company opened an improved pathway to the summit in 1891 and subsequently operated tent and shingled cottages as part of its lodge atop one of the most popular recreational destinations in the Los Angeles area.[46] By the mid-1880s campers had already arrived on the slopes of Mount Wilson, and in 1893 a former miner, William Sturdevant, started what soon became one of the most frequented vacation spots in the San Gabriel Timberland Reserve. Remodeled in 1898, Sturdevant's establishment included not only a tent village, made homelike by adjacent outdoor stone fireplaces, but also a chinked log-cabin sitting room and a dining pavilion with stone foundation and log-and-twig openwork walls. Hammocks complemented other furnishings, "simple and rustic, of necessity, as everything not made in the canyon must be packed up by burros."[47] Sturdevant's Camp was again improved in 1905 as an adjunct of the Mount Wilson Hotel, which consisted of a central building and forty "artistic" mountain cabins, financed by the toll-road company.[48]

The new Mount Wilson facilities drew national publicity, for William T. Comstock pictured one of the bedroom "bungalows" in his 1908 compendium *Bungalows, Camps, and Mountain Houses*. Two years earlier, the *Craftsman* had devoted a well-illustrated article to this "summer home"—"not a hotel, it is not a camp—and yet it is both."[49] Equally praiseworthy were the "low, widespread bungalow"—containing servants' quarters, dining room (plate 64), and library-lounge—and the shingled sleeping "cottages," sporting individual porches punctuated by lattice railings. All the structures were built from native pine or redwood and wainscoted to the plate rail, with burlap, toned in complementary dull reds, yellows, or mossy greens, applied above. Interior coloring was enriched by burning the wooden trim to bring out the grain, and in the main building, the burlap panels were relieved by burnt-wood stripping—"a very Craftsman-like treatment." The principal gathering place was like "the living room of a country home," organized around a ten-foot fireplace of rough granite quarried from the mountain and outfitted with wicker arm- and easy chairs interspersed with cedar- or hickory-pole rockers and side chairs. The rustic furniture may have been purchased from one of the Indiana hickory manufacturers, whose functionally

64. Cooperative dining room in the large bungalow, Mount Wilson Hotel, 1906. From *Craftsman,* August 1906.

65. Mount Lowe Alpine Tavern, c. 1912.

98

designed pieces made of sturdy posts and woven-bark upholstery found favor among Arts and Crafts devotees, despite their origins in factories equipped with modern cutting and bark-splitting machines. Some items, especially tables and case pieces, may have been made on site to avoid the travails and expense of transport to the peak.[50]

Although rustic complexes like the Mount Wilson Hotel invite comparison to compounds in the Adirondacks, significant differences existed between the two, which render the public and private vacation haunts of the Pacific more congruent with Arts and Crafts ideals. The comments by the architectural historian Richard Longstreth concerning The Bend (1898), a hunting lodge near Mount

Shasta conceived by the San Francisco architect Willis Polk, apply equally to Southern California mountain getaways:

> The effect is entirely different from that of Adirondack camp interiors, where the sheer quantity of overscaled logs, roots, and boulders generates a sense of applied decoration. These are primeval versions of gilded Edwardian rooms, where rusticity was pursued with a vengeance, only to result in a rarefied display. . . . While life amid the wilderness was still somewhat alien to the rich New Yorkers who inhabited the camps, such an existence was sufficiently close in time and place for Californians now to be considered as a natural extension of their routine. The Bend suggests the compatibility between civilization and nature, as the largest Adirondack camps tend to perpetuate a sense of struggle and conquest.[51]

Whereas the Adirondack camps were largely private vacation getaways, the Mount Wilson Hotel and its nearby neighbor, the Mount Lowe Alpine Tavern (plate 65) and housekeeping cabins, along with a multiunit building called The Bungalow, were public hostelries ardently promoted in tourist literature such as Charles Keeler's *Southern California* (1898) and Mina Dean Halsey's *A Tenderfoot in Southern California* (1908). The Mount Lowe and Mount Wilson enterprises attracted many more excursionists than all the other resorts in the San Gabriel Mountains combined.[52] The notions about an informal way of life, rustic furnishings, and cooperative housekeeping, which the tourist imbibed along with the balsam-scented air, significantly shaped the material world of early twentieth-century California. As one chronicler of Far Western tourism has explained: "From roughly the 1890s into the 1920s, he [the tourist] was preeminently a potential settler, who after enjoying a sample of the product might place a continuing order."[53]

In the same early twentieth-century period, the bungalow as an unobtrusive summer cottage constructed to enhance the charm of a nonurban landscape enjoyed nationwide promotion and consumer popularity. The house type was linked with "back-to-nature" rustic imagery also seen in the vogue for gardening, camping, and physical culture, and with Arts and Crafts ideals that rejected contemporary consumer culture in favor of a preindustrial, rural idyll. Just as Gustav Stickley's furniture "was founded on a return to the sturdy and primitive forms that were meant for usefulness alone," so too the *Craftsman* viewed the American bungalow as "nothing more or less than a summer residence of extreme simplicity, economic construction and intended for more or less primitive living."[54] Still, as early as 1906 the *Craftsman* ran a feature called "Possibilities of the Bungalow as a Permanent Dwelling," and in 1911 Henry Saylor made an exception to his definition of the bungalow as a "temporary home, shooting lodge, and week-end retreat" in the cases of Los Angeles and Pasadena.[55] There the climate of "perpetual summer," boisterously acclaimed by the writer-outdoorsman George

Wharton James, made the bungalow an appropriate, economical, and artistic house for year-round occupancy in burgeoning suburbs.[56]

Although the prime years of bungalow promotion were 1905–15, the *Los Angeles Examiner* reported in May 1904 that every street in Pasadena had a bungalow, and Los Angeles and Hollywood abounded in the wide-roofed dwellings as well.[57] The typical bungalow that came to dominate in the greater Los Angeles area combined timber construction and rustic siding or shingles with such mountain-camp references as fieldstone foundations or walls, cobblestone chimneys and piers—sometimes randomly interspersed with protruding clinker bricks—and, perhaps, log or pebble-dash accents.[58]

Such "rustic simplicity," deemed the essential bungalow trait by one writer on Southern California domesticity, was reiterated inside.[59] A masonry chimney breast or mixed-media surround (cobblestones, brick, rock, or tile facings) often served as the focal point of a wainscoted living room incorporating built-in benches and bookcases to create a compact but imposing fireside inglenook. The cavernous stone hearth of the Mount Lowe Alpine Tavern was illustrated in a 1909 *House and Garden* article on modern fireplaces that captured the old-fashioned home spirit of the colonial or preindustrial kitchen and living hall. Also featured in the article were a floor-to-ceiling rough clinker-brick model from the Los Angeles mail-order bungalow builder Henry L. Wilson and a Craftsman-like affair of tile, wood buttresses, and beams framing an overmantel mountain landscape.[60] The latter fireplace treatment was the work of Carl Enos Nash's company, "artists as well as craftsmen," who favored scenic, matte-glazed Grueby and Rookwood tiles depicting forest, desert, and pastoral motifs in keeping with the bungalow's mission to maximize the charms of outdoor life.[61] The living-room hearth was the most important emblem of the devoted though informal home life advocated by Keeler and numerous reformer-idealists associated with the Arts and Crafts movement. Nash articulated this linkage between material environment and spiritual state: "As we sit meditating, watching the leaping flames and listening to the crackle of the fire, what can be more conducive to perfect contentment than a well designed fireplace?"[62]

In January 1913 an account by Charles Francis Saunders in the West Coast magazine *Sunset* admirably distilled the interior and exterior hallmarks of the Californian indoor-outdoor house, along with the easygoing, wholesome way of life associated with it. "When you see a cozy one or one-and-a-half storied dwelling, with low-pitched roof and very wide eaves, lots of windows and an outside chimney of cobble or clinker-brick half hidden by clinging vines—that *is* a bungalow, whatever other houses may be."[63] Besides the inviting open fireplace, the interior needed bright-colored oriental or Native American rugs and couch covers, Native or Latin American earthenware pottery serving as flower holders, Indian baskets utilized as receptacles or wall decorations, and pictures of "characteristic California scenes, such as snow-capped mountains, cool canyon depths, the crumbling missions—all such things help to give the unconventional touch which goes with bungalow living." Ease of housekeeping was another bungalow directive, implemented in a compact, airy kitchen utilizing such built-ins as the "California cooler," an ingenious air-conditioning system featuring a screened bottom and top and perforated shelves, through which cool air rose from under the house to the roof. This natural refrigerator, and laundry tubs too, occupied a screen porch appended to the kitchen proper.

Porches of all sorts—for storage, sleeping, dining, and entertaining—were integral to the bungalow way of life. Saunders's favorite "room" was his family's rear veranda, described as a honeysuckle-and-climbing-rose bower looking out on the garden and the Sierra Madre in the distance. It served as an outdoor living and eating area, made comfortable with those staples of resort hotel equipage— hickory chairs, settees, and tables. Henry L. Wilson's *Bungalow Magazine* corroborated not only the primacy of porches but also the preeminence of Old Hickory furniture, which coordinated effectively with reed porch shades and Mourzouk cocoa-fiber rugs or Crex wire-grass carpets.[64] For enclosed rooms Wilson endorsed leather-upholstered, fumed-oak seats, in the style of, but not necessarily manufactured by, the Craftsman Workshops. As a tireless promoter of California's primacy in artistic homebuilding, he lent support to local enterprises such as the Bungalow Furniture Manufacturing Company of Los Angeles, makers of Stickley-look-alike spindle pieces.[65]

Beginning in June 1909, Wilson published a series of four articles in *Bungalow Magazine* in which he traced the transformation of the California bungalow from a one-room frontier log cabin sporting a stone chimney and plank furniture to a tasteful suburban home. Although he gave a nod to those who saw the origin of the Western bungalow in the anglicized East Indian thatched cottage, he stressed the evolution and addition of features in accord with the particular climate and customs of the Pacific Coast.[66] Traits that continued to distinguish "true" California bungalows from related shelters sporting emphatic horizontal lines, wide roofs, and plain trim-work were a very low-pitched roof, feasible in a locality lacking the climatic rigors of ice and snow; an informal plan, omitting an entrance vestibule in favor of a front door opening directly from the outdoors into the family's living room; and "California Style" construction, with boards and battens, sometimes finished on the interior with burlap.[67] This inexpensive "box house," as *Ladies' Home Journal* called it, might be not only roofed but entirely sheathed in shakes—"a distinctive Western product, originally made by sawing the giant redwoods into three foot sections and splitting them off by hand."[68]

Such battened-board and shake- or shingle-covered dwellings conjured up associations with the wooden chalets of the Swiss and Italian mountains, and the alpine connection was reinforced by the hillside siting of so many houses in Pasadena and Los Angeles, as well as in Berkeley and San Francisco. The Park Place Tract on the edge of Pasadena's Arroyo Seco heights became known as Little Switzerland. There were associational as well as topographical reasons for

Californians to adopt the Swiss chalet as their own, since "simplicity of life," quality craftsmanship, democratic institutions, and exceptionally high rates of home ownership and literacy attributed to the Swiss people were principles integral to the theory and practice of the Arts and Crafts movement.[69] Furthermore, the Swiss mountaineer, like his Pacific Coast counterpart, preferred life in the out-of-doors; hence the profusion of porch-balconies on his two- or three-storied abode equipped with wide eaves to shelter these open-air spaces.[70] As in California bungalows, foundations were often of stone continuing half-way up the first story; roofs in upper-valley chalets were flattened to retain the snow; whereas lower-plains types sported steeply sloping roofs to shed water. Thus, there were Swiss prototypes for both the spreading roofs favored by Greene and Greene and the strong vertical rooflines of Maybeck's shingled cottages in the Berkeley hills.[71]

It was neither Greene and Greene nor Maybeck commissions, however, that Henry Saylor chose to illustrate for the West Coast "Swiss chalet" type in his *Bungalows* survey of 1911. The book's frontispiece showed Felsengarten, the home of C. W. Robertson in Nordhoff, California, designed with board-and-batten walls and a cobblestone chimney by the transplanted midwesterners Myron Hunt and Elmer Grey. Even though it was two stories tall, Saylor deemed the structure exemplary for its harmonious blending with the Ventura Valley landscape.[72] Saylor had been made editor of the nationally prominent homemaking magazine *House and Garden* in 1909, and an article on Hunt and Grey's Felsengarten appeared in the journal that year.[73]

Named for the "rocky setting to its flower gardens," Felsengarten nestled snugly among sheltering live oaks (plate 24), one of which supported a platform in the boughs where afternoon tea was served. Inside the house, the tree-loving spirit was maintained with the raftered ceiling and the "velvety brown wooden walls" of russet-stained Oregon pine, which approximated the interiors of real Swiss chalets "finished entirely in natural wood" (plate 66).[74] Stylized pine trees were painted between the rafters; pine trees stenciled in green also adorned the pale brown monk's-cloth draperies. Other painted decoration included German mottoes over doorways and a triptych panel (executed by one of Robertson's daughters) above the entrance to the kitchen, depicting a Tyrolese peasant girl, a mountain climber, and the climber's cry *Glück auf!* (Good luck!). A log chandelier suspended from the rafters by iron chains held wax candles to illuminate the dining table, which was supported on spiral-twist legs evocative of the German-Swiss tradition of ornamental turning and carving. Much of the furniture was handmade and hand-carved, and the stair balustrade was sawed out to emulate the pierced pattern of the gable-end exterior balcony. Similarly, the dining chairs were decoratively sawn to approximate frankly constructed German or Swiss back stools—a form that the decorator Dorothy Tuke Priestman generically labeled a "bungalow chair" and recommended for the simple home, whether or not it was built along chalet lines.[75]

Myron Hunt credited Charles Sumner Greene with having originated the boarded-and-shingled California bungalows that "made one think of a Swiss chalet" but also revealed "a touch of Japan, even a touch of Thibet [*sic*], in their make-up. . . . There was something basic about his method of attack, and something logical in his use of material, with the result that carpenters and builders, not to mention architects, found it possible to emulate him and to do so with remarkable success."[76] Indeed, as early as 1908 California mail-order bungalow companies were offering Swiss-chalet renditions, and Southern California Homebuilders used its redwood-sided and cobblestone-accented Plan No. 119, labeled an adaptation of Swiss and Japanese architecture, as an advertising icon in *Arrowhead* and *West Coast* magazines.[77] Although both the seminality of the Greene brothers and the degree of Japanese influence on California bungalow architecture have been disputed, what remains certain is the Greenes' synthesis of the fundamental oriental sensibilities identified by the Boston Arts and Crafts architect Ralph Adams Cram in his *Impressions of Japanese Architecture and the Allied Arts* (1905): the reverence for inherent texture, grain, and coloring in natural wood; the beauty of constructional ornament; the organic elegance of soft light and matte color evidenced equally in courtyard gardens and translucent-screened rooms opening onto them.[78]

The Greenes' mastery of color and light effects—keying the interior palette to the landscaping and utilizing lighter tones for dark corners, alcoves, and upper sections of walls as opposed to deeper shading for sunny areas—garnered rave reviews and substantial national publicity from the Pasadena bungalow designer and decorator Una Nixson Hopkins.[79] In "The Development of Domestic Architecture on the Pacific Coast" (*Craftsman,* January 1908), she selected photographs of the Greene brothers' Garfield (1904) and Libby (1905) houses to illustrate the rustic shake or shingled category. She claimed that these homes, like the Swiss chalet, adapted to the contours of the land, but their detailing was in the "Japanese spirit." She was especially enthusiastic about the Libby house-and-garden "ensemble," where pergola-porches and Cherokee rose vines nullified distinctions between human artifice and natural ornament. Similarly, in a *Craftsman* case study of Greene and Greene's third house for Josephine van Rossem in Pasadena (1905), Hopkins commended the out-of-door feeling achieved in the redwood-boarded living room (plate 67), with its numerous windows giving a view of "majestic pine trees, throwing a tangle of light and shade below, on roof and doors and window sills."[80] East Indian wicker chairs enhanced the impression of living room as porch, and they were complemented by India-cotton draperies of light buff with a pattern in dull pink. Oriental rugs in a predominant "old rose" hue added liveliness while blending with the reddish color of the wood sheathing and built-in furniture.

Hopkins believed color to be the essential factor in the success or failure of interior decoration. She quoted Ruskin and Morris on the importance of artful gradations and on proper combinations of earthy browns, yellows, greens, and pale copper.[81] Hopkins and other domestic advisers praised homes in which the natural coloring of flowers and leaves was emulated. Since all objects, whether expensive or cheap, possessed color, successful decoration was a matter of tasteful sensibilities rather than wealth and conspicuous consumption. The wide appeal of the bungalow, according to Kate Greenleaf Locke, lay in its moderate cost, for "when furnished with extreme simplicity it may (if sufficiently artistic in its treatment) outrank the most expensive conventional house."[82]

105

67. Charles Summer Greene and Henry Mather Greene, living room of the Josephine van Rossem House, Pasadena, 1905. From Una Nixson Hopkins, "A House of Fine Detail That Conforms to the Hillside on Which It Is Built," *Craftsman,* June 1907.

Locke illustrated as an archetypal bungalow the one-story rambling residence in Pasadena of Arthur Jerome Eddy, built (like Lummis's El Alisal) of concrete in a patio-plan configuration (plate 68). Eddy himself wrote about his home, and color was a major topic.[83] Climbing tea roses were planted against two sides of the house not just to alleviate the starkness of the concrete walls but also to harmonize with the red-tile roof. The native clay utilized for the tiles was fired to a lovely vermilion that changed seasonally—fresh, bright red after the winter rains; dull and dusty in the summer heat. Adobe bricks of the same material paved both patio and hall, but in the latter they were varnished, giving a half-glazed effect due to the irregularities associated with brick making by hand. Ruddy tones prevailed in the redwood front door with a hammered-copper handle and bell push and in the redwood wainscot of the living room. A frieze of warm gray Portland cement showed inherent color gradations as light played in an "unusually interesting" way over the unsmoothed circular trowel marks. Silhouetted against the mist-toned walls, on the shelf atop the wainscoting, were wrought-iron-and-mica electric lights. Such fixtures were used throughout the residence and as patio lanterns. The lampshades reinforced the golden hue of Oregon pine posts, rafters,

68. Arthur Jerome Eddy and Frederick L. Roehrig, Arthur Jerome Eddy House, Pasadena, 1905. From Kate Greenleaf Locke, "Furnishing and Decorating Houses of Moderate Cost," *House and Garden*, June 1907.

⤳ *The dining and living rooms in Eddy's bungalow were furnished en suite. The massive dining table of pine and mahogany featured a redwood border, steel-brushed to accentuate the rough, flat wood grain. The accompanying chairs were upholstered in a heavy tanned leather, with the brown brand marks and large handmade nails serving as intrinsic decoration. Silvery green window hangings complemented the wainscoting, just as foliage relieves the dark hues of tree trunks and boughs. Native American accessories, especially Navajo blankets, radiated the strong colors so well suited to what Eddy called "the dry, hot light of the California summers."*

106

and trusses. The black iron was "a good strong contrast to the redwood," as noted of a similar combination in a *House Beautiful* description of D'Arcy Gaw's own Arts and Crafts house in San Jose, California.[84] Sturdily built furniture "that seems to keep its place" was made from redwood and Oregon pine as well, while the large fireplace was of cement faced in irregular cobbles.

The Eddy bungalow was a success not just in matching color, texture, and materials to local conditions but in implementing the major precepts of a nationwide Arts and Crafts movement—notably, unity in artistic expression derived from nature, straightforward construction and handcraftsmanship, minimal finish and restraint in ornamentation, use of vernacular sources and reference to the indigenous cultural heritage, as well as cultivation of a family-centered domesticity represented in the open plan and imposing central hearth. Yet those very principles, which linked this adobe-cum-concrete home and the wooden bungalows by the Greenes and other designers of board-and-battened or shingled "California Style" houses to the larger American movement, were also the bases for differentiating a distinct regional expression. Mary Austin, one of the "local color" authors initially encouraged and published by Lummis, wrote eloquently about the congruence of the bungalow and the unspoiled California landscape:

> This is the thing that most strikes the attention of the traveler. . . . The Angelenos call them bungalows, in respect to the type from which they developed, but they deserve a name as distinctive as they have in character become. These little thin-walled dwellings, all of desert-tinted native wood and stones, are as indigenous to the soil as if they had grown up out of it, as charming in line and perfection of utility as some of those wild growths which show a delicate, airy florescence above ground, but under it have deep, man-shaped resistant roots. With their low and flat pitched roofs they present a certain likeness to the aboriginal dwellings which the Franciscans found scattered like wasps' nests among the chaparral along the river, which is only another way of saying that the spirit of the land shapes the art that is produced there.[85]

Whereas the Arts and Crafts agenda in much of the United States was reformist, antimodern, and anti-industrial, Californians, especially in the Southland, were still forming, initiating, and defining a social and material culture on the Pacific frontier. In his discussion of bungalow life, Charles Francis Saunders sketched an "old Californian," who asserted that the Golden State was still young, democratic, and preindustrial insofar as farmers were wanted and needed to develop the soil.[86] Although the homesteader might later be bought out, at a handsome price, by suburban developers, the houses subsequently built and furnished on his land would bear witness to the natural, functional, aesthetic traditions of life begun in the days of aboriginal occupation and perpetuated by the mission padres, Spanish rancheros, and Anglo pioneers bent on resuscitating an Arcadia that would be home to the chosen people in the promised land.

The logic of the trend of history for centuries has pointed to Southern California as the final "promised land" of the human race. Natural prosperity, greatness and power have always been confined within a narrow zone of thirty degrees north latitude, between the thirtieth and sixtieth parallels, and the march of natural supremacy has always been westward within these lines. . . . God has destined this [Southern California] to be the home of his newer and better "chosen people." It is the new and better Eden, and to us is entrusted its present care.

George Wharton James, "Southern California," *Mt. Lowe Echo* 1 (June 9, 1894): n.p.

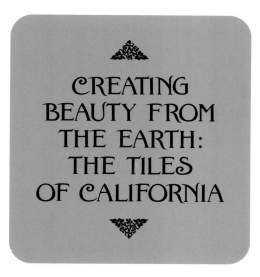

CREATING BEAUTY FROM THE EARTH: THE TILES OF CALIFORNIA

Joseph A. Taylor

The exploration and exploitation of the clay resources of the West has been carried on . . . with the zest of a child with a new found toy. The realization that in clay products lies a future wealth . . . that will dwarf the comparative wonders of the gold exploration has seized upon the imagination of broad-visioned and practical men.[1]

Tile making—the shaping of earthen materials into useful, often beautiful objects—is an ancient craft predating recorded history. Through the centuries many cultures have demonstrated notable skill and artistic achievement in this utilitarian form of ceramic art, the result of a convergence of aesthetic and architectural traditions.

The emergence of the tile industry in California since the turn of the century has paralleled the dramatic growth in population there and has thus been largely an urban and coastal phenomenon, nourished by abundant natural resources and enhanced by the romantic architectural styles of the period. The predominance of ceramic surfaces in the state illustrates a merging of the aesthetic traditions of the western Mediterranean countries with the principles of the Arts and Crafts movement in the eastern United States and Northern Europe.

During the first three decades of this century, the principal ceramists, talented and well trained, were also teachers. They engaged in this ancient craft with a mixture of motives, having to strike a balance between the need for self-expression and a desire for profitability. Inspired by the land, its bounty, and the unencumbered opportunities of the frontier, many maintained a romantic vision of the preindustrial world, espousing Arts and Crafts ideas as a way of life. Working cooperatively with the architectural community, most chose to be personally involved in the process of production and to reveal the handcrafted nature

69. Frontispiece from a catalog for the California Art Tile Company, Richmond, c. 1925.

of their products. Although technological advances were gradually implemented in many of the factories, most of the artisans steadfastly preserved the illusion of a handcrafted product, consciously avoiding the appearance of machined ware. Decorative tiles, signed by the maker, became popular artistic objects, readily available and affordable for the average person to have installed in the home.

California's clay-tile tradition had originated with the sun-dried adobe bricks and the fired roof and floor tiles made by Native Americans under the direction of the Spanish Franciscans, who established the chain of missions along El Camino Real, the major north-south thoroughfare. At the Mission San Antonio de Padua, for example, founded by Father Junipero Serra in 1771, a kiln was erected to fire large tiles, many with finger-impressed designs.[2] The concept of the picturesque Franciscan mission, utilized extensively to promote the development of the territory, sanctified the use of indigenous earthen materials, promulgated the ideal of craftsmanship, and legitimized the inspiration derived from the state's Spanish, Mexican, and Native American heritage.

In the middle of the nineteenth century there began a great influx of people attracted by the discovery of gold. Many of the new settlers brought with them distinct ideas concerning the appropriateness of ceramic tiles in the houses they bought or built for themselves. Clinging to Victorian precepts well into the 1890s, residential architects viewed tiles as suitable only for certain floors or for the fireplace and hearth, the focal point of the home. Most of the decorative tiles employed were ornate in design, often with glossy translucent glazes, supplied by manufactories in several of the eastern states or, less often, by importers of European ware.

The architecture at the turn of the century, both the Craftsman-style bungalow and the Mediterranean derivatives, in large measure determined the genre of tiles chosen. In sharp contrast to the Victorian style, tiles used in bungalows tended to be handcrafted from wet clay, often earthy in appearance, with matte finishes and pictorial designs. Those in the Mediterranean category, especially the Spanish Colonial houses that became increasingly popular after the 1915 Panama-California Exposition in San Diego, were originally pressed from dry clays and were brighter in color, often with geometric or exotic designs. These tiles, referred to generally as Hispano-Moresque, were derived from aesthetic traditions established by the Moors in eighth-century Spain.

As local products began to appear, they encountered a dubious reception by architects, who depended on the imported and East Coast tiles that had long been available and well promoted. The early tile makers in California were also frustrated by the lack of reliable sources of raw materials and by the primitive transportation system. Gradually, however, with the lower prices and immediate availability of local tiles and with a growing acceptance of ceramic surfaces throughout the homes, architects and tile installers were presented with an ever-widening variety of products. By the middle of the 1920s the tile makers were experiencing unprecedented demand.

The crowning touch to the ensemble [at the Panama-Pacific International Exposition] is given by the handsome tile fireplace at the far end of one room. Over the fireplace there is embodied a tile panel in colors, illustrating most splendidly an old castle sequestered in a beautiful garden spot. . . . Hill and dale, trees and shrubbery are represented distinctly and harmoniously. Even the sky and cloud effect is portrayed in true manner.

Pacific Coast Architect (May 1915): 97.

70. Eucalyptus-pattern tile panel made by Los Angeles Pressed Brick Company and displayed at the Clay Products Exposition in Chicago, 1913.

A cornerstone of California's tile manufacturing venture was laid on July 10, 1900, in Tropico, about six miles north of downtown Los Angeles—an area previously known only for its strawberry fields.[3] Joseph Kirkham, a fifty-five-year-old Wedgwood-trained ceramist, the first of many with similar credentials to arrive from England, had gone to the West Coast with high expectations. In just six months he proudly exhibited his Pacific Art Tile products at the Los Angeles Chamber of Commerce.[4] In 1903 Fred H. Wilde, an Englishman with experience in tile potteries in England and the East, was hired to superintend the plant, which was soon renamed Western Art Tile. Years later Wilde would bemoan the difficulties in obtaining materials in those early days: "I found that one sample [of clay] was very good and asked for more. . . . I then found out that it was an outcropping away up in the mountains. They loaded it in sacks and brought it down to the railroad on donkey backs."[5] Over the next two decades this pottery would go through numerous transformations, but the stage was set for what would eventually become one of the largest tile manufactories of the era, Tropico Potteries.

The Los Angeles Pressed Brick Company, founded in 1887, offered both mantel and hearth tiles as early as 1904 (plate 70).[6] Following the 1906 earthquake in San Francisco, Fred H. Robertson was hired, and he encouraged the production of faience tiles—a thickly glazed earthenware with a handcrafted appearance.[7] At the 1915 Panama-Pacific International Exposition in San Francisco, the company erected an elaborate exhibit, which was described in detail in the *Pacific Coast Architect*.[8] Not surprisingly, the matte green tiles closely resembled those of Rookwood and Grueby Faience, both of which were popular among

West Coast architects at that time. However, following this impressive showing, the company chose to focus on other, presumably more profitable, product lines, such as building brick, architectural terra cotta, sewer pipe, and roofing tile.

By 1911 tile manufacturing in the state was beginning to take shape, however tenuously. William Wade and his nephew, George Poxon, both tile makers from J. & W. Wade in England, established factories in the farming community of Vernon, southeast of downtown Los Angeles.[9] Wade's facility would become the West Coast Tile Company, which in 1919 was taken over by the American Encaustic Tiling Company, the manufacturing giant from Zanesville, Ohio.[10]

There is little doubt that American Encaustic's interest in West Coast Tile was due in part to the latter company's consolidation with California China Products Company of National City two years earlier, when West Coast purchased its presses, molds, and glazes as well as the use of its trade name, Kaospar. In 1911 California China Products' founder, Walter Nordhoff, an enterprising businessman with an empathy for the arts, had hired a remarkable staff: Fred H. Wilde, as experienced a tilewright as there was in California at the time; John

71. California China Products Company tiles on the California State Building, Panama-California Exposition, Balboa Park, San Diego, 1915.

ﻌ *These buildings are the largest examples of pure Spanish Colonial style in the United States. Ten thousand feet of brilliant colors, in bright glaze tile, have been used in them. . . . Mr. Goodhue's free use of colored glazed tile . . . marks the dawn of a new era in the architecture of our Western States.*

Architect (June 19, 1915): 237.

72. California China Products Company tiles for the interior of the California State Building, Panama-California Exposition, Balboa Park, San Diego, 1915.

McKnight, a well-known authority on local clays; and Wesley H. Trippett of Redlands Pottery. California China Products Company received the contract to produce the tiles for the new San Diego railroad depot designed by Bakewell & Brown and for Bertram Goodhue's California State and Fine Arts buildings for the Panama-California Exposition. Together, this talented team produced tiles of exceptional brilliance in bold geometric designs (plates 71, 72).[11] The Hispano-Moresque aesthetic was thus established and would play a major part in the Spanish Colonial revival over the next two decades.

In sharp contrast to these early attempts at manufacturing tiles for profit in the southern part of the state, Dr. Philip King Brown chose to use clay as a medium to assist the recuperation of his convalescing tubercular patients at the Arequipa Sanatorium in Fairfax, Marin County. The first director, Frederick Hürten Rhead, headed the pottery from its inception in 1911 and focused his energies on experimentation with glazes while striving to develop a viable commercial enterprise. Rhead had produced some exceptional tiles while under the tutelage of Taxile Doat at University City, Missouri,[12] but at Arequipa he was

preoccupied with the production of pots. Tile making was introduced by Albert L. Solon—an Englishman and, like Rhead, a descendant of several generations of famous potters—who was hired in July 1913 to direct what had become Arequipa Pottery (plate 73). Solon introduced the use of local clays and developed a number of special glazes during his tenure. He was responsible for the comparatively frugal operation of the pottery and received much praise as a result.

Wilde, now sixty years old, was the third director at Arequipa Pottery, and he arrived in September 1916, fresh from his success at California China Products Company.[13] Not surprisingly, tiles became the major focus at the pottery under Wilde's competent guidance. The largest (and final) commission was for the floor of Casa Dorinda in Montecito, the western house of Mr. and Mrs. William H. Bliss of New York. The sixty-five-room Spanish Colonial mansion was designed by Carleton Winslow in 1916, and the tiles that adorn the floors were made from designs submitted by Frank Ingerson,[14] who, with his partner, George Dennison, was charged with the interior decoration and landscape design (plate 74). The glazed tiles in low relief feature a decorative border of entwined leaves and vines, accented by dainty orange-red berries and exotic green-and-blue crested birds. It is hard to believe that this volume of high-quality ware was produced in a remote

OPPOSITE

73. Arequipa Pottery. *Patio Tile,* c. 1917. Fired clay with glazed sgraffito design, 24½ x 20 in. Bothin-Arequipa Collection, Fairfax, California.

BELOW

74. Arequipa Pottery tile designed by Frank Ingerson for Casa Dorinda, Montecito, 1917.

mountain studio in faraway Marin County, and the tiles remain a testimony to Wilde's technical expertise and Brown's enlightened vision.

About 1911 Ingerson and Dennison, both easterners, purchased property at Alma in the Santa Cruz Mountains with the intention of opening a school of arts and crafts called Cathedral Oaks (plate 75). Although never formalized, classes in various subjects, including ceramics, were held at the mountain retreat, which became a gathering place for artists, musicians, and poets. As early as 1912 decorative tiles were handcrafted there and boldly marked with the Cathedral Oaks name. Many depict the beauty of the natural surroundings.

Similarly, Ernest A. Batchelder planned to open a School of Design and Handicraft[15] when he purchased property overlooking the Arroyo Seco in Pasadena in the fall of 1909. His intention was to make not tiles but "works . . . executed in copper and silver, jewelry, enamelling, leather and pottery."[16] In November 1910, having completed the construction of his home on the site, Batchelder took out a permit to build a studio in his backyard; shortly thereafter he began making tiles.

A significant inspiration behind Batchelder's unexpected preoccupation was clearly Henry Chapman Mercer, a successful tile maker from Doylestown, Pennsylvania, whose Moravian tiles Batchelder had first encountered at the Society of Arts and Crafts in Boston.[17] Batchelder later ordered Mercer's tiles for classroom use at Throop Polytechnic Institute in Pasadena, and also used them to decorate the chimney and fireplace of his new home.[18] When interviewed years later in the *Pasadena Star News,* he admitted his indebtedness to Mercer: "Greatest of all American potters . . . is the famous Mercer of Doylestown. . . . 300 years out of his time, probably the only modern artist retaining the glorious touch of the medieval masters."[19]

Batchelder's earliest tiles were in low relief, hand-pressed from plaster molds, and depicted medieval heraldic subjects, which were also favored by Mercer. Romanticized views of the California landscape (plate 76) and numerous other subjects were to follow. Batchelder published his first catalog in 1912; by this time he had moved his tile-making operation out of his backyard and into a warehouse in Pasadena. The company was expanded in 1916 and eventually moved to larger quarters in Los Angeles.[20] Batchelder prided himself on using local clays and on imbuing each tile with a character of its own; he conscientiously signed every piece. Atmosphere was of prime importance. He viewed his employees as family and designed the new factory to be "a wholesome place in which to work— clean and well-lighted."[21] For inspiration, he planted a garden outside the modeling room "where California flowers bloom the year through."[22]

By 1921 Gus Larson, the superintendent at Los Angeles Pressed Brick, was well aware of the demand for handcrafted tiles and saw an opportunity to start his own company. He teamed up with fellow employee Fred H. Robertson (and eventually Fred's son, George) to form Claycraft Potteries, not far from Tropico (see plate 77). Conscious of Batchelder's success with the handcrafted look and

Cathedral Oaks and School of Art, Alma, Santa Cruz Mts. Cal. 2858

ABOVE
75. Promotional postcard for "Cathedral Oaks, School of Art, Alma, Santa Cruz Mts., Cal," dated January 27, 1915.

OPPOSITE
76. Batchelder & Brown. *Tile,* c. 1916. Press-molded fired clay colored with pigmented slip, 18¼ x 12 in. Ceramic Tile Institute, Los Angeles.
❧ *Our tiles are hand wrought, by processes peculiar to our own factory. They have slight variations of shape and size—just sufficient to relieve the monotony of machine pressed tiles. These variations are not sought; they are desirable and inevitable in a hand made product. We make the very best tile we can possibly make by hand.*

Ernest A. Batchelder, *Batchelder Tiles: A Catalog of Figure Tiles* (Pasadena, Calif.: Batchelder & Brown, 1912), p. 3.

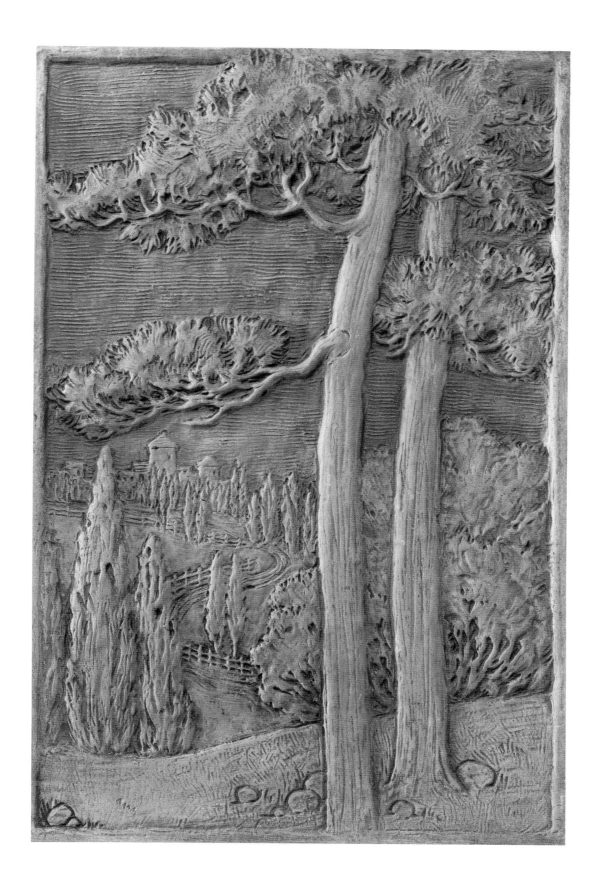

yet appreciative of the advantages of modern machinery, they produced "hand-made tiles . . . to give the true appearance of a hand fashioned article." [23] What was called the Claycraft line, a single-fired glazed tile, was "afterward buffed and sanded [to] produce an interesting irregularly mottled effect."[24] These illusory practices notwithstanding, the press-molded decorative tiles depicting an endless array of romanticized subjects were, in fact, colored by hand with mineral slips, in a technique similar to Batchelder's.

In Northern California, the handcrafted tradition was enhanced by James White Hislop,[25] a wealthy descendant of two generations of brick makers in Scotland. In 1922, together with his sons, Hislop organized the Clay Glow Tile

77. Fred H. Robertson at Claycraft Potteries, Los Angeles, c. 1928.

118

Company, soon to become California Art Tile in Richmond (plate 69). Projecting the family's success and social position, an early brochure emphasized that Caltile, as it was called, "enhances aristocratic individuality. . . . The pastel colors afford most genteel and refined treatment."[26] Aware of the economic advantages to machine-pressed tiles, Hislop, like his counterparts in Southern California, reserved handcrafting for the glazers.

In 1925 A. Clay Myers, one of the original team members at California Art Tile, left the company; approaching the management of Kraft Cheese in Chicago, he received financing for a tile operation in Niles, east of San Francisco Bay. A year later Kraftile began manufacturing a "high fired faience," a single-fired glazed tile, recognized for its economy and durability.[27]

Another Scotsman, William Flynn Muir, immigrated to California via Canada, arriving in the Fresno area in 1913. Having become a successful tile contractor in the area, Muir was familiar with the different tiles being produced in the state. In 1925 he abandoned his business and moved to Oakland, where he leased warehouse space to manufacture Muresque Tiles,[28] a distinctive line of high-relief decorative tiles. The catalog proclaimed: "Because they are hand-made they reflect a quality of fine individual craftsmanship which is at once apparent. The soft, lovely colors . . . readily and harmoniously lend themselves to any decorative scheme. The distinctive hand finish characteristic of Muresque products adds the final note of richness and beauty to every piece."[29] Two other companies in the San Francisco Bay Area, Handcraft and Woolenius, began producing handcrafted tiles during the late 1920s.[30] Both made their tiles by pressing wet clay in plaster molds. Handcraft tiles were heavily glazed and often hand dipped; those from Woolenius had glazes applied more thinly and then rubbed off.

Without exception the makers of handcrafted tiles were involved in creating illusion, in promoting ideas associated with earthen materials: warmth, richness, fertility, and, indirectly, even material wealth. The illusion had little to do with the way the tiles were actually made. As a rule tile makers had great respect for whatever machinery they could afford, but hand labor was unavoidable, and the sequence of stages required to make a tile took the better part of a week. There was no need to accentuate the effect of the process in the finished products; much of it was already obvious.

Many of the tiles were designed for fireplaces and hearths, facades that would blend into the subdued interior of the home. A dull-colored, liquid clay (called "slip") was applied and then rubbed off the plain, undecorated tiles, leaving an uneven or mottled appearance resembling an earthen material, as if to bring the outdoors into the home. Decorated tiles, designed to be symmetrically inserted into a field of plain ones, depicted a wide variety of subjects. The most fascinating combine medieval imagery with the California landscape—as in the Batchelder tiles, where castles form a mystical backdrop for cultivated fields, or in the Muresque mural, where knights are seen riding through the California redwoods. Each scene had a distinct raised border to highlight the subject. The tiles were designed to be looked at, as one would look at a photograph, and they brought an idealized, utopian, albeit illusory, world into the home for contemplation, even inspiration.

The mysterious artwork by the Mayas and Aztecs of Mesoamerica, which had been dramatically displayed in the California State Building at the Panama-California Exposition and later used to adorn the tunnel entrance to the Southwest Museum in Los Angeles, captured the imagination of many tile makers, who identified with the skills of the ancient craftsmen. Ceramic tiles with reproductions of glyphs and ruler-priests in ceremonial garb were increasingly sought by a select group of architects like Stiles O. Clements of Morgan, Walls, and Clements, who designed the Mayan Theater in Los Angeles in 1927. The designs were based on illustrations and photographs in such popular magazines as *National Geographic,* which reproduced the bas-relief stone panels from the temples at Palenque, Yaxchilán, and elsewhere. Individual Mayan- and Aztec-design tiles were used primarily as inserts for floors, stair risers, and fireplace surrounds; elaborate mural work often resembled sacrificial altars (plate 78).

The handcrafting of tiles seems to have been linked to a reverence for the past and a fascination with the mysteries of life and the cosmos. Many of the tile makers (Batchelder, Hislop, Muir, Rhead, Wade, and no doubt others) were practicing Freemasons, a group with spiritual ties dating back to the Middle Ages, when master craftsmen were among the most venerated members of society. The medieval imagery frequently used on tiles embodied the tile makers' recognition of higher ideals and demonstrated their identification with their European predecessors in the Arts and Crafts movement (plate 79).

During the 1920s, the tile industry gradually reached maturity. The successes of the smaller factories were reflected in the growth of the larger firms that were mass producing ceramic ware. Both American Encaustic and Gladding, McBean & Company (plate 80), which purchased Tropico Potteries in 1922, dominated the market by mid-decade. Pomona Tile Manufacturing got under way in 1923 and by the end of the decade offered these companies noticeable competition.

The Hispano-Moresque aesthetic, which had emerged from National City with the tiles for the 1915 exposition in San Diego, determined the decorative output of these larger manufactories. Both color and design were of prime importance. The prevalence of sunlight in the state renders colors more conspicuous. The fact that the most appealing colors were often more vibrant than nature's own can be attributed to what David Gebhard has referred to as the "stage-set atmosphere . . . when so much dream and nostalgia was transposed into living design."[31] Spanish Colonial architecture became the medium and ceramic tiles the means of adding a touch of humanity and tradition, and thus a sense of well-being, to the home.

One of the key players in the post–World War I period was Rufus B. Keeler,[32] as close to a native Californian as anyone who played a major role in the tile industry during this time. In 1917 he established Southern California Clay

78. Advertisement for California Clay Products Company, South Gate, showing the fireplace in the Rufus B. Keeler House in South Gate. From *Pacific Coast Architect,* July 1924.

∽ *Although the advertisement identifies the design as Aztec, it is in fact a reproduction of the Mayan stone relief panels from the Temple of the Cross at Palenque in southern Mexico.*

BELOW

79. Fireplace front and mantel shown in a promotional photograph for California Clay Products Company, South Gate, c. 1924.

PAGES 122–23

80. Gladding, McBean & Company. *Tile Mural—A Child's Storybook World,* 1927. Fired clay with multicolored glaze, 24 x 60 in. The Mitchell Wolfson, Jr., Collection; Courtesy of The Wolfsonian Foundation, Miami.

∽ *Composed of forty 6 x 6–inch tiles, this panel was designed by Gladding, McBean & Company for the Robin Hood Room at the Wilmington Public Library, Wilmington, California. The mural was produced at Tropico Potteries in Glendale, which was then owned and operated by Gladding, McBean. An illustrated advertisement in* Architect and Engineer, *December 1927, reveals familiar elements of Arts and Crafts ideas: "On the shelves of a Public Library, great lovers of history hide and the heroes of chivalry lie unseen. . . . How easily they could change a reading room into a world of romance and adventure."*

121

Products in Vernon[33] and after the war began handcrafting tiles. When additional investors were found, the company was moved to South Gate, greatly enlarged, and renamed California Clay Products—known by its trade name, Calco. Keeler was a promoter, historian, architect, and designer as well as a talented ceramist. In 1925 he wrote an article for the *Bulletin of the American Ceramic Society* in which he described in vivid detail the varied uses of clay products in residential design. For illustration he used his own house, which he had designed and built the year before and where he incorporated his exotic Calco tiles in literally every room.[34]

The Hispano-Moresque tradition clearly captivated Keeler's imagination, just as medievalism had influenced many of his contemporaries. Dedicated to the handcrafted approach, he gave up his prestigious position at Calco in 1926 to establish and manage the Malibu Potteries for the Marblehead Land Company, on what was then an isolated beach west of Santa Monica (see plate 82). In designing the facility Keeler was cognizant of the need for light and fresh air within the factory (plate 81), and once production got underway he incorporated recreational activities for the employees into the daily schedule. By all reports the pottery was an ideal place to work.[35]

Early in the 1920s William Wrigley, Jr., who had purchased Santa Catalina Island off the Southern California coast a few years before, chose to sponsor a local clay-products company to supply building materials for the island's growing community of Avalon and to employ island residents. By the end of the decade, decorative floor and wall tiles were needed to furnish Wrigley's buildings, and colorful tiles were used to adorn many of the storefronts along the beach. Catalina tiles, similar in technique to those made at Malibu, provide a distinct cultural expression, a reflection of Wrigley's utopian vision of a recreational haven for the public.[36]

81. Decorating room at Malibu Potteries, 1926.
 The glazes were applied with rubber-bulb syringes, one color at a time; for convenience the tabletops rotated. The windows to the left face the ocean, and those to the right provide north light.

Beauty and sanitation in the home never before commanded the attention that they do today. This is one of the encouraging proofs that the home itself—the very heart of the ideals and principles which make for a better civilization—is more appreciated as an institution.

Rufus B. Keeler, "The Oldest of the Crafts," lecture presented to the Tile and Mantel Contractors Association of America, 1920s, reprinted in *Ceramic Art of the Malibu Potteries* (Malibu, Calif.: Malibu Lagoon Museum, 1988).

82. Malibu Potteries tile on the exterior of
Serra Retreat, Malibu, c. 1930.

125

In the north Albert L. Solon, after leaving Arequipa and teaching for several years in San Jose, joined with the businessman Frank P. Schemmel in 1920 and began Solon & Schemmel—known as S & S—another company that produced handcrafted tiles in the Hispano-Moresque tradition (plate 83).[37] Although plaster molds were commonly used, Solon introduced linoleum blocks as a means of imprinting designs onto the wet clay. Like many of the other tile makers, he worked closely with the architectural community, designing tiles to precise specifications, and as a result received many notable commissions, including the Steinhart Aquarium in Golden Gate Park, San Francisco.

In addition to the factories, large and small, that principally produced tiles, there were two studios of note—neighbors, in fact, in Berkeley—that produced

83. Solon & Schemmel, tile fountain in the Marina District of San Francisco, c. 1928.

84. California Faience showroom in Berkeley, c. 1928.

I like to work in different mediums and with different but allied materials. It is a fine way to learn about limitations . . . one's own and those of the materials and techniques. My pioneering spirit responds to the challenge of a problem to be solved and I find it fun to blaze a new trail while trying to stay within the rules of good art. All the arts, it seems to me, should be in harmony and complement each other. They should give joy, inspiration and spiritual uplift as well as to reflect the period in which we live.

Gertrude Rupel Wall, "Gertrude Rupel Wall," n.d. A summary by Hazel Bray, Art Department, Oakland Museum.

pots as well as tiles: California Faience and Walrich Pottery. The founders of California Faience, William V. Bragdon and Chauncey R. Thomas, formed their partnership in 1915. Both easterners by birth, it is likely that they had met at the University of Chicago, where both taught ceramics, or at an annual meeting of the American Ceramic Society.[38] By 1916, under the name Thomas & Bragdon, the pair had opened a storefront on San Pablo Avenue with a kiln out back. The studio was known as the Tile Shop (even though both pots and tiles were produced), and the ware itself, California Faience (plate 84).

The pottery maintained a studio atmosphere; fellow artists and would-be potters were welcome participants. The tiles were characterized by highly stylized designs in bright colors, especially vivid blues. As in other tile studios, the design responsibilities were shared among the artists present. According to Stella Loveland Towne, one of the designers during the 1920s: "They were very interesting men . . . not very business-like. . . . They were in it because they loved it."[39] In 1922 the company moved to Hearst Avenue, still in Berkeley, and two years later the name was formally changed to California Faience. Given the modest size of the operation, the commission from William Randolph Hearst to supply most of the decorative tile needed for La Cuesta Encantada (The Enchanted Hill) at San Simeon must have stretched the company to its limit.

Gertrude Rupel Wall and her husband, James Wall, moved their Walrich Pottery to Hearst Avenue in 1924, adjacent to California Faience. Gertrude, the artist of the pair, was from Ohio and had studied at a number of midwestern institutions; she and James married just before going to California in 1912. James, like so many other influential ceramists of the period, came from England, where he had been employed at Royal Doulton. At Walrich, they were experimenters, studio-potters focusing on individual work rather than mass production. "We were pioneers . . . in California. We never wanted to buy anything that anybody else had worked with. We wanted to produce our own . . . as much as we possibly could."[40] The decorative tiles were frequently glazed in two or more colors; and the white clay body tended to soften even the brightest glazes, creating an effect similar to watercolor. Many of the tiles depicted the landscape of California with a distant illumination, which produced a dreamlike effect, as if one were standing at the edge of the world in the land of the setting sun.

By 1930 what had begun at Tropico years before as a rudimentary attempt at manufacturing had mushroomed into more than fifty tile-making operations servicing the pre-Depression marketplace. Integrated into the dominant architectural styles of the period, the tiles of California maintained a distinct, identifiable character, reflecting the resourceful creativity of the ceramists and designers. From the natural subtleties of the handcrafted work to the fanciful brilliance of the more exotic varieties, there remains a legacy of beauty derived from the bounty of the western terrain.

THE ARTS AND CRAFTS MOVEMENT IN THE SAN FRANCISCO BAY AREA

Kenneth R. Trapp

85. Digby S. Brooks. *Monumental Tray,* 1918–23. Hammered and patinated copper with pierced handles, diameter: 30¼ in. The Mitchell Wolfson, Jr., Collection; Courtesy of The Wolfsonian Foundation, Miami.
∾ *Little is known about Digby S. Brooks. Indeed, even his name appears incorrectly, as "Digley Brooks," in San Francisco city directories between 1918 and 1923. One of the most impressive features of this tray is its mark: a bold strike of "Digby S. Brooks" beneath an oak tree in the center of the face of the tray. With their cutout designs of butterflies, the handles of the tray betray an indebtedness to Japanese stencils.*

That San Francisco responded enthusiastically to the Arts and Crafts movement is easily explained. The city had the manufacturing and commercial infrastructure to provide the reliable wealth necessary to support the arts; a well-developed transportation network; a sizable cosmopolitan population that constituted its own market for local manufactures; an industrious, stable, highly educated middle class; and well-defined cultural institutions. With these advantages it would have been a surprise had the Arts and Crafts movement not been accepted and nurtured in San Francisco and the Bay Area.

The history of the Arts and Crafts movement in San Francisco is divided by the great earthquake and fire of April 18, 1906. The earthquake that struck San Francisco on that dawning Wednesday set fires that converged into a firestorm. Three days later, when the fires subsided and San Franciscans could tally their losses, the toll was incomprehensible. The injured, the dying, and the dead numbered in the thousands. Twenty-eight thousand buildings on some four square miles of prime real estate, including downtown and exclusive Nob Hill, were reduced to rubble. In the truest sense, San Franciscans had been tried by fire. And yet there never was any doubt that the city would rise from the ashes.

No American city in the Arts and Crafts period had a better opportunity than San Francisco to reshape and even reinvent itself in a way that took into account human needs and scale. By cruel irony, the City Beautiful plan for San Francisco, drawn up by the architect–city planner Daniel Burnham, had been deposited in city hall on April 17, 1906. The plan—and the dream—burned with city hall. The noted painter Arthur F. Mathews and his wife, Lucia K. Mathews, established Philopolis Press and began to publish the little magazine *Philopolis* (love of the city) in October 1906.[1] Both in the pages of *Philopolis* and in lectures Arthur argued for rebuilding San Francisco in an ethical manner that would pay equal heed to trade, art, and common justice. By the time *Philopolis* ceased publication in 1916, however, it was all too apparent that greedy commercialism had exploited the resurrection of the city by the bay.

The first tangible signs of what would become the Arts and Crafts movement in the San Francisco Bay Area were more imitative than promising of future artistic vitality. Art pottery was one of the earliest manifestations of artistic predisposition, and the first noteworthy concern to be founded in California was the Stockton Art Pottery, incorporated in Stockton, California, in October 1896. It is of interest less for its derivative products than for what it signified: that California had the extensive clay deposits needed to supply local potteries and that the idea of art pottery had reached the West Coast—not merely in concept but in practice.

Rookwood, the prestigious art pottery founded in Cincinnati in 1880 by Mrs. Maria Longworth Nichols, became Stockton's artistic and corporate model. Stockton's Rekston ware (plate 86) is, in fact, an imitation of Rookwood's Standard ware. Both are Victorian in aesthetic, characterized by contrived shapes and earthenware bodies decorated mostly with floral subjects painted naturalistically in colored slips under a high-gloss glaze. Besides copying Rookwood's principal decorative process and even the shapes of its wares, the Stockton Art Pottery copied Rookwood's policy of dividing labor according to gender, with women working only as decorators and men as administrators and technicians.

The Stockton pottery sold its decorated wares at Nathan-Dohrmann & Co. in San Francisco and in New York. Eastern buyers urged that the name "Rekston" be changed: "It will meet with even more ready sale if the name carries with it something of a suggestion that it is a California product."[2] This suggestion, that California's exotically romantic image could be used as a marketing device, was intended to strengthen Rekston's identity in a market where similar decorated ceramics—especially from Ohio—proliferated. Stockton's choice of the name Mariposa Pottery for a decorative line of underglaze, slip-painted pottery may have been made to capitalize on the line's Californian origins.

Poor economic conditions at the turn of the century, combined with a fire of 1902, led to the demise of art-pottery production at Stockton. By this time, however, the Roblin Art Pottery was in full operation in San Francisco. Alexander W. Robertson was a founding partner in this, the second major art-pottery venture in Northern California. Having read Linna Vogel Irelan's essay "Pottery," published in the *Ninth Annual Report of the State Mineralogist* of 1889, Robertson approached her in 1891 to show her some pieces that he had made using California clays. Impressed by Robertson's inventiveness and by the potential of California clays, Irelan agreed to join him in opening a pottery. After two unsuccessful attempts, Robertson and Irelan fulfilled their dream of establishing a viable art pottery when they opened Roblin in San Francisco in 1898.

86. Stockton Art Pottery. *Three Vessels,* 1896–1902. Earthenware painted with underglaze slip. Left: pitcher, 7 x 5½ in. The Oakland Museum; Gift of Mr. and Mrs. Kenneth R. Dane. Center: pitcher, 12½ x 5½ in. The Oakland Museum; Gift of Mr. and Mrs. Kenneth R. Dane. Right: three-handled cup, 4½ x 3¾ in. The Oakland Museum; Bequest of the estate of Helen Hathaway White.

Some time ago a Japanese importer of Yankee manufactures, while visiting San Francisco, purchased a number of vases for his stores in Tokio. These are now offered for sale in the land of the Mikado; thus the first to recognize art value in "Roblin" is the Orient.

Illustrated Glass and Pottery World (September 1902): 15.

Like the Stockton Art Pottery, Roblin was inspired by and modeled on Rookwood. Irelan provided the capital and established the artistic identity for the pottery. Robertson's vast technical knowledge complemented Irelan's artistic talents. He threw the thin-walled, classically inspired shapes that are a hallmark of Roblin pottery, experimented extensively with California clays, formulated and applied the glazes, and attended to the firings.

Whereas Nichols had opened Rookwood with the idea of producing a uniquely American decorative art, Irelan took this idea one step further to create a uniquely Californian art. This quality was derived from the use of California's clays and other materials and of motifs based on the state's flora and fauna. Roblin's clays span the spectrum from light to dark: white, cream, pale sand, orange, and deep red mimic nature's palette (plate 87). Glazes range from transparent high-gloss finishes tinted in greens, blues, and browns to soft matte finishes in green and black and to mottled effects of these colors (plate 88). In addition to simple beading, slip painting, carving, hammering, and incising, Irelan modeled high-relief decoration, using nature as her guide and inspiration.

> Mrs. Irelan's lizards are modelled from life, as are turtles, rabbits, chickens, and beetles, which crawl over the edge of a vase, or nestle cunningly in some nook indented as if for their express protection.
>
> Mushrooms, with all their delicate filaments; lichens as lifelike as if just gathered from some old stone wall; flowers and ferns special to California, are all reproduced in enduring clay. It is the history of a country written in stone.[3]

Despite valiant efforts to expand, Roblin lacked the capital needed to market its wares in the East. Worse still was the surprising lack of patronage suffered by Roblin at home: "San Francisco dealers will have none of it because it is produced within the city limits, consequently cannot be of value, again proving that a prophet is without honor in his own land."[4] Such rejection must have been a bitter pill for Irelan and Robertson, especially since Roblin had received an honorable mention at the Paris Universal Exposition in 1900—high honor indeed for a small pottery so recently founded. Eight years after it opened, the Roblin Art Pottery became one of many casualties of the San Francisco earthquake and fire. With Roblin destroyed, Irelan retired to Berkeley, and Robertson moved to Los Angeles and worked in various potteries in the Southland.

Six years after major Arts and Crafts societies were founded in Boston and Chicago in 1897, two Arts and Crafts organizations were established in San Francisco within days of each other. The San Francisco Guild of Arts and Crafts was organized by the metalworker Douglas van Denburgh in August 1903.[5] On September 10, 1903, the United Crafts and Arts of California was incorporated in San Francisco, with the enigmatic Russian-born mystic Dr. Orlof N. Orlow as one of two principal financial backers and the driving force behind the organization.[6] Whereas the guild—modeled after prototypes in Boston, Chicago, and other eastern cities—was a loose organization of independent craft workers that sponsored annual exhibitions, Orlow's group was a capitalistic enterprise intended to take advantage of a lucrative market.

The guild included 117 members and represented "wood-workers, sculptors, book-binders, workers in metals, tapestry and lace-workers, photographers,

That California is in no degree lacking in craftsmen of ability has long been beyond a matter of doubt, but hitherto they have been scattered, being but little known to one another, nor has the public been able to reach or judge of their work. This fact made apparent the need of some organization that would overcome these difficulties and bring to the craftsmen the advantage of being better known.

Catalogue: Second Annual Exhibition of the Guild of Arts and Crafts (San Francisco: by the Guild, 1904), n.p.

weavers, designers of jewelry, interior decorators, designers in glass and mosaics, and book-illuminators."[7] It was founded as a "reaction from an undue dependence upon machine and factory,"[8] a comment that seems to contradict the retrospective view of California as a preindustrial paradise. It is important to remember, however, that at the turn of the century San Francisco was the major manufacturing city in the West and supported a sizable number of traditional craft industries. A report compiled in 1903 on San Francisco's manufactories serves as a useful reminder of this fact. That year the city boasted thirty-five bookbinderies, thirty-five jewelry and silverware makers, twenty-two marble workers, twelve wood-turners and -carvers, eleven picture-frame makers, eight coppersmiths, and five glass stainers and cutters.[9] The catalog of the guild's second annual exhibition, in 1904, lists 141 members—a rise in membership from the previous year of more than 20 percent. Among the 105 active members were the furniture designer Frederick H. Meyer and Linna Vogel Irelan, who exhibited modeled and illuminated leather.[10]

Orlow's United Crafts and Arts of California was doubtless so-named to avoid confusion with the San Francisco Guild of Arts and Crafts, but equally important is the allusion to United Crafts, founded in 1899 by Gustav Stickley, whose furniture and other designs would establish the norm for an Arts and Crafts look in the early years of the twentieth century. United Crafts and Arts occupied a grand building with workshops and showrooms near the Presidio, commanding a magnificent view of the Golden Gate, the bay, and the hills of Marin County, truly "an ideal shelter for a guild of craftsmen, working in the inspiration of nature."[11]

Although the guild and United Crafts and Arts seem not to have been officially affiliated, Orlow included work by guild members in his showrooms. Frederick H. Meyer, Lucinda Butler, and Lillian Tobey, all active members of the guild, are mentioned as exhibitors with the other group in an article published in June 1904.[12] Not one extant work of art is known to have been created or exhibited by either the guild or Orlow's group, but the rare existing publications relating to those organizations provide some insight into the wealth of talent and the kinds of craftwork being created in San Francisco during the early years of this century. Although the guild survived the earthquake and fire, it did not recover enough to influence perceptibly the burgeoning Arts and Crafts movement in San Francisco. Orlow's venture succumbed in 1907.[13]

A third agent of cultural transmission and one that exerted unique influence on the early Arts and Crafts movement in San Francisco was Paul Elder & Co. In 1903 Elder incorporated his bookshop and printing business and began to publish bulletins illustrating the Arts and Crafts objects available in his shop,[14] which catered to a well-to-do and cultivated clientele. With civic-minded pride Elder, who was himself an associate member of the San Francisco Guild of Arts and Crafts, displayed handicrafts made in San Francisco and elsewhere in California: jewelry by Ferdinand Heiduska; brasswork by Douglas van Denburgh of Los Gatos; copper-, brass-, and ironwork by Victor Toothaker; leatherwork by

Furniture to be of that true use for which it is intended should be remarkable for its simplicity, fine proportion, honest material, sound construction, and harmonious colorings, and whether much adorned or severely simple, it should have all that old excellence of design and execution so marked in medieval craftsmanship. Besides which, the lines should be natural and frank, clean and secure, dignified and convincing, rhythmic of strength in every part, superlatively excellent, and combining rare brilliancy with true expression, and having nothing of that lifeless and monotonous touch, so peculiar to the machine made kind of today. Such furniture, too, has both moral dignity and sanctity, and yet withal a modest spirit of self-approval, being of both plainness and boldness of spirit, speaking frankly and standing for what it is.

Dr. Orlof N. Orlow, quoted in "The Influence of Intimate Surroundings," *Overland Monthly* 44 (September 1904): 390.

89. Showroom of furniture designed by
Frederick H. Meyer, San Francisco,
c. 1904–6.

Anna C. Crane, Lillian Tobey, and Lillian O'Hara and Grace Livermore; furniture
by Frederick H. Meyer; Redlands Pottery from Southern California; and bookbindings from the guild. Also for sale were Arts and Crafts pieces from other
parts of the country, including decorated pottery and embroideries from
Newcomb College in New Orleans; Pewabic pottery from Detroit; Dedham pottery by Hugh Robertson (brother of Alexander W. Robertson) from Massachusetts; and metalwork from the Jarvie Shop in Chicago. An Anglophile, Elder
also displayed in his shop enameled silver jewelry by W. D. Hadaway of London
and bookbindings from the London Guild of Women Binders and from the
Hampstead Bindery.

The German-born furniture designer and maker Frederick H. Meyer was
active in the three organizations founded in San Francisco in 1903. Meyer's work
is known through a few publications, a small number of pieces, and an album of
photographs in The Oakland Museum (plate 89). From 1898 to 1902, when he
moved to San Francisco and married Laetitia Summerville, Meyer was supervisor
of drawing in the Stockton public schools. In San Francisco he joined the
Berkeley architect Bernard Maybeck in designing and making deal tables, chairs,
and chandeliers for the refectory of Wyntoon, Phoebe Apperson Hearst's
Norman-style country estate in Siskiyou County, in far northern California. In
keeping with the medieval character of the mountain castle, the furniture and
other furnishings were boldly rustic, with no attempt at refined detail. From 1902
to 1906 Meyer designed furniture in his Craftsman's Shop, and his business associate Stanley Kopersky made the pieces.[15]

An article of 1904 in the *Overland Monthly,* illustrated with furniture designed
by Meyer, suggests that the furniture and furnishings for Wyntoon were made

under the auspices of United Crafts and Arts of California, as was the furniture for the California exhibit at the Louisiana Purchase Exposition of 1904 in St. Louis. Of the rooms in the United Crafts and Arts building in San Francisco, "the most interesting . . . is the great beamed workshop where the craft idea is expressed in the beautiful native woods of California."[16]

Although Meyer is not named in the *Overland Monthly* article, he is mentioned by name in C. P. Neilson's essay "Applied Art in San Francisco" (1904). Accompanying the essay are drawings of a redwood library table and a hanging studio cabinet, designed by Meyer in a mature Arts and Crafts Mission style.

> Designs for furniture in California redwood will prove one of the most interesting features among the various specimens of the craftsmen's art. Comparatively few people have any idea of the art value of this beautiful wood. This is particularly true of the timber cut from the trees near the base, where the most exquisite graining is usually found.[17]

The use of indigenous woods, as of California clays, was promoted as supporting native industries. There was even hope of establishing a furniture industry using the fast-growing Australian eucalyptus trees that had proved remarkably adaptable to the soils and climates of California.[18]

90. Arthur F. Mathews. *Youth,* c. 1917. Oil on canvas in a carved, painted, and gilded wood frame made by the Furniture Shop. 59½ x 67¾ in., framed. The Oakland Museum; Gift of Concours d'Antiques, Art Guild.

In the second annual exhibition of the Guild of Arts and Crafts, Meyer showed six pieces. Of these, a stool and a Gothic table with three pointed trilobate arches rising from a center stretcher are pictured in the catalog. Like the furniture designed for Wyntoon, the pieces were heavy in form and straightforwardly simple, with direct inspiration from England.

Meyer's life changed abruptly and unexpectedly, along with thousands of other lives, on April 18, 1906, when his shop was destroyed. The Mathewses' lives, too, were redirected by the earthquake and fire. Concurrent with the activities at Philopolis Press, Arthur and Lucia established the Furniture Shop in San Francisco—an ambitious venture in which they began to produce custom-designed furniture and related objects (plate 204). Such an affiliation of shop and little magazine recalls Gustav Stickley, his furniture business, and his magazine the *Craftsman*.

Operated from 1906 to 1920, the Furniture Shop "was not only a successful business venture but was notably successful as an experiment in collaboration between artists and craftsmen under the business guidance of a man of taste." That man of taste was John Zeile, a wealthy art enthusiast turned furniture manufacturer (with Beach-Robinson Company, incorporated in June 1906) and a retailer who doubtless saw the marketing possibilities for furniture immediately following the earthquake and fire. The Furniture Shop "employed sometimes twenty or thirty skilled craftsmen at a time, and the output varied in character from suites for banks, offices and lodge rooms to household furniture and cabinet work, all of unique design."[19] The Mathewses divided their labor in a manner determined more by gender than by talent or ability. Thus, Arthur designed the furniture and supervised the shop's craftsmen, with the assistance of Thomas McGlynn. Lucia applied her talents to the drawing, painting, gilding, and carving of decorative schemes for the furniture, a fact substantiated by the few pieces that she signed. Especially fond of flowers and landscapes, she imaginatively interpreted blossoms and other floral forms and California's scenic vistas as decorative motifs. Both Arthur and Lucia were consummate colorists, and their work was indebted to the atmospheric quality of the light in California (see plate 90).

The shop is known primarily through furniture, frames, small objects, and pieces pictured in a rare photographic album—all in The Oakland Museum—and through the few other pieces in public and private collections. It is evident that there was no "Furniture Shop style" that can be used to identify the shop's prodigious production, which varied widely in type and in sources for its designs. Japanese and Chinese objects—so abundant in San Francisco—were often consulted for decorative motifs and furniture designs (see plate 2).

Perhaps best described as eclectic, the Furniture Shop's productions fall into two general categories—residential and commercial. The larger, artistically decorated pieces, mostly for residential use, include upright drop-front desks inspired by medieval and Renaissance furniture (plates 91, 92), chests of drawers, and tables embellished with richly polychromed and gilded scenes of draped figures in

The atmosphere of San Francisco—I mean the physical atmosphere—is almost exactly the atmosphere of Venice, where so many great painters worked. And, like Venice, we come in touch here with the Orient, only more directly.

Our sun is not so clear or our colors so intense as away from the bay. So much the better. The atmosphere here is thicker and richer for that reason. The sun is disintegrating. The air of San Francisco is filled with its own colors, changing with the time of day and the play of the sun and mist.

Arthur F. Mathews, quoted in George P. West, "Secluded S.F. Painter Revealed as State's Most Famous Artist," *San Francisco Examiner,* March 28, 1925, n.p., on file at the San Francisco Examiner.

PAGES 138–39

91, 92. Furniture Shop (Arthur F. and Lucia K. Mathews). *Desk,* c. 1910–15. Carved and painted maple (?), oak, tooled leather, and (replaced) hardware, 59 x 48 x 20 in. The Oakland Museum; Gift of Mrs. Margaret R. Kleinhans.

arcadian settings. Profuse flowers and fruiting trees represent the natural bounty of California. Whether painted, carved, executed in marquetry, or rendered in a combination of methods, these figural scenes reflect Arthur F. Mathews's academic training in painting in Paris and relate directly to his classically inspired allegorical murals. On a smaller scale but with equal artistry, Lucia executed screens, clocks, covered jars (plate 93), boxes, urns, candlesticks, and frames. Her art often displays an immediacy and a compelling unself-consciousness not found in Arthur's grand vehicles.

The Furniture Shop catered to clients who could afford custom-designed furniture and could await its production. In some instances the Mathewses' interest was more in the art of the decoration than in the craft of cabinetry. Indeed, the craft of the Furniture Shop leaves much to be desired, for the furniture is often poorly made. Still, the shop harks back to the ideal, from mid-nineteenth-century England, of wedding the fine and the applied arts.

Frederick H. Meyer was briefly associated with the Furniture Shop: in late 1906 Zeile sent him east to buy equipment for the shop, and from there he went on to visit his childhood home in Germany. During this trip Meyer journeyed to Norway and Sweden, which, as he recalled years later, "were then coming to the fore in modern furniture."[20] The influence of this trip is evident in a suite of furniture that Meyer designed for his friends James Adam Barr, Sr., superintendent of the Stockton public schools, and Barr's wife, Julia, to grace the Stockton house into which they and their two children moved in April 1908. Writing on November 7, 1909, in the lifebook that she kept for her son James Adam, Jr., Julia Barr commented: "We think our new home is very much more beautiful than the old one. The furnishings certainly are. . . . It was all designed by Frederick Meyer of Berkeley. The furniture in the dining room is dark oak and the living room is in Genesero [Genizero], a South American hardwood."[21] For the living room a side chair and a settle that combines both seating and case furniture (plate 94) betray an indebtedness to Jugendstil design (the German equiva-

ABOVE
93. Furniture Shop (Lucia K. Mathews). *Covered Jar,* c. 1910–15. Carved, painted, gilded, and shellacked maple (?), 11½ x 11½ in. The Oakland Museum; Gift of Concours d'Antiques, Art Guild.

OPPOSITE
94. Frederick H. Meyer. *Settle,* 1908, from the James Adam Barr House, Stockton. Genizero wood, glass, hammered-copper fittings, and (replaced) upholstery of cotton, wool, and nylon, 65¹¹⁄₁₆ x 91½ x 27 in. The Oakland Museum; Gift of Laetitia Meyer.

lent of Belgian-French Art Nouveau). Meyer's furniture for the Barr family represents a rare instance in which a design source in the Arts and Crafts period in the United States can be traced directly to Germany.

A chance remark about his dream for a practical art school, which Meyer made at a dinner for the San Francisco Guild of Arts and Crafts not long after the April disaster, was unexpectedly published in the *San Francisco Call.* Surprised by the positive response to his idea, Meyer and his wife decided to establish a school that would not only offer instruction in the mechanical arts and traditional crafts, as well as drawing, painting, and sculpture, but would also educate future teachers in these disciplines. Beginning with forty-three students and three instructors, the Meyers launched the California School of Arts and Crafts in 1907, thus giving form and systematic direction to what the earlier Arts and Crafts societies in San Francisco had hoped to achieve.

Both San Francisco and California were built, metaphorically speaking, on foundations of gold and silver. The gold rush of 1848–49 and the discovery of silver in the Comstock Lode in western Nevada in 1859 provided the massive infusion of ready capital that transformed San Francisco from an outpost into a center of civilization. Indeed, gold and silver are alloyed with San Francisco's history and folklore and are deeply embedded in the psyche of the city.

95. Shreve & Co. *Coffee Server,* c. 1900–1910. 18-karat-gold-plated brass and ivory, 7 x 8⅜ in. The Oakland Museum; Gift of the Women's Board.

BELOW

96. Shreve & Co. *Water Kettle on Stand,* c. 1900–10. Hammered silver and ivory, 10 x 7½ in. The Norwest Corporation, Minneapolis.

"Silver" to San Franciscans is still synonymous with "Shreve & Co." Founded in 1852 by the half-brothers George C. and Samuel S. Shreve as a retail shop for jewelry, Shreve began to make artistic silverware in 1883 and was incorporated in 1894. In the 1890s Shreve executed major commemorative presentation pieces in gold and silver. A former Shreve employee recalled that "our people could make anything imaginable in hand-crafted precious metals or custom-designed jewelry."[22] The silver produced by Shreve in the late nineteenth century is indeed exceptional in craftsmanship and design.

At the turn of the century Shreve appropriated or adapted from the Arts and Crafts movement certain designs and decorative processes that suited its needs. Shreve's most obvious bow to the movement is its XIV Century pattern, in which slightly hammered, applied silver strapwork stands in relief to the surface it embellishes (plate 95). The strapwork, which includes trefoil flourishes and false rivets, alludes to medieval wrought iron and leatherwork. It also recalls the exaggerated hinges on much Arts and Crafts oak furniture, but whereas in furniture this medievalizing design was meant to complement woods and to suggest boldness and strength, in silver the interpretation is more elegant than forceful.

Shreve used hammering—or the illusion of hammering reproduced in the die—as a decorative process. Hammering, which generally indicates that an object was made by hand, usually appears only on one surface to create a contrast in reflectivity and thus enhance the decorative effect. Shreve's false hammering, however, was produced by a machine but intended to appear created by hand. The hammered surface so common in Shreve's Arts and Crafts productions probably derives from the Japanese influence of the 1870s and 1880s, which Tiffany and Gorham interpreted exquisitely in their silver designs.[23]

So numerous are the sources of Shreve's designs that it is impossible to catalog them. From what is known, however, it is obvious that Shreve was as cosmopolitan as any art manufacturer in the United States or Europe. In the early years of this century Shreve created designs that appealed to Arts and Crafts enthusiasts, Anglophiles, and Francophiles alike. Bowing to the Arts and Crafts, Shreve produced hammered-copper pieces with silver trim (plate 7). Appealing to clients with European tastes in flatware, the company introduced such patterns as Louis XVI, Napoleonic, Norman, Marie-Louise, Buckingham, and Winchester. Because Shreve's customers were well-to-do and well traveled, it was not uncommon for the company to mount coins, ceramics, and lacquer ware they had collected. Nor was it uncommon for Shreve to mount decorative arts imported from Europe, Japan, and China in silver of the company's design, creating hybrids of materials, designs, and cultures. A case in point is a small compote made of a Japanese Satsuma bowl mounted on a Shreve stem; the pierced foot with encircling ivy leaves is indebted to silver made by Liberty & Co. in London (plate 97).

Silversmithing was dominated by Shreve, but the number of companies producing artistic copperwork in San Francisco proliferated in the period following

97. Shreve & Co. *Compote,* c. 1900–1905. Japanese Satsuma earthenware bowl mounted on silver stem with pierced foot, 6⁵⁄₁₆ x 4⁷⁄₈ in. The Oakland Museum; Gift of Judy and Austin Olson and the Chevron Corporation matching fund.

98. Lillian Palmer, undated.

the earthquake and fire of 1906, up to the 1930s. One of the earliest recorded workers in metals after the earthquake was Lillian Palmer (plate 98), who lived in San Jose. Ignoring the gendered roles that obtained in that period, Palmer not only designed pieces but made them as well. Originally attracted to metalwork as a recreation, by 1907 Palmer was devoting herself full time to work in copper, lead, and brass, and she was assisted by a "Miss Gaw, well known in the world of arts and crafts."[24] "Miss Gaw" was D'Arcy Gaw, who had moved from Chicago to San Jose in 1904, where she designed for her father, Henry Gaw, a house that was featured in *House Beautiful* in April 1909. Palmer's lack of formal training in metalworking proved an advantage, for she was not encumbered by tradition or doctrine. She discovered that she could manipulate lead into an upright form and then hammer into it relief and repoussé decorations, much as in copperwork. With a spirited inventiveness, she introduced beach pebbles as decorative elements, just as workers in precious metals and jewelry would use gems to add color and ornamentation.

From what we can surmise from the meager literature, Palmer prospered sufficiently after being featured in the *San Francisco Call* of April 28, 1907, to enable her to study metal crafting in Vienna. There "she learned the technique of her craft and of electric designing." Having returned to the United States via the Orient, Palmer then went to Chicago to learn more about lighting. "She studied how to make fixtures that consumed the minimum rather than the maximum of power, and finally she placed her lighting problem in the hands of a prominent oculist and from him learned how to place lights so as to give the least eye strain."[25] With the opening of her art-metal shop in San Francisco in 1910, Palmer concentrated on making lamps and lighting fixtures designed for the new electrical age.

Dirk van Erp also opened his Copper Shop in San Francisco in 1910. Of the numerous art-copper ventures established in San Francisco after 1906, van Erp's workshop is the best documented. It established an artistic identity rather quickly, lasted the longest, and was the most prolific. The van Erp enterprise set the artistic and technical standards for handwrought copper in San Francisco, provided apprenticeship opportunities for a few students, and became a venerated San Francisco institution that operated for sixty-seven years, until 1977.

Although he was born into a Dutch family whose trade was coppersmithing, twenty-two years elapsed from the time van Erp immigrated to California in 1886 to the time he set up a copper workshop in Oakland in 1908 (see plate 11). In 1909 van Erp formed a brief partnership with Alexander J. Robertson and took as an apprentice Harry Dixon, whom he had met at the large Arts and Crafts exhibition at Idora Park in Oakland in October 1908.[26] Confident of his craft, van Erp sent twenty-seven pieces of copper- and brasswork to the Alaska-Yukon-Pacific Exposition in Seattle in 1909 and was awarded a gold medal.[27] Prices for the pieces shown at the exposition ranged up to sixteen dollars, proof that fine handiwork was not cheap.

145

Buoyed by his success in Seattle and by the prospects of a better future in San Francisco, van Erp moved across the bay in 1910 (plate 99). In March he formed a second, and equally short-lived, partnership, this time with D'Arcy Gaw.[28] Van Erp and Gaw differed markedly in their training. Van Erp had learned the family craft first in the Netherlands and then by practice as an independent artisan. Gaw, by contrast, was schooled in metalworking at the School of the Art Institute of Chicago. An independent woman nearing forty-two when she joined van Erp, Gaw was a professional with experience in architectural and interior design. No doubt at Gaw's suggestion, van Erp exhibited a lamp at the annual exhibition of the Art Institute of Chicago in 1910, its documentation being the first recorded mention of a lamp made at the shop.[29] After less than a year van Erp and Gaw severed their professional relationship, on January 30, 1911.[30] Despite the brevity of Gaw's partnership with van Erp, she is believed to have exerted strong influence on the designs of the van Erp studio.

From 1910, when van Erp opened his San Francisco shop, to 1929, when he retired, the shop produced a wealth of objects—vases, jardinieres (plate 12), bowls, boxes, desk sets, bookends, trays, smoking stands and sets, ashtrays, wastebaskets, fireplace screens and paraphernalia, buckets, kettles and other kitchenwares, and lighting fixtures. A few of van Erp's earliest lamps burned kerosene and have since been electrified, but nearly all of his lighting devices were designed for electricity. They range from floor, desk, and boudoir lamps, all with mica shades (plate 101), to hanging ceiling fixtures and wall lights (plate 100).

LEFT
99. Dirk van Erp and an unidentified woman in his studio in San Francisco, c. 1910–20.

BELOW
100. Dirk van Erp Studio (Dirk van Erp). *Pair of Electrical Wall Lamps,* c. 1910–25. Hammered copper with frosted-glass shades, 11 x 5 x 7⁹⁄₁₆ in.; 11 x 5 x 8¼ in. David Reneric.

OPPOSITE
101. Dirk van Erp Studio (Dirk van Erp and D'Arcy Gaw, designer). *Electrical Lamp,* 1910. Hammered and patinated copper with mica, 27³⁄₁₆ x 26¹⁄₁₆ in. Roger and Jean Moss.

LEFT

102. Left to right: Agatha van Erp, August Tiesselinck, and Dirk van Erp in the Dirk van Erp Studio, San Francisco, c. 1917.

BELOW

103. Dirk van Erp Studio (Dirk van Erp). *Two Warty Red Vases and Small Jardiniere,* c. 1910–25. Left: 10⅞ x 7³⁄₁₆ in. Center: 5¾ x 7 in. Hammered copper patinated deep red. Right: 11⅞ x 7¾ in. Roger and Jean Moss.

The output of the shop is staggering in its quantity, which is no doubt the reason that the quality of craft and design varies from the mundane to the spectacular.

Although most famous for his lamps, many of which are commanding in size and stunning in design, van Erp produced other pieces of such exceptional beauty and strength as to stand unrivaled in American metalwork. The heavily textured surfaces and their patinations in rich blood reds with hints of oranges, golds, browns, and even greens and purples are described aptly by collectors as "warty reds" (plate 103). Often the patinas suggest the subtleties of impressionistic landscapes. They were carefully waxed to keep them from changing color.

Gaw's was not the only departure from the shop in 1911, for van Erp fired Dixon that year; Dixon promptly moved to Lillian Palmer's shop and became her foreman. Van Erp's nephew August Tiesselinck emigrated from the Netherlands in 1911 and began to work for his uncle. Tiesselinck worked in the shop for fifteen years (plate 102), until he left in 1926 to teach metal crafts at Mission High School in San Francisco. In a rare instance when a high-school manual-arts student is known to have found employment in an Arts and Crafts shop, Tiesselinck sent his student Charles Anderson to the van Erp shop in 1931, where he worked continuously, except for the World War II years, until his death in 1975.

In October 1911 the San Francisco physician Dr. Philip King Brown engaged the English-born potter Frederick Hürten Rhead to establish a pottery in conjunction with the Arequipa Sanatorium in Fairfax, across the bay from San Francisco in Marin County. Modeled after the Marblehead pottery in Massachusetts founded by Dr. Herbert J. Hall in 1904, the new pottery was a philanthropic venture intended to provide therapeutic occupation for poor women convalescing from tuberculosis.

The Arequipa Sanatorium building was designed to admit sunlight and fresh air. Expanses of glass replaced gloomy walls. Sleeping porches ran the length of the building so that the women could breathe clean air while sleeping. To complement the benefits of rest and fresh air, Dr. Brown established a program of activities that offered exercise and psychological therapy. Pottery making and decoration, he believed, were not too physically taxing. Sales of the pieces produced by the patients could offer modest remuneration to offset medical expenses. But Dr. Brown's belief that pottery decoration held promise of future employment for recovered patients remained only a hope, for a woman's stay at the sanatorium averaged only four to five months—not long enough to develop sufficient skills for employment in art industries.

Having immigrated to the United States in 1902, Rhead had worked at five potteries in Ohio, New York, and Missouri in various capacities before he and his wife, Agnes, moved to Arequipa. He brought with him considerable knowledge of and experience with clays, glazes, and decorative processes. But Rhead's ambition to build Arequipa into a major art-pottery industry in Northern California conflicted with the central purpose of Arequipa as a refuge and sanatorium. The

149

Our work here is progressing most favorably, we have worked very hard, and have succeeded in establishing what will be an important business. Not only is California a wonderful place for such a business as ours but you know that there is not in this country a pottery like the big European factories. The manufacturers in the United States, all of them, are not learned enough in the work to see the wisdom in paying large salaries to artists, chemists and sculptors.

Frederick Hürten Rhead, quoted in Sharon Dale, *Frederick Hürten Rhead: An English Potter in America* (Erie, Pa.: Erie Art Museum, 1986), pp. 82–83.

Rheads, at Arequipa from November 1911 to May 1913, gave instruction in the basics of pottery making and decoration. Rhead experimented with California clays from Placer County, again making an effort to use California's natural resources to support an art industry, and he encouraged his charges to draw inspiration for decorative motifs from the surrounding landscape. Slip trailing, in which raised lines define the design and hold the glaze in place much as metals do in cloisonné, was introduced by Rhead at Arequipa (plate 104). The shapes and decorations of the pieces were inspired by Chinese temple jars and Italian majolica plates (plate 6). The use of the acanthus leaf in various forms as decoration seems to have derived from a carved-marble flower holder (plate 106), which has since been donated to The Oakland Museum by the estate of Dr. Brown's daughter.

At Rhead's suggestion, Arequipa Pottery incorporated in February 1913, only to dissolve incorporation in November 1915. Asked to resign in May 1913, Rhead moved with his wife to Santa Barbara, where he established an art pottery. Rhead's famed mirror black glaze developed in Santa Barbara has its roots in glazes developed at Arequipa (plate 107). Despite the brevity of his time at Arequipa, Rhead left an indelible and positive mark on the small Marin pottery.

After Rhead's departure, a second English-born ceramist was hired to direct Arequipa: Albert L. Solon took over in July 1913 and directed the pottery until his departure in May 1916, when he moved to San Jose. Solon reduced operating expenses at Arequipa and expanded sales. The extent of his success as a business manager is recorded in the third annual report of the Arequipa Sanatorium: "We have been able to employ more than twice the number of girls employed before, and market our wares in the best known art stores in the East."[31] Arequipa pottery was retailed in San Francisco at Vickery, Atkins, and Torrey, an art-goods shop.

The third, and last, director of Arequipa Pottery was yet another English-born potter. Fred H. Wilde's management of Arequipa lasted from the time he took over the pottery in September 1916 until Arequipa closed in November

OPPOSITE

104. Arequipa Pottery (Frederick Hürten Rhead?). *Vase,* 1912. Earthenware with slip-trailed leaf design and multicolored matte glaze, 10 x 5⅛ in. William Noonan.

ABOVE

105. Agnes and Frederick Hürten Rhead in their studio at Arequipa Pottery, Fairfax, California, c. 1912–13.

RIGHT

106. Left: Arequipa Pottery (Frederick Hürten Rhead?). *Bowl,* c. 1912. Earthenware with deep blue matte glaze, 5 x 9⅜ in. Right: *Flower Holder,* possibly Italian in origin, 19th century (?). Carved white marble, 6 x 10⅞ in. The Oakland Museum; Gift of the estate of Phoebe H. Brown.
∽ *The carved-marble flower holder descended in Dr. Philip King Brown's family. Its form and its carved acanthus-leaf design served as a prototype at Arequipa for pieces that range from small bowls to vertical vases.*

LEFT

107. Arequipa Pottery (Frederick Hürten Rhead?). *Vase,* c. 1912–13. Earthenware with carved leaf design and black semimatte glaze, 5¼ x 2¹¹⁄₁₆ in. Gary Keith.

∾ *This vessel's opaque glaze with a soft sheen is a predecessor of Rhead's famous mirror black glaze, which he perfected in Santa Barbara between 1913 and 1917.*

OPPOSITE

108. Arequipa Pottery (Frederick Hürten Rhead?). *Vase,* c. 1912–13. Earthenware with sgraffito floral design and multicolored glaze, 13 x 10⅜ in. The Oakland Museum; Gift of the estate of Phoebe H. Brown.

∾ *The floral design of this vase is unique among the wares produced by Arequipa. There is little doubt that the inspiration—if not the direct source— of the design was the wallpaper and textiles designs of William Morris.*

1918. Like Rhead and Solon, he brought extensive technical knowledge of clays and glazes to Arequipa. In particular, his experience was in tile production, and Wilde seems to have been responsible for introducing the production of tiles at Arequipa.

Although Arequipa Pottery operated for a brief seven years, it was able to attract three exceptionally qualified men as artistic directors. Despite the problems that plagued the pottery, the small enterprise produced some pieces of exceptional artistic and technical refinement (plate 108).

Arequipa Pottery is one of the few known Bay Area Arts and Crafts producers to have exhibited in the Panama-Pacific International Exposition of 1915 in San Francisco.[32] Others included Dirk van Erp, Lillian Palmer, Shreve & Co., Beach-Robinson (Furniture Shop), and the Tile Shop. The California School of Arts and Crafts in Berkeley and the San Jose State Normal School exhibited, respectively, a model artist's studio (plate 109) and a model nursery.[33] Doubtless because of the outbreak of the war in Europe in 1914 and because of San Francisco's distance from other major cities, the exposition attracted disappointingly few major national Arts and Crafts exhibitors and little attention.

The manual-arts teacher Rudolph Schaeffer moved from Los Angeles to the Bay Area in 1915, in an exception to the more usual movement of Arts and Crafts figures from Northern California to the Southland.[34] Schaeffer's contribu-

And, surely, from this time forward, the resentment felt heretofore by a comparatively few number of people against the defilement of our landscapes and our cities by hideous posters, and the maddening riot of disagreeable pictorial advertisements in the magazines and newspapers, will spread widely among our people, because of the influence of this exposition—which as a whole is a great, unified work of art, showing how art may be applied to daily human life—and also because of the direct lessons afforded by the Arts and Crafts exhibition.

Michael Williams, "Arts and Crafts at the Panama-Pacific," *Art and Progress* 6 (August 1915): 376.

tions to the Arts and Crafts movement as a teacher, artisan, designer, and colorist have gone largely unrecognized. In 1910 he moved from Columbus, Ohio, to Pasadena to teach metal arts and manual training at Polytechnic Elementary School, affiliated with Throop Polytechnic Institute. Having studied with Ernest A. Batchelder at the Handicraft Guild of Minneapolis summer school in 1909, Schaeffer entered into the tight-knit Arts and Crafts communities in Pasadena and Los Angeles, becoming friends with Douglas Donaldson, who had also taught at Polytechnic Elementary School.

In 1914 Schaeffer was appointed by the U.S. Commissioner of Education to visit Munich to "report on the role of color in trade schools curricula."[35] While in Europe he met with Josef Hoffmann, the architect and cofounder, with Koloman Moser, of the Wiener Werkstätte. Having returned to the United States in November 1914, after war broke out in Europe, Schaeffer was in the San Francisco Bay Area by early 1915. He taught design as applied to interior decoration, textiles, metalwork, silversmithing, and jewelry at various schools, from public high school to the university level. In 1915–16 he first taught classes privately in the East Bay cities of Piedmont and Berkeley. In 1917 Schaeffer was made professor of design and handicrafts at the California School of Fine Arts (formerly the Mark Hopkins Art Institute), a position he held until 1923. That Schaeffer taught in public schools in Ohio and in California shows just how widespread the Arts and Crafts ideal of democratizing the visual arts had become within a very brief span of time.

Schaeffer's trip to Germany and Austria had a profound effect on his designs and his use of color. This influence is evident in his design for the announcement

109. Hazel Verrue, *Pen and Ink Sketch of a Model Artist's Studio Exhibit Created by Students at the California School of Arts and Crafts in Berkeley and Shown at the Panama-Pacific International Exposition in San Francisco,* 1915. The Oakland Museum; Gift of Laetitia Meyer.
∾ *The furniture for this exhibit was designed by Margery Wheelock under the supervision of Frederick H. Meyer. The furniture displays obvious medieval influences and is "Arts and Crafts" in the use of oak and the exaggerated and exposed construction.*

110. Rudolph Schaeffer, *Announcement of Rudolph Schaeffer Summer School of Design in Piedmont, California, in 1917.* The Oakland Museum; Rudolph Schaeffer Archive, Archives of California Art.

Design Classes

In this course Mr. Schaeffer will endeavor to stimulate a new appreciation of Applied Art and give a clearer idea of the great fundamental principles governing all artistic expression.

Through an understanding of these principles, and by a simple yet scientific color theory, original interpretations will be evolved from flowers, birds and other nature motifs.

To develop the imagination and to create with the direct use of beautiful light and dark color, will form essential features of the design study.

Mr. Schaeffer was formerly a student of the Royal Arts and Crafts School at Munich, Germany, a pupil of Prof. Hoffmann at Vienna, Ernest Batchelder and Ralph Johonnot of California.

Announcement for "Design in Color: A Course of Eight Lessons with Rudolph Schaeffer," held at the Paul Elder Gallery, 239 Grant Street, San Francisco, 1917. Rudolph Schaeffer Archive, Archives of American Art, Smithsonian Institution.

of the Rudolph Schaeffer Summer School of Design in Piedmont in 1917 (plate 110). As Schaeffer matured, so did his interest in color as applied to design in myriad manifestations, including theater design. In 1926 he founded the Rudolph Schaeffer School of Design in San Francisco and exerted a strong influence on generations of San Francisco students until his death in 1988.

Schaeffer brought direct knowledge of modern design in Central Europe to the San Francisco Bay Area at the very time many Americans were becoming increasingly anti-German because of the war, which the United States entered in 1917. Because the war created an immediate shortage of essential raw materials, the burgeoning artistic handwrought copper movement was interrupted. Van Erp and Dixon were employed in the shipyards, where their talents in metalworking were much needed; Palmer closed her shop; and Arequipa breathed its last. The armistice declared in November 1918 formally ended the hostilities, but it did not signal a return to life as usual. As San Francisco entered the third decade of the twentieth century, the Arts and Crafts movement had already reached its apex. In 1920 the Furniture Shop closed. Shreve bowed to modernism in its designs. Palmer continued metalworking from her home and eventually became an interior decorator. Gaw became an interior decorator in New York City in the 1920s.

A brief look at artistic ceramics and metalwork in San Francisco in the 1920s provides more specific evidence of changes that were occurring across the nation. In 1915 William V. Bragdon had arrived in Berkeley to teach pottery at the California School of Arts and Crafts. Like Gaw and Schaeffer, Bragdon had been trained in his craft. He had studied ceramics at the State School of Clayworking and Ceramics in Alfred, New York, from 1906 to 1908. There he was doubtless influenced by Charles Fergus Binns, who had emigrated from England in 1897 and assumed the directorship of ceramics at the school and who became a charter member of the American Ceramic Society in 1899. Bragdon represented a new generation within the Arts and Crafts movement of artisans whose formal class-room-studio instruction was in a specific medium-oriented discipline. Equally important, like a growing number of men and women from that new generation, Bragdon returned to the classroom as teacher.

In 1916 Bragdon and Chauncey R. Thomas opened the Tile Shop in Berkeley, which became California Faience in 1924. Bragdon offered technical experience in clays and mold making; Thomas was in charge of glazes (plate 111). The firm made both artwares and commercial wares, the latter for florists. Strongly influenced by Binns, the pottery of California Faience emphasizes classic simplicity in shape and in the solid matte or high-gloss finishes (plate 112). The decoration of vessel forms is integrated into the overall design as part of the mold itself and almost always appears in conjunction with matte glazes. Intaglio designs

111. California Faience and West Coast Porcelain Manufacturers. *Lemonade Set*, c. 1925. Porcelain with mottled green-gray glaze: pitcher, 6¾ x 8½ in.; six tumblers, 4½ x 2¾ in., each. The Oakland Museum; Gift of Museum Donors Acquisition Fund.
∾ *In the mid-1920s California Faience contracted with West Coast Porcelain Manufacturers in Millbrae, south of San Francisco, to produce porcelain using molds and glazes from California Faience. This lemonade set exemplifies the confusion of identities that resulted from that brief partnership. The pitcher is incised "California Porcelain," whereas two of the tumblers are incised "California Faience." The body of the pieces is definitely porcelain, and the glaze is one commonly seen on California Porcelain.*

112. California Faience. *Vase,* c. 1925–30.
Slip-cast earthenware with dark green matte
glaze, 6¼ x 3⅞ in. The Buck Collection.

look more graphic than sculptural or pictorial, an aesthetic that is decidedly modern in spirit (plate 113). By about 1930 artistic production at California Faience had ceased.

Like California Faience, Jalan in San Francisco and Walrich Pottery in Berkeley represent the transitional phase from the Arts and Crafts movement into the studio-craftsman movement, in which one artist, perhaps with some assistance, would guide artistic work from conception to execution. About 1918 the Danish-born Ingvardt Olsen and the Mississippi native Manuel Jalanivich formed a partnership to produce ceramics. Around 1920 the two men settled in San Francisco and established Jalan. Like Bragdon and Thomas, Olsen and Jalanivich divided their labor, with Olsen offering technical authority in clays and glazes and Jalanivich providing artistic direction by designing, sculpting, and molding pieces. By using intense primary and secondary colors and sometimes hybrids of these and by combining these hues with high-sheen crackle glazes, Jalan created robust yet elegant wares that recall ancient ceramics at the same time they forecast modernism in the appropriation of Persian and Chinese shapes (plate 114). Jalan's use of ancient cultures to inspire its shapes and glazes and its stunning contrasts between vivid colors bring to mind the ceramics that Rookwood was producing in Cincinnati during the 1920s. The prestigious San Francisco department store Gump's sold Jalan's ceramics.

Another pottery that created both artistic and commercial wares was the Walrich Pottery. Established in Berkeley in 1922 by Gertrude Rupel Wall and her husband, James, the small venture eventually succumbed to the Great Depression. James threw pieces and cast others from molds he made. Both earthenware and

113. California Faience. *Two Vases,* c. 1925–30. Left: slip-cast earthenware with in-mold design and red and blue matte glaze, 6⁷⁄₁₆ x 4 in. Brandon Allen. Right: earthenware with slip-trailed design and multicolored glaze, 8³⁄₁₆ x 4 in. Stephanie Lynn and David Mills.

RIGHT
114. Jalan (Manuel Jalanivich and Ingvardt Olsen). *Vase,* c. 1920–30. Earthenware with red and white crackle glaze, 5⅛ x 8¼ in. The Oakland Museum; Gift of Mr. and Mrs. Elliott Peterson.

porcelain bodies were used, finished primarily with matte glazes (plate 115). In addition to vessel forms, the pottery issued small sculptural items—bookends, paperweights, figurines, busts, candlesticks, ashtrays—plaques, and tiles. Like its nearby competitor, California Faience, Walrich produced wares for a limited market at a time when major socioeconomic changes were occurring that would doom such potteries.

Two small metalworking firms established in San Francisco in the 1920s appealed to a market for handwrought metals at the same time that they used machines to give the appearance of handwork. Ye Olde Copper Shop, owned by Hans Jauchen, and Old Mission Kopperkraft, by Fred Brosi, bore names that allude to the romantic past before industrialization had reduced workers to mere tenders of machines. Yet both shops used lathes to spin metal forms (the equivalent of casting in ceramics) and the appearance of handiwork, achieved most commonly by dies that yielded "hammered" surfaces, was only an illusion. Even pieces that were in fact later handworked presented nothing more than surface embellishment. That the use of machines was not in itself inimical to the creation of well-designed and even artistic objects is demonstrated in some of the pieces created by Ye Olde Copper Shop and Old Mission Kopperkraft, pieces that are harmonious in proportion and appealing in design.

Brosi used the facade of Mission Dolores as a mark to identify his copperwork as a California product; Jauchen used the eucalyptus. He cast eucalyptus sprays with leaves and pods, painted them green to approximate nature, and then applied these "naturalistic" decorations to forms (plate 8) that were little more than supporting vehicles for the decoration. Brosi's proud claim in Old Mission Kopperkraft's mark, "Made by Hand," was true only in that human hands did tend the machines that spun the form (plate 116). Astute entrepreneurs knew that "Made by Hand" was an appealing phrase that would help to sell products. Such misleading marks did violence to the tenets of honesty and sincerity, the most sacred virtues of the Arts and Crafts movement.

In 1921 Harry Dixon opened a metal shop in San Francisco that operated until 1932. During the 1920s his metalwork reached maturity in its superb crafts-

manship and design. He could easily hammer and manipulate a sheet of copper to create a form that fulfilled modern utility and at the same time embodied the appeal of handicraft. Dixon's designs frequently transcend the humbleness of base metals in their sophistication (plate 117).

The character of the Arts and Crafts movement in San Francisco and the Bay Area was shaped by people who mostly came from some other place. Indeed, of some thirty principal figures, only Lucia K. Mathews was born in San Francisco and received her formal education there. The number of foreign-born proponents and practitioners of the movement is surprisingly large, with at least twelve known to have been born in Canada, Great Britain, the Netherlands, Germany, or Denmark. The degree of British influence on the Arts and Crafts movement in San Francisco—an ocean and a continent away—testifies to the cosmopolitan spirit of the city and shows how strong the initial impetus of the movement must have been.

The Arts and Crafts movement in Northern California can be seen as a regional phenomenon that was limited to its own regional market. It was not led by any one charismatic individual whose theories provided an ideological foundation. Nor did it revolve around any cohesive organization that gave participants a system for exhibiting regularly and an outlet to sell their work. Most Arts and Crafts producers in San Francisco and the Bay Area failed to survive long enough to establish strong artistic identities, and they lacked the capital needed to market their wares aggressively in the populous East.

It may seem, at the other extreme, that the Arts and Crafts movement in San Francisco and the Bay Area was little more than a scattering of individuals who worked alone in isolated shops or as members of a small team of workers, but this perception is inaccurate. It is obvious that the principals constituted an active network and enjoyed a lively exchange of ideas. San Franciscans and their Bay Area neighbors created an Arts and Crafts movement that reflected their unique climate, their special resources, and their strong desire to establish their independence as Californians.

THE ARTS AND CRAFTS MOVEMENT IN THE SOUTHLAND

Leslie Greene Bowman

California has as it were a civilization and an art of its own, independent
of the East. It produces its own geniuses, measures them by its own standards,
and makes their fame itself, without waiting for the aid or consent of any
wiseacre on the other side of the Rockies.[1]

Isabel McDougall,
House Beautiful, 1905

McDougall's amused assessment of California's Arts and Crafts movement was startlingly accurate, with one exception. The geniuses
were not produced there—the majority came from the other side of
the Rockies, seeking opportunity or better health. Their arrival
marked a rejection of the East; few sought to make California or
their own careers over in an eastern image.

The Arts and Crafts movement in the Southland (an area comprising Los
Angeles, Santa Barbara, Pasadena, and the desert communities to the east), and
in all of California, was a phenomenon of receivership, a vision transplanted from
elsewhere. California was a land unspoiled by industrialization—the purest possible test for Arts and Crafts experiments. In this place apart, nurtured by easterners anxious to keep it so, the movement was carefully groomed to enhance the
California dream. "Here in the Far West men and women of wide vision are gathering craftsmen and artists together in working centers housed in beautiful
California architecture with sunny patios and convenient outdoor courts for work-
rooms. Playing fountains, blooming plants and works of art, intimate and
friendly, add their inspiration to the aroused talent of the designers."[2]

The Arts and Crafts movement in California is distinctive more in process

118. Charles Frederick Eaton and Robert
Wilson Hyde. *Guest Book,* c. 1904. Hinged
covers with natural suede overlaid with cut
and hammered copper, ink and paint on vellum, and paper, 18¼ x 12½ in. The Oakland
Museum; Timken Fund.

than in style. The patronage for local craftspeople was largely upper class, since the middle-class markets for Arts and Crafts goods were supplied by numerous large-scale eastern firms, like Gustav Stickley's Craftsman Workshops, that could keep prices low through prescribed designs, mass production, and volume sales. In responding to this discriminating clientele, artisans tended to produce limited quantities in small studios or workshops, sometimes out-of-doors in natural settings. Custom commissions were commonplace; machinery was only a minor component, and designers, if not themselves the makers, worked directly with those who were. Well-heeled easterners found this alliance with Ruskinian ideals delightfully consistent with the California dream that had beckoned them west.

Historically, virtuoso craftsmanship has been demonstrated in ornament, not structure. Though eschewed by Gustav Stickley and too expensive for the middle class, ornament enjoyed a more important role in the West. The fascination of the region's upper-class patrons with custom design and highly skilled workmanship explains California's departure from the national norm of simple, chaste designs. Untroubled by economic or social concerns, the patrons of the Arts and Crafts movement in Southern California applauded its intention to preserve and revive richly ornamented old-world craftsmanship. Accordingly, a study of Southern California Arts and Crafts can be organized by its three affluent areas—Los Angeles, a prosperous city outstripping San Francisco with a population of 577,000 by 1920, and the two posh resorts of Pasadena and Santa Barbara. The potteries of the inland desert region are discussed at the conclusion of this essay.

Pasadena combines the conservatism of the East with the big and broad horizons that you get only in Southern California.[3]
James A. B. Scherer, President, Throop Polytechnic Institute, 1909

Pasadena was an ideal enclave for Arts and Crafts experimentation. Its strong sense of community was aided by its topography. Tucked along the oft-snow-capped San Gabriel Mountains and distinguished by the Arroyo Seco, a picturesque dry riverbed strewn with sand-washed boulders and rocks, Pasadena was a scenic and well-promoted resort. Wealthy easterners migrated west every winter to the beautiful and healthful Crown City (so called because *Pasadena* is a Chippewa word meaning "crown of the valley"). The rustic landscape, the gentle climate, and the romance of the ranchos suggested outdoor living spaces and more informal architecture and appointments. Architects and craftspeople alike were quick to seize on the patronage of a carriage trade that could afford their labors. Nowhere in America was the bungalow better suited to landscape, climate, and way of life. And nowhere did bungalows so artfully disguise mansions, many of them appointed with art pottery, handwrought silver, hammered copper, and Mission furniture.

Greene and Greene were among the first to reap success from Pasadena's advantages. Products of the Arts and Crafts emphasis on manual training, Charles

RIGHT

119. Charles Sumner Greene and Henry Mather Greene. *Desk,* 1904, from the Adelaide M. Tichenor House, Long Beach. Ash, 50 x 31 x 16 in. Randell L. Makinson.

BELOW

120. Charles Sumner Greene and Henry Mather Greene, inglenook and benches in the living room of the Adelaide M. Tichenor House, Long Beach, 1904.

Sumner Greene and his younger brother, Henry Mather Greene, had been introduced to the movement's concepts of design, materials, and artisanry at the Woodwards Manual Training High School in St. Louis.[4] Their architectural study at the Massachusetts Institute of Technology followed in natural succession. Recently graduated, in 1893 they visited the World's Columbian Exposition in Chicago en route to Pasadena. One of the exhibits in Chicago, the Japanese timber-frame temple with exposed construction, was to stimulate their evolving design sense and inspire an avid investigation of Far Eastern artifacts, books, and designs. Equally influential were magazines featuring the avant-garde Arts and Crafts look, such as Gustav Stickley's publication, the *Craftsman,* and *Ladies' Home Journal,* from which Charles took clippings for his scrapbook. The brothers began designing furniture en suite with their commissions in 1903.

Their designs for the Adelaide M. Tichenor House in 1904 are among the most successful of this early period, when their style was still reliant on Stickley's example but also expressive of their study of oriental art and architecture. Nowhere is the marriage of these two concepts more palpable than in the Tichenor furniture, which is muscular and forthright in its materials and construction but quietly assertive of oriental refinement in its lines and design. On the desk (plate 119), the rounded edges of the planks, the stepped arch of the Far Eastern cloud-lift motif, and the subtle shaping of the sides counterbalance the strong grain of the ash and the bold applied battens. The butterfly joinery seen on the sides of the desk was interpreted decoratively as well as structurally on the Tichenor benches, which form an inglenook around the fireplace (plate 120).

The influence of oriental design became increasingly apparent in subsequent commissions, and the structurally outspoken, Stickleyesque character receded. Whereas Stickley expounded on the rigidity and power of wood, the Greenes celebrated its pliancy and sculptural character. The mature Greene and Greene style in furniture was more refined, its structure apparent but less emphatic, with its focus on quality of line; subtle, exquisite details; and eloquent aspect. The Greenes abandoned oak and ash in favor of fine-grained mahoganies and teaks. The results bespeak their genius as well as the talents of their cabinetmakers, Peter and John Hall, whose superb woodworking and joinery skills gave life to the Greenes' vision.

For the Robert R. Blacker House (1907), the first of their four greatest commissions, they designed a massive bungalow of twelve thousand square feet, elaborately outfitted and landscaped. The furnishings were masterfully orchestrated with one another and with the architecture, each room set apart from the next by special details, all expressive of the Greenes' reverence for oriental design. The hallway furniture was entirely of teak, for example (plate 122), while that of the dining and living rooms was of mahogany (plate 121). A visitor to the Blacker House around 1908 wrote, "Mr. Greene's woodwork is a delight for the softness

121. Charles Sumner Greene and Henry Mather Greene. *Breakfast Table,* 1907, from the Robert R. Blacker House, Pasadena. Made by Peter Hall Manufacturing Company, Pasadena. Mahogany and ebony with inlay of mother-of-pearl and silver, 30 x 36 x 22¼ in. The Oakland Museum; Gift of the Women's Board, Donors Acquisition Fund, and Marjorie Eaton, Elizabeth Elston, and Mr. and Mrs. Harold E. Sherman, by exchange.

122. Charles Sumner Greene and Henry
Mather Greene. *Hall Armchair,* 1907, from
the Robert R. Blacker House, Pasadena.
Made by Peter Hall Manufacturing Company,
Pasadena. Teak, oak, and (replaced) leather,
40¼ x 24 x 23⅞ in. Los Angeles County
Museum of Art; Museum Acquisition Fund.

of its finish. It is like fresh butter or paste squeezed out of a tube—so soft are the surfaces and the corners."[5]

The David B. Gamble (see plates 26, 42) and the Charles M. Pratt house commissions followed in close succession to the Blacker, in Pasadena and Ojai, respectively. The last of the architects' great bungalows was the William R. Thorsen House in Berkeley, built in 1909. As with the Blacker House, all three of these commissions included a comprehensive design scheme, ranging from landscape to furnishings. The dining-room furniture of the Thorsen House was designed en suite, of mahogany with shared details such as the pierced stretchers. The sideboard (plate 124) is among the Greenes' finest case pieces. A commanding six and a half feet in length, it has eight legs girded by pierced stretchers that support the piece visually as well as structurally. Illustrative of the Greenes' design subtleties is the repetition of the stepped cloud-lift line of the stretchers in reverse on the vestigial splashboard. The focal points of the cabinet are its doors, framed in ebony to set off oriental floral compositions of delicate inlay. The reputed "spell of Japan" is evident in all four of these houses and their interiors.[6]

Another Pasadena architect designing Arts and Crafts furniture was Louis B. Easton. Though not the equal of the Greenes as an innovator, he was important as one of numerous easterners who transported the Arts and Crafts movement west and cultivated it to fruition in the land of sunshine. A manual-arts teacher from Illinois, Easton went west to improve his health, becoming a self-styled contractor for "bungalows and furniture." His cabinetmaking (plate 125)

168

BELOW

123. Charles Sumner Greene and Henry Mather Greene. *Dining-Room Sideboard,* 1909, from the Charles M. Pratt House, Nordhoff (now Ojai). Made by Peter Hall Manufacturing Company, Pasadena. Walnut and ebony, 36 x 64½ x 21¼ in. High Museum of Art, Atlanta; Virginia Crawford Collection.

OPPOSITE

124. Charles Sumner Greene and Henry Mather Greene. *Dining-Room Sideboard,* 1909, from the William R. Thorsen House, Berkeley. Made by Peter Hall Manufacturing Company, Pasadena. Fruitwoods, ebony, and mother-of-pearl, 40 x 80 x 24 in. The Gamble House, USC, Pasadena.

is imitative of similar designs by Stickley and other Arts and Crafts furniture manufacturers.

The Greenes and Easton were by no means alone in their homage to Arts and Crafts principles. Pasadena boasted its own manual-training institution. Founded in 1891, Throop Polytechnic Institute was committed to a balanced education. "Character, culture, and good craftsmanship might well spell our creed."[7] Throop's curriculum included wood turning, wood carving, carpentry, forging, clay modeling, and pattern making.[8] After 1910, however, when it was renamed the California Institute of Technology, the school deemphasized manual arts in favor of engineering.

The Throop ideal of developing both aspects of the person by inculcating a love and respect for manual work as a balance to intellectual labors was certainly fulfilled by at least one of its early students. Harold L. Doolittle was a successful engineer who remained devoted to the arts throughout his life. Notable as one of the few native California craftsmen in the region's movement, Doolittle graduated from Throop's college-preparatory academy in 1903. With no other art training, he became a notable etcher and an amateur wood- and metalworker. His surviving furniture is Arts and Crafts in design, some of it with delightful passages of Celtic-style ornament (plate 126). Doolittle combined his hobby and career interests in a single project when, in 1912, he designed a house for George and Susan Howell in Altadena, a hillside community neighboring Pasadena. Howell was a local patron of the Arts and Crafts community, and Doolittle provided him with a gabled,

ABOVE

125. Louis B. Easton. *Bench,* 1906. Redwood, 15⁹⁄₁₆ x 37¼ x 15½ in. Barbara Curtis Horton.

OPPOSITE

126. Harold L. Doolittle. *Chest,* 1907. Carved and varnished oak with hammered-and-pierced-brass hinges and hammered-brass handles, 22½ x 45½ x 25 in. Mr. and Mrs. Edward Bunting.

shingle-sided bungalow with exposed construction and a broad veranda. The interior featured extensive woodwork, leaded-glass cabinets, a fireplace inglenook, and specially designed light fixtures (plate 127). Doolittle represents the frequently overlooked amateur aspect of the movement, both nationally and in California, which placed strong emphasis on arts and crafts as a healthful avocation.

Throop's reputation as a bastion of Arts and Crafts doctrine was enhanced when, in 1901, Ernest A. Batchelder joined the faculty, teaching ceramics, drawing, and design. His national stature made Batchelder a seminal figure for the Southern California Arts and Crafts movement. In 1904 he was invited to select Californian submissions for the applied-arts section of the Louisiana Purchase Exposition in St. Louis. When Batchelder left Throop in 1909, undoubtedly because of its changing doctrines, he began the School of Design and Handicraft at his home on the Arroyo Seco. The faculty included Douglas Donaldson,[9] one of Batchelder's most important protégés. Donaldson had studied with Batchelder at the Handicraft Guild of Minneapolis and was an accomplished metalworker in his own right by the time he joined his teacher in California. He crafted the lighting fixtures for Batchelder's bungalow in 1910, wrought of copper with chased birds and flora, designs specified by Batchelder. A table lamp from this period is believed to be a collaboration by the two of them (plate 128), the ceramic base by Batchelder and the shade by Donaldson. Following Batchelder's example, Donaldson became an important teacher as well as a craftsman and a major figure in Southern California Arts and Crafts circles. After his tenure with Batchelder's school, however, his story is no longer associated with Pasadena but with Los Angeles.

Batchelder's school on the arroyo was in close proximity to other Arts and Crafts institutions. The Arroyo Guild published one issue of its journal, *Arroyo Craftsman,* in 1909. A self-proclaimed "hive" of craftsmen, whose work was scrutinized by "the heads of all the Departments of the Guild,"[10] the organization was evidently the brainchild of George Wharton James, a colorful proselytizer for California and the Arts and Crafts movement and a former editor for Stickley's *Craftsman.* Despite its avowed compendium of talents—producing stained glass, wall and ceiling treatments, carpets, furniture, mantels, lighting fixtures, pottery, pictures, bookbindings, jewelry, metalwork, leatherwork, paintings, prints, photographs, and even landscape design—no objects or commissions can be firmly attributed to the guild.[11] Its Ozymandian fate is probably explained in part by literary hyperbole; the guild may never have grown into James's ambitious descriptions.

In contrast to the guild's promotional rhetoric were the quieter activities of artisans like Clemens Friedell. Not a card-carrying member of any Arts and Crafts organization, Friedell was simply a consummate silversmith, a chaser to be precise, in the European tradition. In Pasadena he found wealthy patrons for his expensive labors, patterned after Gorham's response to the Arts and Crafts movement, a handwrought line called Martelé. Friedell had worked as a chaser for Gorham, before economic downturns inspired him to seek opportunity in California in

127. Harold L. Doolittle, inglenook fireplace in the Howell House, Altadena, 1912.

128. Ernest A. Batchelder and Douglas Donaldson. *Electrical Lamp,* c. 1908–10. Earthenware base colored with pigment, opalescent glass in copper frame, 21 x 23⅝ x 20⅝ in. Jack Moore.

172

1910.[12] Working alone or with a single assistant, he specialized in trophies (plate 129) and custom commissions for affluent patrons. For the millionaire brewer Eddie R. Maier, Friedell completed his masterpiece, a 107-piece holloware dinner service, each piece chased with California orange blossoms and the patron's initials. A similar design is found on the Turkish-coffee service (plate 130).

Elaborate chasing, accomplished by hammering the design into the surface with blunt tools, was laborious and expensive—such work could exceed the cost of the silver. For less affluent patrons or for those with a cleaner design sense, Friedell produced handwrought silver more typical of the Arts and Crafts idiom, with exquisite proportions and texture, ornamented only by hammer marks and chased initials (plate 131). Friedell's entries in the 1915 Panama-California Exposition in San Diego—a punch bowl, a coffee set, and several portrait plaques—won a gold medal. His shop in Pasadena's prestigious Hotel Maryland was so successful that he retired to Texas in 1921. He returned to business in

129. Clemens Friedell. *Trophy Vase,* c. 1915. Presented to Anita Baldwin at the Panama-Pacific International Exposition, San Francisco, 1915. Hammered and engraved silver with chased peacock, 18 x 9 in. Neil Lane and Bob Rehnert.

OPPOSITE

130. Clemens Friedell. *Coffee Service,* c. 1910. Hammered silver with chased orange blossoms, gilt, and ivory. Coffee server, 10½ x 8 in.; covered sugar bowl, 5½ x 6¾ in.; creamer, 4¾ x 4 in. June and Robert Berliner.

1 7 4

Pasadena in 1927, but his works from this later period are more souvenir oriented and exhibit less costly workmanship.

The Arts and Crafts movement in Pasadena coincided with the resort's heyday, when affluent residents and tourists could afford pricey handcraftsmanship. The Greenes enjoyed fewer and fewer grand commissions in the teens, and Charles moved to Carmel in 1916. Also that year, Batchelder moved to Los Angeles, having developed his pottery into a large commercial enterprise. Friedell maintained a livelihood, but his best works date before 1921.

In our fifteen years' residence in this wonderful land [Los Angeles] we have watched with increasing admiration the blossoming of a crude western town into a full-fledged city. Two characteristics that . . . make it a paradise for the artist are, first, a remarkable spirit of democratic comradery among our workers; and secondly, and almost as important, a free atmosphere as yet not much suppressed by the deadening conventions that have gripped most of the older art centers of the east.[13]

Douglas Donaldson, 1924

Douglas Donaldson was one of the most influential proponents of the Arts and Crafts movement in Los Angeles. He left Pasadena in 1912 when he became head of the crafts department at Manual Arts High School in Los Angeles, where he taught "hammer work, repoussé work, etching, enameling, coloring processes, gilding, stone polishing, and casting."[14] In 1919 he joined the staff of Otis Art Institute and founded his own summer school shortly thereafter, offering courses in decorative design and color theory.

Donaldson and his wife, Louise Donaldson, were appointed to select applied-arts entries for the Southern California section of the Panama-California Exposition in San Diego. The exhibit included their own metalwork as well as pieces by Batchelder, Cornelius Brauckman (of Grand Feu Pottery), Robert Wilson Hyde, Frederick Hürten Rhead, Alexander W. Robertson (of Alberhill Pottery), and Rudolph Schaeffer.[15] Donaldson's gold-medal-winning entry for the fair was a covered chalice (plate 132), distinguished by elaborate repoussé and enamel work and crowned by a delicate opal finial carved in the shape of a bird. Donaldson explained its composition: "The opal bird that surmounts the cover supplied the motif for the design. Moon stones, turquoise, emeralds, and peridots were used with enamel bosses to add a note of color to the gray of the silver, and to repeat the bird motif in the band about the bowl, and in the base."[16] Not surprisingly, certain of the cup's motifs, including the bird finial, relate to designs published by Donaldson's teacher, Batchelder.[17] The student surpassed his instructor, however, in craftsmanship: Batchelder's tiles do not approach the technical virtuosity of Donaldson's silver. An enameler, jeweler, and silversmith, Donaldson successfully blended all three crafts on the chalice, a marriage typical of his finest work.

131. Clemens Friedell. *Coffee Service,* c. 1910. Hammered silver, gilt, and ivory. Tray, diameter: 11¹¹⁄₁₆ in.; coffee server, 6⅞ x 7³⁄₁₆ in.; sugar bowl, 2¼ x 4⅛ in.; and creamer, 3 x 3⅝ in. Dorothy and Richard Sherwood.

132. Douglas Donaldson. *Covered Chalice* (also known as *Freshman Singing Cup*), 1914. Silver, parcel-gilt, champlevé enamels, opal, moonstones, turquoise, emeralds, and peridots, 8⅜ x 3⁵⁄₁₆ in. President and Fellows of Harvard College, Cambridge, Massachusetts.

133. Douglas Donaldson. *Tea Caddy,* c. 1915. Silver, enamels, and carnelian, 6¼ x 2⅝ in. Cranbrook Academy of Art Museum; Gift of George G. Booth.

134. Douglas Donaldson. *Covered Bowl,* 1945. Silver and carnelian, 4½ x 6½ in. Nancy Daly.

Donaldson's silver was usually handwrought, mounted with semiprecious stones, and worked with stylized designs from nature, as in his tea caddy (plate 133) exhibited with the Detroit Society of Arts and Crafts in 1916.[18] Donaldson illustrated the vessel in his brochure with the accompanying entry:

> William Morris said: "Have nothing in your home that you do not know to be useful and believe to be beautiful." A tea caddy may be a very humble affair or it may through its art be made to justify its presence not only as an object of use, but of beauty as well.
> The smoothly planished surface of this caddy is ornamented with a border of birds and flowers. The enamel bosses of orange and green enamel are made to harmonize with the sardonyx used in the settings.[19]

Stylized birds like those on the chalice and the caddy appear consistently throughout his brochure, suggesting that they were Donaldson's emblem, as the rabbit was Batchelder's.

Donaldson's penchant for enameling and mounting stones is traceable to the influence of Charles R. Ashbee's Guild of Handicraft in England. Emphasizing beauty in common materials, Ashbee's silver designs were simple and clean, often adorned only with enamels and semiprecious stones, a conscious rejection of the period's ornately worked and jewel-encrusted silver. Ashbee's designs were known and adapted by American silversmiths, but Donaldson may have had more direct knowledge of them through Batchelder, who spent six months studying metalsmithing and enameling with the guild in 1905–6.[20]

In December 1923 Louise Donaldson established the Decorative Arts Guild in Los Angeles "to build up a Craft Movement and Artists Directory." Included in the list of exhibitors at the guild's shows were Porter Blanchard, Harry Dixon, and Douglas Donaldson.[21] This was probably the forerunner of the Arts and Crafts Society of Southern California, founded the following May, with Blanchard as president and Donaldson as vice president. Founded to "stimulate the love for the Crafts, to increase the number of Craft workers and to provide a place in which to exhibit and sell Craft-work," the society boasted over one hundred members at its first meeting. Despite its numbers, the society disappeared from the pages of local art publications in eighteen months.[22]

As fellow officers of the society and fellow metalsmiths, it was not surprising that Donaldson and Blanchard should join forces, as announced in 1927: "Mr. Donaldson will supplement the hand-wrought silver and pewter of Mr. Blanchard with specially designed jewelry and art metal objects of various kinds." By September of that year they had assembled a traveling exhibition of their works and sent it to "art centers of the East."[23] The two men had easily distinguishable styles. Donaldson's penchant for ornament contrasted with Blanchard's more minimal, heavily wrought style, which rarely admitted any applied decoration. Whether influenced by Blanchard's simpler style, or by changing tastes, Donaldson's covered bowl from 1945 (plate 134) has only the mounted carnelian in common with his earlier designs. In place of enameling and stylized repoussé designs, the bowl relies on its superb proportions and the subtle texture of its hammer marks for aesthetic effect. The design suggests a dialogue with Native American silverwork.

Porter Blanchard was a product of the Arts and Crafts movement. The son of a Massachusetts silversmith, he learned the craft in his father's workshop in Gardner before succumbing to wanderlust and heading for California in 1923.[24] He shared his impressions as a "rank easterner" the following year, calling himself:

> one of the first million in Southern California. We're here sure enough, and "no fooling" in the much advertised and criticized (advertised East— criticized West) land of sunshine and sandstorms (last not advertised). That's why we're here (and the other 999999 also I believe) to see if what you talked so much about, your wonderful California, was, in fact or fiction. . . .
>
> On my trip across . . . there were many sick at heart wishing they were home but gritting their teeth and smiling through the dusty windshield of a flivver straining their eyes toward the promised land.[25]

Blanchard went on to advise Californians how to cope with the eastern influx, chiding them, "do be careful to remember it's YOUR advertising that has brought [them] here." He was more outspoken than most of his contemporaries, but nearly all the Arts and Crafters profiled here went west for the same reasons; and despite the frustrations they encountered with sandstorms or their businesses, most of them remained, for as Blanchard concluded, "when California smiles, all is forgiven."

Blanchard settled in Burbank; his father and brother joined him, and by 1925 there were eight men in the studio, which Blanchard promoted as an idyllic Arts and Crafts setting: "Sunshine and flowers surround [our] shop; scented breezes, tempered by the Pacific, blow through it. It has expanded wonderfully under this influence." In contrast with Friedell, Blanchard spurned ornamentation, citing Ruskin and professing an appreciation for "simpler, finer lines and plainer surfaces."[26] Blanchard continued the restrained Colonial Revival style of his Boston years but soon added more progressive designs, of even simpler lines (plate 135). Applied ornament is largely absent from Blanchard's work; he relied on his medium and its form for aesthetic effect, aided only by the texture of his hammer marks and the satin finish he preferred.

Blanchard is one of the few California craftspeople who marketed himself nationally through standard retail channels, much as Stickley did. Blanchard exhibited in the usual Arts and Crafts arenas, but he also contracted with department stores, "usually the most exclusive in the particular city."[27] Such expansion required the same predictable compromises that Stickley had encountered: standardized designs and machine assistance. Blanchard also maintained a retail

135. Porter Blanchard. *Matching Coffee and Tea Servers,* c. 1930. Silver with ebony handles. Coffee server, 7½ x 9¼ in. The Oakland Museum; Gift of the Architectural Council. Tea server, 4¾ x 10⅜ in. The Oakland Museum; Gift of the Collector's Gallery, Sandra G. and Steven Wolfe, and Kenneth R. Trapp.

studio that specialized in custom commissions for the Hollywood film community, earning him the moniker "silversmith to the screen stars."[28]

Los Angeles hosted art potters as well as silversmiths. The scarcity of timber meant that little Arts and Crafts furniture was made locally, but Southern California boasted superb clay deposits in Riverside County, east of the city. Among the earliest to take advantage of these resources was Fred H. Robertson, a sixth-generation potter whose family had founded Chelsea Keramic Art Works near Boston. Fred grew up in the business and worked with his father, Alexander W., and his uncle, Hugh, at Chelsea. Hired as a clay specialist by the Los Angeles Pressed Brick Company in 1906, Robertson developed an art-pottery line with his own mark, F.H.R./Los Angeles.

Having been longer in the tutelage of his uncle than of his father, Robertson made pottery that reflects Hugh Robertson's emphasis on form and glaze to the exclusion of surface manipulation (plate 137). Fred H. Robertson may also have been trying to compete with Fulper pottery, which was marketed in Los Angeles. His crystalline and luster glazes bear comparison with Fulper variations, and one of his lamps copies a known Fulper model (plate 213). Robertson's entries in the applied-arts exhibit at the Panama-California Exposition won a gold medal.

The most sophisticated art pottery in Los Angeles came from Grand Feu, the only Southern California pottery to produce high-fired wares such as stoneware and porcelain (the other local potteries made low-fired earthenwares). Indeed, the

136. Robertson Pottery (Fred H. Robertson). *Vase,* c. 1913–16. Stoneware with green crystalline glaze, 7⅝ x 5¾ in. David Reneric.

ABOVE

137. Robertson Pottery (Fred H. Robertson). *Three Vases,* c. 1913–16. Stoneware with metallic glaze. Left: 6 x 2½ in., Stephanie Lynn and David Mills. Center: 4¼ x 2⅝ in., The Oakland Museum; Bequest of the estate of Helen Hathaway White. Right: 6⁵⁄₁₆ x 3⅜ in., Caroline and Gary Kent.

name is French for "high (or large) fire" and was probably inspired by a seminal publication in the field, *Grand Feu Ceramics,* by Taxile Doat, the renowned French art potter. Grand Feu was the creation of Cornelius Brauckman, a Missouri native who studied art in St. Louis. Brauckman founded his venture about 1912,[29] producing a high-fired, vitrified stoneware called *grès.* Like Fred H. Robertson, Brauckman specialized in the unity of form and glaze (see plates 138, 139), as a surviving sales brochure explains:

> Grand Feu uses no applied or painted decorations. The wonderful play of colors blending harmoniously one with the other are created by the firing effects and various glazes as in the Turquois, Mission, Tiger Eyes, Blue, Yellow, Green, Red and Moss Crystals, Green and Blue Ramose, Moss, Agate, Multoradii, Venetian Green and Sun Rays.[30]

Brauckman was among several American potters of the period who sought to control and codify exotic glazes, which resulted not only from self-taught recipes but also from the conditions and temperature of the kiln itself. European and

ABOVE

138. Grand Feu Pottery. *Three Vases,* c. 1913–16. Stoneware with transmutation glazes. Left: 10¾ x 4⅝ in., Gary Keith. Center: 6⁵⁄₁₆ x 9⅛ in. Stephanie Lynn and David Mills. Right: 8⅝ x 4³⁄₁₆ in. Stephanie Lynn and David Mills.

OPPOSITE

139. Grand Feu Pottery. *Vase,* c. 1913–16. Stoneware with dark green semimatte glaze, 7 x 3½ in. Stephanie Lynn and David Mills.

Chinese wares were usually the inspiration, but the secrets of their surfaces had been lost or were closely guarded. Brauckman's entries in the Panama-California Exposition were awarded a gold medal, but despite its artistic success, Grand Feu closed about 1916.

> *Among her rivals the city of Santa Barbara sits the queen on the amphitheatre of the Santa Ynez Range. Here within a radius of 40 miles, is found all that can delight the seeker for health and pleasure, knowledge and profit. Land and sea, mountain and island, cañon and arroyo, tree and flower, under a cloudless sky, combine to realize the artist's dream of the earthly Paradise.[31]*
>
> Julius Starke,
> a Santa Barbara woodworker, 1905

Santa Barbara, like Pasadena, was a resort community patronized by wealthy easterners. The seaside village enjoyed an enviable setting, nestled between the Santa Ynez Mountains and the Pacific Ocean. Eastern Arts and Crafts aficionados transplanted their ideologies to the idyllic setting. Anna Sophia Cabot Blake was a Boston philanthropist (and relative of the founder of Arequipa Pottery in Northern California) who established Santa Barbara's first manual-arts training school in the early 1890s. Ralph Radcliffe Whitehead (a student and friend of John Ruskin better known as the founder of Byrdcliffe, an Arts and Crafts colony in Woodstock, New York) founded another manual-arts training school on his estate in neighboring Montecito in 1898.[32] Whitehead and his wife, Jane Byrd McCall, had built their Tuscan villa, called Arcady, in 1892, and filled it with Morris and Company appointments.

Arcady was rivaled by another Arts and Crafts villa in Montecito, Riso Rivo. Charles Frederick Eaton was a wealthy dilettante in his mid-forties when he arrived in Montecito in 1886 after nearly twenty years abroad. A painter, craftsman, and landscape architect, Eaton built his own artistic paradise on several hundred acres. Riso Rivo was a magnificent estate with renowned gardens surrounding an Arts and Crafts home of stone and weathered oak, "which with its contents give expression to the owner's desire for substantial handiwork of merit and distinctive artistic design."[33]

The 1906 description goes on to note that Eaton's real fame rests in his Arts and Crafts studio (plate 140), located above his carriage house, "open on all sides, free to any inspiration that may be gathered from Nature, and from it have gone forth such exquisite productions that they have attracted the attention of the art loving public at all the recent exhibitions." Such productions included handmade books of illuminated parchment or vellum, bound in leather with wrought-metal mounts (plates 118, 141, 142); tooled-leather chests; silver caskets with semi-precious stones; "honest Furniture . . . made by hand"; "Brass[,] Copper and Iron Devices wrought with all the thoughtfulness and cunning of the Mediaeval craftsmen"[34]; and shell-mounted lamps and lighting fixtures.

140. Charles Frederick Eaton in his studio at Riso Rivo, Montecito, c. 1904. From *Craftsman,* July 1904.

141, 142. Charles Frederick Eaton and Robert Wilson Hyde. *Wedding Album,* 1903, with marriage certificate for Robb de Peyster Tytus and Grace Selley Henop, May 19, 1903. Hinged brass covers with mother-of-pearl, windowpane oyster, natural suede, and ink and paint on vellum, 12¾ x 9¼ in. The Mitchell Wolfson, Jr., Collection; Courtesy of The Wolfsonian Foundation, Miami.

Most notable to eastern audiences was Eaton's use of regional materials: "Their novelty is the abundant and ingenious decoration with California products—the streaked abalone shell, or stones found on the Pacific beaches. Sometimes the coffer or frame is made of red cedar or sequoia, and sometimes it has strange rosettes applied to its surface, formed from the scales of giant pine-cones."[35]

Eaton's designs are characteristically of multiple materials and detailed workmanship, as seen in his tea screen from about 1904 (plate 143). They relate not to the simple, clean aesthetic of Stickley's democratic art but to a revival of intricate craftsmanship in humble, vernacular materials, but not inexpensive. Eaton sent fourteen pieces to the 1904 world's fair in St. Louis—serving pieces, coffers, books, and manuscripts—including a jewelry cabinet of "Port Orford Cedar covered outside & inside with Sheep skin trimmed with mottled copper—Pine Cone decorations," for seventy-five dollars, and a book, "Christ Teaching . . . Illuminated in parchment. Covers brass. Squares Philippine shell. Studded with Abalone Shells cut as stones," for ninety dollars. Eaton was assisted with his designs by Robert Wilson Hyde, who also did all the book illumination.[36]

Eaton probably began producing electric lighting fixtures with his intriguing shell mounts in 1903. He wrote to the supervisor of the St. Louis exposition, "I could send some very novel electric light shades made of shell."[37] A reviewer of the 1903–4 applied-arts exhibition at the Art Institute of Chicago raved: "The crowning glory of the California section is the lamp-shade. It is a wonderfully harmonious thing. . . . The marvelous shimmering gray of the abalone shell, the duller, lifeless gray of the iron frame, and the soft, velvety gray of the wire cloth with which it is lined."[38]

These distinctive lamps and shades have traditionally been attributed to Eaton's daughter, Elizabeth Eaton Burton. Which one of them first introduced translucent shells into lampshades remains a mystery, but both made use of the idea. When Stickley reviewed Eaton's home and work in an issue of the *Craftsman* in 1904, he also commented on Elizabeth's work: "Like her father, she is also a metal worker, using bronze in a gamut of greens and yellows, in combination with the abalone, melon, and Philippine shells, to produce lamps and sconces in floral forms."[39]

Born in Paris in 1869, Eaton's eldest daughter was educated in Europe and pursued many interests in common with her father—landscape architecture, painting, and craftwork. The earliest mention of her craft pursuits occurs in an earlier *Craftsman* article on California leatherwork, which notes that her work "has for some years been sold in New York."[40] In a style assimilated from her father, Burton combined various techniques and materials to produce elaborate designs of medieval, Japanese, and Art Nouveau inspiration. Her leather screens, chests, and frames were variously tinted, embossed, carved, burned, gilded, stitched, and inlaid with mother-of-pearl.[41]

Curiously, Burton was never mentioned as one of Eaton's associates, and when selected by Batchelder to exhibit at the St. Louis exposition of 1904, she

143. Charles Frederick Eaton. *Tea Screen,*
c. 1901–4. Patinated repoussé tin and windowpane oyster, 8 x 15½ in. The Buck
Collection.

did so under her own name, exhibiting a chest of leather, "illuminated with silver leaf, bound with iron," two lampshades and a tea screen mounted with shells, and two leather table mats, also shell-mounted.[42] Burton actively engaged in leather- and metalwork in Santa Barbara until about 1910. She operated a studio on State Street near her home and published a catalog, *Hand-Wrought Electric Lamps and Sconces,* sometime during this period. She won a gold medal at the Alaska-Yukon-Pacific Exposition in 1909 in Seattle, where she again exhibited separately from her father, though their repertoire of leather- and metalwork lighting fixtures, chests, books, and accessories was quite similar.[43]

Burton's catalog features lighting devices with shells mounted in handwrought metal that could be ordered in brass or copper, "either plain or greened finish." The Medusa, the largest and most expensive model in the catalog, was recommended in greened brass and featured "Philippine Shell combined with Pearl Abalone Shell"; its price was $175.00. Not all the designs offered were as organic as Medusa, but nearly all incorporated shells in the shades—abalone, chiton, limpet, pearl, and Philippine of varying colors—contrasted with silk and wire gauze spanning the handwrought metal (plates 5, 144, 145). Smaller lamps and sconces ranged in price from fifteen to forty dollars.[44]

A third Santa Barbara craftsman of note was Eaton's associate, Robert Wilson Hyde. Another transplanted easterner, Hyde went to Santa Barbara in 1902. Hyde's specialty was described in the local newspaper in 1906 as "a revival of the quaint though laborious art of the medieval cloisters; not a plagiarism, but

ABOVE

144. Elizabeth Eaton Burton. *Hanging Electrical Lamp,* c. 1910. Hammered, cut, and pierced copper with Gumboot chiton shells and mantles, mica, and chain link, 10⅞ x 25¾ in. D. J. Puffert.

OPPOSITE

145. Elizabeth Eaton Burton. *Electrical Lamp,* c. 1910. Hammered and pierced copper, painted black, 19½ x 22 in. Tazio N. Lombardo.

giving the essence of the old work in an original way." Listing illuminating (see plates 142, 146) and book making as his pursuits, the article continued:

> Mr. Hyde's greatest work, however, is illuminating special books to order, the making of guest books, family registers, wedding books and marriage certificates, child records, and Christmas and Easter books from original designs. Guest books of which only one copy is made from the special design, with cover bound in natural calf, hinged with brass in gothic style, and title page illuminated with allegorical scenes, perhaps give wider range for the exercise of the talent of this artist and designer, said to be the first in America to adapt to modern purposes and ideas the work of the monks of the middle ages.[45]

146. Robert Wilson Hyde. *Illumination,* c. 1904. Gold leaf, ink, and paint on vellum, 16¾ x 20¾ in. Gary Breitweiser.

147. Group of illuminated books by Robert Wilson Hyde, photographed c. 1910.

Handmade books of leather, parchment, watercolor, and calligraphy (plate 147) were not a middle-class item. The St. Louis entries mentioned above ranged in price from $60.00 to $90.00, while an accompanying marriage certificate in white calf on illuminated parchment cost $125.00. Hyde exhibited a wedding book in the Alaska-Yukon-Pacific Exposition, under Eaton's aegis, priced at $85.00.[46] In the same period one could buy a chest of drawers from Stickley that was considered not inexpensive for $40.00. But Hyde's work was also available for far less money, in published form. The San Francisco Arts and Crafts printer and bookseller Paul Elder offered books and cards designed by Hyde and printed in elaborate colors. Cards were ten to fifteen cents apiece, and guest and wedding books ranged from $3.50 to $15.00, depending on the choice of binding.[47] Hyde had likely become acquainted with Elder through the latter's satellite shop in Santa Barbara, which probably retailed works by Hyde, Eaton, and other Santa Barbara craftspeople.[48] Hyde may also have been associated with the Gift Shop of the Craft-Camarata (*Camarata* means "friends" in Italian). The shop was recorded in city directories from 1912 to 1917, and Hyde advertised at the same address in 1917.[49]

The most famous member of Santa Barbara's Arts and Crafts community, Frederick Hürten Rhead, had visited Santa Barbara while still employed at the Arequipa Pottery in Northern California, to assist Anna Sophia Cabot Blake in establishing pottery classes at her manual-arts school. Having distinguished himself at several American potteries in others' employ,[50] Rhead selected the resort as a suitable place to start his own enterprise, explaining:

> The selection of the place and site of the studio had nothing to do with the proximity of materials, or market considerations. It was a beautiful place; I would locate here, make my pots, and then decide what to do with them. . . . I happened to have chosen a residential resort within easy distance of other resorts, and of half a dozen fairly large cities, and incidentally in a tourist district which was a regular hotbed for craft shops.[51]

Rhead established his pottery in 1914 with the help of two shareholders.[52] Ralph Radcliffe Whitehead, then living in Woodstock, invested $250, a minor amount compared to the $1,750 supplied by Christoph Tornoe, a carpenter, cabinetmaker, and metalworker of some repute in local newspapers. Indeed, Rhead's picturesque site was on Tornoe's property in artist-frequented Mission Canyon.[53] Although formally titled Rhead Pottery, Rhead's venture was also known as the Pottery of the Camarata,[54] suggesting a relationship with the aforementioned Gift Shop of the Craft-Camarata.

Rhead continued to decorate pottery with variations on sgraffito, a technique he had introduced to American art potteries, in which the surface is covered with a colored slip and then carved to reveal the contrasting body beneath (plate 148). He frequently added more colors with inlaid slips or glazes, so the results were highly textural and richly hued (plate 152). On the whole Rhead's designs in this

193

period are looser and more flowing than the tight, repetitive compositions of his earlier work in the East. He was aided in design and decoration by his first wife, Agnes Rhead, and he continued to employ assistants for throwing as well as decorating, allowing him to focus on designs and glaze development.

This last concern was a major aspect of Rhead's Santa Barbara years. A proponent of the highly decorated surface when he came to the United States, Rhead was introduced to the possibilities of exotic glazes by Taxile Doat when the two worked together from 1909 to 1911 at Edward Lewis's state-of-the-art laboratory pottery, University City Pottery, near St. Louis. Doat's approach had long been preached in America by the pioneering ceramist Charles Fergus Binns; both subscribed to an oriental tradition—unity of form and glaze without applied decoration (plates 150, 151). Santa Barbara offered firsthand opportunities to study this approach. Ednah Anne Rich, a contemporary of Rhead's and a native of the city, noted in her memoirs, "Surely I could not grow up in Santa Barbara with its Chinese pottery always at hand without developing a love for form and color and glaze."[55] Rhead devoted himself to experimentation with glazes, attempting to recreate various Chinese formulas, especially the elusive mirror black glaze (plate 149). He employed his results as the sole decoration on shapes that were equally derivative of Far Eastern prototypes.

Rhead's workshop on the Tornoe property was as sylvan as the one he had enjoyed at Arequipa, and as he had there, he encouraged working out-of-doors, even selling wares under Japanese umbrellas when weather permitted.[56] Local landscapes are depicted on a number of pieces, the best example of which is a statuesque vase (plate 152). Probably in an effort to stay solvent, Rhead also conducted pottery classes; Ralph Whitehead's wife, Jane, was among his students. Although ultimately an unsound business venture, the pottery, with entries

OPPOSITE

148. Rhead Pottery. *Low Bowl and Vase,* 1913–17. Earthenware with sgraffito design and multicolored glaze. Lois [Loiz] Whitcomb, decorator of low bowl; Frederick Hürten Rhead (?), decorator of vase. Low bowl, 1⅛ x 8¾ in. The Oakland Museum; Bequest of the estate of Helen Hathaway White. Vase, 7¾ x 4¼ in. The Oakland Museum; Kahn Collection.

BELOW

149. Rhead Pottery (Frederick Hürten Rhead). *Vase,* 1913–17. Earthenware with mirror black glaze, 12 x 9½ in. The Oakland Museum; Bequest of the estate of Helen Hathaway White.

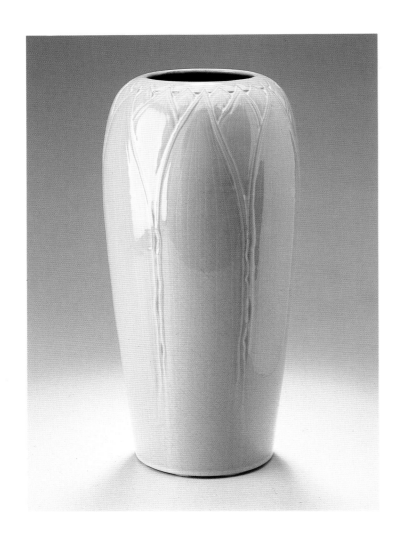

150. Rhead Pottery (Frederick Hürten Rhead). *Vase,* 1913–17. Earthenware with sgraffito design and colorless glaze, 15⁵⁄₁₆ x 7³⁄₈. The Oakland Museum; Gift of Rod and Lynn Holt.

151. Rhead Pottery (Frederick Hürten Rhead). *Vase,* 1913–17. Glazed earthenware, 8³⁄₄ x 5¹⁄₄ in. Carolyn and John Grew-Sheridan.

152. Rhead Pottery (Frederick Hürten Rhead). *Vase,* 1913–17. Earthenware with incised design and inlaid multicolored glaze, 11½ x 6¼ in. Isak Lindenauer.

selected by Douglas and Louise Donaldson, earned a gold medal at the Panama-California Exposition in San Diego.

Another eastern potter, Alexander W. Robertson, was working at the Halcyon cooperative colony, north of Santa Barbara near Pismo Beach. California was the chosen land for a number of utopian communities, for all the same reasons that made it attractive to Arts and Crafts proponents. A Theosophical splinter group from Syracuse, New York, founded Halcyon in 1903.[57] The organizers established Halcyon Art Pottery as one of the community's industries, and the colony's newspaper reported progress on the pottery in May 1910:

> Apparatus, work benches and tools are being assembled. Two kilns are now en route by freight from the east. These kilns have been presented by Mrs. Robineau, who is associated with Taxile Doat of University City, in the Ceramic Department of that institution.
>
> Mr. A. W. Robertson, an expert potter of national renown, will be the specialist in charge of the Pottery Department of the School of Arts and Crafts.[58]

The pottery had enviable connections. Adelaide Alsop Robineau was among the most talented ceramists in the country; she had been invited to work with Taxile Doat at University City Pottery, and in 1910 she won the grand prize at the international exposition in Turin, Italy. Robertson was also a luminary in the ceramics field, having founded Chelsea Keramic Art Works near Boston and having most recently been associated with the ill-fated Roblin Art Pottery in San Francisco.

Robertson arrived later in 1910; the first kiln firing was on display in January 1911.[59] Using local red clays found in the county, Robertson continued in the Roblin style, with applied decoration of regional flora and fauna—lizards, flowers,

153. Pottery made by Alexander W. Robertson at Halcyon Art Pottery, 1912. ❧ *The verso of this vintage photograph is dated 9/17/12 and inscribed "made from local red brick clay."*

154. Alberhill Pottery (Alexander W. Robertson). *Triangular Vase,* 1913. Biscuit-fired buff earthenware with modeled lizard, 6 x 3¼ x 3½ in. The Oakland Museum; Bequest of the estate of Helen Hathaway White.

and so forth (plate 153). The majority of Halcyon's production was bisque-fired only, without applied glazes. This surface accentuated the fine-grained texture of the clay and maintained the sharpness of the applied decoration. It may also have been a cost- or labor-saving device. Aesthetically, it was wonderfully consistent with the arid climate and the reptilian ornament. Halcyon produced vases, pitchers, candlesticks, bowls, incense burners, whistles, paperweights, toothpick holders, match holders, and "useful and artistic 'catch alls.' "[60]

Despite its propitious beginning, the pottery fell victim to problems within the community. Robertson left in 1912 to join Alberhill Coal and Clay Company, near Riverside; the pottery closed in 1913, although it was reopened in 1931 for summer classes with the Northern California ceramist Gertrude Rupel Wall, of Walrich Pottery. The summer program could not sustain itself, however, and the equipment was dismantled in the early 1940s.[61]

California's inland desert region, with its excellent clay deposits, hosted art potteries in addition to its other Arts and Crafts activities (see pages 77–87). One of the earliest in the area was Redlands Pottery, founded by Wesley H. Trippett, who came from New York for health reasons around 1895. An art metalworker formerly with Tiffany Studios, Trippett settled in Redlands.[62] He began experimenting with local clay deposits and by 1904 had founded Redlands Pottery. Trippett specialized in molded designs of "subjects peculiar to this coast" (plate

155).[63] Native plant and animal motifs adorned his red bisque vases and bowls, sometimes enhanced with a hint of color wash, suggesting the patinas of his metalwork (plate 156). When Trippett left Redlands in 1911 to head the art department of the California China Products Company in National City, near San Diego, a local newspaper reported the move, noting that "his wares, bearing the 'Tadpole Mark,' have sold as readily in New York and Boston as in California."[64]

The same year that Trippett joined California China Products Company, Alexander W. Robertson was hired by the Alberhill Coal and Clay Company to promote their high-grade clays with a line of art pottery (plates 154, 206). Alberhill was located in neighboring Riverside County, not far from Redlands. Robertson's style may have influenced Trippett's; the white bisque surfaces favored by Robertson contrast with the red bodies of Halcyon wares, but the applied reptilian designs are similar. Robertson did glaze some of the wares and incise designs in addition to applying molded ornament. He was among those selected by Douglas and Louise Donaldson to exhibit in the Panama-California Exposition, where his work for Alberhill was awarded a gold medal.

There is no discernible style associated with Southern California Arts and Crafts. Some of the Southland's artisans, like Doolittle and Easton, were clearly influenced by the Stickley example of simple, solid workmanship, with minimal decoration. But others subscribed to the movement's emphasis on reviving old-world traditions and distinguished themselves in the more demanding craftsmanship of ornamental techniques—Burton, Donaldson, Eaton, Friedell, Hyde, and in some pieces, Rhead. And a third group was clearly influenced by oriental traditions—Brauckman, Greene and Greene, Rhead, and Fred H. Robertson. All but Doolittle came from somewhere else, and most of them were already proponents of the Arts and Crafts movement when they arrived. Seeking the good life, they collectively forged Southern California's contribution to an international phenomenon.

THE ARTS AND CRAFTS MOVEMENT IN SAN DIEGO

Bruce Kamerling

157. Reginald Machell, designer and carver. *Folding Screen,* c. 1905–10, for the Theosophical Society, Point Loma. Carved and painted wood, 78¼ x 81⅛ in. Archives, Theosophical Society Library, Pasadena.

Spain established San Diego in 1769 as its first outpost in Alta California, but by the time California achieved statehood in 1850 the town still had not developed into anything more than a small Mexican village. Throughout the early years of its existence as an American city, San Diego attempted to compete with San Francisco and particularly Los Angeles to become an important commercial center on the West Coast. Unfortunately, despite San Diego's outstanding harbor and numerous enthusiastic promoters, its isolation and lack of natural resources continually undermined the town's efforts to become a major industrial center. One natural resource, however, turned out to be of great value. San Diego was blessed with an unusually temperate climate, which became a definite factor in attracting a wide variety of people to the area, including health seekers, utopian groups, and others committed to the reform agenda of the Arts and Crafts philosophy.

The health benefits resulting from the mild weather were an important part of the city's early promotions. By the 1870s several hotels had set aside rooms specifically for invalids. Some health claims became so outrageous that an editorial in the *San Diego Union* of March 10, 1870, pronounced: "This climate, good as it is, will not raise the dead." After a visit in 1872 the famous scientist Louis Agassiz wrote of the climate: "This is your capital, and it is worth millions to you."[1] The climate became the key to living the good life in Southern California, offering an extended growing season to the farmer, year-round flowers to the gardener, continuous employment to the seasonal worker, a vacation spot to the tourist, and perhaps most significantly, the hope of recovery to the invalid or health seeker.

Dr. Peter C. Remondino became one of the major promoters of the Southern California climate. Born in Italy, he served as a doctor during the Civil War, during which he contracted typhomalarial fever. His condition abated while he resided in France for a time but returned when he moved back to Minnesota. Inspired by his brief European respite, Remondino began to study climatology, which resulted in his decision to move to San Diego in 1873. One of the most prominent doctors in Southern California, Remondino also became a prolific writer. Two of his books had a substantial impact on the future growth of San Diego as a health resort. *The Mediterranean Shores of America: Southern California: Its Climatic, Physical, and Meteorological Conditions* (1892) and *The Modern Climatic Treatment of Invalids with Pulmonary Consumption in Southern California* (1893) helped establish the region's climate as ideal for relief, if not full recovery, from numerous respiratory ailments, particularly tuberculosis. Fresh air, rest, and outdoor occupations were considered to be essential factors in the effective treatment of pulmonary disorders.

In *Modern Climatic Treatment*, Remondino set out to create a guidebook for the layman health seeker, advising that "None come too early." He warned against expectations of a complete or instant cure. "Because the climate cannot replace a departed lung or degenerated kidney, do not vote it down as a fraud." Remondino pointed out that it would be useless for invalids to come to California for the climate and then to lock themselves in an overheated hotel room, to "breathe as foul an air as they could have done in their Pennsylvania home." "The main remedial faculty in the Southern Californian climate," he wrote, "consists in the fact that it allows the greatest facility for an out-of-door life and for the greatest freedom in ventilation, conjoined to the greatest possible amount of sunshine."[2]

The ill began to arrive by the trainload. Naturally, not all San Diegans were thrilled with the idea of living in a city full of sick people, but others recognized the possibilities offered by the invalid trade. Sanatoriums, preventoriums, and other treatment centers sprang up around San Diego, which began to promote itself as the ideal place to live for those who were well and the perfect place to recover for those who were not.

In 1905 the Rancho Guajome Health Company proposed one of the most ambitious plans for treating invalids. Originally established in 1848, Rancho Guajome was located near Oceanside, adjacent to Mission San Luis Rey. A group of leading Southern California doctors, including Remondino, incorporated the company "for the purpose of providing, at rates within the reach of persons of moderate means, homes where they can live under the best sanitary conditions, and at the same time earn all or the larger part of their living, while they are seeking to recover their health."[3] The plan called for converting the old adobe hacienda into offices and club rooms, building a twenty-four-room hotel designed by William S. Hebbard and Irving Gill, and constructing five hundred canvas cottages. Under expert supervision, invalids could rent a cottage together with an acre or two of irrigated land and there, in the healthy out-of-doors, grow at least part of their livelihood. An elaborate promotional brochure claimed that over forty thousand invalids with pulmonary troubles were then living in Southern

San Diego's long-standing rivalry with Los Angeles is evident in the sarcasm of these lyrics written by Humphrey J. Stewart, the official organist for the Panama-California Exposition of 1915.

LUNG LAND
An Ode to Los Angeles

I.
There's a land that's dear to me,
South of old Tehachapi,
Where the people cough and hack
For the lung that can't come back!

CHORUS
Lung-land! Lung-land!
Wonderful realm of lung-land!
Cons and cripples gather there,
Where the climate's always fair,
In the open, or by stealth.
There they scrap for health and wealth;
There they raise their stand-by yell,
"Cough it up, both sick and well,"
All together, cheer like hell,
For dear lung-land!

II.
There we breathe the balmy breeze,
Beautiful Los Angeles!
There the sucker's cash we steal,
Waiting for our lungs to heal.

CHORUS
Lung-land! Lung-land!
Beautiful realm of lung-land!
There beneath the cloudless skies
Real estate doth soar and rise,
There we sell, but seldom buy,
Always knock the other guy;
Pat each other on the back,
Though we cough, and spit, and hack;
Yet for boosting we've the knack
In dear lung-land!

California and projected an excellent return on stock investments. The plan, however, never obtained the necessary backing.

Not all those who came to San Diego were ill. Many arrived healthy and wanted to stay that way. Concern for healthful living and working environments encouraged architects to design buildings that were well lighted and ventilated. Gill, who himself had gone to San Diego to recover his health, is perhaps the best known of these architects. Appalled at the number of poorly constructed cottages that were being tossed together, he wrote: "The family of health- or fortune-seekers who comes out here generally expects to camp in these poor shacks for but a short time and plans to sell the shiftless affair to some other impatient newcomer."[4] Gill set out to develop an architecture that was well constructed, simple in design, easy to maintain, and that encouraged healthful living.

Taking special note of the architectural possibilities afforded by the area's climate and inspired by the U-shaped adobe haciendas of San Diego's Hispanic past, Gill began to design houses with courtyards as an integral part of the living space. The Thomas Hamilton residence (1908), featured in the February 1915 issue of the *Craftsman,* contained an open central court enclosed on all four sides. Considered the main room of the house, this inner garden court included furniture, carpets, a wall fountain, and a copper-wire fly-screen cover. In 1911 Gill designed an even larger screen-covered court for the Henry H. Timken residence. This U-shaped plan allowed nearly every room on the main floor to open onto the court, which Gill surrounded with three spacious loggias. Writing for the *Craftsman,* Eloise Roorbach felt that "the construction of this house makes possible a much-needed return to home privacy."[5] Architecture could thus contribute to mental as well as physical health.

Among the many health seekers attracted to San Diego was the family of Ulysses S. Grant, Jr., who arrived in 1893. Anna Held, governess of the Grant's five children, accompanied them to San Diego. A hearty, down-to-earth woman, she was frequently amused when people later confused her with the petite Ziegfeld girl of the same name. Anna did, however, have some theatrical background, as she had been secretary and companion to the famous Shakespearean actress Ellen Terry and had even posed for the costume portion of John Singer Sargent's well-known portrait of the actress (National Portrait Gallery, London). After moving to San Diego, Held purchased a section of hillside above the ocean at La Jolla. About 1894 she hired Gill to design a sixteen-by-sixteen-foot room of redwood board-and-batten construction with Dutch doors and mullioned windows. Held shared the cottage with the writer Beatrice Harradan, who named it the Green Dragon, after her story of the same name.

Held's dynamic personality attracted numerous musicians, actors, writers, and artists to La Jolla. To accommodate them, she built additional cottages, each with its own name and individual character. The Den was constructed as a retreat for the famous Polish tragedienne Helena Modjeska and her husband, Count Bozenta. Other cottages were named the Wigwam, the Eyrie, the Doll House, and the Jack-O'Lantern. She built the Ark to resemble a ship, complete with porthole windows, deck chairs, life preservers, and a swing made from a lifeboat. Many of the cottages had mottoes carved or burned into the beams and mantels, and Held encouraged her guests to add their own. By 1901 the fame of the pseudo-bohemian colony had spread to such an extent that the *San Francisco Chronicle* proclaimed, "La Jolla is The Green Dragon and The Green Dragon is La Jolla."[6]

The famous baritone and pianist Max Heinrich visited the colony in 1904. Later that year he married Held, with Count Bozenta and Helena Modjeska acting as best man and matron of honor. When Anna and Max traveled in Europe, they left the Green Dragon Colony, as it became known, under the management of John and Frances Schroeder (plates 158, 159). The Schroeders purchased and leased property adjacent to the Green Dragon and constructed the Tyrolean Terrace Colony, which opened at the end of 1912. Unlike the Green Dragon group, whose cottages were scattered across the landscape, the Tyrolean

158. The Tyrolean Terrace Colony (foreground) and the Green Dragon Colony; photographed c. 1915.

LEFT
159. Wahnfried House, the Green Dragon Colony, c. 1910.
∾ *At the Green Dragon Colony, Anna Held built a grand cottage called The Wahnfried (Spirit-Peace) as a wedding present for her husband, Max Heinrich. The Wahnfried's interior featured Mission furniture, Indian rugs, and the spinning wheel that the actress Ellen Terry had used in Henry Irving's production of* Faust. *Over the large ocean-view windows, Held inscribed "Winter Storms Will Disappear before the Moon of My Delight."*

160. Grossmont Inn, 1913.

~ *Ed Fletcher commissioned Emmor Brooke Weaver to design the Grossmont Inn in 1913. The inn's French chef served breakfast, lunch, tea, and dinner to visitors, who took the stage from the El Cajon train depot. Fletcher later converted the inn into his family home.*

A Cottage in God's Garden

There's a cottage in God's garden,
Upon a mountain high,
Away from strife and turmoil
And all life's din and cry.
Away from care and sorrow,
From all life's tears and woe,
A cottage in God's garden
Where I am free to go.

There's a cottage in God's garden,
Where my tired feet may rest,
And weary though my soul may be,
My spirit there is blessed.
The wild birds chant their carols,
And wild flowers bloom galore
Out in God's lovely garden—
How could I ask for more?

Carrie Jacobs-Bond
Memoirs of Ed Fletcher (San Diego: privately printed, 1952).

Terrace cottages lined the streets, perhaps anticipating the increasing number of travelers with their own automobiles. The Swiss theme of the colony was carried through to the cottage names, such as Tyrol, Geneva, Lucerne, and Matterhorn. Frances Schroeder included a restaurant and an Arts and Crafts gift shop, which sold "hand-made jewelry, coppers, brasses, blankets, stencils and all the unique things in handicraft work at its best."[7]

Far inland from La Jolla's breezy shores another "artists' colony" was taking shape. In 1910 *Southwest Builder and Contractor* declared: "The little resort of Grossmont in El Cajon valley, near San Diego, is destined to become the center of a brilliant literary, musical and artistic colony, if the present plans of property holders are realized."[8] Unlike the Green Dragon Colony, which grew as if by accident, the Grossmont Art Colony was intended from the beginning to be the home of personalities from the worlds of literature and music. The partners in this venture were the San Diego real-estate developer Ed Fletcher and William Gross, a theatrical agent who had himself spent some time on the stage. Partly motivated by the hope of enriching San Diego's cultural life, the developers realized that famous personalities could attract other buyers.

Fletcher and Gross filed the subdivision, named Grossmont Park, in 1910 with the local authorities. They installed water and electrical lines and planted numerous trees, including eucalyptus and rare Torrey pines. In 1913 the actress Lillian Russell opened the first road. In order to launch the colony, Fletcher and Gross gave one lot to the famous operatic contralto Ernestine Schumann-Heink, who in 1913 constructed on it a home designed by Del Harris. Other artists looking for a quiet refuge from their demanding careers soon followed.[9] Carrie Jacobs-Bond, the writer of such well-known songs as "I Love You Truly," also joined the colony. She described her redwood cottage, which she christened Nestorest, in *House Beautiful* of June 1914. The dimensions of the cottage had to be twenty-five by twenty-nine feet because "that was the only space between the boulders." To create a silvery effect in the interior, she had the redwood painted gray and then had most of the paint rubbed off before it dried. Using the eucalyptus as the inspiration for her color scheme, she had the wicker furniture painted a soft gray green and repeated the color in the fireplace tiles. Her fondness for Grossmont inspired Jacobs-Bond to write "A Cottage in God's Garden," which she published as sheet music in 1917.

Most of the homes constructed at Grossmont were built of redwood in the Arts and Crafts style. In 1911 Richard S. Requa designed a cottage for Owen Wister, the author of *The Virginian*. Clad in shingles, the bungalow featured three screened sleeping porches. Emmor Brook Weaver designed a small train depot and the Grossmont Inn for Ed Fletcher in 1913 (plate 160). A rambling redwood structure with heavy beam construction, the inn looked picturesque against the huge granite boulders on the site.

In addition to the artists' colonies developing in La Jolla and Grossmont, several utopian communities also blossomed in San Diego at this time. Katherine

Tingley established the International Brotherhood and Theosophical Society on Point Loma in 1897. Theosophy, founded in 1875 by Helena P. Blavatsky—whose writings *Isis Unveiled* (1877) and *Secret Doctrine* (1888) became the original texts for the movement—did not claim to be a new religion. It attempted to search through the collected wisdom of all peoples to draw out certain basic, universal truths. Theosophical doctrine did not include an anthropomorphic god, positing instead that all beings were expressions of Universal Divinity. The concepts of karma and reincarnation were basic to Theosophical thought.

Katherine Tingley had taken over as leader of the organization in 1896. Her agents purchased 132 acres on Point Loma, the peninsula that forms the outer boundary of San Diego Bay. Eventually the property grew to over five hundred acres. In *Our Italy* (1891), Charles Dudley Warner had described the view from the summit of that site as one of the three finest in the world. After laying the cornerstone for her School for the Revival of the Lost Mysteries of Antiquity, Tingley traveled to New York to obtain the needed backing for the venture. Her reform agenda included improving the conditions of orphans and "unfortunate" women, assisting prisoners to become useful citizens, helping working men and women realize the "nobility of their calling," creating understanding between so-called savage and civilized races, abolishing capital punishment, and generally relieving human suffering.[10]

A charismatic woman, Tingley garnered the financial support of many wealthy people, including the diamond broker E. August Neresheimer and Albert G. Spalding of sporting-goods fame. Soon a White City, known as Lomaland, with

161. Point Loma Theosophical Society, c. 1906.
～ *An Egyptian-style gate frames the main buildings of Katherine Tingley's White City.*

162. Benjamin Gordon. *Untitled [Moonlight Landscape],* c. 1910. Oil on board in carved and gilded wood frame, 25¼ x 31½ in., framed. San Diego Historical Society; Gift of Mrs. Iverson Harris in memory of her husband.

architecture unlike anything previously seen in the United States, began to take shape on the peninsula (plate 161). The diamond-shaped Homestead (later renamed the Râja Yoga Academy) and the round Temple, both with colored-glass domes, were among the earliest built. (They no longer exist, but other structures from the complex survive as part of Point Loma Nazarene College.) The year 1901 saw the completion there of the first open-air Greek theater in America. Some early plans for structures are labeled "Original design by Katherine Tingley," though her architectural training seems to have come more from occult studies than from any course in known architectural styles. Clusters of round, wood-frame Lotus Homes were constructed to house orphans arriving from war-torn Cuba and other places. In later years several trained architects were among the residents of Lomaland.

As the community developed, the diverse activities at Point Loma attracted many accomplished people to the movement. Tingley placed strong emphasis on cultural pursuits such as music, dance, drama, literature, and art. Artists were encouraged to move to Point Loma, and their work done there, frequently full of symbolism, shows an interest in ethereal effects and "hidden" qualities (plate 162).[11] Reginald Machell, Lomaland's most important artist, had been introduced to Theosophy by Blavatsky herself. He became the main artistic influence on the community, providing numerous paintings, carvings, and wall decorations.

Originally a painter, Machell began to make heavily carved and detailed frames for some of his works. After he arrived at Point Loma his interest in carving turned to other forms, and he created a remarkable collection of screens, chairs, stools, plant stands, and other furnishings for use at the headquarters (plates 157, 164). The flowing lines are a hybrid of Celtic and Art Nouveau influences, recalling the design work of Edward Burne-Jones. Apparently matching pieces are frequently of slightly different size and varying detail, and the individual panels of his screens often exhibit different patterns. Some of the earliest examples of his furniture were finished in metallic gold paint, but all of them were eventually painted a cream color and antiqued. One suspects some deep symbolism in the carving of even the humblest piece.

In addition to Machell, a number of other artists worked at Lomaland. Several of these were instructors at the Râja Yoga Academy. Others learned skills to produce goods for sale in the Woman's Exchange and Mart, which had a branch outlet in Tingley's Isis Theater building in San Diego. An Arts and Crafts Department was established in 1903, which produced decorated china, gesso-work panels, wood and copper plaques decorated with images of Buddha, fancy leatherwork, and novelties made from dried kelp and silkworm cocoons. Grace Betts, sister of the prominent New York portrait painter Louis Betts, learned the ancient art of batik dying using the wax-resist method, and she taught the skill to Marian Plummer. The two women produced some outstanding examples on silk (plate 165) for sale in the Mart. The isolating nature of the Theosophical Society encouraged some of its artists to work in styles that elsewhere had become outdated. The Symbolist trends found in their paintings continued long after the

BELOW

163. Reginald Machell teaching woodcarving at the Râja Yoga Academy, c. 1905–10.

OPPOSITE

164. Reginald Machell, designer and carver. *Katherine Tingley's Throne Chair with Two Other Chairs,* c. 1905–10, for the Theosophical Society, Point Loma. Carved and painted wood. Left: 37¾ x 16 x 16 in., San Diego Historical Society; Gift of the Theosophical Society, Pasadena. Center: 52½ x 29½ x 25 in., Archives, Theosophical Society Library, Pasadena. Right: 37 x 17½ x 17¼ in., San Diego Historical Society; Gift of the Theosophical Society, Pasadena.

Symbolist movement had subsided elsewhere. Batiks signed by Plummer after her 1931 marriage to Leonard Lester are still strongly influenced by the design aesthetic of the Arts and Crafts movement.

The Theosophical Society survived the death of Katherine Tingley in 1929 and struggled through the Depression until World War II; changes in property-tax laws made it impossible to continue at Lomaland. In 1942 the Theosophical Society moved to the Los Angeles area, and it remains active in Pasadena to this day.

A different type of utopian experiment appealed to those interested in independence: the American dream of owning one's own house and making a living from one's own property. William E. Smythe, a well-known leader of the national land-reclamation movement, relocated to San Diego in 1901. In the hope of settling the area surrounding San Diego and at the same time diverting some of the midwestern immigrants heading for Los Angeles, he became interested in the concept of "little lands" as expressed by Bolton Hall in *A Little Land and a Living* (1908). Smythe gave a back-to-the-land speech at San Diego's Garrick Theater on July 28, 1908, where he proclaimed, "I believe God made Southern California to be the paradise of the common man—the chosen home of those who would work and live in the midst of the most ideal condition nature ever devised."[12] A few days later, Smythe helped establish the Little Landers Corporation.

The corporation purchased 550 acres of land south of San Diego, near the Mexican border, and named it San Ysidro. Home sites in the village were available for $250, and acre lots were sold for $350 to $550, depending on the location and the quality of the soil. The colony was based on the principle that one man, through intensive cultivation of a single acre of land, could produce more than enough to provide for his family. Although it was claimed that the community was open to everyone, in fact Asians, African-Americans, and Mexicans were excluded.[13] Dissatisfaction with the general management led the colonists to separate from the original corporation and create their own company. They organized an irrigation district and established the Little Landers Market in San Diego to sell their surplus produce.

The colony appeared to be succeeding despite its problems, and it began to receive wide attention. In August 1912 an article in the *Craftsman* reported: "If we should accept the theory of the Littlelander, and we must because it has been conclusively proved . . . then we have a solution to some of the most widespread and pressing problems of our day." Also that year several distinguished visitors praised the experiment, including a statesman from Australia, a leader of Palestine's Zionist colonies, and a Progressive politician from Wisconsin, where a settlement patterned after Little Landers had been established.

To spread the word further, in January 1916 Smythe began to publish a magazine called *Little Lands in America* (plate 166). It contained practical hints on gardening, beekeeping, raising fur-bearing rabbits, building a mushroom cellar, and other articles of interest to Little Landers. Bernard Maybeck agreed to write a series of articles entitled "Maybeck Homes for Little Lands." A second colony, Los

165. Marian Plummer Lester. *Batik of Landscape with Trees,* c. 1910–20, for the Theosophical Society, Point Loma. Batik dye on pongee silk, 14 x 9 in. San Diego Historical Society; Gift of the artist.

Little Lands in America

February, 1916   Price 10 Cents

A MAYBECK HOUSE---Sketch by the Designer of
the Palace of Fine Arts, Panama-Pacific Exposition

Terrenitos ("Little Lands" in Spanish), was founded in the suburbs of Los Angeles in the area now known as Tujunga. The San Francisco Bay Area became home to a third colony, called Hayward Heath, near the town of Hayward.[14]

Despite Smythe's claims that the experiment was a success, increasing problems began to undermine the original colony at San Ysidro. Many of the colonists discovered that they needed outside employment to make ends meet. Some residents were older and retired, without proper knowledge of gardening. When the Industrial Workers of the World actively supported the socialist insurrection against the Mexican government in 1911 and much of the fighting took place directly across the border, the colonists grew uneasy and the unrest discouraged newcomers. A disastrous flood in 1916 left 150 Little Landers homeless, two dead, and much of the usable farmland ruined. Many of those not yet disheartened, particularly the younger members, left to join the war effort during World War I. By 1918, the year Smythe left California, the Little Lander experiment at San Ysidro had ended.

ABOVE

166. Cover of *Little Lands in America,* February 1916.

OPPOSITE, TOP

167. Advertisement from *California Garden,* October 1912.

OPPOSITE, BOTTOM

168. Anna and Albert Valentien at work on pottery in their San Diego plant, with Arthur Dovey in the background, c. 1912.

San Diego's involvement with reform ideals and the Arts and Crafts aesthetic began to manifest itself in other ways. The progressive architecture of Irving Gill and his followers and other innovative designers created the need for compatible furnishings. Several prominent local retailers began to carry the products of national Arts and Crafts manufacturers. The Marston Company department store, owned by George W. Marston, who lived in a large Craftsman-style house designed by Hebbard and Gill, began to advertise that it was "sole agent" in San Diego for Gustav Stickley's Craftsman furniture (plate 167). Promotional material for the Roycroft shops stated that their goods were available through J. Jessop and Sons, Jewelers. Alfred Stahel and Sons, retailers of fine home furnishings, carried selections from Teco and other art potteries.

The local artist and designer Alice Klauber helped establish the Torii Shop with Robert G. Nichols in 1910, which specialized in artistic home furnishings and wall coverings. Klauber's special interest in oriental art accounts for the shop's being named after a type of Japanese gateway and for the Asian origin of some of their merchandise. When the shop closed in 1913, the Coronado photographer Harold A. Taylor opened a store on Sixth Street in San Diego and announced, "Mr. John Skidmore Bush, formerly of The Torii Shop, will have in connection his display of Art Craft Pottery, Jewelry and Electric Fixtures."[15] Taylor's gallery began to carry Rookwood pottery; Paul Elder books (some illustrated with Taylor's photographs); desk sets, candlesticks, and bowls made of California laurel and redwood burl; hand-tooled leather bags, purses, and book covers; and painted wicker baskets and trays.

In addition to its sunshine, San Diego had another natural resource that proved to be of value to a small local industry. San Diego County contained excellent clay beds as well as the feldspar and pegmatite necessary for the manufacture of the finest pottery and porcelain. North of San Diego, the Elsinore Pottery and Fire Clay Company had incorporated in 1885. In 1888 Henri and Wilfrida Fairweather constructed a kiln at their home in San Diego and christened it the New Palissy, after the sixteenth-century French ceramic artist Bernard Palissy. By 1890 some optimists were predicting that San Diego would exceed both Cincinnati, Ohio, and Trenton, New Jersey, in the production of high-quality pottery.[16] Unfortunately, this and many other notions became victims of the nationwide economic depression of the 1890s. Not until the decade of the 1910s did San Diego achieve any real distinction in the ceramic arts.

In 1905 Anna and Albert Valentien ended their long association as decorators for the Rookwood Pottery in Cincinnati. Settling in San Diego in 1908, the Valentiens eventually established a pottery there (plate 168). The local banker Joseph W. Sefton, Jr., provided the financial backing for the venture and hired Gill to design a pottery plant in 1910. Sefton served on the committee for San Diego's upcoming 1915 Panama-California Exposition, and part of his interest in establishing the pottery may have been to provide a source of tiles for the Spanish Colonial–style buildings being designed for the fair. Since both Anna and Albert were decorators, an experienced potter was necessary for the new venture. The Valentiens contacted Arthur Dovey, who had worked with them at Rookwood before moving to the Niloak Pottery in Arkansas. Dovey arrived early in 1911, and production probably started shortly thereafter.[17]

Not surprisingly, the pottery produced by the Valentiens in San Diego shows the influence of their years with Rookwood. Many of the shapes and design elements are similar to those found in Rookwood pieces, some of which may have originated with the Valentiens. The Valentien shape book records the outlines of forty-three basic shapes and another forty-seven shapes prefixed with the letter "Z," indicating decoration in low relief. Both Valentiens had traveled to Paris for the 1900 international exposition there, and many later Valentien pieces show the influence of Art Nouveau design, with swirling plant forms, peacock feathers, dragonflies, and fish. Trained as a sculptor, Anna had experimented with sculptured shapes at Rookwood and continued this interest in San Diego, executing several figural pieces (plate 169). Albert created some fine painted vases and others with complicated linear patterns in low relief (plate 170). The Valentiens preferred soft to dead matte glazes, often with very subtle gradations of atomized color.

The experimental nature of some of the Valentien pottery leads to speculation about what they might have achieved had the venture survived. Unfortunately, the area around the pottery plant began to develop as a residential neighborhood, and people complained about smoke from the kiln. Although some of the tiles for the 1915 exposition did come from the Valentien Pottery, the operation proved too small to fill the fair's needs. California China Products Company obtained the con-

BELOW

169. Valentien Pottery Company (Anna Valentien, decorator). *Vase,* 1911–13. Earthenware with three modeled figures; dull finish, 16¾ x 16½ in. Mr. and Mrs. Albert A. Jaussaud.

OPPOSITE

170. Valentien Pottery Company (Albert Valentien, decorator). *Vase,* 1911–13. Earthenware with low-relief interlace design; dull finish, 10 x 4¼ in. San Diego Historical Society; Purchase from the Mrs. William A. Edwards Curatorial Fund.

tract for the exposition's tiles, and by the end of 1913 the Valentien plant was being dismantled.

California China Products Company had been incorporated by Walter and Charles B. Nordhoff in 1911. The company purchased a factory site on the railroad in National City as well as a kaolin mine on top of El Cajon Mountain. The plant included facilities for reducing and preparing the raw material, three eighteen-foot kilns, and a test laboratory. California China Products Company adopted the tradename Kaospar for its wares.

An extensive article in the *San Diego Union* claimed that California China Products Company was the only white-ware pottery in America that mined and prepared the crude material for its own use as well as being the first porcelain factory in the Far West.[18] The article went on to state that the company produced tiles, electrical porcelain, and high-voltage insulators and also manufactured porcelain tableware, "Beleek art ware," Rockingham ware, and both enameled and faience tiles for mantels and mural decoration. In January 1912 Wesley H. Trippett from Redlands joined the firm, and the *National City News* reported that he would "make shapes in vases and decorative porcelain as well as a line of decorated mantel tile."[19] Since nothing other than tiles and a few yellow bowls marked KAOSPAR have ever been identified, it seems likely that the other types of ware mentioned were never actually put into production. Trippett's final illness and death from tuberculosis in 1913 may have precluded further work in this area. Tile production became the main focus at California China Products Company.

The Nordhoffs apparently did not abandon the idea of producing artware. In 1913 Herman and Kenneth Markham of Ann Arbor, Michigan, moved their pottery operation to National City. Having already decided to relocate to the Pacific Coast, the Markhams toured the California China Products Company plant; Walter Nordhoff convinced them of the advantages of National City and provided them with space in his facilities, although the Markhams' entity still remained independent.

Herman Markham's initial attempts at making pottery originated in his interest in growing roses. Using clay from his own yard, he created a porous pottery vase that kept the water cool by evaporation, helping the flowers to stay fresh longer. As his experiments progressed, he developed a type of surface decoration, the exact process of which still remains a mystery. In the October 1905 issue of *Sketch Book,* Lillian Gray Jarvie noted that the pottery gave the impression of great age and that it "does not tell all of its story with the first inspection . . . but is ever revealing new delights, colors not before discovered, unexpected combinations of the delicate traceries, and latent tones of light and shade."

Two main types of surface finish were developed by the Markhams. Reseau ware has a fine texture of slightly raised weblike traceries (plate 171). Arabesque ware is coarser in texture, with an intricate maze of fossillike lines in low relief (plate 172). Both types have a matte glaze in dark muted browns, greens, and pur-

171. Markham Pottery. *Vase,* c. 1913–21. Earthenware with dark brown glaze, 5 x 3 in. The Oakland Museum; Gift of the estate of Helen Hathaway White.

172. Markham Pottery. *Three Vases,* c. 1913–21. Earthenware with pigmented dull finish. Left: 9⅞ x 9 in. Center: 5⅛ x 3¼ in. Right: 6¾ x 5⅜ in. Stephanie Lynn and David Mills.

ples and occasionally vibrant oranges, reds, and yellows. Sometimes the glazes exhibit a metallic appearance. Shapes are simple in outline and often copy oriental forms because Markham felt that these types would not detract from his unique surface patterns and textures. No two pieces were alike and each received an individual number, those numbered higher than 6,000 being made in National City.

After moving to California, Markham Pottery received a gold medal at the Panama-California International Exposition of 1916. Unfortunately, California China Products Company began to experience difficulties and in 1917 sold most of its equipment to the West Coast Tile Company in a stock exchange. Forced to

relocate their pottery operation, the Markhams moved to a new location in National City, filing incorporation papers in 1921 in an attempt to raise new capital. The plan failed, and the corporate charter was suspended the following year, shortly before Herman's death.[20]

A few San Diego craftspeople tried their hand at metalwork. Although J. Jessop and Sons, Jewelers, operated primarily as a retail store, their manufacturing department did produce a few outstanding objects. About 1905 Jessop decided to build a large ornamental street clock to stand outside his store. Using San Diego tourmaline and other local gemstones for the jewels, the Jessop manufacturing department designed and created every part of the clock mechanism, which won a gold medal at the California State Fair in 1907. Although not particularly Arts and Crafts in design, the twenty-one-foot-tall clock remains a remarkable achievement for a small retail jewelry store.

While working on the street clock, the Jessop manufacturing department was also engaged on another unusual object. For the Church of Saint James in La Jolla, a Mission Revival structure designed by Irving Gill in 1907, they created a baptismal font using a pair of giant clamshells donated by Virginia Scripps. Jessop's craftspeople rimmed the shells in silver and inlaid a silver dedication plate.[21] A stand made of wrought iron nicely harmonized with Gill's architectural setting.

In 1907 President Theodore Roosevelt sent twenty-seven warships on a round-the-world cruise as a demonstration of military might. He particularly intended this display to impress the Japanese, as there was a growing fear of increased military strength in the Far East. The Jessop firm obtained the commission to produce a silver presentation box for Rear Admiral Robley D. Evans, commander of the Great White Fleet (plate 173). Designed to be a suitable memento of the admiral's visit to San Diego, the box is lined with wood cut from one of the ancient olive trees at the San Diego mission. Low reliefs in silver of Evans's flagship, the U.S.S. *Connecticut,* as well as images of San Diego's Hispanic past, decorate the ends and sides of the box. The top supports a minutely detailed replica of Juan Cabrillo's ship *San Salvador.* At the four corners of the lid are branches of grapes, olives, oranges, and lemons symbolizing the bounty of Southern California.[22]

Although the details of the box may seem a bit excessive, the basic shape shows the influence of contemporary English craftwork, particularly the designs of Charles R. Ashbee and the Guild of Handicraft. The bracket feet attached with silver rivets and the flying corner handles set with turquoise cabochons are reminiscent of similar features on English metalwork of the period. A gold brooch in the shape of a key to the city set with local gems originally accompanied the box—a gift for Mrs. Evans, the admiral's wife—but now is missing.

The Jessop company retailed the work of other craftspeople, including Anna Valentien, who produced handwrought jewelry for them. Valentien's interest in crafts other than pottery had started before she left Cincinnati. Soon after her

173. J. Jessop and Sons, Jewelers. *Covered Box,* 1908. Presented to Rear Admiral Robley D. Evans, commander of the Great White Fleet, by the citizens of San Diego in 1908. Silver, olive wood, and cabochon turquoise, 7½ x 7¼ x 4½ in. The Oakland Museum; Gift of Florence Dixon in honor of Hazel V. Bray, the Tribute Fund, and Martha and William Steen.

arrival in San Diego, she created a decorative metal plaque for the Holly Sefton Memorial Hospital for Children (1909), one of Gill's most modern designs.

In 1911 Valentien became involved in creating one of the most beautiful Arts and Crafts buildings in San Diego. The Wednesday Club, a local women's organization, commissioned Hazel Wood Waterman to design a new clubhouse for them. She in turn asked her friend Alice Klauber to assist with the interiors. Waterman designed a low, Gill-like stucco structure fronted by a broad, open terrace with columned pergolas at either end. Klauber created the club's logo, a caravel-type sailing vessel. Ernest A. Batchelder produced four different tile panels, depicting caravels, that were inset across the facade. He also supplied tiles for the immense recessed fireplace in the auditorium and for the smaller fireplace in the drawing room. Klauber's Torii Shop provided the wallpapers for the interiors, which featured beautiful openwork air-vent tiles designed by Waterman and art-glass wall sconces. Anna Valentien's contribution included the club's sign and door plates in etched copper and a pierced brass-and-art-glass lantern depicting a caravel, which hung from a decorative bracket next to the entry.

174. Looking over the model farm at the Panama-California Exposition, Balboa Park, San Diego, 1915.

ও *The exposition featured a nearly seventeen-acre model farm with a citrus grove and a bungalow, all sponsored by the seven counties of Southern California. The farm had been planted several years before, so that by the time the fair opened in January 1915, it had already become productive. Daily demonstrations of the actual work of maintaining the farm were intended to inspire converts to the back-to-the-land movement. Blueprints for the handsome modern bungalow, built at a cost of $4,000, could be had for one dollar per set.*

175. Anna Valentien. *Wall Mirror with Sconces,* c. 1910–20. Patinated copper with cutout overlay design and mirror, 18 x 10 x 3 in. San Diego Historical Society; Gift of Mavina McFeron.

176. Paul Lohman, decorator. *Vase,* c. 1915–20. Austrian porcelain blank painted overglaze in persimmon red and black, 9¾ x 4¼ in. San Diego Historical Society; Gift of Florence D. Hord.

After the unsuccessful Valentien Pottery venture, Anna taught elementary manual training and arts and crafts at the San Diego State Normal School. She listed among her skills wood carving, weaving, beadwork, metal craft (plate 175), leather craft, basketry, jewelry, batik, macramé, and wickerwork. At the 1915 Panama-California Exposition, her crafts display received a gold medal; the following year at the international extension of that exposition she won another gold medal for crafts. In 1919 her batik opera bags won the highest award and cash prize at the California State Fair.

When it was announced that the Panama Canal would be completed in 1915, San Diegans took notice. To celebrate their city's status as the first U.S. port of call for ships traveling through the canal, they decided to hold a world's fair. San Francisco also made a bid for an exposition and eventually won out over San Diego for the officially sanctioned international fair. Undeterred, San Diego proceeded with its own plans, making it the smallest city ever to host a world's fair (see plate 174). Naming their fair the Panama-California Exposition, the governing committee decided to concentrate on cultural rather than industrial exhibits, emphasizing land reclamation, horticulture, and the "history of man."

Surprisingly few records of the exhibits and awards for San Diego's exposition survive. Much confusion has arisen from the fact that the fair reopened for a second year as the Panama-California International Exposition (some of the foreign exhibits were moved down after the close of the San Francisco fair because the war in Europe prevented their return). The Foreign Arts Building included displays from Japan and China, and Japanese craftsmen constructed a tea garden and pavilion. An Indian Arts Building and a full-scale reconstructed pueblo, complete with Native Americans from New Mexico, featured their crafts and customs. The Pala Chief Gem Mine sold picture frames, letter openers, and other souvenirs made of hammered copper set with local tourmaline cabochons. Awards listed for 1916 include gold medals in arts and crafts to Frederick Hürten Rhead, Douglas Donaldson, Ernest A. Batchelder, Fred H. Robertson, the Markham and Alberhill potteries, and Anna Valentien (in the Women's Department). Silver medals went to Douglas Donaldson and to Arequipa Pottery.[23]

For the Women's Headquarters at the fair, Alice Klauber designed a reception room in persimmon red, black, and gray, known as the Persimmon Room. Its decor included comfortable rattan furniture and persimmon branches in jardinieres. The persimmon color seems to have gained particular local significance. The German-born china decorator Paul Lohman arrived in San Diego about the time of the exposition. He achieved recognition for originating decorated china called Persimmon Red, a color that proved very difficult to use and often came out uneven (plate 176). Lohman's color studies and surviving examples of Persimmon Red ware show a strong interest in Arts and Crafts design motifs with geometric patterns and stylized plant forms. From his San Diego studio, Lohman created extensive hand-decorated dinner services for European royalty.[24]

Most of the furniture produced in San Diego that can be classified as Arts and Crafts related directly to architectural commissions. One of the earliest of these, a house for Wheeler J. Bailey spectacularly sited on the cliffs at La Jolla, was designed by Irving Gill and Frank Mead in 1907 (plates 46, 47, 178). To complement the rustic redwood board-and-batten interior, the architects designed a complete suite of furniture made of the same wood. Gill liked redwood for its practical qualities, preferring to leave it hand-polished without stain, wax, or varnish (plate 177). Writing about the Bailey House for the *Craftsman,* Natalie Curtis indicated that "the chairs were the most original note in the room . . . and were a sort of camp-chair with back and seat of cow-skin, the hide with all its decorative markings of black, white or red, being uppermost, tacked to the wooden frame with big brass nails" (plate 179).[25] A line engraved around the edge of the tabletops and large iron-loop drawer pulls eased the severity of the furniture's straight lines.

177. Irving Gill and Frank Mead. *Desk,* 1907, from the Wheeler J. Bailey House, La Jolla. Redwood with wrought-iron pull, 28¾ x 41¼ x 27¹⁵⁄₁₆ in. Mrs. Sim Bruce Richards.

ABOVE

178. Irving Gill and Frank Mead, Wheeler J. Bailey House, La Jolla, California, 1907.

RIGHT

179. Irving Gill and Frank Mead. *Chair,* 1907, from the Wheeler J. Bailey House, La Jolla. Redwood and (replaced) cowhide, 38⅛ x 19⅞ x 19½ in. Mrs. Sim Bruce Richards.

In 1914 Bailey decided to construct a guest house on property adjoining his residence. He hired Mead, now in partnership with Richard S. Requa, to create a pueblo-style structure called Hopi House, complete with exposed beam ends and ladders to the roof. The architects designed a full set of redwood furniture, including an ingenious armchair in which the seat and back recline as a unit. Decorated with cutout chevrons and Indian stair-step designs, the suite includes a chest of drawers whose pulls are made of rawhide strips extending through slots cut in the drawer fronts (plate 180). Hopis were commissioned to produce woven shades for the light fixtures and a large rug.[26]

Custom-furniture designs were often created for specific ecclesiastical projects. In 1920 the Mission Hills Congregational Church asked Irving Gill's nephew Louis J. Gill to draw up plans for a new building to replace the redwood chapel that Emmor Brooke Weaver had designed in 1911. Apparently over Gill's objections, the building committee asked him to maintain the flavor of the old structure. He later scribbled defensively across one of his presentation sketches, "They wanted a 'bungalow' church."[27] Louis J. Gill designed a sturdy communion table, two massive altar chairs (plate 181), and a lectern for the church. The bold forms of these pieces were finished in flat sheets of carefully joined mahogany veneer. He softened the design by adding an inlaid line of lighter-colored wood

226

180. Frank Mead and Richard S. Requa. *Chest of Drawers,* 1915, from the Wheeler J. Bailey "Hopi House," La Jolla. Redwood with (replaced) leather pulls, 31 x 41⅞ x 19½ in. San Diego Historical Society; Gift of Wheeler G. North.

181. Louis J. Gill. *Altar Chair,* 1920, one of a pair from the Mission Hills Congregational Church, San Diego. Mahogany veneer, 53⅛ x 25⅛ x 21¾ in. Mission Hills First Congregational Church–United Church of Christ, San Diego.

182. View of Torrey pines, with the Pacific Ocean in the background.
 The rugged profile of the rare Torrey pine became an inspiration for many artists and crafts-people, symbolizing far Southern California as much as the Monterey cypress and redwood symbol-ized Northern California.

that traced an arch-topped rectangle in the center of the chair backs and front of the lectern.

Another project that included custom furnishings was the Torrey Pines Lodge. After purchasing several lots north of La Jolla to protect the finest stands of rare Torrey pines (plate 182), Ellen Scripps financed the construction of a lodge for the San Diego Board of Park Commissioners in 1922. Designed in the pueblo style by Requa and Herbert Jackson, the adobe structure was built by a crew of Native American workmen. The lodge provided quarters for the park's caretaker as well as public dining facilities. The *San Diego Union* noted: "The lodge's furnishings will be of Hopi Indian design. Indian blankets, rugs, and pottery will be used for drapery and decoration. Pottery, rugs, baskets, blankets, and other products of Indian artisans will be offered for sale, as well as baskets made from needles of the Torrey pine."[28] The architects designed furnishings for the lodge, including brass bracket-lanterns with a cutout stair-step design that was

ABOVE

183. William Templeton Johnson, designer, and attributed to Harry Brawner, maker. *Chest,* 1926–28. Carved redwood with hammered-iron hinges and handles, 22 x 52 x 24¾ in. Connie and George Beardsley.

RIGHT

184. William Templeton Johnson, designer, and attributed to Harry Brawner, maker. *Desk,* 1926–28. Carved redwood, 51 x 38 x 14⅝ in. Connie and George Beardsley.

repeated on the porch columns and display cases in the lounge.[29] Made of red-wood wire-brushed to give the appearance of weathered wood, the cases were assembled with large-head wrought-iron nails. Lampshades were made of Torrey pine needles.

In 1926 George W. Marston and his family decided to upgrade their property by adding a garden to the north. John Nolen's office prepared preliminary plans for a formal garden, and the local architect William Templeton Johnson supplied drawings for some of the architectural details. In 1928 Johnson's office created a handsome eucalyptus-leaf-and-pod design used to decorate the hand-carved corbels on the garden fountain and the capitals on the columns of the garden house. He repeated this design as a decorative panel in a suite of garden furniture that included a bench, storage chest, and drop-front desk (plates 183, 184). Well versed in Spanish architecture and furniture design, Johnson found his prototypes in the long bench, *arca* chest, and *vargueño* desk typical of early Spanish interiors. The use of redwood and the eucalyptus motif added a California touch to this beautiful and appropriate blending of contemporary and historical design.

These special-order furniture commissions can frequently be assigned to specific architectural firms through surviving drawings. Determining the actual manufacturers is a different story. In some cases, the furniture could have been made by the finish carpenters on the construction crew. Other pieces may have been subcontracted to specialized cabinet shops. One building contractor, Roy F. McCrary, also listed himself in the 1908 and 1909 San Diego city directories under furniture manufacturers as a maker of "Mission furniture." The cabinet-maker William F. Franzen operated a shop in San Diego from 1909 to 1923. The San Diego Historical Society owns a large and impressive Arts and Crafts–style library table signed by Franzen that uses Stickley hammered-copper hardware and demonstrates that high-quality work was indeed available from local shops.

San Diego also produced some excellent presswork during this period. The Theosophical Society operated an extensive publishing operation (see plate 185), and their exhibit of printing and graphic arts received the gold medal at the Leipzig Exposition of 1914. In 1917 Phineas Packard and Charles Kessler acquired the press operation that had been functioning as an exhibit at the San Diego exposition. It was called Arts and Crafts Press, but not enough examples of its early work are yet known to determine how well the product suited the name.

The local press most consistent with the design ideals of the Arts and Crafts movement was Denrich Press of Chula Vista. James D. Marsden, a wealthy engineer, retired to a five-acre citrus ranch in Chula Vista, which he named Liptuswood. After the novelty of retirement wore off, he took up printing as a hobby, having studied the trade in his youth. Working out of his barn, Marsden did his printing for free, for friends and neighbors. When word spread about the quality of his work, Denrich Press was born. His son, Hillis, joined him in the venture, as did his daughter, Virginia Goodrich, who provided beautiful ink illustrations for many of their printing jobs.

229

The earliest work carrying the Denrich Press imprint dates to about 1908. In 1910 the Marsdens produced an attractive booklet on the newly restored Casa de Estudillo, the so-called Ramona's Marriage Place. One of their finest productions was the Cabrillo memorial souvenir album, published for the Order of Panama in 1913 in an edition of one hundred numbered copies. With text by Charles Fletcher Lummis, illustrations by Virginia Goodrich, and an embossed cover medallion by the British sculptor Allen Hutchinson, it is an outstanding example of fine presswork.

Most of the stained glass used in San Diego in the late nineteenth century came from manufacturers and designers in San Francisco. John Mallon and his successors and the artist Bruce Porter created numerous windows in Southern California. San Diego's first stained-glass artist, William F. Jungk, set up business about 1907 after having worked in Dubuque, Iowa, and briefly in Los Angeles. Jungk executed work for Gill, Requa, and other local architects, including the boldly patterned windows for Gill's Church of Christ, Scientist (1909). He also made windows for Ernestine Schumann-Heink's home in Grossmont as well as fancy mirrors for San Diego's infamous red-light district. Besides windows, Jungk did mosaic work and made leaded-glass lampshades and jewelry boxes. Jungk's nephew, Fred Wieland, joined him in the mid-1920s and became the leading art-glass maker of the next generation in San Diego.

In San Diego, as in most of America, involvement in the Arts and Crafts movement reached its peak during the years between 1905 and 1915. Even then,

185. Cover of Lomaland Souvenir Album, 1913.

there probably was never a very large local market for Arts and Crafts goods. Early interior photographs illustrate some modern tendencies embodied in occasional pieces of Mission furniture, but only rarely does one find a consciously Arts and Crafts interior. Even the presumably enlightened owners of some of Gill's most progressive designs frequently furnished their homes with highly ornamental furniture and Victorian bric-a-brac. More modest homeowners who might be able to purchase a new bungalow could not always afford to furnish it in the latest style.

During the years of Prohibition (1920–33), San Diego changed dramatically as it became a gateway to the liquor and gambling available across the border. The city began to reject the modern trends initiated by Gill and others in favor of an artificial Spanish-Mexican look that would enhance its association with Mexico. The post–World War I affluence of prospective home buyers created little sympathy for the austere designs promoted by Stickley and Gill. Some of Gill's followers, particularly Richard S. Requa, and other local architects, including William Templeton Johnson, adapted the more romantic details of Spanish and other Mediterranean styles to suit Southern California. Annoyed by the misuse of the term "Spanish architecture," Requa announced that what he and the others were doing was completely modern, writing: "There are no Spanish houses in California, unless we consider as such the crude buildings erected by the early settlers during the period of Spanish occupation."[30] Requa began to promote the term "California Architecture," fully admitting that it took the best of Spanish design and made it appropriate for modern use. This became the popular new style of residential architecture in Southern California for the next generation, complete with interiors full of pseudo-Spanish furnishings.

Although San Diego's contributions to the Arts and Crafts movement were limited compared to those made by other areas of the state, they are not without significance. The artists and designers of the Theosophical Society sought tangible forms for their deeply felt beliefs, creating art objects unlike anything else produced in this country. Ceramics made by the Valentien and Markham potteries and the California China Products Company stand up well to comparisons with work by other potteries of the period. In architecture the highly respected critic and historian Henry-Russell Hitchcock, Jr., wrote as early as 1934 that Frank Lloyd Wright and Irving Gill were the only modern architects of consequence during the first quarter of the century in America.[31] Perhaps initially drawn by the climate, these designers and craftspeople were held by the prospects that Southern California offered, by what Gill had called "the newest white page turned for registration."[32] They used this opportunity to add a small but noteworthy chapter to the history of art in America.

THE ARTS AND CRAFTS AFTER 1918: ENDING AND LEGACY

Richard Guy Wilson

186. Claycraft Potteries. *Wall Sconce,* c. 1926. Press-molded fired clay colored with pigmented slip, 12¾ x 9 x 3 in. The Oakland Museum; Gift of Bob Jessup.

The bittersweet epitaph "brief fleeting fame" would be suitable for many Californian designers and craftspeople who had risen to prominence at the turn of the century. One looks in vain in publications of the interwar years for the names of the earlier leaders: Dirk van Erp, Charles Sumner Greene, Irving Gill, Bernard Maybeck. The legendary penchant of Californians for the latest fad offers one explanation for their absence, but these artists suffered equally from a nationwide amnesia, as others such as Frank Lloyd Wright, Gustav Stickley, and Will Bradley either were written off as has-beens or completely forgotten. Similarly, the name of William Morris was seldom invoked by writers concerned with art and craft reform. When he was noted, his progeny, the "Craftsman wave," were lampooned as being too much of "a cult, and ran, also too exclusively to fumed oak, colored burlap, and beaten copper."[1] A new climate of taste in design swept the country, with values—consumerism, historicism, and a Machine Age modernism—antithetical to many of the core beliefs of the Arts and Crafts movement. For many Arts and Crafters the movement appeared to be over or, at the least, lacking its former energy.

There is no precise death date for the American Arts and Crafts; rather, as is common with vital art movements that encompass a wide variety of individuals and modes of expression, it just slowly faded away. World War I, from 1914 to 1918, marked a watershed in American culture, and during it the Arts and Crafts began its decline. Within a few years some of the movement's leaders slipped away: Charles Sumner Greene moved to Carmel, California, in 1916; Frank Lloyd Wright began spending time in Japan in 1915; and the last issue of Gustav Stickley's *Craftsman* appeared in December 1916. The architecture of the Panama-Pacific International Exposition of 1915 was the most outward manifestation of Arts and Crafts metaphysics, but it housed no comprehensive display of crafts.[2]

Complex reasons, ranging from personal choices and problems to broader economic, technological, and cultural shifts, lay behind these changes. Yet many of the features of the Arts and Crafts persisted in an altered form well into the 1920s and beyond.

Many forms and motifs of the Arts and Crafts became popularized in the late 1910s and 1920s. Bungalows, some in direct imitation of buildings by style leaders such as the Greenes or Maybeck, were still constructed in California and elsewhere. Plan books continued to extol the "California Bungalow," even though, as one historian has noted, bungalows lost their exotic image in the 1920s and became known as "cheap" housing.[3] Another form that endured was the simple oak furniture pioneered by Stickley, now produced by mass-marketing firms such as Sears Roebuck. Such popularization forced Stickley (never an astute businessman) to find new alternatives. He finally selected an awkward, reinterpreted colonial style, which failed and forced him into bankruptcy. A few new craftspeople appeared who were inspired by prewar ideals; Ward Ritchie had learned fine printing from Clyde Brownie at the Abbey San Encino during the late 1920s and, working in the Los Angeles area, became California's leading typographer-designer and fine printer (plate 187).

At the national level, Rookwood pottery was still produced in Cincinnati and Van Briggle in Colorado Springs, and in California a number of extremely active potteries—Claycraft and Ernest A. Batchelder, both in the Los Angeles area, and California Faience and Walrich, both in Berkeley—traced their roots to the prewar period. Practitioners of other crafts such as weaving, silverwork, and metalwork survived, in some cases for many years. However, when the later objects are examined, differences from earlier products frequently become apparent: the colors of the 1920s are generally brighter or more pastel, and historical or foreign references abound. In tile production, instead of native fauna and flora, Hispano-Moresque or French Art Deco forms are dominant, indicating new directions of American design in these years (plate 186).

In architecture similar shifts occurred. The new leaders in California were not particularly aligned with the Arts and Crafts, but they were willing to use Arts and Crafts mannerisms. Reginald Johnson, Gordon B. Kaufmann, Julia Morgan, and Wallace Neff, for example, exploited explicit historical and native vernacular images, adapted their buildings to the landscape, and fitted them out with handcrafted details. However, the scale and the furnishings often grew beyond the domestic to the extravagantly large, in seeming mimickry of Hollywood sets, as with Kaufmann's Gothic Revival Greystone for Edward Doheny in Beverly Hills, Morgan's castle for William Randolph Hearst at San Simeon (plate 188), and Neff's Regency-style Pickfair in Los Angeles for Mary Pickford and Douglas Fairbanks, Sr. Two major landmarks created in California in the 1920s, the Ahwahnee Hotel at Yosemite (1926) and the Santa Barbara County Court House (1929), extensively utilized handcrafted details. With their regional references these two buildings are pure Arts and Crafts, even though

BELOW
187. Ward Ritchie, *First Book: Robinson Jeffers,* 1932.

OPPOSITE
188. Julia Morgan, front view of La Casa Grande, Hearst Castle, San Simeon, California.

FIRST BOOK : ROBINSON JEFFERS

I AM WILLING to tell the history of my first book, though it is not clear why it should interest anyone; certainly it does not interest me. In 1912 I came into possession of a little money, a little more than was immediately required, a novel ex-.

their designers, Gilbert Stanley Underhill and William Mooser and Company, respectively, had no apparent ties to the movement. Arts and Crafts features became part of an academic design vocabulary in the 1920s. Frank Lloyd Wright designed five houses in the Los Angeles area in the years 1918 to 1924 that displayed a new, defensive personality consciously at odds with his earlier Arts and Crafts mode. Across the country the Tudorbethan and various regional colonial revivals of the 1920s, although heavily indebted to earlier Arts and Crafts imagery, were now being designed by architects with academic allegiances.

This increasing historicism had a certain irony, especially in California, for much of the Spanish Colonial Revival grew from Bertram Goodhue's work at the Panama-California Exposition in San Diego in 1915 (plates 71, 189). A New York–based, conservative, Arts and Crafts–oriented architect, Goodhue had designed a number of buildings in California between 1901 and 1915. He even had a vacation house in Montecito. Yet he also had a modern side, for he recognized that new methods of construction—the steel frame, reinforced concrete— abrogated all past styles of architecture. But Goodhue found himself "too conservative . . . to abandon the language of ornament," and he tried to modernize traditional styles through abstraction and by borrowing elements from advanced European design such as that of the Vienna Secession.[4] His late works (he died in 1924)—particularly the Nebraska State Capitol (1920–31) and the Los Angeles Public Library (1922–26)—contain vestiges of the Arts and Crafts, but they also represent a new urbanity and international modernity, with traces of classicism that were foreign to the original Arts and Crafts.

Regionalism, a key feature of the Arts and Crafts movement, continued with 1920s design but with an increasingly historicist bent. Depression-era regionalism of the 1930s was different, and although the Works Projects Administration crafts and arts projects may have owed a tenuous debt to the Arts and Crafts,

189. Bertram Goodhue, California State Building at the Panama-California Exposition, Balboa Park, San Diego, 1915.

another popular regionalist mode exemplified by Thomas Hart Benton, John Steuart Curry, and Grant Wood drew nothing from the Arts and Crafts and was politically conservative and backward-looking.

Formal Arts and Crafts organizations had a tendency to be short-lived; the initial enthusiasms of the founders quickly dissipated, as, for example, with the Arroyo Guild of Pasadena, which had only a brief existence around 1909. Nationwide, many of the Arts and Crafts clubs were equally ephemeral. A few did persist, such as the Society of Arts and Crafts in Boston, which is still alive ninety-four years after its founding. The National League of Handicrafter Societies was organized in 1907, and the Arts and Crafts movement as a whole became increasingly focused on the individual artisan. New groups sprang up. The Southern Highland Handicraft Guild, although organized in 1929 to revive folk handicrafts, grew out of efforts that began in the 1890s at Berea College in Berea, Kentucky, and the Home Missions of the Presbyterian church near Asheville, North Carolina. In New Hampshire, Sandwich Home Industries, formed in 1926, led to the statewide League of Arts and Crafts, founded in 1932.[5] In Los Angeles, the Arts and Crafts Society of Southern California was organized in 1924, and within a year had a membership of 250. Though claiming to encompass all the arts and crafts, the Los Angeles group was dominated by weavers and batik artists and concentrated on making unique decorative objects; formed to support individual handicrafters, it lacked the reformist zeal of earlier societies.[6]

The Pure Design approach advocated by Arthur Wesley Dow, Denman W. Ross, and Ernest A. Batchelder came to dominate craft and commercial-design education in the United States for many years, though it never made much of an impact on painting and sculpture. Ironically, given the anticommercial bias of many earlier Arts and Crafters, the principles of Pure Design found a home in the new field of advertising design in the 1920s. Otis Shepard, the wunderkind of advertising art in the 1920s, ran a studio in San Francisco for Foster and Kleiser, the outdoor-billboard firm, and used graphics derived from Pure Design to sell oil, typewriters, and cigarettes (plate 190). In the early 1930s Shepard became the

190. Otis and Dorothy Shepard, *Drawing for Chesterfield Cigarettes*, 1930.

art director of the Wrigley Chewing Gum Company and in that capacity remodeled much of Santa Catalina Island, which was owned by William Wrigley, Jr.[7]

Many schools with Arts and Crafts objectives, such as the California School of Arts and Crafts, remained. The concept that educated people worked with their hands as well as their minds resulted in shop and crafts training extending from grade school to college, beginning in the 1880s. With the emergence of the Arts and Crafts movement, crafts for the educated gained great currency and continued into the 1950s. Such ideas found an ally in John Dewey, the major philosopher of learning by doing and experiential education. A legacy of the Arts and Crafts was the growth among urban professionals of "do-it-yourself" activities, with men working in their home shops and reading *Popular Mechanics* and with women quilting, knitting, and weaving. Whereas such activities on a farm might be life supporting, in most urban or suburban homes they filled the new leisure time.

One factor in the eventual demise of the Arts and Crafts movement was simply the inexorable passage of time. By 1915 the Arts and Crafts movement in the United States had been a force for at least twenty years; for a modern art movement, this is tantamount to old age. The look that was new in 1900—dark wood, fawn and green colors, stylized plant forms—had become old-fashioned. What had been stylish in 1900 now was seen as a sea of mud, as a younger generation coming of age sought—as young people always do—something different from what their elders had. Rooms were remodeled, and furniture and objects that had been prized twenty years earlier disappeared, were sold off, moved up to the attic, the maid's room, or the summer house. (Years later it would all be rediscovered and moved back onto display.) The designers who had become dominant in the Arts and Crafts around 1900 had all matured by 1915; could they adjust to new tastes and requirements? Many tried, but most failed.

A signal transforming feature of the early twentieth century was the increasing mechanization of life. Everywhere the machine seemed to dominate, and perhaps the most notable example is the automobile. The numbers of automobiles grew almost exponentially: from no motorized vehicles in 1900, to fewer than five hundred thousand in 1910, to nearly ten million in 1920, and over twenty-six million by 1930. An entirely new landscape in which to operate the automobile was created almost overnight. Electrification of the home, while not new, was more widely applied: from about 16 percent of American houses in 1912, the number grew to over 80 percent of urban dwellings by 1930. Joining electric lamps, washers, toasters, and refrigerators was a new entertainment form, the commercial radio, which appeared in the early 1920s. Radio transformed the leisure habits—and tastes—of millions of Americans, as did another new mechanized entertainment, the movies. Many Arts and Crafts individuals had tried to seek an accommodation with the machine, but the idea of a Machine Age, which entered the popular consciousness in the 1920s, was totally at odds with the credo that had been passed down from Morris.[8] The reaction to the Machine Age took two forms: avoidance and a retreat into the safety of historical images; and full acceptance, leading to modern design.

The Machine Age apotheosized not just machine operators and their creators, engineers and scientists, but also businessmen and what were viewed as new economic principles—mass production and mass consumption. The notion of a cornucopia of new goods and the related need to stimulate consumption led in the 1920s to the annual model change as a tenet of business. Increasingly, Americans were bound together by words and images that had been massaged by advertising executives and artists.

Although the American Arts and Crafters never had a consolidated political agenda, most adherents subscribed to progressivism and government by experts; they were anti–big business and corporations, and a few flirted with soft socialism. But in the 1920s, lack of talent seemed a prerequisite for national office, and progressivism and reform were out of favor. Any exposition of leftist economics was labeled communistic, and the country moved to the right. The hero of the 1920s was the corporate leader, an idea totally unthinkable one or two decades earlier. One of the best-sellers of the 1920s was *The Man Nobody Knows* by Bruce Barton (an advertising executive), a novel in which Jesus Christ is described as a business executive. The Arts and Crafters' essentially beneficent view of people and nature found little following in the intellectual community of the 1920s as a darker view of humankind appeared, exemplified by T. S. Eliot's pessimistic images of the modern age in *The Wasteland.* Robinson Jeffers—working at Tor House, his craftsy hand-built house in Carmel—wrote poetry in which people were accidental, nature indifferent.

Some designers experienced personal crises. Charles Sumner Greene, for example, worked for years at peak intensity and suffered at least one nervous breakdown. His distraction intensified as he saw builders copy and cheapen the carefully crafted forms that he and his brother Henry had developed. Unhappy with the conservative and—he felt—stodgy artistic climate of Pasadena, Charles sought a more liberal artistic community in Carmel, where he devoted himself to mysticism. Although Henry and Charles continued to design in the 1920s—the D. L. James House in Carmel Highlands and the Fleishhacker estate in Hillsborough—they found their work had little widespread appeal.

Broad changes in taste affected many other designers. Those who had recently done substantial buildings, such as Irving Gill with his Dodge House in Los Angeles and Bernard Maybeck at the Panama-Pacific International Exposition, found it increasingly difficult to get work in the 1920s. Gill kept dreaming and getting small jobs in spite of ill health until his death in 1936. Maybeck kept busy up to the mid-1920s, but then commissions decreased and he retreated into a cerebral world.

All of these forces, and others, conspired to undermine one of the essential features of the Arts and Crafts movement, the metaphysics of a higher life and a search for a divine excellence. Mysticism continued in the 1920s, and in California it actually experienced growth along with other religious cults—ranging from Aimee Semple McPherson's Evangelicalism to more exotic forms of Buddhism and Rosicrucianism. The state became known for its liberal attitude toward religious "experimentation"; it was the place where anything went.[9] Theosophy gained a greater foothold in California when a Theosophist magazine announced that the next step in human spiritual evolution, "a new sixth sub-race," would emerge in the Ojai Valley. Annie Besant, the Theosophist leader, purchased 465 acres in Ojai and brought the "new Messiah," or the "literally Perfect One," Krishnamurti, to hold classes there and throughout Southern California, including at the Hollywood Bowl. Among the rapt listeners to Krishnamurti at Ojai in May 1929 was the seventeen-year-old aspiring artist Jackson Pollock, who would revolutionize American art in ways unthought of by the Arts and Crafters.[10] What relation existed between the earlier leaders of the Arts and Crafts and Besant and Krishnamurti is unclear; Charles Sumner Greene in Carmel continued to study various forms of oriental and occult religions and philosophies. His essay "Symbolism" (1932) outlines "the hidden kernel of the oneness of all that exists" and displays Theosophical elements.[11]

Although mysticism retained a following in the 1920s and even beyond, it gained an increasing reputation as a refuge for charlatans. Those artists and designers interested in metaphysics went underground. Freudianism, introduced to the United States in the late 1910s, grew substantially among intellectuals and artists in the following two decades; it was unsympathetic to mysticism, which it interpreted as a subterfuge for deeper childhood and sexual dysfunctions. A consumer-oriented culture would not see windows, pottery, and houses as mediums for contemplation of higher truths but as material objects expressing status. The good life became not higher thought, but possession. And finally, the growth of Hollywood and its product presented an alternative to the more difficult task of contemplation and mysticism. Movies presented a fantasy world available to all at little cost or effort.

The Arts and Crafts had always embraced sentiment but, as Robert W. Winter has observed, it turned into sentimentality in the 1920s.[12] Instead of looking at the past as a source for inspiration and transformation, designers now sought a more literal transcription of historical prototypes. In California the Spanish Colonial or Renaissance supplanted the more humble mission or adobe house. Bertram Goodhue's great Churrigueresque entry screen for the California State Building at the San Diego exposition of 1915 (Gill's loss of that commission was the beginning of his end) was the most immediate prototype, though Myron Hunt had designed the Congregational Church in Riverside in 1912 using the same elements. The other major feature of the new historicism was a cloying, sweet-faced romanticism, a total fiction that at its best could be remarkably convincing, as in the new town of Santa Barbara. The rebuilding of downtown Santa Barbara after the 1925 earthquake (several of the best buildings had actually survived from earlier days, such as the multiuse El Paseo) into a movieland image of Old Spain or *The Mark of Zorro* (a popular book and several movies of 1924–25 starring Douglas Fairbanks, Sr.) showed how far it could go.[13] A Spanish Colonial fantasy became the dominant image in California (plate 191).

A development in product design, at least partially an outgrowth of the Arts and Crafts and yet antithetical to it in several ways, centered on the industrial-arts movement of the late 1910s and 1920s. Beginning in 1917 the Metropolitan Museum of Art in New York sponsored an annual exhibition of manufactured products that were inspired by objects in museums or designed by artists. Across the country during the next few years, similar "Art in Trade" exhibitions took place in museums, department stores, and exhibition halls, showing Maxfield Parrish photolithographs, Cadillacs, and Cheney silks based on Japanese patterns. Despite the evidence offered in such exhibitions, articles and books were written decrying the low quality of American goods, the lack of native designers, and the fact that "a great industrial nation [is] without an industrial art."[14] Various commentators claimed that World War I and the restriction of immigration meant that American industry could no longer count on European-trained designers. American commercial products suffered from a lack of design, and the solution was to be sought in an alliance between schools, industry, and the government, as in England, Germany, and France.[15] Only a few commentators claimed the Arts and Crafts movement as a native precedent to be followed, since its emphasis on handmade products made it seem to them peripheral.[16]

Initially, most of the art-in-industry supporters accepted the viability of copying historical examples and motifs.[17] This attitude changed in the mid-1920s

241

191. Lutah Marie Riggs. *George Washington Smith Project, East Side of de la Guerra Plaza, Santa Barbara,* 1922. Pencil on vellum, 17¼ x 36⅜ in. Architectural Drawing Collection, University Art Museum, University of California, Santa Barbara.

SUGGESTION FOR CITY HALL PLAZA · LOOKING EAST ·
SUBMITTED BY COMMUNITY ARTS ASSOCIATION

as objects from the *Exposition internationale des arts décoratifs et industriels modernes* in Paris (1925) began to be exhibited across the country. Herbert Hoover, who as secretary of commerce decreed that the United States possessed no modern art and hence declined the invitation for Americans to display their wares in Paris at the *Exposition internationale,* nonetheless sent an official team of observers. Although the team report did not inspire any action by the federal government,

192. Kem Weber, furniture designed for Barker Brothers, Los Angeles, c. 1926–27. Architectural Drawing Collection, University Art Museum, University of California, Santa Barbara.

many of the observers, along with other Americans, were shocked to discover that a modern-art movement had grown up in Europe and was making a substantial impact on product design. Historically based product design continued unabated in the United States despite this knowledge, yet the way was clear for modernism.[18]

The roots of American modernism as it developed in the 1920s are more complicated than French Art Deco imports. Although some Arts and Crafts designers viewed themselves as "modern" (Charles Sumner Greene, for example) and although Arts and Crafts–derived decorative patterns do appear in 1920s modernism, the Arts and Crafts emphasis on handicraft made it seem old-fashioned. Into the breach stepped a new individual, the industrial designer. Joseph Sinel (who later taught at the California College of Arts and Crafts) was apparently the first to use the term. Tentatively in the 1920s and then with a rush in the 1930s, American companies discovered the value of design. Few, if any, of America's industrial designers had an Arts and Crafts background. Instead, the best known—Norman Bel Geddes, Henry Dreyfus, Raymond Loewy, and Walter Dorwin Teague—came to the new field from advertising and theater-set design, experiences that well served the new age.[19] The few industrial designers who did have an Arts and Crafts background came from Europe, and specifically from Germany and Austria and had worked in those countries' Jugendstil or Secessionist styles. Kem Weber was the major California representative of this Germanic wave and had little patience for the earlier Arts and Crafts. He emerged in the early 1920s as one of the leading modern stylists in Los Angeles, producing a furniture line for Barker Brothers and designing store interiors (plate 192). In the 1930s Weber was joined by Paul Frankl, who had arrived from Germany in 1915. Frankl, however, had stayed on the East Coast designing Art Deco interiors and his line of skyscraper furniture while writing his important books, *New Dimensions* (1928) and *Form and Re-Form* (1930). In Los Angeles in the mid-1930s he introduced a softer modernistic look.

The important feature of the new modernism was the dominance of the machine. From abroad came choruses of praise for the United States as the great land of industry and machinery, and at home younger artists and intellectuals rushed to portray and utilize machines in poems, novels, photographs, paintings, buildings, and furniture. European architects like R. M. Schindler and Richard Neutra became dominant figures in the United States, where they had the chance to create a genuinely modern architecture based on new materials and techniques. Schindler's Kings Road House, in Los Angeles (1921–22), utilized a construction system derived from Irving Gill in creating a house open to nature and filled with furniture he designed himself. But neither the image of the house nor the furniture had anything to do with the Arts and Crafts; instead it was part of a modernist glorification of the machine (plate 193). The setback skyscrapers that came to dominate American cities in the 1920s, including San Francisco and Los Angeles, were seen as both products and representatives of the Machine Age.

193. R. M. Schindler, Kings Road House, Los Angeles, 1921–22. Architectural Drawing Collection, University Art Museum, University of California, Santa Barbara.

243

Later, in the 1930s, the streamline dominated much of American design, from gas stations to vacuum cleaners, and again the source was a perception of the machine as clean, efficient, and smooth.

With the rise of a machine-based modernism, the Arts and Crafts no longer played a central role in American life and design. Only a very few younger designers found inspiration in the turn-of-the-century Arts and Crafts. The historicist design agenda contained traces of the Arts and Crafts in its emphasis on well-crafted details and respect for the past, but commitment to a higher life was missing. Metaphysics was replaced by the costumed historical romance. For the most part the new regionalism that surfaced in the 1930s appears not to have been indebted to the earlier Arts and Crafts, though more research may show some ties.

An Arts and Crafts legacy began to appear in the 1940s, when a reaction against the dominance of mechanophile modernism began to develop. Charles Eames and Eero Saarinen, who had both studied at the Arts and Crafts–inspired Cranbrook Academy in Bloomfield Hills, Michigan, developed molded-plywood furniture in biomorphic shapes during the early 1940s. Eames, who moved to California, and his wife, Ray Eames, became two of the most important mid-twentieth-century furniture designers. Then, after World War II, came a thin-legged wooden furniture from Scandinavia, which emphasized natural grain. This inspired a number of American craftspeople, including Sam Maloof, of Alta Loma, California, who also looked closely at earlier Arts and Crafts furniture, such as the elegant work of the Greenes (plate 194).

194. Sam Maloof. *Settle,* 1969. Walnut with (replaced) leather seats, 30½ x 39½ x 20¼ in. The Oakland Museum; Bequest of Mrs. Dorothea Adams McCoy.

195. Harwell Hamilton Harris, Ralph
Johnson House, Bel Air, 1948.

In architecture Cliff May, located in the Los Angeles area, had by the late 1930s begun to produce low-slung ranch houses that betrayed a debt to the Greenes' Bandini bungalow. Also in Southern California, Jean Bangs, an architectural journalist, helped rediscover the work of the Greenes, who by then had been ignored for years. Bangs was married to the architect Harwell Hamilton Harris, himself the son of a Redlands-area Arts and Crafts architect.[20] Harris designed a number of houses after World War II, such as those for Ralph Johnson in Bel Air (plate 195) and Clarence Wyle in Ojai, which are openly dependent on the structural elaboration and woodwork of the Greenes. Lewis Mumford, the critic-historian and writer for the *New Yorker,* wrote a column in 1947 identifying a Bay Area wooden style—"native and humane"—and traced its roots to the turn-of-the-century Arts and Crafts.[21] Mumford's observations led to an exhibition two years later in which contemporary, low-slung houses by William Wurster and Gardner Dailey were linked with the earlier work of Maybeck, Louis Christian Mullgardt, and others.[22] The importance of the Bay Area Arts and Crafts was further recognized when in 1951 the American Institute of Architects awarded their gold medal, the highest honor possible, to Bernard Maybeck. Maybeck was then eighty-nine years old, and the buildings for which he was honored—the Palace of Fine Arts, the First Church of Christ, Scientist, and individual houses—had been done at least thirty years earlier. And the next year, 1952, the same group of architects gave a special citation to Greene and Greene, noting their contributions of over thirty years before.[23]

A full examination of the subsequent rediscovery of the Arts and Crafts movement beginning in the mid-1960s is beyond the scope of this essay. Many publications and exhibitions on the subject have since appeared, at the same time that a resurgence in the crafts has taken place. With more research perhaps other legacies, elsewhere, will be found. The reasons for this renewed interest in the Arts and Crafts movement are still unclear and require more perspective; however, a number of forces are clearly at work. Some individuals have responded to the political radicalism and counterculturalism of many of the earlier Arts and Crafters. Certainly the recent interest contains both a nostalgia for an earlier, and supposedly more tranquil, time and a general appreciation for the high quality of many of the objects: their beauty, good design, and fitness to purpose. In our era of rampant commercialism and hucksterism, when integrity seems lacking in so many aspects of art and life, when artists are best known for their outrageous behavior, the Arts and Crafts idealism is a breath of fresh air. Yet objects that were meant to be used in daily life and to be symbols of higher thought have, ironically, been degraded into commercial collectibles in which possession is the only goal: their original meanings need to be restored.

Although the original Arts and Crafts movement in America had spent most of its energy by 1920, it left an important legacy to future generations. The Arts and Crafts did provide the concept that simplicity is better than overly ornate and pretentious design. It announced the ideal that craftsmanship was an integral element of design and that the maker should not just understand the techniques involved but should also be concerned with how an object was marketed and sold, as well as with its ultimate use. There is a morality of design that goes far beyond materials and texture to purpose. The Arts and Crafts meant many things to its practitioners, and even though some of the original ethos and ideas have been forgotten and only the stylistic features carried on, it may yet offer a path to real reform in design based not only on material reality but on a metaphysical content.

NOTES

"DIVINE EXCELLENCE": THE ARTS AND CRAFTS LIFE IN CALIFORNIA
Richard Guy Wilson

1. Unless otherwise noted, this and all further Ashbee quotes are from Charles Robert Ashbee, Journals, January 1909, King's College Library, Cambridge. See also Alan Crawford, *C. R. Ashbee: Architect, Designer, and Romantic Socialist* (New Haven: Yale University Press, 1985), pp. 151–53; Robert W. Winter, "American Sheaves from 'C.R.A.' and Janet Ashbee," *Journal of the Society of Architectural Historians* 30 (December 1971): 317–22.

2. *Daily Palo Alto,* January 20, 1909, p. 1, quoted in Peter Stansky, "C. R. Ashbee Visits Stanford University," *Imprint of the Stanford Libraries Associates* 3 (April 1977): 16–23.

3. George Wharton James, "The Arroyo Craftsman," *Arroyo Craftsman* 1 (October 1909): 52.

4. Gustav Stickley, "The Colorado Desert and California," *Craftsman* 6 (June 1904): 236, 255, 259.

5. Gustav Stickley, "Nature and Art in California," *Craftsman* 6 (July 1904): 370–90.

6. Gustav Stickley, "Als Ik Kan: What the West Means to the Nation," *Craftsman* 22 (August 1912): 569–71.

7. Liberty Hyde Bailey, "California," *Country Life in America* 1 (January 1902): 71–75.

8. "A House with a Garden Room," *Craftsman* 27 (February 1915): 564.

9. Ralph Adams Cram, preface to *American Country Houses of Today* (New York: Architectural Book Publishing Company, 1913), pp. iv–v. See also A. W. Alley, "House in Japanese Style," *House Beautiful* 25 (March 1909): 76–77.

10. Elizabeth G. Graham, "The Swiss Chalet: Its Influence on American Home Architecture," *Craftsman* 28 (April 1915): 220–23; "California Barn Dwellings and the Attractive Bungalows Which Have Grown Out of the Idea," *Craftsman* 15 (February 1909): 598–600; Ernest Peixotto, *Romantic California* (New York: Charles Scribner's Sons, 1910), p. 3.

11. Peter B. Wight, "California Bungalows," *Western Architect* 27 (October 1918): 92. This myth has been disproved by later authors; see Clay Lancaster, *The American Bungalow* (New York: Abbeville Press, 1985); and Robert W. Winter, *The California Bungalow* (Los Angeles: Hennessey & Ingalls, 1980).

12. For songs, see Winter, *Bungalow,* pp. 8–10; Henry H. Saylor, *Bungalows* (Philadelphia: John H. Winston Co., 1911). For the bungalow's appearance in a novel, see Sinclair Lewis, *Main Street* (1920; New York: Signet, New American Library, 1961), p. 139.

13. [Gustav Stickley], "How 'Mission' Furniture Was Named," *Craftsman* 16 (May 1909): 225. Alwyn T. Covell, "The Real Place of Mission Furniture," *Good Furniture* (March 1915): 359–68, reproduces on p. 361 "Sketches of the First Three Pieces of Real 'Mission' Furniture Made in the East" and claims it was made of ash, not maple. "San Francisco, the Home of Mission Type of Furniture," *Architect and Engineer of California* (August 1906): 68; Catherine Zusy, in Wendy Kaplan et al., *"The Art that is Life": The Arts and Crafts Movement in America, 1875–1920* (Boston: Museum of Fine Arts; New York Graphic Society, 1987), p. 185, no. 71, side chair.

14. Virginia Robie, "Mission Furniture: What It Is and Is Not," *House Beautiful* 27 (May 1910): 162.

15. Charles Keeler, *San Francisco and Thereabout,* 2d ed. (1902; San Francisco: California Promotion Committee, 1906), p. 93. Excellent background sources on which I have depended are Kevin Starr, *Americans and the California Dream, 1850–1915* (New York: Oxford University Press, 1973); and Kevin Starr, *Inventing the Dream: California through the Progressive Era* (New York: Oxford University Press, 1985).

16. Bernard Maybeck, quoted in Louis J. Stellmann, "Interesting Westerners," *Sunset* 35 (November 1915): 952.

17. William Morris, "Making the Best of It," in *The Collected Works of William Morris,* ed. May Morris, 24 vols. (London: Longmans Green, 1910–15), vol. 22, p. 83.

18. K. Porter Garnett, "The 'Arts and Crafts': Its First Exhibition in San Francisco," *Overland Monthly,* 2d ser., 27 (March 1896): 292–302.

19. Ernest A. Batchelder, "The Abiding Lesson of Gothic Architecture: All Its Beauty and Inspiration the Outgrowth of Sound Construction," *Craftsman* 15 (February 1909): 545; Batchelder, quoted in Mabel Urmy Seares, "Ernest Batchelder and His Tiles," *International Studio* 58 (April 1916): liii.

20. Ernest A. Batchelder, *The Principles of Design* (1904; Chicago: Inland Printer, 1911), p. 53; originally published as articles in the magazine *Inland Printer.*

21. See "Some Hints on Pattern Designing," [1881], in Morris, *Collected Works,* vol. 22, pp. 206–34. See also Walter Crane, *The Bases of Design* (London: G. Bell and Sons, 1898). On Dow and Batchelder, see below.

22. Henry George's *Progress and Poverty* appeared in 1879 and by 1906 had gone through at least one hundred editions. Thorstein Veblen popularized the concept of "conspicuous consumption" in his *Theory of the Leisure Class,* first published in 1899.

23. Hazel V. Bray, *The Potter's Art in California, 1885–1955* (Oakland, Calif.: Oakland Museum Art Department, 1978), p. 11.

24. Walt Whitman, *Leaves of Grass,* ed. Scully Bradley (New York: Holt, Rinehart and Winston, 1949), p. 174.

25. Keeler, *San Francisco,* p. 41.

26. [Charles Keeler and Bernard Maybeck], *Berkeley Homebuilding as Hillside* (Berkeley, Calif.: Hillside Club, [1907]), [p. 8]. Charles Sumner Greene, "California Home Making," *Pasadena Daily News,* January 1, 1905, p. 26.

27. [George Wharton James], "The Dawn of the Spiritual Era," *Arroyo Craftsman* 1 (October 1909): 55–58.

28. This was the motto of the magazine *Land of Sunshine,* which Lummis edited. See Starr, *California Dream,* pp. 387–401; Starr, *Inventing the Dream,* chaps. 3, 4, and p. 346; Edwin R. Bingham, *Charles F. Lummis, Editor of the Southwest* (San Marino, Calif.: Huntington Library, 1955).

29. Robert Michael Craig, "Maybeck at Principia: A Study in Architect-Client Relationship" (Ph.D. diss., Cornell University, 1973), p. 128.

30. Maybeck did the set for the play and the frontispiece for Isaac Flagg's book *Circe: A Dramatic Fantasy* (East Aurora, N.Y.: Roycrofters, 1915).

31. Helen Hunt Jackson, *Ramona* (1884; Boston: Little, Brown and Co., 1926), p. 26.

32. Charles Fletcher Lummis, "The Patio" and "The Grand Veranda," *Land of Sunshine* 3 (1895): 13–16 and 64–67. [Keeler and Maybeck], *Berkeley Homebuilding as Hillside,* [p. 6].

33. Lelia A. Mather Greene, letter to Charles Sumner Greene, dated January 1, 1893, Greene and Greene Center for the Study of the Arts and Crafts Movement in America, the University of Southern California and the Huntington Library, Art Collections, and Botanical Gardens, San Marino, Calif.

34. Stickley, "Colorado Desert," p. 237.

35. Edwin Markham, *The Man with the Hoe and Other Poems* (1899; New York: McClure, Phillips & Co., 1902), p. 17; see also Starr, *Inventing the Dream,* pp. 213–15.

36. Keeler, *San Francisco,* pp. 53–54.

37. Charles Keeler, *Southern California* (Los Angeles: Passenger Department, Santa Fe Route, 1898); Keeler, *San Francisco.* Between 1895 and 1903 Lummis edited *Land of Sunshine/Out West,* and although it promoted Arts and Crafts causes it was also a voice for substantial landholding and banking interests and has a chamber-of-commerce promotional air.

38. Greene, "California Home Making," pp. 26–27.

39. "The House Beautiful," in Jack London, *Revolution and Other Essays* (New York: Macmillan, 1910), pp. 159–76; Clarice Stasz, *American Dreamers: Charmian and Jack London* (New York: St. Martin's Press, 1988).

40. George Santayana, "The Genteel Tradition in American Philosophy," in *Selected Critical Writings of George Santayana,* ed. N. Henfrey, 2 vols. (Cambridge: Cambridge University Press, 1968), vol. 2, pp. 85–107.

41. *Mysticism* and *spiritualism* can have different meanings. Strictly defined, mysticism is a direct link with an absolute (i.e., God, unifying principles), and spiritualism is the survival beyond death and sometimes a communication with the beyond. However, the terms were used interchangeably along with others such as "symbolism" at the turn of the century, and I have followed that practice. The only substantial study of mysticism and art does not treat the Arts and Crafts; see Maurice Tuchman et al., *The Spiritual in Art: Abstract Painting, 1890–1985* (Los Angeles: Los Angeles County Museum of Art; New York: Abbeville Press, 1987).

42. William R. Lethaby, *Architecture, Mysticism, and Myth* (1891; New York: George Braziller, 1975). The extent of Lethaby's influence in America is unclear, but he certainly was known; see B.G.G. [Bertram Grosvenor Goodhue], review of *Architecture, Mysticism, and Myth,* in *Knight Errant* 1 (January 1893): 31.

43. Worcester is treated below; on Point Loma, see Emmett A. Greenwalt, *California Utopia: Point Loma, 1897–1942,* rev. ed. (San Diego: Point Loma Publications, 1978); Bruce Kamerling, "Theosophy and Symbolist Art: The Point Loma Art School," *Journal of San Diego History* 26 (Fall 1980): 230–55.

44. "The Revival of Mysticism," *Current Literature* 47 (November 1909): 532.

45. Oscar Wilde, *The Picture of Dorian Gray* (1891; Oxford: Oxford University Press, 1981), p. 133. Claude Bragdon claimed, "It transforms inanimate, common, familiar things into symbols." (Bragdon, "The New Mysticism," *Reader's Magazine* 4 [July 1904]: 189.)

46. "American Mysticism from a European Standpoint," *Atlantic Monthly* 85 (March 1900): 431.

47. Michael Williams, quoted in "The New Spiritual American Emerging," *Current Literature* 46 (February 1909): 180, originally published in *Van Norden's Magazine* (1908).

48. Michael Williams, "The Pageant of California Art," in *Art in California* (San Francisco: R. L. Benier, [1915]), p. 61.

49. Bernard Maybeck, quoted in Stellmann, "Interesting Westerners," p. 952.

50. Arthur Wesley Dow, *Composition* (Boston: J. M. Bowles, 1899); and Arthur Wesley Dow, "A Note on Japanese Art and What the American Artist May Learn Therefrom," *Knight Errant* 1 (January 1893): 114–16. See also Frederick C. Moffatt, *Arthur Wesley Dow, 1857–1922* (Washington, D.C.: Smithsonian Institution Press, 1977), pp. 49, 74–78. Frank Lloyd Wright, "In the Cause of Architecture," *Architectural Record* 23 (March 1908): 155; Sidney K. Robinson, "The Romantic Classicism of the Prairie School," *Inland Architect* 35 (May–June 1991): 42–45.

51. Denman W. Ross, *A Theory of Pure Design* (1907; New York: Peter Smith, 1933), p. 6; Denman W. Ross, "The Arts and Crafts: A Diagnosis?" *Craftsman* 7 (December 1904): 335–43.

52. Ernest A. Batchelder, *Design in Theory and Practice* (New York: Macmillan, 1910), p. vii; originally published in *Craftsman* 13 (October 1907–March 1908): 82–89, 206–13, 332–40, 458–68, 578–87, 689–96; 14 (April–September 1908): 89–99, 201–11, 316–20, 426–35, 542–50, 666–71.

53. William van Erp, quoted in [Bonnie Mattison], "Metal Work," in Timothy J. Andersen, Eudorah M. Moore, and Robert W. Winter, eds., *California Design, 1910* (Pasadena, Calif.: California Design Publications, 1974; reprint, Salt Lake City: Peregrine Smith, 1989), p. 78.

54. George Wharton James, "William Keith," *Craftsman* 7 (December 1904): 306, 307.

55. Richard Longstreth, *On the Edge of the World: Four Architects in San Francisco at the Turn of the Century* (New York: Architectural History Foundation; Cambridge, Mass.: MIT Press, 1983), pp. 273–74; Leslie Mandelson Freudenheim and Elisabeth Sacks Sussman, *Building with Nature: Roots of the San Francisco Bay Region Tradition* (Santa Barbara, Calif., and Salt Lake City: Peregrine Smith, 1974), chap. 1. Worcester's importance was first recognized in print in Charles Keeler, "Municipal Art in American Cities," *Craftsman* 8 (August 1905): 592. For background, see Marguerite Beck Block, *The New Church in the New World: A Study of Swedenborgianism in America* (1932; New York: Octagon Books, 1968).

56. Othmar Tobisch, *The Garden Church of San Francisco* (San Francisco: San Francisco Church of the New Jerusalem, 1982), pp. 7, 6.

57. *New York Evening Post,* quoted in "San Francisco, the Home of Mission Type of Furniture," p. 68.

58. Mabel Clare Craft, "A Sermon in Church Building," *House Beautiful* 9 (February 1901): 125–33. See also A Stranger [George Wharton James?], "A Departure in Church Building: The Second New Jerusalem Church in California," *Craftsman* 10 (June 1906): 330–34.

59. Bernard Maybeck, *Palace of Fine Arts and Lagoon* (San Francisco: Paul Elder & Co., 1915), pp. 1–2.

60. Louis Christian Mullgardt, *The Architecture and Landscape Gardening of the Exposition* (San Francisco: Paul Elder & Co., 1915), p. v; see also Cora Lenore Williams, *The Fourth-Dimensional Reaches of the Exposition* (San Francisco: Paul Elder & Co., 1915).

61. Maybeck, *Palace of Fine Arts,* pp. 2–13; Bernard Maybeck, "Architecture of the Palace of Fine Arts at the Panama-Pacific International Exposition," in *Art in California,* pp. 161–64.

62. Irving Gill, "The Home of the Future: The New Architecture of the West: Small Homes for a Great Country," *Craftsman* 30 (May 1916): 142, 146, article reprinted in *Architect and Engineer of California* 45 (May 1916): 77–86. See also "A New Architecture in a New Land," *Craftsman* 22 (August 1912): 465–73.

63. Charles Sumner Greene, "Thais Thayer" (typescript, 1913, Greene and Greene Center).

64. Greene, "California Home Making," p. 26; A. C. David, "An Architect of Bungalows," *Architectural Record* 20 (October 1906): 310.

65. Randell L. Makinson, *Greene and Greene: Architecture as a Fine Art* (Salt Lake City: Peregrine Smith, 1977); Randell L. Makinson, "Greene and Greene: The Gamble House," *Prairie School Review* 5 (Fourth Quarter, 1968): 5–23.

THE ARTS AND CRAFTS GARDEN IN CALIFORNIA
David C. Streatfield

1. Ben C. Truman, *Semi-tropical California: Its Climate, Healthfulness, Productiveness, and Scenery* (San Francisco: A. L. Bancroft & Co., 1874).

2. Carey McWilliams, *Southern California: An Island on the Land* (Salt Lake City: Peregrine Smith, 1974), p. 7.

3. Patricia Trenton and William H. Gerdts, eds., *California Light, 1900–1930* (Laguna Beach, Calif.: Laguna Art Museum, 1990).

4. Harold F. Heady, "Valley Grassland," in *Terrestrial Vegetation of California,* ed. Michael G. Barbour and Jack Major (New York: John Wiley & Sons, 1977), pp. 491–514.

5. *Pacific Rural Press* 7 (May 30, 1874).

6. David C. Streatfield, " 'Paradise' on the Frontier: Victorian Gardens on the San Francisco Peninsula," *Garden History* 12 (Spring 1984): 58–80.

7. Grace Ellery Channing, "The Meeting of Extremes," *Out West* 19 (1903): 243–45.

8. John McLaren, *Gardening in California: Landscape and Flower* (San Francisco: A. M. Robertson, 1909).

9. Herbert D. Croly, "The Country House in California," *Architectural Record* 34 (1913): 485–519.

10. *American Country Houses of Today* (New York: Architectural Book Publishing Company, 1913), pp. 1–5; Mac Griswold and Eleanor Weller, *The Golden Age of American Gardens: Proud Owners, Private Estates, 1890–1940* (New York: Harry N. Abrams, 1991), pp. 319, 321, 331.

11. Diane Balmori, "The Arts and Crafts Garden," *Tiller* 1 (1983): 17–27.

12. Tom Turner, *English Garden Design: History and Styles since 1650* (Woodbridge, England: Antique Collectors' Club, 1986), pp. 166–95; Jane Brown, *Gardens of a Golden Afternoon. The Story of a Partnership: Edwin Lutyens and Gertrude Jekyll* (London: Allen Lane, 1982), pp. 41–53.

13. Leslie Mandelson Freudenheim and Elisabeth Sacks Sussman, *Building with Nature:*

Roots of the San Francisco Bay Region Tradition (Santa Barbara, Calif.: Peregrine Smith, 1974), pp. 10, 45.

14. Karen J. Weitze, *California's Mission Revival* (Los Angeles: Hennessey & Ingalls, 1984), pp. 21–24; Charles E. Beveridge, "Introduction to the Landscape Design Reports: The California Origins of Olmsted's Landscape Design Principles for the Semiarid American West," in *The California Frontier, 1863–1865,* ed. Victoria Post Ranney (Baltimore: Johns Hopkins University Press, 1990), pp. 457–60.

15. Myron Hunt, *Los Angeles Evening News,* October 7, 1907.

16. Clay Lancaster, *The Japanese Influence in America,* new ed. (New York: Abbeville Press, 1983), pp. 97–103, 207.

17. Charles Keeler, *The Simple Home* (San Francisco: Paul Elder & Co., 1904; reprint, Santa Barbara, Calif.: Peregrine Smith, 1979), p. 11.

18. Florence Dixon, "Japanese Effects for Small Gardens," *Craftsman* 18 (September 1910): 631–37. See also Lancaster, *Japanese Influence in America,* pp. 104–25, 207–13.

19. Alfred D. Robinson, "Wanted—A Greater Garden for San Diego," *California Garden* 4 (January 1913): 4; Alfred D. Robinson, "The Fitness of Things," *California Garden* 4 (April 1913): 4; "Tiles from the Potters of Tunis: Suggestions for the American Landscape Gardener," *Craftsman* 27 (February 1915): 584–86.

20. Freudenheim and Sussman, *Building with Nature.*

21. *What the Club Advocates,* 1898, in *Hillside Club Yearbook, 1911–12,* pp. 6–7, Fred H. Dempster Papers, Bancroft Library, University of California, Berkeley.

22. Keeler, *Simple Home,* p. 12.

23. Bernard Maybeck, "Program for the Development of a Hillside Community," *Journal of the American Institute of Architects* 15 (1951): 250–52.

24. Eaton, quoted in Gustav Stickley, "Nature and Art in California," *Craftsman* 6 (July 1904): 370–90.

25. Kate O. Sessions published numerous articles in the *California Garden* advocating hardy and drought-tolerant plants. One of her most important articles is "Horticulture in San Diego County" (submitted for the Creative Day Contest of the A.A.U.W., 1933). Kate Olivia Sessions Collection, San Diego Public Library.

The quotation cited in my text is from Kate O. Sessions, "Bulbs for Rainless Winters," *California Garden* 3 (August 1911): 5.

26. Randell L. Makinson, *Greene and Greene: Architecture as a Fine Art* (Salt Lake City: Peregrine Smith, 1977), pp. 160–67; "California's Contribution to a National Architecture: Its Significance and Beauty as Shown in the Work of Greene and Greene, Architects," *Craftsman* 22 (August 1912): 532–47.

27. Helen Hunt Jackson, *Glimpses of California and the Missions* (Boston: Little, Brown and Company, 1902); George Wharton James, *Through Ramona's Country* (Boston: Little, Brown and Company, 1912), pp. 94–115, 305–13; Harold Kirker, *California's Architectural Frontier* (Salt Lake City: Peregrine Smith, 1986).

28. Arthur Burnett Benton, "The Patio," *Land of Sunshine* 7 (1897): 109; Charles Fletcher Lummis, "The Patio," *Land of Sunshine* 3 (1894): 12; Grace Ellery Channing, "What We Can Learn from Rome. III—Garden Homes," *Out West* 5 (1903): 473; Henrietta P. Keith, "Swimming Pools That Snare the Sun," *Craftsman* 29 (December 1915): 312–17; Charles Francis Saunders, letter to Señora del Valle, Charles Francis Saunders Papers, Huntington Library, Art Collections, and Botanical Gardens, San Marino, Calif.

29. *Myron Hunt, 1868–1952: The Search for a Regional Architecture* (Los Angeles: Hennessey & Ingalls, 1984), pp. 24, 70, 74–75; *American Architect* 108 (December 8, 1915): 375–79, and photographic plates; "The California Bungalow: A Style of Architecture Which Expresses the Individuality and Freedom Characteristic of Our Western Coast," *Craftsman* 13 (October 1907): 68–80.

30. "California's Contribution," pp. 150–53; Charles Sumner Greene, "California Home Making," *Pasadena Daily News*, Tournament of Roses edition, January 1905, pp. 26–27.

31. E. M. Roorbach, "The Garden Apartments of California. Irving J. Gill . . . Architect," *Architectural Record* 34 (1913): 525–27, 530; for Homer Laughlin House, see *Architectural Record* 32 (1912): 374–76.

32. *Irving Gill, 1870–1936* (Los Angeles: Los Angeles County Museum, 1958), p. 26. Richard S. Requa, a San Diego architect, argued that the color of the house needed to be carefully related to the landscape; see his "Importance of the Garden in Home Planning," *California Garden* 2 (September 1910): 11.

33. For the Theosophical Society Building, Krotona Court, Los Angeles, see *Western Architect* 20 (1914): 97–102.

34. Charles Fletcher Lummis, "The Carpet of God's Country," *Out West* 22 (1905): 306–17. See also Theodore Payne's "California Wild Flowers," *California Garden* (October 1912): 10–11; (November): 8–10; (December): 8–9; (January 1913): 9–10; and "Wildflowers on Vacant Lots Which Cannot Be Watered," *California Garden* 6 (November 1914): 15.

35. Arcady, the George Owen Knapp estate, and Pepper Hill, the Gwethalyn Jones estate in Montecito, also had extensive collections of wildflowers and other native plants. See David F. Myrick, *Montecito and Santa Barbara: From Farms to Estates,* 2 vols. (Glendale, Calif.: Trans Anglo Books, 1987), vol. 2, pp. 348, 311–23; Porter Garnett, "Stately Homes of California. II—Anoakia," *Sunset* 32 (1914): 145.

36. Eugene O. Murmann, *California Gardens* (Los Angeles: Eugene O. Murmann, 1915).

37. Ernest Braunton, *The Garden Beautiful in California* (Los Angeles: Cultivator Press, 1915), pp. 16, 21.

38. E. J. Wickson, *The California Vegetables in Garden and Field: A Manual of Practice,* 5th, rev. ed. (San Francisco: Pacific Rural Press, 1923), pp. 16–21; Charles Francis Saunders, "Bungalow Life: The Cost of Living It," *Sunset* 30 (January 1913): 33. See also Charles Francis Saunders, "Decorative Uses in the Garden of Vegetables," Saunders Papers.

39. E. J. Wickson, *California Garden Flowers, Shrubs, Trees, and Vines,* 3d, rev. ed. (San Francisco: Pacific Rural Press, 1926), p. 48.

40. J. E. Gould, "Designing Entrances to Grounds of the Bungalow and Small House Is Difficult Problem," *Bungalow Magazine* 5 (1916): 514–21.

41. Braunton, *Garden Beautiful,* p. 21.

42. Channing, "What We Can Learn from Rome," p. 473.

43. Lummis, "Patio," p. 12.

44. Persis Bingham, "Ruddy Bungalow, Los Angeles, Sanitary House, Rooms Reversed Bring Garden Nearer Home," *Bungalow Magazine* 5 (1916): 492–99; Roorbach, "Garden Apartments," pp. 521–29. For Gill's double houses, see David Gebhard, "Irving Gill," in Timothy J. Andersen, Eudorah M. Moore, and Robert W. Winter, eds., *California Design, 1910* (Pasadena, Calif.: California Design Publi-

cations, 1974; reprint, Salt Lake City: Peregrine Smith, 1989), p. 113.

45. Charles Francis Saunders, "The Small California Garden," *House and Garden* 19 (1911): 70–81, 120–22.

46. Mrs. Francis King, *Pages from a Garden Note-Book* (New York: Charles Scribner's Sons, 1921), pp. 196–204.

47. Elmer Grey, "Some Country House Architecture in the Far West," *Architectural Record* 52 (1922): 309–16; David C. Streatfield, "Echoes of England and Italy 'On the Edge of the World': Green Gables and Charles Greene," *Journal of Garden History* 2 (1982): 377–98.

48. William C. Tweed, Laura E. Soulliere, and Henry G. Law, "National Park Service Rustic Architecture, 1916–1942" (typescript, 1977, National Park Service, Western Regional Office).

UTOPIAN PLACE MAKING: THE BUILT ENVIRONMENT IN ARTS AND CRAFTS CALIFORNIA
Karen J. Weitze

1. The writer Carey McWilliams popularized Jackson's phrase in his *Southern California: An Island on the Land* (1946; reprint, Santa Barbara, Calif.: Peregrine Smith, 1973).

2. Leo Marx, *The Machine in the Garden: Technology and the Pastoral Ideal in America* (New York: Oxford University Press, 1964).

3. Robert W. Winter, "The Arroyo Culture," in Timothy J. Andersen, Eudorah M. Moore, and Robert W. Winter, eds., *California Design, 1910* (Pasadena, Calif.: California Design Publications, 1974; reprint, Salt Lake City: Peregrine Smith, 1989), pp. 9–29; Jean Pfaelzer, *The Utopian Novel in America, 1886–1896: The Politics of Form* (Pittsburgh: University of Pittsburgh Press, 1984); Peter J. Schmitt, *Back to Nature: The Arcadian Myth in Urban America* (New York: Oxford University Press, 1969).

4. Karen J. Weitze, *California's Mission Revival* (Los Angeles: Hennessey & Ingalls, 1984).

5. Paul V. Turner, Marcia E. Vetrocq, and Karen J. Weitze, *The Founders and the Architects: The Design of Stanford University* (Palo Alto, Calif.: Department of Art, Stanford University, 1976).

6. Kevin Starr, *Americans and the California Dream, 1850–1915* (New York: Oxford University Press, 1973), pp. 307–44; Weitze, *Mission Revival.*

7. Richard Longstreth, *On the Edge of the World: Four Architects in San Francisco at the Turn of the Century* (New York: Architectural History Foundation; Cambridge, Mass.: MIT Press, 1983), pp. 273–76, 389.

8. Ibid., pp. 316–25.

9. Kenneth H. Cardwell, *Bernard Maybeck: Artisan, Architect, Artist* (Santa Barbara, Calif.: Peregrine Smith, 1977), pp. 56–61.

10. Dimitri Shipounoff, introduction, in Charles Keeler, *The Simple Home* (San Francisco: Paul Elder & Co., 1904; reprint, Santa Barbara, Calif.: Peregrine Smith, 1979), pp. vii–xli.

11. Joaquin Miller, *The Building of the City Beautiful* (Chicago: Stone & Kimball, 1894); and Starr, *California Dream,* pp. 288–90.

12. *Hillside Club Yearbook, 1906–07,* Bancroft Library, University of California, Berkeley. Shipounoff, introduction, in Keeler, *Simple Home,* pp. xxv–xxviii.

13. Cardwell, *Maybeck,* pp. 58, 98–100, 129; Longstreth, *On the Edge,* pp. 353–54; Esther McCoy, *Five California Architects* (New York: Praeger Publishers, 1975), pp. 20–35; Norman Beasley, *The Cross and the Crown: The History of Christian Science* (New York: Duell, Sloan and Pearce, 1952).

14. Cardwell, *Maybeck,* pp. 115, 163–64, 171, 214–15, 242–46.

15. The Palo Alto bungalow was designed by either Bolton Coit Brown or Arthur Bridgman Clark: both had been with the Stanford art department since its founding in 1896 and both were referred to as "founder" or "head," although Clark functioned as the true department chair and was an architect as well. Brown, however, left for New York about 1901–2 to become one of the three cofounders of the art colony Byrdcliffe at Woodstock in the Catskills, at just the time the Palo Alto house was sold. Whether the house belonged to Clark or Brown, it is likely that its indoor-outdoor aesthetics were passed on via Stanford art department camaraderie to Byrdcliffe. E. A. Needles, "A Little House with Five Fireplaces," *House Beautiful* 21 (April 1907): 23–24; Pat White, Department of Special Collections, Stanford University Libraries, telephone conversation with the author, August 5, 1991; Coy L. Ludwig, *The Arts and Crafts Movement in New York State, 1890s–1920s* (Layton, Utah: Peregrine Smith, 1983), pp. 32, 45–46.

16. Robert W. Winter, *The California Bungalow* (Los Angeles: Hennessey & Ingalls,

1980), pp. 14, 58; Helen Lukens Gaut, "Tent Houses for Summer Days," *Ladies' Home Journal* 36 (July 1909): 23; "Out-Door Sleeping," *Fresno Republican,* August 1, 1907, p. 4; Allene Archibald, "William Alexander Sharp: Artist of the Mission Inn" (master's thesis, University of California, Riverside, 1989), pp. 50–51. Sharp worked with the architect Arthur B. Benton in Arts and Crafts Riverside. After devising a tent residence, Sharp made a treehouse for his family on their Alhambra property, east of Pasadena. Parents and children slept outdoors for many years, true practitioners of the simple life.

17. "Arthur Martin Cathcart," *Stanford Observer* 36 (May–June 1991): 22; and Helen Lukens Gaut, "Summer Homes in the Woods," *Ladies' Home Journal* 36 (June 1909): 27.

18. Karen J. Weitze, "Architect Hart Wood: Prologue and Early Career, 1880–1918," in *The Architecture of Hart Wood: Toward a Hawaiian Style,* forthcoming.

19. Portland Art Association and Portland Architectural Club, *Year Book: Second Annual Exhibition in the Galleries of the Museum of Fine Arts, March 22–April 10, 1909* (Portland, Oreg.: Irwin, Hodson Co., 1909).

20. Architectural League of the Pacific Coast: *Los Angeles Architectural Club Yearbook, January 13–17, 1910* (Los Angeles: George Rice and Sons, 1910); *Seattle Architectural Club Yearbook, April 16–30, 1910* (Seattle: Lowman and Hanford Co., 1910); *Portland Architectural Club Yearbook, June 3–19, 1910* (Portland, Oreg.: Irwin, Hodson Co., 1910).

21. Wanda M. Corn, *The Color of Mood: American Tonalism, 1880–1910* (San Francisco: M. H. de Young Memorial Museum and the California Palace of the Legion of Honor, 1972).

22. Harvey Ellis, "A Note of Color," *Craftsman* 5 (November 1903): 152–63.

23. August G. Headman, "A Review of the San Francisco Architectural Club's Exhibition," *Architect and Engineer of California* (November 1909): 53.

24. Una Nixson Hopkins, "Houses Designed Relative to Their Situation," *Keith's* 32 (December 1914): 416.

25. Weitze, "Hart Wood"; Eileen Michels, "Late Nineteenth-Century Published American Perspective Drawing," *Journal of the Society of Architectural Historians* 32 (1972): 291–308.

26. Ralph S. Fanning, "Consideration of Color in Architectural Design," *American Architect* 109 (May 1916): 310–11.

27. Harvey L. Jones, *Mathews Masterpieces of the California Decorative Style* (Layton, Utah: Gibbs M. Smith, 1985).

28. Architectural League of the Pacific Coast, *Year Book: San Francisco Architectural Club, June 7–19, 1915* (San Francisco: Hansen Co., 1915). Dr. Goddard, like many other Bay Area Arts and Crafts clients, taught at the University of California at Berkeley. Goddard worked in the Department of Geology as a colleague of Andrew C. Lawson—the two-time client of Maybeck's.

29. Arthur J. Burdick, *The Mystic Mid-Region: The Deserts of the Southwest* (New York: G. P. Putnam's Sons, 1904).

30. Mary Austin, *The Land of Little Rain* (Boston: Houghton Mifflin and Company, 1903).

31. Randell L. Makinson, *Greene and Greene: Architecture as a Fine Art* (Salt Lake City: Peregrine Smith, 1977), pp. 70–74.

32. Kevin Starr, *Inventing the Dream: California through the Progressive Era* (New York: Oxford University Press, 1985), pp. 18–19; William E. Smythe, *History of San Diego, 1542–1908* (San Diego: History Company, 1908), pp. 164–67.

33. California Federation of Women's Clubs, *Women's Clubs of California: Official Directory* (San Francisco: Chas. C. Hoag, 1904); Redlands Indian Association, Minute Book 2, April 1904–November 1928, in the A. K. Smiley Library Archives, Redlands, Calif.; hereafter cited as *AKSL.*

34. Mildred Brooke Hoover, Hero Eugene Rensch, and Ethel Grace Rensch, *Historic Spots in California,* 3d, rev. ed. (1966; reprint, Stanford, Calif.: Stanford University Press, 1970), p. 341; George Wharton James, *In and Out of the Old Missions of California* (1905; reprint, Boston: Little, Brown and Company, 1916), pl. xvii.

35. Makinson, *Greene and Greene,* pp. 88–91, 94–99.

36. "The California Bungalow: A Style of Architecture Which Expresses the Individuality and Freedom Characteristic of Our West Coast," *Craftsman* 13 (October 1907): 68–80; "A Small Bungalow Worth Studying," *Craftsman* 14 (August 1908): 534–36; Laura Rinkle Johnson, "A California Bungalow Planned for Comfort," *Craftsman* 23 (November 1912): 218–21.

37. Winter, *Bungalow,* pp. 40–43.

38. Arnold L. Gesell, "A California Bun-

galow Treated in Japanese Style," *Craftsman* 18 (September 1910): 696.

39. "California Bungalow," *Craftsman* 13 (October 1907): 80.

40. Ira Brown Cross, "Socialism in California Municipalities," *National Municipal Review* 1 (October 1912): 611–19.

41. Winter, "Arroyo Culture"; Starr, *Inventing the Dream,* pp. 99–127, 212–13.

42. Mariane Babal, "Frederick Hürten Rhead," *Noticias* 36 (Spring 1990): 16–22; *San Luis Obispo Telegram,* August 19, 1913, p. 2; "Celebrated Artists," *Santa Barbara Press,* August 21, 1913, p. 10; Starr, *Inventing the Dream,* pp. 120–21.

43. Susan B Anthony and Ida Husted Harper, eds., *The History of Woman Suffrage, 1883–1900,* vol. 4 of *The History of Woman Suffrage* (1902; reprint, Salem, N.H.: Ayer Company, 1985), p. 499.

44. Reyner Banham, introduction, in Makinson, *Greene and Greene,* p. 17.

45. Florence Williams, "The Southern California Bungalow: A Local Problem in Housing," *International Studio* 30 (December 1906): lxxvi–lxxxi; "Wooden Dwellings in California on the Lines of the Old Spanish Adobe," *Craftsman* 13 (February 1908): 568–71.

46. *Builder and Contractor,* citations of 1908–12; Williams, "Southern California Bungalow," p. lxxvi.

47. Makinson, *Greene and Greene;* Randell L. Makinson, *Greene and Greene: Furniture and Related Designs,* 2d ed. (Salt Lake City: Peregrine Smith, 1982).

48. William R. Current and Karen Current, *Greene and Greene: Architects in the Residential Style* (Fort Worth: Amon Carter Museum of Western Art, 1974), pp. 68–111.

49. Winter, "Arroyo Culture," p. 24. David Gebhard and Robert W. Winter, *A Guide to Architecture in Los Angeles and Southern California* (Santa Barbara, Calif.: Peregrine Smith, 1977), p. 322.

50. From about 1906 to 1920 the California Section of the California State Library (Sacramento) developed a biographical card file for California artists, writers, and musicians. Handwritten by the subjects, these cards still exist only as unique originals: "Olive May Graves Percival," 1907; "Una Nixson Hopkins," n.d.; "Helen Lukens Gaut," 1908. See also Starr, *Inventing the Dream,* p. 105. Gaut and Hopkins often wrote articles in the same journals, some-

times on related topics in the same issue. See Una Nixson Hopkins, "If a Woman Must Earn Her Living at Home" and "Four Well-Furnished Rooms," *Ladies' Home Journal* 28 (February 15, 1911): 23, 43. All three of these influential Pasadenans arrived in Southern California between 1880 and 1895, Gaut as a child, Percival and Hopkins as young women.

51. Helen Lukens Gaut, "A Charming and Inexpensive Cottage in the Bungalow Style," *Craftsman* 18 (July 1910): 489; William Phillips Comstock and Clarence E. Schermerhorn, *Bungalows, Camps, and Mountain Houses* (1908 and 1915; reprint, Washington, D.C.: American Institute of Architects Press, 1990); Harvey H. Kaiser, *Great Camps of the Adirondacks* (Boston: David R. Godine, 1982). The Adirondack and Catskills rustic camps of New York, increasingly popular from the 1850s into the Arts and Crafts period, offered America's robber-baron aristocracy a welcome imagery of American architectural rusticity. The New York camps paralleled the bungalow clusters and the Mission Revival estates in Pasadena and Santa Barbara in that their site was remote and exotic, and the vacationing patrons were all extremely wealthy. Small, inexpensive bungalows—including tent bungalows—contributed to the California vacation landscape.

52. Southern California Panama Exposition Commission, *Southern California* (San Diego: Southern California Panama Exposition Commission, 1914), pp. 67, 207–33; James, *In and Out,* p. 389; Smythe, *San Diego.*

53. Grace Louise Miller, "The San Diego Progressive Movement, 1900–20" (master's thesis, University of California, Santa Barbara, 1976); Frederick L. Ryan, "The Labor Movement in San Diego, 1887–1957" (unpublished paper, 1959, for the Bureau of Business and Economic Research, San Diego State College); Donald Worster, *Rivers of Empire: Water, Aridity, and the Growth of the American West* (New York: Pantheon Books, 1985), pp. 118–24; William E. Smythe, *The Conquest of Arid America* (rev. ed., 1905; reprint, Seattle: University of Washington Press, 1969).

54. Smythe, *Conquest,* p. ix.

55. Weitze, *Mission Revival,* pp. 112–29.

56. Miller, "San Diego"; Mary Gilman Marston, *George White Marston* (Los Angeles: Ward Ritchie Press, 1956). *Journal of San Diego History* (hereafter cited as *JSDH*) 36 (Spring–Summer 1990): Gregg R. Hennessey, "George

White and Anna Gunn Marston: A Sketch," pp. 96–105; Mary Dutton Boehm,"The Arts and Crafts Movement in America," p. 93.

57. *JSDH* 36 (Spring–Summer 1990): Bruce Kamerling, "The George White and Anna Gunn Marston House," pp. 130–43; Vonn-Marie May, "The Marston Garden: The Southwest Interprets English Romantic," pp. 162–77; Bruce Kamerling, "Hebbard and Gill, Architects," pp. 106–29. See also McCoy, *California Architects,* pp. 58–99.

58. "Balboa Park Chosen as Name," *San Diego Union,* October 28, 1910, p. 1.

59. Bruce Kamerling, "Self-Guided Walking Tour of Seventh Avenue," *JSDH* 36 (Spring–Summer 1990): 144–61; Bruce Kamerling, "An Inventory of Buildings by Irving J. Gill" (typescript, January 5, 1989, San Diego Historical Society [hereafter cited as *SDHS*] files); "A Full Measure of Life," *Western Woman* 4 (July–August 1942), in SDHS biographical files. Lee's family had previously developed the Adirondack resort community of Westport on Lake Champlain and was directly responsible for designing one of the prototypical Adirondack chairs, c. 1903. Greene and Greene also designed a house for a Marston relative in 1912 near Seventh Avenue at the edge of Balboa Park.

60. Sally Bullard Thornton, *Daring to Dream: The Life of Hazel Wood Waterman* (San Diego: San Diego Historical Society, 1987).

61. Makinson, *Greene and Greene,* p. 146.

62. Thornton, *Daring to Dream;* Smythe, *San Diego,* pp. 133, 150; Hazel Wood Waterman, *Estudillo Adobe Garden Site Plan,* watercolor of September 1908, in the SDHS Archives; Hazel Wood Waterman, "The Restoration of a Landmark" (manuscript, filed as MSS 226, "Estudillo House 1910–34," SDHS Archives).

63. Larry E. Burgess, *The Smileys* (Redlands, Calif.: Moore Historical Foundation, 1991).

64. *Redlands City Directory,* 1902–3, p. 233.

65. "Hotel Men Delighted with Sights of the Gem City," *Redlands Facts,* April 11, 1910, p. 4.

66. "'Squirrel Inn,' California," *House Beautiful* 4 (August 1898): 82–88.

67. Charles Dudley Warner, *Our Italy* (New York: Harper & Brothers, 1891), p. 15.

68. For Redlands, see *John L. Stoddard's Lectures,* 10 vols. (Boston: Balch Brothers Co., 1898), "Southern California," vol. 10, pp. 53–60.

69. Charles William Wooldridge, *Perfecting the Earth: A Piece of Possible History* (1902;

reprint, New York: Arno Press and the New York Times, 1971); Harold Bell Wright, *The Eyes of the World* (Chicago: Book Supply Company, 1914); Sidney H. Burchell, *Jacob Peek* (London: Gay and Hancock, 1915). Catherine Cressey Dunn, "A Study of Redlands, California, as Characterized by Its Novelists" (master's thesis, University of Redlands, 1957). In real life Redlanders encouraged both nature and the machine, much as Henry Adams would reflect on the Virgin and the Dynamo in his 1907 *Education of Henry Adams*. Redlands was not only a premier Arts and Crafts landscape but also the site of the first three-phase hydroelectric plant in the United States (in 1893). Extreme modernism graced crafted rusticity.

70. Daniel Smiley to Burt and Hugh Smiley, Redlands, California, January 8 and 10, 1913, AKSL.

71. Burchell, *Jacob Peek,* p. 160.

72. Redlands Indian Association, Minute Book 1, citations of February 27, 1899, and February 11, 1900.

73. Redlands Indian Association, Minute Book 1, March 1894–December 1903, AKSL. Quilt-making citations of March 5 and 26, 1894, and April 30, 1894.

74. Redlands Indian Association, Minute Book 2; active citations run through December 1914; a closure citation of September 1916 ends the work of the association, with passage in November 1928 of the minute books to the Smiley Library. See also *Redlands Indian Association, Constitution, By-Laws, and Membership* (Redlands, Calif.: Daily Review Press, 1910), and *Indian Industries Committee of the Redlands Indian Association (Redlands),* AKSL.

75. Redlands Indian Association, Minute Book 2.

76. Larry E. Burgess, "First the Smiley Brothers, Then the Phelps-Stokes Sisters," *Redlands Facts,* September 15, 1985, p. A5.

77. "Carnegie Gives $500 to Library," *Redlands Facts,* October 5, 1910, clipping in AKSL.

78. "With a Grain of Salt," *Redlands Facts,* February 9, 1980, clipping in AKSL.

79. Elmer Wallace Holmes, *History of Riverside County, California* (Los Angeles: Historic Record Company, 1912), pp. 92–96; San Pedro, Los Angeles, and Salt Lake Railroad, *Riverside the City Beautiful* (Los Angeles: Home Printing Co., 1907); *Picturesque Riverside* (c. 1902), in the Riverside Municipal Museum Archives (here-

after cited as *RMM*); Tom Patterson, *A Colony for California* (Riverside, Calif.: Press-Enterprise Company, 1971), pp. 193, 322.

80. "City Beautiful," *Los Angeles News,* January 4, 1913, clipping in Frank Miller Scrapbook, 1909–16, RMM; Holmes, *Riverside,* p. 93.

81. Charles H. Cheney, *Major Traffic Street Plan and Report, Riverside, California* (June 1928); "Ornamental Concrete Electroliers," *Western Engineering* (August 1912), clipping in Miller Scrapbook.

82. David V. Hutchings, *The Story of Mount Rubidoux* (Riverside, Calif., 1926), in the Mission Inn Collection, Riverside, Calif.; hereafter cited as *MIC.*

83. Photographs, published drawings, and postcards of the Mission Inn, MIC; Michael Rounds, "A Booster in Paradise: Frank Augustus Miller's Early Career, 1874–1902" (master's thesis, University of California, Riverside, 1988).

84. Arthur Burnett Benton, "The California Mission and Its Influence upon Pacific Coast Architecture," *Architect and Engineer of California* 24 (February 1911): 34–75.

85. In mid-1902 Frank Miller journeyed east to study how other entrepreneurs had captivated their clientele through an Arts and Crafts view of life. In a later interview Miller related that the New York resorts, particularly those of Paul Smith and the Smileys—along with Hubbard's Roycroft—had made profound impressions on him. Smith played the shrewd impresario on Lower Saint Regis Lake. A contemporary of the Smiley twins, he was nearly eighty at the time of Miller's visit and was getting rich from the cult of rusticity. Paul Smith kept an eye to the West, just as Miller did to the East: both before and after Miller's trip to New York, Smith visited Riverside and bought property there. In Smith's obituary of 1912 a reporter commented: "When he went to the Adirondacks many years ago the woods were full of Indians; when he died they were full of millionaires." A similar statement could be applied to the Southern California desert, because of Miller and others.

See Rounds, "A Booster," pp. 68–70; Theresa E. Hanley, "'Tourists and Art Lovers': The Mission Inn as Museum, 1903–1925" (manuscript, 1991, Mission Inn Foundation, Riverside, Calif.); "Back from Eastern Trip," *Riverside Press,* August 16, 1902, p. 4; "Famous Hotel Man Visiting Riverside," *Riverside Press,*

February 27, 1902, p. 4. Also Kaiser, *Great Camps,* pp. 42–49, 115; Mildred Phelps Stokes Hooker, *Camp Chronicles* (Blue Mountain Lake, N.Y.: Adirondack Museum, 1964).

86. The Mission Inn also had a burned-in stamp, "Glenwood," which appears to have been used indiscriminately to mark furniture owned as well as made by the inn.

87. "Fra Elbertus Shown Sights of Riverside," *Riverside Enterprise,* April 18, 1909, p. 1. It is likely that he had visited in c. 1906–7 as well.

88. "The Glenwood," *Fra* (1908), and "Elbert Hubbard Compliments the Glenwood," *Philistine* (December 1909), clippings in Miller Scrapbook.

89. Archibald, "Sharp."

90. Arthur B. Benton, *California Mission Inn* (Los Angeles: Senogram Publishing Co., 1907–8).

91. *Riverside County, California* (Riverside, Calif.: Cloister Print Shop, [c. 1914]).

92. Elbert Hubbard, *Days of Peace and Rest at the Glenwood by Those Who Know* (East Aurora, N.Y.: Roycrofters Print Shop, 1907), RMM; Elbert Hubbard, *Music at Meals* (East Aurora, N.Y.: Roycrofters Print Shop, 1912), MIC.

93. Redlands Indian Association, Minute Book 2, citation of April 26, 1913.

94. "Pottery Kiln To Be Considered by Miller," *Riverside Enterprise,* December 23, 1919, p. 3.

95. Holmes, *Riverside,* pp. 119–20; *Historical Highlights* and "Announcement of Summer Institute" (Washington, D.C., 1916), in vertical files of the Riverside Public Library (hereafter cited as *RPL*); *Sherman Institute Scrapbook,* c. 1902, RMM.

96. Ludwig, *Arts and Crafts Movement in New York,* pp. 55–56; David M. Cathers, *Furniture of the American Arts and Crafts Movement: Stickley and Roycroft Mission Oak* (New York: New American Library, 1981), pp. 126–41; Wendy Kaplan et al., *"The Art that is Life": The Arts and Crafts Movement in America, 1875–1920* (Boston: Museum of Fine Arts; New York Graphic Society, 1987), pp. 43, 79; Leslie Greene Bowman, *American Arts and Crafts: Virtue in Design* (Los Angeles: Los Angeles County Museum of Art; Boston: Little, Brown and Company, 1990), pp. 66–81.

97. Gilborn, *Adirondack Furniture,* pp. 251, 255.

98. Vincent Moses, Curator of History, Riverside Municipal Museum Archives, inter-

view with the author, June 28, 1991; photograph files provided by Chris Moser, Curator of Anthropology, Riverside Municipal Museum. Rumsey's basket collection became the basis for the Cornelius Earl Rumsey Indian Museum of 1924, which in 1925 became the Riverside Municipal Museum.

99. "Tea Room in Old Adobe," *Picturesque Riverside,* c. 1902, RMM; "Students of Sherman Institute Present a Japanese Operetta 'Princess Chrysanthemum,'" announcement card of May 11, 1914, RPL vertical files.

100. Mark Howland Rawitsch, *No Other Place: Japanese-American Pioneers in a Southern California Neighborhood* (Riverside: Department of History, University of California, Riverside, 1983). In January 1912 Mamoru Kish, assistant manager of the Imperial Hotel in Tokyo, went to the Mission Inn to observe Miller's operation. Kishi was looking for ideas for a new Imperial Hotel. Interestingly, the Chicago architect Frank Lloyd Wright ultimately landed the commission to design the new hotel, 1916–22. "Here to Study Hotels," *Hotel Registry* (January 1912), clipping in Miller Scrapbook.

101. Bolton Hall, *Three Acres and Liberty* (New York: Macmillan, 1907); Bolton Hall, *A Little Land and a Living* (New York: Arcadia Press, 1908).

102. Karen J. Weitze, "Midwest to California: The Planned Arts and Crafts Community" (paper submitted to the Winterthur Museum for "The Substance of Style: New Perspectives on the American Arts and Crafts Movement" conference, October 18–20, 1990, publication forthcoming); Pauline Meyer, *Keep Your Face to the Sunshine: A Lost Chapter in the History of Woman Suffrage* (Edwardsville, Ill.: Alcott Press, 1980); *The American Woman's Republic* (University City, Mo.: Lewis Publications, 1911).

103. *Keramic Studio* 12 (September 1910): 89; Frederick Hürten Rhead, letter to Taxile Doat, October 15, 1911, and Taxile Doat, letter to E. G. Lewis, dated by contextual information to April 1913, in University City Public Library, Special Collections, University City, Mo.; E. G. Lewis Diary, 1905–15, private collection; photograph collections of the Atascadero Historical Society and the Saint Louis Art Museum.

104. "Primary Election Notice," *San Luis Obispo Telegram,* August 11, 1914, p. 2, and August 12, 1914, p. 4. Liberal politics were also found to the east, across the San Joaquin Valley

at Fresno, where Chester Harvey Rowell commissioned Maybeck in 1909 to design a bungalow adapted to the semiarid climate. Rowell was a founder of the Lincoln-Roosevelt Republican League and is also credited with being the intellectual force behind the unfolding of the Progressive party in California. His politics paralleled those surrounding Atascadero. Fresno's Arts and Crafts enclaves (notably that of North Park) sat enframed by miles of irrigated raisin vineyards, with the revered Arts and Crafts retreat of Yosemite farther to the east. Its Arts and Crafters also regularly encamped west of Atascadero at Morro Bay and north at Carmel.

105. University City, Mo.: Colony Holding Corporation, February 1913–September 1915: *Bulletin 1–7,* including two published versions of *Bulletin 5,* Atascadero Historical Society and Bancroft Library, University of California, Berkeley; "Atascadero Colony," *Templeton Times,* August 7, 1913, p. 2; Ida Husted Harper, *The History of Woman Suffrage, 1900–1920,* vol. 6 of *History,* pp. 847–60.

106. Lewis Diary.

107. Weitze, "Midwest to California"; Atascadero *Bulletins 1–7;* Atascadero Historical Society photograph albums; *Atascadero News,* April 22, 1916, p. 4.

108. Starr, *Inventing the Dream,* pp. 137–40.

THE RESORT TO THE RUSTIC:
SIMPLE LIVING AND THE CALIFORNIA
BUNGALOW
Cheryl Robertson

This essay is a short version of work in progress on domesticity and the pursuit of the simple life in California at the turn of the century.

1. David E. Shi, *The Simple Life* (New York: Oxford University Press, 1985), p. 11.

2. Ibid., p. 177. See Anthony D. King, *The Bungalow: The Production of a Global Culture* (London: Routledge & Kegan Paul, 1984), p. 141, on the Los Angeles boom, 1900–30, when population grew from 100,000 to 1,000,000 residents.

3. Karen J. Weitze, *California's Mission Revival* (Los Angeles: Hennessey & Ingalls, 1984), p. 16.

4. Daniela P. Moneta, ed., *Charles F. Lummis: The Centennial Exhibition* (Los Angeles: Southwest Museum, 1985), p. 11. On Lummis's coining the term "the Southwest," see Lawrence Clark Powell, "Charles Fletcher Lummis and The

Land of Sunshine," *Westways* 62 (January 1970): 21–22.

5. David E. Shi, *In Search of the Simple Life* (Salt Lake City: Gibbs M. Smith, 1986), pp. 178–79, 182–85. See also Tom Lutz, *American Nervousness, 1903* (Ithaca, N.Y.: Cornell University Press, 1991).

6. Charles Fletcher Lummis, "The Making of Los Angeles," *Out West* 30 (April 1909): 234–35.

7. Alice J. Stevens, "A Hand-Made House," *Harper's Weekly* 44 (September 1, 1900): 825. On concrete's simulation of adobe, see Lummis, quoted in Weitze, *Mission Revival,* p. 118. El Alisal has been preserved as a museum, and it serves as the headquarters of the Historical Society of Southern California.

8. Turbese Lummis Fiske and Keith Lummis, *Charles F. Lummis: The Man and His West* (Norman: University of Oklahoma Press, 1975), pp. 98–99; Kevin Starr, *Inventing the Dream: California through the Progressive Era* (New York: Oxford University Press, 1985), p. 84.

9. Stevens, "Hand-Made House," p. 825; Dudley Gordon, "Lummis and Maynard Dixon: Patron and Protégé," *Westerners: Los Angeles Corral* 102 (September 1971): 9.

10. Stevens, "Hand-Made House," p. 825.

11. Fiske and Lummis, *Lummis,* p. 111. Lummis briefly described his "ranch" workdays in letters to Charles Keeler, 1898–99, Keeler Papers, Huntington Library, Art Collections, and Botanical Gardens, San Marino, Calif.

12. Stevens, "Hand-Made House," p. 825.

13. Lummis to Keeler, August 22, 1898, Keeler Papers.

14. Marc Simmons, *Two Southwesterners: Charles Lummis and Amado Chaves* (Cerrillos, N.Mex.: San Marcos Press, 1968), pp. 11–13. The "Little Lion" was so nicknamed for his fierce tenacity in skirmishes with the Navajos. Lummis's title "In the Lion's Den" for his *Land of Sunshine* editorials may have been a tribute to Don Miguel Antonio Chaves. For other speculations on the term "Lion's Den," see Edwin R. Bingham, *Charles F. Lummis: Editor of the Southwest* (San Marino, Calif.: Huntington Library, 1955), p. 79.

15. Ibid., pp. 139–40.

16. Ibid., p. 21.

17. Charles Keeler, "Some Contemporary California Writers," *Personal Impressions* 1 (July 1900): 73.

18. Dimitri Shipounoff, introduction, in Charles Keeler, *The Simple Home* (San Francisco: Paul Elder & Co., 1904; reprint, Santa Barbara, Calif.: Peregrine Smith, 1979), pp. xix, xxx.

19. Ibid., pp. xxv, xxxi; George Wharton James, "Charles Keeler, Scientist and Poet," *National Magazine* 35 (November 1911): 47–48, 49.

20. Shipounoff, introduction, in Keeler, *Simple Home,* p. xxi.

21. Keeler, ibid., p. 4.

22. Ibid., pp. 3, 5. Keeler quoted Emerson: "The ornament of a house is the friends who frequent it."

23. James, "Keeler," p. 42; Shipounoff, introduction, in Keeler, *Simple Home,* p. xxi.

24. Keeler, ibid., p. 25.

25. James, "Keeler," p. 47.

26. Leslie Mandelson Freudenheim and Elisabeth Sacks Sussman, *Building with Nature: Roots of the San Francisco Bay Region Tradition* (Santa Barbara, Calif.: Peregrine Smith, 1974), p. 98.

27. Ibid., p. 46; Shipounoff, introduction, in Keeler, *Simple Home,* p. xxxiv.

28. James, "Keeler," p. 51; Shipounoff, introduction, in Keeler, *Simple Home,* p. xxxii.

29. James, "Keeler," p. 49.

30. Ruskin, quoted in John F. Sears, *Sacred Places: American Tourist Attractions in the Nineteenth Century* (New York: Oxford University Press, 1989), p. 141.

31. Ibid., p. 148.

32. The architect was given as "John" White in W. E. Colby, "The Completed Le Conte Memorial Lodge," *Sierra Club Bulletin* 5 (January 1904): 69, but the clubhouse is described, illustrated, and reattributed in William C. Tweed, Laura E. Soulliere, and Henry G. Law, "National Park Service Rustic Architecture, 1916–1942" (typescript, February 1977, National Park Service, Western Regional Office), p. 5.

33. Colby, "Le Conte Memorial Lodge," pp. 66–67.

34. Shi, *Simple Life,* p. 209.

35. Earl Pomeroy, *In Search of the Golden West: The Tourist in Western America* (New York: Alfred A. Knopf, 1957), p. 203.

36. Ibid., p. 7.

37. Thomas Starr King, *A Vacation among the Sierras: Yosemite in 1860,* ed. John A. Hussey (San Francisco: Book Club of California, 1962),

p. 26; Margaret Sanborn, *Yosemite* (New York: Random House, 1981), p. 87.

38. Sanborn, *Yosemite,* pp. 94, 98; Peter J. Blodgett, "Visiting 'The Realm of Wonder': Yosemite and the Business of Tourism, 1855–1916," *California History* 69 (Summer 1990): 122.

39. H.H. [Helen Hunt Jackson], *Ah-Wah-Ne Days: A Visit to the Yosemite Valley in 1872* (San Francisco: Book Club of California, 1971), pp. 34, 40.

40. "Yosemite—Sentinel Hotel/Camp Yosemite," [c. 1901] , Huntington Library ephemera collections (hereafter cited as *HLEC*).

41. Blodgett, "Yosemite and Tourism," p. 132; "Curry of Yosemite," [c. 1915], HLEC.

42. "Yosemite—Camp Curry," 1917, HLEC.

43. *The Yosemite Story,* 3d ed. (Santa Ana, Calif.: F. H. Scott/Western Resort Publications, 1957), p. 26.

44. Elsie Leonard, "The Utility of the Bungalow," *American Homes and Gardens* 5 (May 1908): xiii, xiv; "Some California Bungalow and Residence Interiors," *Architect and Engineer* 14 (October 1908): 71. On California as the birthplace of, and ideal physical locale for, the American bungalow, see Robert W. Winter, *The California Bungalow* (Los Angeles: Hennessey & Ingalls, 1980), pp. 7, 11.

45. Charles Keeler, "The Impress of Nature on California," *Impressions* 1 (November 1900): 172.

46. "Wilson Peak Park, above the Clouds: The Alps of America," 1910, HLEC; John W. Robinson, *The San Gabriels: Southern California Mountain Country* (San Marino, Calif.: Golden West Books, 1977), pp. 36–39.

47. "Sturdevant's Camp on the San Gabriel Forest Reserve," 1900, pp. 7, 9, 10, 12–13, HLEC. See also Robinson, *San Gabriels,* pp. 119–25.

48. "Mt. Wilson: Strain's Camp, Sturdevant Camp," 1910, HLEC.

49. "A Summer Home above the Clouds," *Craftsman* 10 (August 1906): 642, 647. Unless otherwise noted, ensuing description of the Mount Wilson Hotel is from the *Craftsman.*

50. *Craftsman* 10 (August 1906): 642, claimed "the larger pieces of furniture were made on the mountain-top." In the same issue was the second of three woodworking articles on home construction of rustic furniture.

51. Richard Longstreth, *On the Edge of the World: Four Architects at the Turn of the Century*

(New York: Architectural History Foundation; Cambridge, Mass.: MIT Press, 1983), pp. 175–76.

52. Abraham Hoffman, "Mountain Resorts and Trail Camps in Southern California's Great Hiking Era," *Southern California Quarterly* 58 (Fall 1976): 383.

53. Pomeroy, *Tourist,* p. 132. Space has not permitted discussion of other California alpine resorts, notably Lake Tahoe and, in the San Diego area, Pine Hills. Materials on lodges, cabins, and vacation residences in those locales can be found in the Huntington Library and the San Diego Historical Society. Also consult George Wharton James, *The Lake of the Sky, Lake Tahoe, in the High Sierras of California and Nevada* (Boston: L. C. Page, 1915).

54. Gustav Stickley, *Craftsman Homes* (New York: Craftsman Publishing Co., 1909), p. 156; "How to Build a Bungalow," *Craftsman* 5 (December 1903): 253.

55. Harlan Thomas, "Possibilities of the Bungalow as a Permanent Dwelling," *Craftsman* 9 (March 1906): 859–63; Henry H. Saylor, *Bungalows* (Philadelphia: John H. Winston Co., 1911), pp. 20–21.

56. George Wharton James, *California Romantic and Beautiful* (Boston: L. C. Page, 1914), p. 256. On California as the American pioneer in suburban bungalow development, see "Bungalow Building in California," *Pacific Coast Architect* 8 (November 1914): 177.

57. "Architecture Is Attractive and Pretty," *Los Angeles Examiner,* May 22, 1904, p. 43; King, *Bungalow,* p. 132.

58. "Some California Houses That Show an Interesting Use of the Popular and Adaptable Cobblestone," *Craftsman* 13 (November 1907): 192–98, reworked as "The Effective Use of Cobblestones as a Link between House and Landscape," in Stickley, *Craftsman Homes,* pp. 102–8.

59. Florence Williams, "Homes in the Land of Sunshine," *Indoors and Out* 4 (August 1907): 205; "Interiors of California Bungalows," *Bungalow Magazine* 1 (November 1912): 17–24; *Southern California Bungalow Plans* (Los Angeles and San Diego: Southern California Home Builders, 1913), pp. 6, 13, 63; "Interiors of Wilson Bungalows," *Bungalow Magazine* 2 (March 1910): 16–17, 21. Henry L. Wilson published *Bungalow Magazine* out of Los Angeles from 1909 through 1910 (the first issue was called *California Bungalow*). Jud Yoho published

255

another version of *Bungalow Magazine* out of Seattle, from August 1912 through March 1918.

60. Charles Alma Byers, "Modern Fireplaces and Mantelpieces," *House and Garden* 15 (June 1909): 205, 206, 203. Wilson founded and edited *Bungalow Magazine* as a vehicle for publicizing his plans and interior fittings; Design No. 600 for a "Dutch clinker brick mantel," in living room or den, with the brick "laid in black mortar with raised joints, giving a rustic effect," appeared in *Bungalow Magazine* 1 (April 1909): 44. Design No. 600 was the lead illustration in Louise Shrimpton, "Furnishing the Camp or Summer Home," *House and Garden* 17 (June 1910): 230.

61. This fireplace was in the South Pasadena home of P. G. Gates, designed by the Pasadena architect J. J. Blick, who published an illustrated compendium of his commissions (*Pasadena Homes,* [c. 1910], Huntington Library). Nash advertised in *Pasadena Homes* and gave a list of Nash-Blick clients, including P. G. Gates. Mantels and other tiling in Grueby faience were a specialty, according to this ad and another in *Architect and Engineer of California* 4 (April 1906): 128, which utilized the "artists" and "craftsmen" terminology. For executed examples in Grueby and Rookwood tile, see Carl Enos Nash, "The Fireplace: A Neglected Part of the House," *Architect and Engineer of California* 8 (March 1907): 85–87.

62. Ibid., p. 85.

63. Charles Francis Saunders, "Bungalow Life: The Cost of Living It," *Sunset* 30 (January 1913): 33.

64. H. J. Slater, "Furnishing Bungalow Porches," *Bungalow Magazine* 1 (May 1909): 86–87.

65. Philip Savary, "Bungalow Mission Furniture," *Bungalow Magazine* 1 (May 1909): 88–89. "Furnishing a California Bungalow," *Bungalow Magazine* 1 (April 1909): 56–58, showcased a Wilson bungalow decorated by Barker Brothers of Los Angeles that, if unattributed, would pass muster as a model Stickley interior. The Mission Fixture Company of Los Angeles, producers of lanterns and sconces after Craftsman prototypes, advertised in *Bungalow Magazine* 1 (July 1909): 157.

66. [Henry L. Wilson], "The California Bungalow: What It Is, What It Is Not, and What It May Be," *Bungalow Magazine* 1 (June 1909): 115–16. For a sampling of literature con-

troverting the kinship between the Bengalese hut and the Californian/American bungalow, see E. W. Stillwell, *Representative California Homes,* 7th ed. (Los Angeles: E. W. Stillwell Company, 1912), p. 2; Charles E. White, Jr., *The Bungalow Book* (New York: Macmillan, 1923), p. 1; J. Lockwood Kipling, "The Origin of the Bungalow," *Country Life in America* 19 (February 15, 1911): 310.

67. [Wilson], "California Bungalow" (June 1909): 117, 119; (July 1909): 149; and (September 1909): 209. On "our California custom of entering the living room directly from the front door," see *California Bungalow Homes* (Los Angeles: Bungalowcraft Company, 1910), p. 93; on pages 3 and 7 are examples of "California Style" battened-board houses.

68. Helen Lukens Gaut, "A Very Modest Little Cottage," *Ladies' Home Journal* 26 (April 1909): 59; *"Ye Planry" Bungalows* (Los Angeles: "Ye Planry" Company, 1910), p. 7. "Shakes" resembled "shingles," and the words were often used interchangeably in popular housing literature, although "Ye Planry" distinguished the former as untapering, of uniform width, and longer than the latter.

69. Wendell G. Corthell, "The Use of Wood in Switzerland," *Craftsman* 5 (October 1903): 31, 35, 39, 41.

70. Ibid., p. 39; Louis J. Stellmann, "The Swiss Chalet Type for America," *House and Garden* 20 (November 1911): 290.

71. Corthell, "Wood in Switzerland," p. 39, discusses the varying roof types; he also mentions the National Exposition in Geneva in 1896, reported by the American journal *Architectural Record,* where reproductions of chalets from the various cantons were on display.

72. Saylor, *Bungalows,* pp. 29–30, 61.

73. Helen Ray, "A California Chalet," *House and Garden* 16 (November 1909): 168–69. Ensuing description of Felsengarten interiors is from Ray, unless otherwise specified. Ray's article was reprinted in Henry H. Saylor, ed., *Distinctive Homes of Moderate Cost* (New York: McBride, Winston, 1910), pp. 139–40.

74. Corthell, "Wood in Switzerland," p. 39, describes the natural pine woodwork of period rooms in the museum in Basel.

75. Dorothy Tuke Priestman, "Furnishings for the Bungalow," *Country Life in America* 19 (February 15, 1911): 323.

76. Myron Hunt, "Personal Sources of

Pacific Coast Architectural Development," *American Architect* 129 (January 1926): 52.

77. *"Ye Planry" Bungalows* (Los Angeles: "Ye Planry" Company, 1908), pp. 44–45, 70–71; *Southern California Bungalow Plans,* pp. 26–29. Plan No. 119 was one of the few catalog models shown with furnished interiors; the white wicker furniture complemented the white-painted wood finish inside and out. Corthell, "Wood in Switzerland," p. 39, noted that whitewashing was common on the stone portions of Swiss chalets. See also Southern California Home Builders, advertisement, *Arrowhead* (June 1914): 1; *West Coast* 14 (January 1914): 19.

78. On Greene and Greene not as the originators but as the outstanding practitioners of bungalow architecture, see Robert Gregory Brown, "The California Bungalow in Los Angeles: A Study in Origins and Classification" (master's thesis, University of California, Los Angeles, 1964), p. viii. Concerning the internationality of timber building in mountain regions—the Alps, the Himalayas, and Japan—see Clay Lancaster, "The American Bungalow," *Art Bulletin* 40 (September 1958): 248. Cram is reviewed in "Japanese Architecture and Its Relation to the Coming American Style," *Craftsman* 10 (May 1906): 192–212. Greene and Greene dwellings, notably Charles's own home and the Irwin House (both 1906), are the subject of Henrietta P. Keith, "The Trail of Japanese Influence in Our Modern Domestic Architecture," *Craftsman* 12 (July 1907): 446–51.

79. Una Nixson Hopkins, "The California Bungalow," *Architect and Engineer of California* 4 (April 1906): 36–37; Una Nixson Hopkins, "A Study for Home-Builders," *Good Housekeeping* 42 (March 1906): 259–64. Hopkins wrote for all the major homemaking periodicals, including *Ladies' Home Journal, House Beautiful,* and *Keith's.* On light and color, see also William R. Current and Karen Current, *Greene and Greene: Architects in the Residential Style* (Fort Worth: Amon Carter Museum of Western Art, 1974), p. 18.

80. Una Nixson Hopkins, "A House of Fine Detail That Conforms to the Hillside on Which It Is Built," *Craftsman* 12 (June 1907): 330. Exterior and interior also illustrated in "Some California Bungalow and Residence Interiors," p. 72.

81. Una Nixson Hopkins, "The Decoration of Our Homes," *Keith's* 29 (February 1913): 79, 80.

82. Kate Greenleaf Locke, "Furnishing and Decorating Houses of Moderate Cost," *House and Garden* 11 (June 1907): 223. On the inexpensiveness of bungalows and the contention that Greene and Greene homes cost no more than the average small suburban house, see Arthur C. David, "An Architect of Bungalows in California," *Architectural Record* 20 (October 1906): 311.

83. [Arthur Jerome Eddy], "A California House Modeled on the Simple Lines of the Old Mission Dwelling," *Craftsman* 11 (November 1906): 208–20. Ensuing comments on color and furnishings are from this article unless otherwise noted. Eddy's bungalow was also illustrated and described, with particular reference to the "blending colors," in Williams, "Homes in Sunshine," pp. 204, 205. The Eddy living room and library were pictured again in Charles Francis Osborne, ed., *Country Homes and Gardens of Moderate Cost* (Philadelphia: John H. Winston Co., 1907), p. 78.

84. "An Arts and Crafts House," *House Beautiful* 25 (April 1909): 102.

85. Mary Austin, *The Lands of the Sun* (Cambridge, Mass.: Riverside Press, 1927), pp. 33–34.

86. Saunders, "Bungalow Life," p. 40.

CREATING BEAUTY FROM THE EARTH: THE TILES OF CALIFORNIA
Joseph A. Taylor

1. *Clay-Worker* (October 1925): 309.

2. Robert L. Hoover, "The Mission San Antonio de Padua in California," *Archaeology* 32 (November–December 1979): 57–58.

3. "The Tropico Tile Works," *Builder and Contractor* (August 16, 1900): 1.

4. "Tile Exhibit," *Builder and Contractor* (January 3, 1901): 1.

5. Fred H. Wilde, quoted in Everett Townsend, "Development of the Tile Industry in the United States," *Bulletin of the American Ceramic Society* 22, no. 5 (1943): 148.

6. Heinrich Ries and Henry Leighton, *History of the Clay-Working Industry in the United States* (New York: John Wiley & Sons, 1909), p. 70.

7. "Off the Wire," *Mantel, Tile and Grate Monthly* (April 1910): 33.

8. "Many Firms Display Products at Exposition," *Pacific Coast Architect* 9 (May 1915): 197.

9. For details on the development of Vernon as a tile-manufacturing center, see "Tile Factory," *Southwest Builder and Contractor* (March 21, 1912): 9; "Art Tile Factory," *Southwest Builder and Contractor* (January 11, 1912): 3; "Vernon Becoming Unique Clay Products Center," *Southwest Builder and Contractor* (November 30, 1917): 9. Also Maxine Feek Nelson, *Versatile Vernon Kilns* (Costa Mesa, Calif.: Rainbow Publications, 1978), p. 9.

10. Townsend, "Development," p. 149.

11. "Colored Glazed Tile at the Exposition," *Architect* (June 19, 1915): 220.

12. Rhead, together with his first wife, Agnes Rhead, produced a tiled fireplace surround depicting a handsome peacock in full plumage and another with a stylized landscape for the John J. Meachem House in University City, consigned and dated 1910 and 1911, respectively. Rhead would once again produce tiles at his studio in Santa Barbara after leaving Arequipa.

13. Albert L. Solon lists his address as "General Delivery, National City," in the 1912 membership directory of the American Ceramic Society. It is likely that he and Wilde met at that time, and Solon may well have recommended the senior ceramist to Dr. Brown as his replacement.

14. Arequipa Sanatorium, "Sixth Annual Report," September 1917, p. 19.

15. Advertisement, *Pasadena Daily News*, September 16, 1909, p. 10. This information and that in the following note have been extracted from Robert W. Winter's unpublished biography of Ernest A. and Alice Batchelder. I am most grateful to Dr. Winter for his enthusiastic assistance from the inception of this project.

16. "The Scope and Plan of Ernest Batchelder's Work Shop–School," *Pasadena Daily News,* June 3, 1909, p. 8.

17. See Cleota Reed, *Henry Chapman Mercer and the Moravian Pottery and Tile Works* (Philadelphia: University of Pennsylvania Press, 1987).

18. Twenty-four different tiles were sent to Batchelder (at Throop) from the Moravian Pottery on July 30, 1907. The existing fireplace in Batchelder's house, which contains both Moravian and Batchelder tiles, is not original. According to Robert W. Winter, this fireplace facade was likely installed in 1912, a wedding gift from Ernest to his wife, Alice Coleman.

19. E. B. MacLaughlin, "Expert Tile

Worker Prefers Small Pasadena Pottery to Large Factory," *Pasadena Star News,* April 11, 1948, p. 14. This quote came to me thanks to the kindness of Robert W. Winter.

20. Contrary to many published reports, Batchelder moved his factory to Los Angeles in 1920, the first directory listing on Artesian Street being in 1921. Batchelder himself gives the date as 1920 in *A Little History of Batchelder Tiles* (Los Angeles: Batchelder-Wilson Company, [c. 1923]). In his recent research, Robert W. Winter also discovered that Batchelder had obtained a permit to expand his Pasadena factory on November 7, 1916.

21. Batchelder, *Little History.*

22. *A Litle* [sic] *Journey through the Batchelder Factory* (Los Angeles: Batchelder-Wilson Company, n.d.).

23. *Tiles* (Los Angeles: Claycraft Potteries, n.d.).

24. Ibid.

25. Biographical sketches of James White Hislop and his sons may be found in *History of Contra Costa County* (Los Angeles: Historic Record Company, 1926), pp. 1079–80, 1086–87, 1091.

26. *Two Generations of Claycraft* (Richmond, Calif.: California Art Tile Corporation, [c. 1928]).

27. *Kraftile: High Fired Faience* (San Francisco: Kraftile Company, n.d.).

28. Irene Knops, interview with author, Fresno, July 23, 1991. This interview with Muir's daughter revealed what little is known about Muir and his brief career as a tile maker.

29. *Muresque Tiles: Mantel Catalogue* (Oakland, Calif.: Muresque Tiles, n.d.).

30. Handcraft is listed as "San Jose Tile Company" in Waldemar Fenn Dietrich, *The Clay Resources and the Ceramic Industry of California,* Division of Mines and Mining, bulletin no. 99 (San Francisco, January 1928), p. 221. For Woolenius, see ibid., p. 49; also *Woolenius Tile Co.* (Berkeley, Calif.: Woolenius Tile Co., [c. 1930]).

31. David Gebhard, *Kem Weber: The Moderne in Southern California, 1920–1941* (Santa Barbara: Art Galleries, University of California, Santa Barbara, 1969), p. 24.

32. For a detailed account of the life of Keeler, see Joseph A. Taylor, "Rufus B. Keeler: A Tile Wizard," *Flash Point* 2 (January–March 1989): 1, 8, 9, 12.

33. Rufus B. Keeler left his job at Gladding,

257

McBean in September 1916 at the same time that Fred H. Wilde left California China Products Company for Arequipa. The membership roster of the American Ceramic Society lists Keeler's address as "National City" in 1917, the year during which California China Products Company closed its factory and consolidated with West Coast Tile in Vernon. Keeler may have worked at California China Products Company and assisted during the transition. He established his own business adjacent to West Coast Tile in October 1917.

34. Rufus B. Keeler, "The Use of Clay Products in the Modern Home," *Bulletin of the American Ceramic Society* 4 (July 1925): 310–21.

35. See the excerpts from memoirs of former employees in Ronald L. Rindge, *Ceramic Art of the Malibu Potteries, 1926–1932* (Malibu, Calif.: Malibu Lagoon Museum, 1988).

36. Information taken from Lee Rosenthal's unpublished manuscript on the history of Catalina tile forthcoming from Windgate Press, Sausalito, Calif.

37. For a detailed account of the life of Albert L. Solon, see Lynn Downey, "Albert Louis Solon: Ceramist with a Sense of Humor," pts. 1–3, *Flash Point* 3 (October–December 1990): 1, 8, 10; 4 (January–March 1991): 9–11; 4 (April–June 1991): 5–7.

38. In the membership roster of the American Ceramic Society, Chauncey Rapelje Thomas is first listed as "Ceramic Student, Amherst" in 1906; William Victor Bragdon as "Student, New York State School of Clayworking and Ceramics" in 1907.

39. Stella Loveland Towne, interview with Hazel Bray, April 14, 1969, transcript, p. 3, Oakland Museum Art Department. Towne gives an insider's view of California Faience and its founders.

40. Gertrude Rupel Wall, interview with Hazel Bray and Lewis Ferbrache in Montara, Calif., October 14, 1965, transcript, p. 4, Oakland Museum Art Department. Wall reflects in detail on her life and work.

THE ARTS AND CRAFTS MOVEMENT IN THE SAN FRANCISCO BAY AREA
Kenneth R. Trapp

1. Arthur F. Mathews's name has entered the literature incorrectly as Arthur Frank Mathews, when in fact his given name was Arthur Francis Mathews. See Arthur Francis

Mathews biographical card file, 1914, California Room, California State Library, Sacramento; Mathews himself provided the information.

2 . Quoted in Paul Evans, *Art Pottery of the United States: An Encyclopedia of Producers and Their Marks* (New York: Charles Scribner's Sons, 1974), p. 277 n. 15.

3. Alice Chittenden, "The Romance of the Roblin Pottery," *Modern Priscilla* 17 (October 1902): 5.

4. "Roblin Art Pottery," *Illustrated Glass and Pottery World* (September 1902): 15.

5. C. P. Neilson, "Applied Art in San Francisco," *Sunset* 13 (June 1904): 140. Neilson was a member of the Judgement Committee of the guild; Guild of Arts and Crafts, *Catalogue: Second Annual Exhibition of the Guild of Arts and Crafts* (San Francisco: Guild of Arts and Crafts, 1904), n.p. The earlier Guild of Arts and Crafts of San Francisco, established in the mid-1890s, exhibited paintings, sketches, architectural renderings, and the arts of the book and printing; see *Wave* 15 (May 23, 1896): 9.

6. For more about Orlow's group, see "The Influence of Intimate Surroundings," *Overland Monthly* 44 (September 1904): 5, 388–90.

7. Neiison, "Applied Art," p. 140.

8. Guild of Arts and Crafts, *Second Annual Exhibition,* n.p.

9. *San Francisco: Her Great Manufacturing, Commercial, and Financial Institutions Are Famed the World Over* (San Francisco: Pacific Art Company, 1904), p. 44.

10. Guild of Arts and Crafts, *Second Annual Exhibition,* n.p.

11. "Influence of Intimate Surroundings," p. 388.

12. Neilson, "Applied Art," pp. 138–39.

13. Orlow lost a suit filed against him "for rent and restitution of premises" and was evicted from the United Crafts and Arts headquarters at 147 Presidio Avenue. *San Francisco Call,* June 11, 1907, p. 16.

14. Two bulletins of especial interest are *An Arts and Crafts Bookshop* (San Francisco: Paul Elder & Co., [c. 1904–5]) and *An Arts and Crafts Book Shop in Greater San Francisco* (San Francisco: Paul Elder & Co., 1906). The latter bulletin has a Van Ness Avenue address, which indicates it was published after the earthquake and fire. Elder, along with other businesses, moved to Van Ness Avenue to await the rebuilding of downtown San Francisco.

15. See full-page advertisement for Meyer's

Craftsman's Shop in the back of Guild of Arts and Crafts, *Second Annual Exhibition,* n.p.

16. "Influence of Intimate Surroundings," p. 388. On his biographical card of 1908 Meyer wrote: "Designed & made furniture for 1. Dining room, Mrs. Hearst McCloud River Castle 2. Faculty Club U. C. Berkeley 3. Former offices of the Sunset Magazine S. F. 4. Furniture for San Francisco House, St. Louis Exposition 5. Furniture for former rooms of the Sequoia Club S. F." Frederick H. Meyer biographical card file, 1908, California Section, California State Library, Sacramento.

17. Neilson, "Applied Art," p. 138.

18. *Eucalyptus* (St. Louis: Sacramento Valley Improvement Co., [1908]), pp. 14–16.

19. *San Francisco Chronicle,* August 20, 1922, p. 41.

20. [Frederick H. Meyer], "Why an Art School? An Unfinished Autobiography by Frederick H. Meyer," in *Remembering Dr. Meyer* (Oakland: California College of Arts and Crafts, 1960), n.p. Frederick Henry Meyer file, Archives of California Art, Oakland Museum.

21. Julia Inez Mann Barr, "Lifebook of James Adam Barr, Jr.," entry for November 7, 1909, collection of Dr. and Mrs. James Adam Barr, Jr. I wish to thank Dr. Barr for bringing his lifebook to my attention and for sharing information about Meyer.

22. Quoted in Edgar W. Morse, "Silver in the Golden State," in *Silver in the Golden State: Images and Essays Celebrating the History and Art of Silver in California* (Oakland, Calif.: Oakland Museum History Department, 1986), p. 17.

23. I wish to thank Michael Weller, silver historian and dealer, for this suggestion.

24. Mira Abbot Maclay, "An Ingenious Girl Worker in Metals: The Story of the Workshop of Miss Lillian Palmer of San Jose Who Has Hammered Out a Vastly Interesting Occupation for Herself," *San Francisco Call,* April 28, 1907, magazine section, part II.

25. Louise M. O'Hara, "She Evolves Art from Scraps: Woman Worker 'Eats Up' Iron Pipe," *San Francisco Call,* June 23, 1923, p. 3.

26. "Art Exhibit at Idora Proves Success," *Oakland Tribune,* October 24, 1908, p. 9. Beach-Robinson Co. exhibited hand-carved furniture at the Idora Park exhibition. No doubt this furniture was made by the Mathewses' Furniture Shop. Beach-Robinson and the Furniture Shop both operated at 1717 California Street in San Francisco.

27. *Catalogue of Fine Arts Gallery and Exhibit of Arts and Crafts* (Seattle, 1909), pp. 25–26, items 188–214. The exhibit comprised six bowls, fourteen vases, two candlesticks, four jardinieres, and one "placque."

28. Van Erp Family Archive, scrapbook, no pagination, Archives of California Art, Oakland Museum. What little is known about Gaw is compiled in her file in the Archives of California Art. Using census records and other sources, I was able to establish Gaw's birth and death dates and places.

29. Art Institute of Chicago, *Catalogue of the Ninth Annual Exhibition of Original Designs for Decorations and Examples of Art Crafts Having Distinct Artistic Merit* (Chicago: Art Institute of Chicago, 1910), no. 492.

30. Van Erp Family Archive, scrapbook, n.p.

31. Quoted in Evans, *Art Pottery,* p. 18.

32. *Official Catalogue of Exhibition: Panama-Pacific International Exposition,* rev. ed. (San Francisco: Wahlgreen Co., 1915); see Department E, Domestic Varied Industries. United States: Shreve & Co., pp. 63–64; Arequipa, pp. 65 and 68; Tile Shop, pp. 65 and 69; Dirk van Erp, p. 65; and Beach-Robinson Co. [Furniture Shop?], pp. 67–68.

33. Michael Williams, "Arts and Crafts at the Panama-Pacific," *Art and Progress* 6 (August 1915): 375–76.

34. Schaeffer's papers are deposited in the Archives of American Art, Smithsonian Institution, Huntington Library, Art Collections, and Botanical Gardens, San Marino, Calif., and in the Rudolph Schaeffer Archive, Archives of California Art, Oakland Museum.

35. "Highlights of Rudolph Schaeffer," data sheet (curriculum vitae), Schaeffer Archive, Archives of American Art. Schaeffer's uncataloged papers were studied at the Archives of American Art when the archives were housed at the M. H. de Young Memorial Museum, Fine Arts Museums of San Francisco.

THE ARTS AND CRAFTS MOVEMENT IN THE SOUTHLAND
Leslie Greene Bowman

1. Isabel McDougall, "A Craftsman of the Pacific Slope," *House Beautiful* 17 (February 1905): 15.

2. "California Develops Handicrafts," *California Arts and Architecture* (November 1932): 15.

3. James A. B. Scherer, "The Throop Idea," *Arroyo Craftsman* 1 (October 1909): 30.

4. Randell L. Makinson, "Charles and Henry Greene," in Timothy J. Andersen, Eudora M. Moore, and Robert W. Winter, eds., *California Design, 1910* (Pasadena, Calif.: California Design Publications, 1974; reprint, Salt Lake City: Peregrine Smith, 1989), p. 99. Factual information relating to the Greenes was derived from this source and from Randell L. Makinson, *Greene and Greene: Furniture and Related Designs* (Salt Lake City: Peregrine Smith, 1979).

5. Quoted in Robert Judson Clark, ed., *The Arts and Crafts Movement in America, 1876–1916* (Princeton, N.J.: Princeton University Art Museum, 1972), p. 83.

6. So Charles R. Ashbee described the Greenes' work in 1909, as quoted in Makinson, *Greene and Greene: Furniture and Related Designs,* p. 150.

7. Scherer, "Throop Idea," p. 30. I am grateful to Joan Ploetz and Shelley Erwin for their research assistance with Throop.

8. Advertisement, *Out West* 18 (May 1903).

9. Antony E. Anderson, "Art and Artists," *Los Angeles Sunday Times,* November 14, 1909, pt. III, p. 15.

10. "What Is the Arroyo Guild?" *Arroyo Craftsman* 1 (October 1909): 52–54. I am grateful to Inger Feeley for her research assistance with the guild.

11. Ibid., pp. 53–54. For more information on James and the guild, see Andersen, Moore, and Winter, eds., *California Design,* p. 39; and Robert W. Winter, "The Arroyo Culture," ibid., pp. 21–22.

12. For more information on Friedell, see Leslie Greene Bowman, "Arts and Crafts Silversmiths: Friedell and Blanchard in Southern California," in Edgar W. Morse, ed., *Silver in the Golden State: Images and Essays Celebrating the History and Art of Silver in California* (Oakland, Calif.: Oakland Museum History Department, 1986), pp. 41–46.

13. Douglas Donaldson, "Craftsmanship Comments," *California Southland* (February 1924): 24.

14. *The Donaldson Summer School* (Los Angeles: Manual Arts High School, 1915), [p. 2], Oakland Museum Archives. I am grateful to Sherri Birdsong for her assistance with Donaldson research.

15. *Southern California Exhibition of Applied Arts by Southern California Craftsmen at the Panama-California Exposition, San Diego, 1915* (Los Angeles: Lang Press, 1915); copy obtained from Doe Library, University of California, Berkeley.

16. [Douglas Donaldson], *Douglas Donaldson, Craftsman,* [c. 1917], [p. 4]; Library, Los Angeles County Museum of Art.

17. William Scott Braznell, in Wendy Kaplan et al., *"The Art that is Life": The Arts and Crafts Movement in America, 1875–1920* (Boston: Museum of Fine Arts; New York Graphic Society, 1987), pp. 330–31, and n. 7. Designs similar to the bird finial are found in Ernest A. Batchelder, *Design in Theory and Practice* (New York: Macmillan, 1910), p. 253, fig. 149.

18. *Arts and Crafts in Detroit, 1906–1976: The Movement, the Society, the School* (Detroit: Detroit Institute of Arts, 1976), p. 85, cat. no. 49.

19. *Douglas Donaldson, Craftsman,* [pp. 10–11].

20. "Throop's New Art Instructor Arrives," *Pasadena Evening Star,* August 7, 1906, p. 9.

21. "Decorative Arts Guild," *California Southland* (February 1924): 24.

22. Quoted in Marion Hugus Clark, "The Arts and Crafts Society," *California Southland* 7 (January 1925): 11. The last reference to the society is in *California Graphic,* November 28, 1925.

23. *California Southland* (May 1927): 5; (September 1927): 5.

24. For more information on Blanchard, see Bowman, "Arts and Crafts Silversmiths," in Morse, ed., *Silver in the Golden State,* pp. 46–55.

25. Porter Blanchard, "An Easterner Comes West," *California Southland* 6 (May 1924): 24.

26. Blanchard, quoted in Bowman, "Arts and Crafts Silversmiths," in Morse, ed., *Silver in the Golden State,* pp. 48, 49.

27. Ibid., p. 52.

28. Newspaper clipping, unrecorded citation, c. 1948, Porter Blanchard Papers, Archives of American Art, Smithsonian Institution, Washington, D.C.

29. See Leslie Greene Bowman, *American Arts and Crafts: Virtue in Design* (Los Angeles: Los Angeles County Museum of Art; Boston: Little, Brown and Company, 1990), p. 150, for information relating to Grand Feu.

30. *Grand Feu Art Pottery* (Los Angeles: Grand Feu Art Pottery, n.d.), pp. 1–2. Copy generously supplied by Paul Evans.

31. Julius Starke, *California Woods: Grandeur of the Yosemite* (Santa Barbara, Calif.: A. G. Rogers, 1905), p. 18.

32. "Exhibition of Art at Arcady School," *Santa Barbara Morning Press,* June 15, 1902, p. 3. I am grateful to Kim Cooper for her assistance with this reference and many more throughout this essay.

33. Katherine Louise Smith, "A California Craftsman and His Work," *House and Garden* 9 (January 1906): 33. I am grateful to Elizabeth Nesbitt for her assistance with Eaton research.

34. Charles Frederick Eaton, *The Arts and Crafts* (Santa Barbara, Calif.: Self-published, [c. 1905]), [p. 3]. The author is grateful to D. J. Puffert for introducing her to this rare pamphlet and permitting her access to his personal copy.

35. Isabel McDougall, "Some Recent Arts and Crafts Work," *House Beautiful* 14 (July 1903): 74–75.

36. *Official Catalogue of Exhibitors, Universal Exposition . . . Art* (St. Louis: Official Catalogue Company, 1904), p. 78. Rolls 1752 and 1748 (Charles Frederick Eaton, letter to F. A. Whiting, May 16, 1904), Louisiana Purchase Exposition Records, Department of Art Papers, Archives of American Art, Smithsonian Institution, Washington, D.C. (hereafter cited as *LPER*).

37. Charles Frederick Eaton, letter to F. A. Whiting, May 3, 1904, roll 1748, LPER. Such lighting was not included in Eaton's entries in exhibitions in Minneapolis and Chicago in 1902, but was shown in Chicago in 1903. Katherine Louise Smith, "An Arts and Crafts Exhibition at Minneapolis," *Craftsman* 3 (March 1903): 373–74; Art Institute of Chicago, *Catalogue of the First [and Second] Annual Exhibition of Original Designs for Decorations and Examples of Art Crafts Having Distinct Artistic Merit* (Chicago: Art Institute of Chicago, 1902, 1903). I am grateful to Sid Bernstein for providing the Chicago research.

38. Elizabeth Emery, "Arts and Crafts, Some Recent Work," *House Beautiful* 15 (February 1904): 134.

39. Gustav Stickley, "Nature and Art in California," *Craftsman* 6 (July 1904): 370–90, quote on p. 388. I am grateful to Judy Anderson for her research assistance with Burton.

40. Arthur Inkersley, "The Californian Art of Stamping and Embossing Leather," *Craftsman* 6 (April 1904): 52.

41. Stickley, "Nature and Art," pp. 375, 377, 379, 380, 381, 382, 384–89.

42. Roll 1752, LPER; and *Official Catalogue of Exhibitors, Universal Exposition . . . Art,* p. 70.

43. M. Banks, *Catalogue of Fine Arts Gallery and Exhibit of Arts and Crafts* (Seattle, 1909), pp. 18, 27, 31 (obtained from Special Collections and Preservation, University of Washington Libraries, Seattle); *Los Angeles Times,* November 14, 1909, pt. III, p. 15.

44. Elizabeth Eaton Burton, *Hand-Wrought Electric Lamps and Sconces* (Santa Barbara, Calif.: Self-published, [c. 1905]); copy in archives, Oakland Museum.

45. [H. M. Howard], "Parchment Illuminating," *Santa Barbara Morning Press,* May 27, 1906, p. 6. I am grateful to Julia Perry for her research assistance with Hyde.

46. Roll 1752, LPER; *Catalogue of Fine Arts Gallery and Exhibit of Arts and Crafts* (Seattle, 1909), p. 27. The author is grateful to Carla Rickerson and John Medlin in the Special Collections and Preservation division of the University of Washington Libraries, Seattle, for providing photocopies of the latter.

47. *Pleasant Pages, Books, and Cards Worth Giving from the Presses of Paul Elder & Company* (San Francisco: Paul Elder & Co., [1901]), pp. 13–16, 42, 46, 50.

48. For the definitive study of Elder and his various enterprises, see Ruth I. Gordon, *Paul Elder: Bookseller-Publisher, 1897–1917: A Bay Area Reflection* (Ann Arbor, Mich.: University Microfilms International, 1978).

49. *Santa Barbara City Directory, 1917–18* (Santa Barbara, Calif.: Santa Barbara Directory Company, 1917), p. 423.

50. For a complete study of Rhead in the United States, see Sharon Dale, *Frederick Hürten Rhead: An English Potter in America* (Erie, Pa.: Erie Art Museum, 1986).

51. [Frederick Hürten Rhead], "Planning and Operating a Studio Pottery," *Potter* 1 (January 1917): 62.

52. Articles of Incorporation of Rhead Pottery, filed in the office of the Secretary of State of the State of California, January 15, 1914, bk. 309, p. 157, corp. no. 75627. Whitehead's directorship of Rhead Pottery was discovered by Kim Cooper, Oakland Museum, and is confirmed by the articles of incorporation preserved in the Santa Barbara Historical Society.

53. Mrs. Hugh Weldon [Helen Tornoe Weldon], interview with Paul Evans, February 17, 1970, Paul Evans California Art Pottery Research Collection, Oakland Museum.

54. Gussie Packard du Bois, "The Pottery of Camarata," *Santa Barbara Morning Press,* November 4, 1914, p. 4.

55. Ednah Anne Rich, "An Account of the Santa Barbara State Normal School of Manual Arts and Home Economics from the Date of Its Establishment, March 27, 1909, until June 30, 1916, during the Period When Miss Ednah Anne Rich Was President" (manuscript, Special Collections, University of California, Santa Barbara), p. 78.

56. [Rhead], "Planning and Operating a Studio Pottery," p. 96.

57. Robert V. Hine, *California's Utopian Colonies* (Berkeley: University of California Press, 1983), p. 54.

58. *Temple Artisan* 10 (May 1910): 243.

59. "Making Pottery," *San Luis Obispo Tribune,* January 6, 1911.

60. "The Halcyon Art Pottery," *Temple Artisan* 12 (March 1911): 186.

61. The author is grateful to Ruth Penka and Sherri Birdsong for their extensive research on Halcyon. Birdsong is to be credited for the Robineau discovery and the Gertrude Rupel Wall connection.

62. "Pottery Expert Heads Art Department," *National City News,* January 13, 1912. I am grateful to Joseph A. Taylor for sharing this reference.

63. Trippett, quoted in Bowman, *American Arts and Crafts,* p. 174.

64. "Pottery Expert Heads Art Department."

THE ARTS AND CRAFTS MOVEMENT IN SAN DIEGO
Bruce Kamerling

1. Louis Agassiz, quoted in John E. Baur, *The Health Seekers of Southern California* (San Marino, Calif.: Huntington Library, 1959), p. 10.

2. Peter C. Remondino, *The Modern Climatic Treatment of Invalids with Pulmonary Consumption in Southern California* (Detroit: George S. Davis, 1893), pp. 3, 30, and 32.

3. *Rancho Guajome Health Co.,* promotional pamphlet, 1905, p. 3, Rancho Guajome file, San Diego Historical Society.

4. Irving Gill, "The Home of the Future: The New Architecture of the West: Small Homes for a Great Country," *Craftsman* 30 (May 1916): 141.

5. Eloise Roorbach, "Outdoor Life in California Houses, as Expressed in the New

Architecture of Irving J. Gill," *Craftsman* 24 (July 1913): 438.

6. *San Francisco Chronicle,* quoted in Roberta Ridgely, "Anna Held and the Green Dragon," *San Diego Magazine* 21 (June 1969): 47.

7. La Jolla Chamber of Commerce, *La Jolla* (La Jolla, Calif.: Chamber of Commerce, 1913), n.p.

8. *Southwest Builder and Contractor* (February 24, 1910): 9.

9. For a full account of the Grossmont Art Colony, see Kathleen Crawford, "God's Garden: The Grossmont Art Colony," *Journal of San Diego History* 31 (Fall 1985): 298–319.

10. Emmett A. Greenwalt, *California Utopia: Point Loma, 1897–1942,* rev. ed. (San Diego: Point Loma Publications, 1978), p. 36.

11. For a detailed account of the artists at Lomaland, see Bruce Kamerling, "Theosophy and Symbolist Art: The Point Loma Art School," *Journal of San Diego History* 26 (Fall 1980): 230–55.

12. William E. Smythe, quoted in Sandra L. Stanley, "Historical Perspective on the Little Landers of San Ysidro" (paper, 1977, submitted to the San Diego Historical Society Institute of History), p. 3.

13. Ibid., p. 7, and Lawrence B. Lee, "The Little Landers Colony of San Ysidro, *Journal of San Diego History* 21 (Winter 1975): 36.

14. Henry S. Anderson, "The Little Landers' Land Colonies: A Unique Agricultural Experiment in California," *Agricultural History* 5 (October 1931): 145–49.

15. This advertisement appeared in *California Garden* from April to October 1913.

16. For information on San Diego's early ceramic industries, see Bruce Kamerling, "Anna and Albert Valentien: The Arts and Crafts Movement in San Diego," *Journal of San Diego History* 24 (Summer 1978): 343–66.

17. Ibid., p. 351.

18. *San Diego Union,* January 1, 1912, sec. 7, p. 5.

19. *National City News,* January 13, 1912, p. 1.

20. For more information on San Diego's potteries, see Bruce Kamerling, *San Diego and the American Art Pottery Movement* (San Diego: San Diego Historical Society, 1987).

21. *San Diego Union,* March 3, 1908, p. 5.

22. Ibid., February 22, 1908, p. 12.

23. Awards were reported in *Potter* 1

(December 1916): 38, and the *San Diego Sun,* September 9, 1916, p. 12.

24. Lohman's grandson Fritz Nachant, interview with Betty Quayle, April 10, 1989, Oral History Collection, San Diego Historical Society.

25. Natalie Curtis, "A New Type of Architecture in the Southwest," *Craftsman* 25 (January 1914): 333.

26. Architectural Records Collection, San Diego Historical Society; *Western Architect* 29 (June 1920): pl. 4.

27. Louis J. Gill, presentation sketch, Architectural Records Collection, University of California, Santa Barbara.

28. *San Diego Union,* quoted in *The Cultural Resources of the Torrey Pines Units,* State of California Department of Parks and Recreation (March 1983), p. 30.

29. Working drawings for Torrey Pines Lodge, Architectural Records Collection, San Diego Historical Society.

30. Richard S. Requa, "My Idea of a Real California Home," *Modern Clubwoman* (San Diego) 3 (December 1929): 8.

31. Henry-Russell Hitchcock, Jr., "Wright and the International Style," in *Art in America in Modern Times,* ed. Holger Cahill and Alfred H. Barr, Jr. (New York: Museum of Modern Art, 1934), p. 71.

32. Gill, "Home of the Future," p. 141.

THE ARTS AND CRAFTS AFTER 1918: ENDING AND LEGACY
Richard Guy Wilson

1. Matlack Price, "Industrial Art and the Craftsman," *Arts and Decoration* 16 (January 1922): 186–88.

2. H. Percy Macomber, "The Future of the Handicrafts," *American Magazine of Art* 9 (March 1918): 193.

3. Robert W. Winter, *The California Bungalow* (Los Angeles: Hennessey & Ingalls, 1980), p. 77.

4. Bertram Goodhue, quoted in Fiske Kimball, "Goodhue's Architecture: A Critical Estimate," *Architectural Record* 62 (December 1927): 538.

5. Allen H. Eaton, *Handicrafts of the Southern Highland* (New York: Russell Sage Foundation, 1937); Allen H. Eaton, *Handicrafts of New England* (New York: Harper & Brothers, 1949).

6. Nancy Dustin Wall Moure and Phyllis Moure, *Artists' Clubs and Exhibitions in Los Angeles*

before 1930 (Los Angeles: Dustin Publications, 1975), n.p.

7. Dorothy Shepard, interviews with the author, April 7, 1988, and July 31, 1990.

8. Richard Guy Wilson, Dianne Pilgrim, and Dickran Tashjian, *The Machine Age in America, 1918–1941* (New York: Brooklyn Museum; Harry N. Abrams, 1987).

9. On religion, see Carey McWilliams, *Southern California: An Island on the Land* (New York: Duell, Sloan and Pearce, 1946), pp. 248–58; on California in general, see Kevin Starr, *Material Dreams* (New York: Oxford University Press, 1990).

10. Steven Naifeh and Gregory White Smith, *Jackson Pollock* (New York: Harper Perennial, 1990), pp. 126–41.

11. Charles Sumner Greene, "Symbolism" (typescript, dated November 1932, Carmel; Greene and Greene Center for the Study of the Arts and Crafts Movement in America, the University of Southern California and the Huntington Library, Art Collections, and Botanical Gardens, San Marino, Calif.).

12. Robert W. Winter, "Arroyo Culture," in Timothy J. Andersen, Eudorah M. Moore, and Robert W. Winter, eds., *California Design, 1910* (Pasadena, Calif.: California Design Publications, 1974; reprint, Salt Lake City: Peregrine Smith, 1989), p. 28.

13. David Gebhard, *Santa Barbara: The Creation of a New Spain in America* (Santa Barbara: University Art Museum, University of California, Santa Barbara, 1982).

14. James Parton Haney, "Our Needs and Opportunities in the Industrial Arts," *American Magazine of Art* 11 (December 1919): 58. See also Florence N. Levy, "St. Louis Exposition of Industrial Arts and Crafts," *American Magazine of Art* 11 (January 1920): 166–67; Charles R. Richards, "The Third International Exhibition of Industrial Art," *American Magazine of Art* 21 (November 1930): 609–32; Richard F. Bach, "What Is the Matter with Our Industrial Art?" *Arts and Decoration* 18 (January 1923): 14–15, 46, 49; E. Armitage McCann, "A Significant Showing of Industrial Art," *Arts and Decoration* 19 (October 1923): 33–35.

15. W. Frank Purdy, "American Needs Co-operation in Industrial Art," *Arts and Decoration* 14 (January 1921): 208, 250, 252; Hermann Sachs, "How Europe Has Capitalized Art in Industry," *Arts and Decoration* 14 (January 1921): 209, 248; Richard F. Bach, "A Note on

Producers of Industrial Art and Their Relation to the Public," *Arts and Decoration* 18 (December 1922): 82, 84, 96.

16. Price, "Industrial Art and the Craftsman," pp. 185–87.

17. Richard F. Bach, "A Note of Progress in Industrial Art," *Arts and Decoration* 14 (February 1921): 302, 338; Richard F. Bach, "A Museum Exhibit as a Spur to Industrial Art," *Arts and Decoration* 18 (February 1923): 10, 62; "The Machine as an Art Medium," *Arts and Decoration* 13 (September 1920): 227, 275.

18. Wilson, Pilgrim, and Tashjian, *Machine Age,* pp. 49–50, 65, 277.

19. For background, see Jeffrey Meikle, *Twentieth-Century Limited: Industrial Design in America* (Philadelphia: Temple University Press, 1979).

20. Jean Murray Bangs, "Greene and Greene," *Architectural Forum* 89 (October 1948): 80–89; Jean Murray Bangs, "New Appreciations of Greene and Greene," *Architectural Record* 103 (May 1948): 138–40. See also Lisa Germany, *Harwell Hamilton Harris* (Austin: Center for the Study of American Architecture, School of Architecture, University of Texas, 1985).

21. Lewis Mumford, "Skyline," *New Yorker,* October 11, 1947, pp. 94–96, 99.

22. *Domestic Architecture of the San Francisco Bay Region* (San Francisco: Museum of Art, 1949). See also Sally B. Woodbridge, ed., *Bay Area Houses,* new ed. (Salt Lake City: Peregrine Smith, 1988).

23. Esther McCoy, *Five California Architects* (New York: Reinhold, 1960), p. 146. McCoy was also important in the recovery of the Arts and Crafts in California.

BIOGRAPHIES AND COMPANY HISTORIES

Kenneth R. Trapp
Kim Cooper

These chronologies are the result of more than a year's research into the Arts and Crafts movement in California from the 1890s through the 1930s. The best single source of information on the artists, studios, and businesses of the era is the Archives of California Art at The Oakland Museum, especially with the recent addition of The Paul Evans California Art Pottery Research Collection and The Elliott Evans–The Paul Evans California Silver Research Collection. Additional information came from the San Francisco Room of the San Francisco Public Library, the Oakland Public Library's Oakland History Room, the libraries of the University of California, Berkeley, and the morgue of the *San Francisco Examiner*. The California census proved an important resource for pinpointing the location of artists, although it sometimes contained inaccurate information. Also important were the entries for shops and individuals in city directories. An excellent collection of national city directories is in the California State Sutro Library, San Francisco.

Leslie Greene Bowman of the Los Angeles County Museum of Art shared her files on Southern California artists. Bruce Kamerling of the San Diego Historical Society provided invaluable information for the San Diego histories, and Joseph A. Taylor of the Tile Heritage Foundation, Healdsburg, California, was equally generous with the foundation's files on California tile makers. The Santa Barbara Historical Society graciously opened its library to us when we spent two weeks in that city researching the legacy of the Arts and Crafts movement there.

Much of what is presented here has been painstakingly gathered from numerous sources, and every attempt has been made to find corroborating evidence. It is nonetheless possible that some of the information is inaccurate. Misinformation is especially common in city directories, which attempted to record all settled individuals and businesses in a community, listed alphabetically by name and cross-referenced by type of business. City directories were published in April—hence, the 1906 directory for San Francisco is missing, since the earthquake struck on April 18 of that year. Directories contain gross typographical errors and incorrect or outdated addresses; they also omit many residents and businesses. In the chronologies that follow, information culled solely from city directories has been itali-

cized to indicate its source. Names in CAPITAL LETTERS are cross-references to other entries.

Sometimes misinformation has been passed from source to source over the years, until errors are universally reported as fact. Such is the case with Ernest A. Batchelder, about whom a remarkable amount of false data has circulated. Our entry on Batchelder differs from most accounts of his life and supplies the results of new research.

Few of these artists received the sort of extensive media attention accorded to, say, Dirk van Erp and Arthur F. Mathews. Thus it is difficult to document them on a year-to-year basis, much less to trace their movements from month to month. A newspaper clipping may tell us something of an artist's career; but how much credence should be given to the words of a reporter who spoke with the subject for perhaps twenty minutes and was working against a deadline? Although many of these artists doubtless kept records of their careers in some detail, in all our research we have managed to discover only a few caches of personal data: the Dirk van Erp Archive at The Oakland Museum; the Lillian O'Hara papers owned by Dr. Harold Copp; and the Rudolph Schaeffer and Porter Blanchard papers in the Smithsonian Institution's Archives of American Art. Where are the records of other creators? Are they held by descendants, or do they lie uncataloged in library basements? Have they long since been consigned to the dump or the furnace? It is distressing to accept that we will probably never be able to record accurately the lives and careers of such intriguing yet little-known figures as Victor Toothaker, Douglas van Denburgh, Digby Brooks, and Clara and Mildred Holden.

These histories represent a work in progress: the development of The Oakland Museum's archives on the Arts and Crafts movement in California. The gathering of information will continue after the publication of this book and the end of the exhibition tour. These histories must therefore be seen as a call for additional information. It is the hope of all involved in this project that it will lead to the retrieval of more information about the artists featured and perhaps even to the discovery of presently unknown California workers in the Arts and Crafts movement.

ALBERHILL POTTERY

1882   Alberhill Coal and Clay Company begins mining coal at Alberhill, California.

1895   Alberhill begins selling clay from its site.

1912   ALEXANDER W. ROBERTSON leaves his job at HALCYON ART POTTERY to experiment with Alberhill clays for a possible art pottery.

1914   Alberhill and Los Angeles Pressed Brick Company sue the State of California to prevent a highway from being built through the Alberhill clay deposit. Robertson leaves Alberhill late in the year, the planned art pottery never having materialized.

1915   Robertson displays his work in Alberhill clay at the Panama-California Exposition, San Diego, where he is awarded a gold medal.

1920   Alberhill again considers entering the commercial pottery business, but the plan is not pursued.

196. Alberhill Pottery (Alexander W. Robertson). *Double-Handled Vase,* 1914. Biscuit-fired buff earthenware, 11¼ x 6¼ in. Private collection.

CHARLES ANDERSON (1913–1975)

1913   August 16—Charles Everett Anderson born in Mankato, Minnesota.

c. 1929   Begins studying metalwork under August Tiesselinck at Mission High School, San Francisco.

1931   On Tiesselinck's recommendation, joins the DIRK VAN ERP studio as an apprentice. This is during the Depression, and Anderson is the only person in his family with a job.

early 1940s   Attempts to join the navy as a sailor but is rejected because his skills are needed for repairing ships at the Hunter's Point shipyard, San Francisco.

mid-1940s   Although the wages and benefits at the shipyard are far superior to those at the van Erp studio, Anderson feels compelled to remain an art metalsmith. He returns to van Erp, where he remains for the rest of his career.

1975   June 27—dies in San Francisco, two months before his planned retirement from the van Erp studio.

AREQUIPA POTTERY

1911   September—the Arequipa Sanatorium for tubercular women is opened in Fairfax, California, by Dr. Philip King Brown (1869–1940). November—FREDERICK HÜRTEN RHEAD and Agnes Rhead implement a pottery program founded there to encourage physical activity and to generate revenue for the patients.

1913   February—the pottery is incorporated. Frederick Hürten Rhead takes over the financial management of the pottery but does not perform to the directors' satisfaction. May—Rhead resigns. July—ALBERT L. SOLON takes over as pottery manager.

1915   Arequipa hosts a sales booth in the Education Building at the Panama-Pacific International Exposition, San Francisco, in which patients demonstrate their decoration methods. Former patient Verena Ruegg demonstrates throwing techniques. For their work, the sanatorium and Brown are awarded gold medals, and Ruegg a bronze medal. November—the Arequipa Pottery corporation is dissolved. (Arequipa Sanatorium continues to operate until 1957.)

1916   April—a benefit exhibition of the pottery is held at 550 Sutter Street, San Francisco, the site of the Vickery, Atkins, and Torrey art-goods shop; a group of pots is shown at the Boston Society of Arts and Crafts gallery. May—Solon leaves Arequipa to take a position at San Jose State Normal School. September—FRED H. WILDE is hired as manager.

1917   Arequipa begins producing handmade tiles in the Hispano-Moresque tradition. The tiles are promoted to the architectural community in San Francisco.

1918 World War I makes continued production unfeasible. November—Arequipa Pottery closes.

ABOVE, TOP

197. Arequipa Sanatorium, Fairfax, California, c. 1911–20.

ABOVE, BOTTOM

198. Women decorating pottery at Arequipa, c. 1911–13.

ERNEST A. BATCHELDER (1875–1957)

1875 January 22—Ernest Allan Batchelder born in Nashua, New Hampshire.

1895 Graduates from Massachusetts Normal Art Institute, Boston.

1901 Studies under Denman W. Ross, former president of the Boston Society of Arts and Crafts, at the Harvard Summer School of Design. Moves to California and is employed as an instructor of manual arts at Throop Polytechnic Institute, Pasadena.

1904 Collects art objects in California for display at the Louisiana Purchase Exposition, St. Louis.

1904–9 Teaches design theory and manual arts intermittently at the Minneapolis Handicraft Guild.

1905 Visits Charles R. Ashbee at Chipping Campden, England, and works in the guild shops there.

1905–6 Attends Central School of Arts and Crafts in Birmingham, England.

1907 Named director of art at Throop.

1908 Publishes *The Principles of Design,* a book of articles originally published in the magazine *Inland Printer.* Attends the International Congress of Art Education in London.

1909 Leaves Throop. Buys property overlooking the Arroyo Seco in Pasadena and builds a house there.

265

1910 Begins giving classes at his house and produces decorative tile there by the end of the year. Publishes *Design in Theory and Practice,* a book of articles originally published in the *Craftsman.*

1912 Makes Frederick L. Brown a partner. Moves tile operation from his house to 769 South Broadway, Pasadena. July 12—marries Alice Coleman.

1915 Exhibits tiles in the Southern California Exhibition of Applied Arts by Southern California Craftsmen at the Panama-California Exposition, San Diego.

1916 April—a group of his architecturally inspired tiles are shown at the Boston Society of Arts and Crafts gallery. November 7—takes out a building permit to expand the Pasadena factory.

1920 Moves the tile business to a new location on Artesian Street in Los Angeles, with Lucien H. Wilson as his partner.

1932 The tile company fails during the Depression.

1936 Begins making Kinneloa ware, a line of art pots, slip-cast and glazed in matte pastel colors.

1948 Alice Batchelder dies.

1949 Kinneloa Pottery is sold.

1957 August 6—dies in Pasadena.

NATHAN BENTZ (1861–1942)

1861 October 5—Nathan Bentz born in Erie County, New York.

1871 August—brother Philip born in New York State.

BIOGRAPHIES AND COMPANY HISTORIES

| 1885 | *Employed by the Ichi Ban shop, a San Francisco dealer in Japanese goods.* |

| 1887 | Employed by G. T. Marsh & Co., a San Francisco dealer in Japanese art. |

| 1891 | Moves to Santa Barbara. At about this time, marries Alice Cooper. |

| 1892 | Opens oriental art-goods shop in Santa Barbara. |

| 1896 | Makes his first annual buying trip to China and Japan. |

| 1902 | With his brother Philip opens the Nathan Bentz & Co. shop at 211 Fourth Street, Los Angeles. |

| 1906 | *Nathan Bentz shop opens at 1229 State Street, Santa Barbara.* |

| 1911 | GREENE AND GREENE design home for Bentz on Olive Avenue (now Prospect Avenue), Santa Barbara. |

| 1912 | *Shop moves to 1236 State Street.* |

| c. 1913–17 | Becomes friendly with the potter FREDERICK HÜRTEN RHEAD and allows his shop to be used as a gallery for the display of Rhead's pots. Lends oriental pottery to Rhead for study purposes. |

| 1918 | Philip closes the Los Angeles shop to open a branch of Nathan Bentz & Co. at 570 Sutter Street, San Francisco. |

| 1922 | *First listing of wife, Winifred Roberts Bentz, in Santa Barbara directory.* |

| 1923 | *The San Francisco shop moves to 437 Grant Avenue.* |

| 1928 | *Philip becomes a partner in the San Francisco shop.* |

| 1942 | February 8—Nathan dies in Santa Barbara. Philip briefly runs the Grant Avenue shop as Philip Bentz Antiques, then manages the Santa Barbara shop. |

| 1945 | Philip closes the Santa Barbara shop. |

PORTER BLANCHARD (1886–1973)

| 1886 | February 28—Porter George Blanchard born in Gardner, Massachusetts. His father, George Porter Blanchard, trains him as a silversmith. |

| 1909 | George Blanchard opens a flatware shop in his barn with his sons, Porter and Richard. |

| 1912 | Porter exhibits at the Detroit Society of Arts and Crafts. |

| 1914 | Porter takes over his father's shop. Joins the Boston Society of Arts and Crafts. Marries Elizabeth Flood. |

| 1923 | The Porter Blanchards move to California, setting up shop at 3921 Magnolia Boulevard, Burbank. |

| 1924 | Porter is involved in founding the Arts and Crafts Society of Southern California. His work is retailed by Gump's of San Francisco. |

199. Porter Blanchard. *Four Matching Cordials,* c. 1930. Silver with gilt, 4³⁄₁₆ x 1¹⁵⁄₁₆ in., each. The Oakland Museum; Gift of the Art Guild.

| 1925 | George and Richard join Porter in his Burbank shop. |

| 1933 | Porter opens a retail shop at 6605 Sunset Boulevard, Los Angeles, a location convenient for film-industry clients. |

| 1936 | The shop moves to 8626 Sunset Boulevard, a more prestigious location. |

| 1973 | November 6—Porter dies in Studio City, California. The Porter Blanchard firm continues to produce its founder's designs. |

HENRY P. BOWIE (1848–1920)

| 1848 | March 5—Henry Pike Bowie born in Maryland. |

| c. early 1850s | Moves to San Francisco with his father, Dr. Augustus Bowie. |

| c. 1860s | Studies law in San Francisco under Hall McAllister and General W.H.L. Barnes. |

| 1879 | Marries the widowed Agnes Poett Howard, who is fifteen years his senior and extremely wealthy. They live at El Cerrito, her San Mateo, California, estate. Bowie landscapes the property. |

| 1886 | Begins construction on his house, Severn Lodge, in Burlingame, California. Opens the Severn Lodge Dairy. |

| 1890 | Retires from legal practice. |

| 1893 | Agnes dies. Bowie travels to Japan. |

| 1894 | Returns to Japan, where he remains for a number of years, devoting himself to scholarship and art. Studies the Japanese language in Kyoto under Hirai Kinza, and begins his study of Japanese painting under Torei Nishigawa. |

1896   Begins study of landscape painting under Kobuta Beisen.

1901–3 In Tokyo, studies painting under Shimada Sekko and Shimada Bokusen. His grasp of Japanese language and art is so great that his work is generally assumed to be that of a native. He is twice honored when the emperor requests Bowie's works for his own collection.

1904   Returns to Burlingame, where he completes work on Severn Lodge. Although the house itself is in the Mission Revival style, it is surrounded by traditional French and Japanese gardens.

1905   January—travels to Tahiti, where he gathers rare fish for the United States National Museum. Forms the Japan Society of America to promote international understanding.

1906   According to an article in the January 21 *San Francisco Chronicle,* Bowie and his neighbors Charles W. Clark and Eugene de Sabla, Jr., plan to go into the art-pottery business. Fine clay deposits have been found on Bowie's property by his Japanese guests Matsuo and Kawase. An experimental firing of pots made by the Japanese is a great success, and Shimada Sekko is brought in to decorate the ware. The subsequent obscurity of this venture can be attributed to the upheaval following the April earthquake and fire in San Francisco.

1909   November 27—the Japanese garden at Severn Lodge is officially opened with a dedication ceremony when the touring Honorable Japanese Commercial Commissioners visit Bowie's home.

1910   When the town of Hillsborough, California, is incorporated, Severn Lodge falls within its boundaries.

1911   PAUL ELDER publishes Bowie's book *On the Laws of Japanese Painting.*

1916   December—Severn Lodge is sold.

1918   Becomes special Japanese emissary for the Department of State. October—goes to Japan.

1920   October—returns from Japan. December 21—dies in San Mateo. A scandal erupts when it is found that he has left his considerable estate to his secret Japanese family and nothing to his stepchildren by Agnes Howard Bowie.

CORNELIUS BRAUCKMAN (1864–1952)

1864   October 20—Cornelius Walter Brauckman born in St. Louis.

c. 1909 Moves to Los Angeles.

c. 1912 Founds Grand Feu Pottery on the south side of West Ninety-sixth Street, two blocks west of South Main Street, Los Angeles.

1915   Grand Feu awarded gold medal at Panama-California Exposition, San Diego.

1916   Grand Feu work exhibited at First Annual Arts and Crafts Salon, Los Angeles.

c. 1916 Grand Feu closes.

1952   December 3—dies in Los Angeles.

WILLIAM V. BRAGDON. *See* CALIFORNIA FAIENCE

ELIZABETH EATON BURTON (1869–1937)

1869   January 20—born in Paris, the daughter of CHARLES FREDERICK EATON.

1886   Moves to Montecito, California, with her family.

1893   Marries William Waples Burton.

c. 1898 Opens decorative-art studio in Santa Barbara.

1902   Designs and landscapes the garden at Miravista, a Montecito estate.

1904   Exhibits at Louisiana Purchase Exposition, St. Louis.

c. 1905–9 Exhibits at the galleries of Doll & Richards, Boston, and Tilden-Thurber Galleries, Providence, Rhode Island.

1909   Exhibits fifteen objects at the Alaska-Yukon-Pacific Exposition, Seattle, including lamps and miscellaneous leatherwork; receives a gold medal. Shows her exposition work at the Blanchard studio building, Los Angeles.

1910   Possibly holds a crafts exhibition in Santa Barbara. Moves to Los Angeles to pursue interior decoration and leatherwork. Opens a large shop in Los Angeles.

c. 1921 William Waples Burton dies.

1924–26 Lives in Paris.

1927   Leaves Paris for Newport, Rhode Island.

1928   Returns to Los Angeles. Publishes her book, *Paris Vignettes.*

1936   February—exhibits watercolors on Japanese themes at the Schwartz Galleries, New York.

1937   November 15—dies in Los Angeles.

CALIFORNIA CHINA PRODUCTS COMPANY
WALTER H. NORDHOFF (1858–1937)
CHARLES B. NORDHOFF (1887–1947)

1858   May 27—Walter H. Nordhoff born in Brooklyn.

1879   Walter graduates from Yale University's Sheffield Scientific School with a degree in mining engineering.

1880s   Walter is employed as foreign correspondent for the *New York Herald,* in charge of the offices in Berlin, Constantinople, Madrid, and Paris. Marries Sarah Cope Whitall of Philadelphia.

1887 February 1—son, Charles Bernard Nordhoff, born in London.

1890 The Nordhoffs move to Baja California to manage Walter's father's ranch near Ensenada. The family also maintains a house in Redlands, California, where the children are educated.

1911 The Mexican Revolution causes the family to leave Mexico. They settle in National City, California. Walter and Charles establish California China Products Company and begin producing tiles with the trade name Kaospar.

1912 January—WESLEY H. TRIPPETT begins working at CCPCo (until January 1913). September—FRED H. WILDE employed at CCPCo (until September 1916).

1913–15 Kaospar tiles used in new Santa Fe Railway depot in San Diego and the California State and Fine Arts buildings for the Panama-California Exposition, San Diego. Charles leaves CCPCo to pursue other interests.

1914 Kaospar tiles available through Henry Gardner, Inc., New York, and selected for use in the New York State Building at the Panama-Pacific International Exposition, San Francisco, 1915.

1917 CCPCo equipment and the Kaospar trade name are sold to West Coast Tile Company, Vernon, California, in a stock exchange. Walter remains with the business.

1919 West Coast Tile Company and the Kaospar trade name are sold to American Encaustic Tiling Company of Zanesville, Ohio. Walter is probably still involved with the business.

1923 Walter moves to Santa Barbara.

1932 Charles and coauthor James Norman Hall begin a series of South Seas adventure books, which includes the trilogy *Mutiny on the Bounty* (1932), *Men against the Sea* (1933), and *Pitcairn's Island* (1934).

1933 Under the pseudonym Antonio de Fierro Blanco, Walter publishes *The Journey of the Flame,* now ranked as a California literary classic.

1937 February 25—Walter dies in Santa Barbara.

1947 April 11—Charles dies in Santa Barbara.

CALIFORNIA FAIENCE
WILLIAM V. BRAGDON (1884–1959)
CHAUNCEY R. THOMAS (1877–1950)

1877 August 21—Chauncey Rapelje Thomas born in New York.

1884 November 19—William Victor Bragdon born in Pittsburgh.

1905–8 Thomas lists himself in the directory of the American Ceramic Society as a ceramics student residing in Amherst, Massachusetts.

1906 Bragdon begins his studies at the State School of Clayworking and Ceramics, Alfred University, Alfred, New York.

1908 Bragdon graduates with a B.S. in ceramics. Thomas teaches ceramics in the School of Education of the University of Chicago.

1909 Bragdon teaches ceramics at the University of Chicago, through 1912. Thomas establishes the Deerfield Pottery in Deerfield, Massachusetts.

1911 Suffering from ill health, Thomas closes his Deerfield Pottery.

1912 Bragdon teaches ceramics at University City Pottery, University City, Missouri, through 1914. *Thomas lists his address as the P. F. Thomas dry-goods firm in Boston, through 1914.*

1915 Bragdon goes to Berkeley to teach pottery at the CALIFORNIA SCHOOL OF ARTS AND CRAFTS. Thomas and Bragdon exhibit at the Panama-Pacific International Exposition under the name the Tile Shop.

1916 Thomas and Bragdon open the Tile Shop at 2336 San Pablo Avenue, Berkeley.

1918 Thomas begins teaching the pottery course at CSAC.

1921 Bragdon teaches pottery at CSAC for final year.

1922 Tile Shop relocates to 1335 Hearst Avenue, Berkeley. Both tile and art pottery are now known as California Faience.

1924 Firm name is changed to California Faience.

mid-1920s California Faience receives the tile commission for the Hearst estate at San Simeon, California.

c. 1930 Firm's production of artware ceases.

1932 Tile making briefly resumes for the Century of Progress International Exposition in 1933 in Chicago.

late 1930s Bragdon buys out Thomas. Thomas goes to the Los Angeles area to work as a pottery consultant for Mrs. H. T. Epperson, former owner of the California Bisque Doll Company in Berkeley.

1950 August 21—Thomas dies in Glendale, California.

early 1950s Bragdon sells the pottery, continuing to work for the new owners for a time.

1959 October 26—Bragdon dies in Palo Alto, California.

CALIFORNIA SCHOOL OF ARTS AND CRAFTS

1907 The California School of Arts and Crafts is opened at

Shattuck Avenue and Addison Street, Berkeley, by founders FREDERICK H. MEYER, Laetitia Meyer, Perham W. Nahl, and Isabelle Percy West.

1908 CSAC moves to 2130 Center Street.

1909 Xavier Martinez joins the staff of CSAC. First jewelry courses taught.

1911 CSAC moves to 2119 Allston Way, the site of the old Berkeley High School.

1912 Weaving and embroidery are added to the curriculum.

1915 The CSAC Alumni group, under MARGERY WHEELOCK, is awarded the gold medal for their model of an artist's studio at the Panama-Pacific International Exposition, San Francisco.

1922–25 The CSAC Oakland site at College Avenue and Broadway is purchased. A transitional period ensues in which both the Berkeley and Oakland campuses are used. The school is incorporated as a nonprofit institution.

1926 CSAC is in full residence in Oakland.

1936 CSAC is renamed California College of Arts and Crafts.

CATHEDRAL OAKS
GEORGE DENNISON (1873–1966)
FRANK INGERSON (1880–1968)

1873 November 20—George Austin Dennison born in New Boston, Illinois.

1880 Charles Frank Ingerson born in Victory Mills, New York.

c. 1895 Dennison moves to California. Employed as assistant secretary of the California State Board of Trade.

c. 1900 Ingerson attends Pratt Institute in Brooklyn and studies under Marshall Fry.

1904 Dennison serves as secretary to the California Commission at the Louisiana Purchase Exposition, St. Louis. He installs the San Francisco Room at the exposition.

1909 Ingerson begins teaching decorative design at the California School of Design, San Francisco Institute of Art. Dennison serves as secretary to the California Commission at the Alaska-Yukon-Pacific Exposition in Seattle. Ingerson exhibits eight modeled-leather objects at the AYP; receives a grand prize for his modeled-leather screen and a gold medal for the rest of the display.

c. 1910 Dennison purchases property in Alma, California.

1911–12 Partnership of Dennison and Ingerson begins. They build their studio at Cathedral Oaks, Alma. Ingerson travels to England, France, and Germany; studies in London under Nelson Dawson and W. Lee Hankey.

1913 Dennison appointed chief of the Department of Horticulture for the Panama-Pacific International Exposition, San Francisco.

1917–18 The artists spend one year decorating Casa Dorinda, home of Mr. and Mrs. William H. Bliss in Montecito, California, designed by Carleton Winslow.

c. 1920 They decorate the Samarkand Hotel, Santa Barbara.

1925 The Koshland family of San Francisco commissions Dennison and Ingerson to build a model of the biblical Ark of the Covenant in memory of Marcus S. Koshland. The artists travel to Paris to study the Baron de Rothschild's collection of Jewish art, and to London, where they research the ark in the British Museum. Work begins at A. B. Burton's traditional bronze foundry in London, where it continues for fourteen months.

1927 February 5—The Ark of the Covenant is formally dedicated at Temple Emanu-El, San Francisco.

1966 March 26—Dennison dies in Los Gatos, California.

1968 March 15—Ingerson dies in Los Gatos.

HARRY DIXON (1890–1967)

1890 June 22—Harry Robert de Roos St. John Dixon born in Fresno, California.

1908 October—meets DIRK VAN ERP at the Idora Park Arts and Crafts Exposition, Oakland.

200. Harry Dixon. *Desk Set,* c. 1921–30. Hammered, patinated, and enameled copper: pair of bookends, 5¹¹/₁₆ x 5⅛ x 4½ in., each; pen tray, 13¼ x 3¹³/₁₆ in.; letter opener, 8¹/₁₆ x 1⁹/₁₆ in. The Oakland Museum; Gift of the William F. and Helen S. Reichell Trust.

1909   Enrolls at the CALIFORNIA SCHOOL OF ARTS AND CRAFTS, where he studies metalwork under Eulora Jennings. Begins an apprenticeship with Dirk van Erp that will last through May 1911, when Dixon is fired.

c. 1911 Begins a five-year stint for LILLIAN PALMER as foreman of her metal shop in San Francisco and possibly Carmel, California.

1912   Makes his first jewelry.

1912–35 Teaches sporadically at CSAC.

1914   Graduates from CSAC.

1915   Contributes a fireplace hood and shield to the CSAC alumni group's model of an artist's studio; it is a gold-medal-winning exhibit at the Panama-Pacific International Exposition, San Francisco.

1916   Marries MARGERY WHEELOCK, a fellow CSAC graduate and designer of the PPIE exhibit.

1918   Begins a two-year tenure as a shipboard coppersmith, Union Iron Works shipyard, San Francisco. March 21—son, Dudley Newhall Dixon, born.

1920–21 Returns to CSAC to teach metalwork and jewelry.

1921   Opens metal shop at 3 Tillman Alley (now Tillman Place), San Francisco. Has a brief partnership around this time with Fred Brosi.

1926   Exhibits at the California Palace of the Legion of Honor decorative-arts exhibition (again in 1927).

1928   Receives a certificate of honor for metalwork from the San Francisco chapter of the American Institute of Architects. Exhibits at Women's City Club, San Francisco (also in 1929).

1929   Receives a commission for a San Francisco Stock Exchange elevator door.

1930   Solo show at Casa de Mañana Gallery, Berkeley. Makes silver in the style of the Mexican-colonial era for the mining engineer Raymond Guyer.

c. 1932 The Dixons divorce.

1932   Dixon closes shop and moves to a studio in the Montgomery Block artists' building, San Francisco (remains through 1950).

1933   *Listed in city directory as a metalworker working out of the Dirk van Erp shop for this year only.*

1953   Marries Florence Fullmer Couper; they settle in Santa Rosa, California.

1967   September 4—dies in Santa Rosa.

DOUGLAS DONALDSON (1882–1972)

1882   August 24—Douglas Donaldson born in Detroit.

1907   Studies design and metalsmithing in Joliet, Illinois. Studies jewelry making and enameling at the Minneapolis Handicraft Guild, where he meets and studies under ERNEST A. BATCHELDER.

1908   December—exhibits five pieces in copper, enamel, and turquoise in the Handicraft Guild display at the Seventh Annual Exhibition of Original Designs and Decorations and Examples of Art Crafts Having Distinct Artistic Merit, Art Institute of Chicago.

1909   Summer—probably teaches a course at the Minneapolis Handicraft Guild. Follows Batchelder to Pasadena, where he takes Batchelder's former post as instructor of manual arts at Throop Polytechnic Institute. December—exhibits an etched-copper cigar set in the Handicraft Guild display at the Eighth Annual Exhibition of Original Designs.

1910   Lives with his older sister Margaret and two female cousins in Pasadena. As his jewelry work becomes successful, he seeks a respite from daily teaching. Leaves Throop for a post at the new Chouinard School of Art in Los Angeles.

1911   Summer—teaches course in art metal, design, and jewelry at the Institute of Mechanic Arts at Mount Hermon, Santa Cruz, California.

201. Cover of Douglas Donaldson's catalog, c. 1916. The Oakland Museum; Rudolph Schaeffer Archive, Archives of California Art.

1912   Named head of the Art Department at Manual Arts High School, Los Angeles, a post he holds through 1918.

1915   With his wife, Louise Towle Donaldson, collects objects for and installs the Southern California Exhibition of Applied Arts by Southern California Craftsmen at the Panama-California Exposition, San Diego. The couple exhibit metalwork, jewelry, and enameling. His elaborately jeweled and enameled chalice receives a gold medal.

1916   April—metal, jewelry, and enamel are shown at the Boston Society of Arts and Crafts gallery on a national tour with other objects by Southern Californians who had shown at San Diego, and examples of his work are purchased by the Boston Society of Arts and Crafts. Receives the Albert H. Loeb Prize for best original design in silverware from the Art Institute of Chicago (again in 1917).

1917   Commended as a master metalworker by the Boston Society of Arts and Crafts.

1918   March 21—awarded a bronze metal for excellence of work by the Boston Society of Arts and Crafts.

1919   Begins teaching metalwork, jewelry, and decorative design classes at Otis Art Institute, Los Angeles.

1921   Summer—Douglas and Louise Donaldson begin giving classes in color theory and design at their Hollywood house.

1924   Elected first vice president of the Arts and Crafts Society of Southern California.

1972   November 15—dies in Los Angeles.

HAROLD L. DOOLITTLE (1883–1974)

1883   May 4—Harold Lukens Doolittle born in Pasadena.

c. 1890–1900 Studies art at Throop Polytechnic Institute in Pasadena and civil engineering at Cornell University, Ithaca, New York.

1903   Graduates from Throop's college-preparatory academy.

1906   Employed as a mechanical engineer by Southern California Edison.

1908   Marries Vestina Scobey in Altadena, California.

1912   Designs Howell House, Altadena.

1920   Shows at exhibitions of the California Society of Etchers and the San Francisco Art Association.

1924   Exhibits prints at the galleries of Cannell and Chaffin, Los Angeles.

1929   Named chief designing engineer for Southern California Edison.

1936   Takes early retirement to concentrate on his graphic art, photography, metalwork, and furniture construction.

1938   April—awarded the Purchase Prize by the Chicago Society of Etchers.

1943   Serves as president of the Pasadena Society of Artists (through 1944).

1945   The Pasadena Society of Artists introduces the Harold L. Doolittle Award for printmaking.

1950–52 Again serves as president of the Pasadena Society of Artists.

1974   January 9—dies in Temple City, California.

CHARLES FREDERICK EATON (1842–1930)

1842   December 12—Charles Frederick Eaton born in Providence, Rhode Island.

1854   Designs his first garden.

late 1850s Prepares for college with tutors in France and Italy.

1860–62 Attends Brown University in Providence.

mid-1860s Attends the Sorbonne, Paris.

1867   April—marries Helen J. Mitchell of Philadelphia, a fellow student at the Sorbonne.

1869   January 20—daughter, ELIZABETH EATON (BURTON), born.

1873–76 Studies painting under Léon Bonnat in Paris.

late 1870s–early 1880s Studies landscape gardening in Italy and the south of France, as well as architecture, carving, and antique furniture.

1884   Visits Santa Barbara and Montecito, California.

1886   Moves to Montecito permanently. Builds crafts workshop on his estate, Riso Rivo, sometime before 1900.

1892   Helen Mitchell Eaton dies.

1898   June—marries Florence Baxter in Santa Barbara.

1902   November—participates in first exhibition of the Bookbinders' Guild of California in San Francisco. Exhibits thirty-five pieces—including illumination, bookbinding, metal- and leatherwork—at the First Annual Exhibition of Original Designs and Decorations and Examples of Art Crafts Having Distinct Artistic Merit at the Art Institute of Chicago.

1903   With his associates ROBERT WILSON HYDE, Guadaloupe Buelna, Henry Roland Johnson, and Alonso Shad exhibits forty-nine pieces—including shell lampshades, metalwork, and manuscript illumination—at the Second Annual Exhibition of Original Designs.

1904   Exhibits at the Louisiana Purchase Exposition, St. Louis. Shows twelve pieces in the Third Annual Exhibition of Original Designs, including two books illuminated by Hyde.

271

1905 Exhibits six lamps in the Fourth Annual Exhibition of Original Designs.

1909 Exhibits eleven objects at the Alaska-Yukon-Pacific Exposition, Seattle, and receives a grand prize for his display.

1915 March—shows twenty-three pieces in various media in the Santa Barbara Art Committee art exhibition at the State Normal School of Manual Arts.

1930 August 21—dies in Montecito.

PAUL ELDER (1872–1948)

1872 January 1—David Paul Elder born in Harrisburg, Pennsylvania.

c. 1875 Family settles in San Jose.

c. 1889 After graduating from or leaving Lowell High School, San Francisco, Elder works briefly as a clerk for Wells Fargo Express.

1890 Works as a clerk in William Doxey's bookshop, San Francisco.

1896 May 5—marries Emma Moore in San Francisco.

1897 August—establishes himself as a publisher's agent and opens his small Book Room. Meets MORGAN SHEPARD, an unhappy Bank of America clerk with a bookman's ambitions.

1898 March—Elder and Shepard open the Book and Art Shop at 238 Post Street, San Francisco. They publish books under the Elder & Shepard imprint, sell books, and deal in art objects.

1899 Elder and Shepard begin designing ephemera for sale, including cards, bookmarks, broadsides, and stationery.

202. Frontispiece and title page from *Into the Light,* by Edward Robeson Taylor. Published by Elder & Shepard, 1902. Mrs. Scott Elder.

1899–1901 The firm's literary magazine, *Personal Impressions,* is published.

1902 A charter member of the Bookbinders' Guild of California, Elder serves as its secretary-treasurer. Shepard is president. March—*Personal Impressions* becomes a quarterly and is renamed *Impressions Quarterly.* November—the first exhibition of the Bookbinders' Guild is held at the Elder & Shepard shop.

1903 May—Elder & Shepard absorbs the Twentieth-Century Press and renames it Tomoyé Press. The printers John Henry Nash and Bruce Brough stay on to work for Elder. Shepard leaves the partnership, which is incorporated as Paul Elder & Co. on May 8.

1905 December—final issue of *Impressions Quarterly* is published.

1906 March—Tomoyé fails and is refinanced by Elder. April—the Book and Art Shop and Tomoyé Press are destroyed in the earthquake and fire. Elder commissions BERNARD MAYBECK to build a new store at the corner of Bush and Van Ness while he moves the publishing arm to New York. September—Elder goes east, leaving John Howell to oversee general West Coast operations and Theodore Keane to manage the art section. Paul Elder & Co. opens the Arts and Crafts Book Room at 43–45 East Nineteenth Street, New York.

1909 February—after three years in New York, financial problems force Elder to shut down the eastern branch and return to San Francisco. The Paul Elder Building at 239 Grant Avenue opens, designed by Maybeck, containing the bookshop, publishing headquarters, and design studio. August—the Arts and Crafts Book Store of Santa Barbara, a small subsidiary, is sold to its manager, Sarah W. Redfield.

1911 An attempt is made to revive the literary magazine as *Impressions Annual,* but only two issues are produced.

1914 January—Elder offers his creditors half of all money owed in exchange for a two-year extension on the remainder of his debts.

1915 Hosts a bookshop display in the Liberal Arts Building at the Panama-Pacific International Exposition, San Francisco.

1917 Tomoyé Press books are remaindered for ready cash. Soon after, Elder abandons publishing except for occasional volumes.

1921 Paul Elder & Co. moves to 239 Post Street, a new shop with a Maybeck-designed Gothic Revival interior.

1948 Dies. New shop opens at Sutter and Stockton streets. Son, Paul Elder, Jr., manages shop for the next twenty years.

CLEMENS FRIEDELL (1872–1963)

1872   December 19—Clemens Friedell born in Gretna, Louisiana.

1875   Family moves to Vienna, where his parents were born. Apprentices with a silversmith for seven years and also studies music.

1892   Family returns to America, settling near San Antonio. Unable to find work as a silversmith, Friedell teaches music until 1901.

1901   Marries Jeanette Marcee. Employed as a silversmith by the Gorham Manufacturing Company in Providence, Rhode Island.

1907   The financial panic of this year leads Gorham to lay off many of its workers, including Friedell.

1908   Opens his own shop, probably in Providence. It is unsuccessful; he returns to Texas to farm.

1910   Moves to Los Angeles. Sells consignment silver through the Broadway Department Store.

1911   Moves to Pasadena, where he does silver work out of his home.

1912   Receives commission for 107-piece silver dinner service for the millionaire brewer Eddie R. Maier.

1915   Awarded a gold medal for his silver display at the Panama-California Exposition, San Diego.

1916   Sets up shop at the Hotel Maryland on East Colorado Boulevard, Pasadena.

1921   Retires to Texas, where he buys a ranch.

1927   The Friedells divorce. He returns to Pasadena, where he works out of an oriental-imports store on Colorado Boulevard.

1928   Marries Eva Woodard.

1929   Opens own shop at 626 East Colorado Boulevard.

1963   October 21—dies in Pasadena.

D'ARCY GAW (1868–1944)

1868   May 4—Elizabeth Eleanor D'Arcy Gaw born in Montreal.

1875   Moves with her family to Idaho Springs, Colorado.

1878   Family moves to Leadville, Colorado.

1898   Enters the School of the Art Institute of Chicago.

1901   Graduates. Is a founding member of the Crafters design firm, housed in Steinway Hall, Chicago.

1902   December—the Crafters exhibit in the Art Institute's First Annual Exhibition of Original Designs and Decorations and Examples of Art Crafts Having Distinct Artistic Merit. They also exhibit at the Chicago Architectural Club.

1903   October—begins taking evening courses in metalwork at the School of the Art Institute. December—shows an electric-light shade and desk fixture in the Second Annual Exhibition of Original Designs.

1904   April—leaves the School of the Art Institute. Moves to San Jose with her family. Collaborates with Crafters associate Lawrence Buck on the design of her father's home in San Jose. Maintains her association with the Crafters group.

1907   In San Jose, works as assistant to the coppersmith LILLIAN PALMER in Palmer's basement studio.

1908   December—shows two embroideries and a sketch for a copper box at the Seventh Annual Exhibition of Original Designs.

1909   March—shows interior decorations in Oregon at the Portland Art Association and Portland Architectural Club exhibitions. December—shows a design for a trophy treasure box at the Eighth Annual Exhibition of Original Designs.

1910   Serves as president of the San Francisco Guild of Arts and Crafts. March 1—joins the DIRK VAN ERP Copper Shop in San Francisco as partner and designer. A Gaw-designed lamp and two woven scarves are shown at the Ninth Annual Exhibition of Original Designs.

1911   January 30—the partnership with van Erp is dissolved.

1911–14   Returns to Illinois, where she lives at the artists' colony Ravinia, possibly with Lawrence Buck. Buck and Gaw share studio space at 64 East Van Buren Street, Chicago. *She is listed in city directories as interior decorator (1913) and designer (1914).*

1915   Returns to San Jose, possibly with Buck, *and is listed as a designer there through 1919.*

1928   December—after her nephew Henry's murder in New York, Gaw claims the body and gives her address as 229 East Forty-eighth Street.

1933   *Listed as an interior designer in Carmel, California.*

1933–34   *Listed as an interior decorator residing at 229 East Forty-eighth Street, New York.*

1944   November 12—dies in Pacific Grove, California.

IRVING GILL (1870–1936)

1870   April 26—Irving John Gill born in Tully, New York.

1889   Begins his architectural training in the office of Ellis G. Hall, Syracuse, New York.

1890	Relocates to Chicago, where he is employed by the architect Joseph L. Silsby.

1890 Relocates to Chicago, where he is employed by the architect Joseph L. Silsby.

1891 Employed in the office of Adler and Sullivan, Chicago.

1893 Moves to San Diego for health reasons. Completes first independent project, the Daniel Schuyler residence, San Diego.

1894 Becomes the partner of Joseph Falkenham in San Diego for about one year.

1896 December—enters into an architectural partnership with William S. Hebbard in San Diego.

1902–5 Makes several trips to Newport, Rhode Island, to supervise the construction of a number of large residences.

1907 Takes FRANK MEAD as a partner for seven months. Gill and Mead design the Melville Klauber, Wheeler J. Bailey, and Russell Allen residences. Gill designs the Homer Laughlin House, Los Angeles.

1910 Designs Lewis Courts in Sierra Madre, California, a low-income garden-court housing project.

1911 Selected as associate architect for the Panama-California Exposition, San Diego, with Bertram Goodhue as consulting architect and Frank P. Allen as director of works.

1912 Gill moves his office to Los Angeles and becomes architect for model industrial town of Torrance, California, working with Olmsted Brothers. Twenty-one Gill-designed structures are built, including residences, hotels, office buildings, industrial buildings, a school, and a train station.

1913 Begins to use tilt-slab construction for several projects.

1914–19 Takes as partner his nephew Louis J. Gill, who had maintained the San Diego office since 1912.

1916 May—writes an influential article, "The Home of the Future," for the *Craftsman*.

1922–23 Employed by Horatio Warren Bishop on the Carthay Circle project, Los Angeles.

1924 Suffers a heart attack.

1927 Returns to San Diego County to work. Designs the Christian Science church, Coronado, California.

1928 May 8—marries Marion W. Brashears at Palos Verdes Estates, California.

1929 Works with John Siebert on several school designs in San Diego County.

1929–36 Designs a civic center, a fire station, and two schools in Oceanside, California.

1932 Designs a church and cottages for the Rancho Barona Indian resettlement at Lakeside in San Diego County.

1936 October 7—dies in San Diego.

GREENE AND GREENE
CHARLES SUMNER GREENE (1868–1957)
HENRY MATHER GREENE (1870–1954)

1868 October 12—Charles Sumner Greene born in Brighton, Ohio.

1870 January 23—Henry Mather Greene born in Brighton, Ohio.

1874 Family moves to St. Louis.

1887 Charles graduates from Woodwards Manual Training High School, St. Louis.

1888 Henry graduates from Woodwards Manual Training High School with honors. The brothers begin a shortened course in architecture at the Massachusetts Institute of Technology.

1891 March—the Greenes complete their studies at MIT.

1893 August—on their way to visit their parents, who have moved to Pasadena, the Greenes visit the Chicago World's Columbian Exposition and are introduced to Japanese architecture. They arrive in Pasadena and decide to settle there.

1894 The Greenes open an architectural office in Pasadena. They visit the California Midwinter Fair in San Francisco and see the Japanese hill-and-water gardens.

1899 Henry marries Emeline Augusta Dart in Rock Island, Illinois.

1900 Charles designs and makes first piece of furniture, a table for his fiancée, Alice Gordon White.

1901 Charles marries Alice, and they honeymoon in England and Italy. Work begins on Charles and Alice's home at 368 Arroyo Terrace, Pasadena. The Greenes open a second office in the Potomac Building in downtown Los Angeles.

1903 The Greenes close their Pasadena office and move to the Grant Building at Fourth and Broadway, Los Angeles. Design Arturo Bandini House, 1149 Pasqual Street, Pasadena. Design their first furniture for clients, Charles's sisters-in-law.

1904 Design furniture for the Adelaide M. Tichenor House, Long Beach, California.

1906 Design John C. Bentz House, 657 Prospect Square, Pasadena. The Greenes meet contractor Peter Hall and stained-glass artisan Emil Lange. June—Hall begins construction of his carpentry shop, where he will execute the Greenes' furniture designs.

1907 Design Robert R. Blacker House, 1177 Hillcrest Avenue, Pasadena. Hall's brother John begins overseeing Greene furniture construction.

1908 Design David B. Gamble House, 4 Westmoreland Place, Pasadena.

1909	Charles spends the year in England. The firm designs Charles M. Pratt House, 1330 Fairview Road, Nordhoff (now Ojai), California. Designs William R. Thorsen House, 2307 Piedmont Avenue, Berkeley.
1911	Design Nathan Bentz House, 1708 Olive Avenue (now 1741 Prospect Avenue), Santa Barbara.
1916	June—Charles moves to Carmel, California.
1918	Charles begins work on the D. L. James House, Carmel Highlands.
1922	The brothers' partnership is dissolved.
early 1930s	Henry closes his Pasadena office and begins working out of his home.
1954	October 2—Henry dies in Los Angeles.
1957	June 11—Charles dies in Carmel.

ARMENAC HAIRENIAN (1892–1981)

1892	Born in the Ottoman (now Syrian and Turkish) province of Aleppo, of Armenian descent.
1915	Five of Hairenian's six sisters are killed in the Turkish massacre of the Armenians.

203. Armenac Hairenian in his San Francisco shop, c. 1930.

1916	Marries a woman he rescued from the Turks; they divorce several years later.
1921	Immigrates to the United States.
1925	Opens his Art Copper Shop at 2484 Sacramento Street, San Francisco. Specializes in copper but also works in silver and brass. Becomes best known for the elaborate jewelry he makes for opera singers.
1981	Closes his shop in August. October 1—dies in Castro Valley, California.

HALCYON ART POTTERY

1903	William H. Dower and Francia A. LaDue, leaders of a Theosophical group, found the Temple of the People community at Halcyon, near Pismo Beach, California. The Temple Home Association is incorporated in California.
1909	The association announces plans to form a pottery school and commercial art pottery at Halcyon.
1910	ALEXANDER W. ROBERTSON opens the Pottery Department of the Industrial School of Arts and Crafts at Halcyon. Leon Awerdick is named manager of the art pottery. September—exhibition held of the pottery produced at the school. The September issue of *Keramic Studio* announces that some Halcyon students plan to go to Missouri to take the University City course in pottery under FREDERICK HÜRTEN RHEAD.
1912	Robertson leaves to work for ALBERHILL Coal and Clay Company, Alberhill, California.
1913	Halcyon Art Pottery shuts down.
1931	An attempt is made to revive the pottery courses at Halcyon. Summer—GERTRUDE RUPEL WALL gives instruction in pottery making and plastic art.
1932	Summer—Wall returns, this time under the direction of the University of California Extension Department.
early 1940s	Halcyon Art Pottery is dismantled.
1949	Temple Home Association is formally dissolved.

ROBERT WILSON HYDE (1875–1951)

1875	November 6—Robert Wilson Hyde born in Goshen, Indiana. He is raised in Washington, D.C.
1890s	Attends the University of Michigan, in Ann Arbor, where he studies to be a minister. Meets fellow student Susan McKee, who persuades him not to pursue the ministry.
1899	April 12—marries Susan McKee in Michigan.
1902	The Hydes move to Santa Barbara.

1909   With CHARLES FREDERICK EATON, exhibits an illuminated wedding book at the Alaska-Yukon-Pacific Exposition, Seattle.

1915   Exhibits "parchments" in the Southern California Exhibition of Applied Arts by Southern California Craftsmen at the Panama-California Exposition, San Diego.

1916   April—a group of illuminated manuscripts is shown at the Boston Society of Arts and Crafts gallery.

1920   *Hyde opens an antique shop in Carrillo Adobe, 11 East Carrillo Street, Santa Barbara.*

1951   April 25—dies in Santa Barbara.

FRANK INGERSON. *See* CATHEDRAL OAKS

LINNA VOGEL IRELAN (1846–1935)

1846   April 23—Linna Vogel born in Leipzig, Germany, a grandniece of Otto von Bismarck. Her ancestors founded the University of Leipzig in 1550 and the Meissen china works in Saxony.

c. 1870 November 14—marries William Irelan, Jr., an American student of mining and chemistry, in Leipzig. They move to California.

1873   Son, Oscar, born.

1886   William named state mineralogist for California.

1889   Linna publishes her article "Pottery" in the *Ninth Annual Report of the State Mineralogist.*

1891   Linna meets ALEXANDER W. ROBERTSON. They make several attempts over the next seven years to found a pottery together.

1893   William serves as the manager of the California mining exhibition at the World's Columbian Exposition in Chicago. Linna, inspired by the exhibits of American ceramics, is determined to found a distinctly Californian art pottery.

1898   With Robertson, Linna establishes the Roblin Art Pottery in San Francisco. The ware is thrown and glazed by Robertson and decorated by Linna.

1900   Roblin pottery is exhibited at the Universal Exposition, Paris, where it receives a special mention and award.

1901   Linna opens a carved-leather studio on Pine Street, possibly in her home at 1829 Pine Street, San Francisco.

1903   Roblin Art Pottery wins the gold medal at the California State Fair in Sacramento, where Robertson has been demonstrating his throwing technique.

1906   April 18—Roblin Art Pottery is destroyed by the earthquake and fire. Robertson moves to Southern California. Linna retires permanently from the pottery business, *but she is listed*

as an artist in city directories throughout her life.

c. 1908 *The Irelans move to Berkeley.*

1923   Irelan house destroyed in Berkeley fire.

1925   November 9—William dies.

1935   March 25—Linna dies in Berkeley.

JALAN
MANUEL JALANIVICH (1897–1944)
INGVARDT OLSEN (1888–1959)

1888   Ingvardt Olsen born in Copenhagen.

1897   June 24—Manuel E. Jalanivich born in Biloxi, Mississippi.

c. 1900s Olsen studies at the Royal Danish Copenhagen Chinese Kilns.

1908   Olsen immigrates to the United States.

c. 1910s Jalanivich studies under George Ohr in Biloxi, and under Leon Volkmar of Durant Kilns, New York. Possibly a student at the State School of Clayworking and Ceramics, Alfred University, Alfred, New York.

c. 1918 Olsen and Jalanivich meet and form a ceramics partnership, Olsen specializing in clays and glaze, Jalanivich in throwing the ware.

c. 1920 Jalanivich and Olsen move from New York to San Francisco.

c. 1926 Jalanivich and Olsen open a studio at 2840 Baker Street.

1928   Jalanivich and Olsen establish a new studio at 2930 Baker Street.

1929–38 Jalanivich gives weekly private lessons in ceramics.

1935   Jalan exhibits pottery at California-Pacific International Exposition, San Diego. At about this time, Jalan begins producing some molded pots based on thrown prototypes.

1936   Exhibits pottery at National Ceramic Exhibition, Museum of Fine Art, Syracuse, New York, and at Amberg-Hirth Gallery, San Francisco.

1937   Exhibits pottery at Contemporary Crafts Exhibition in Philadelphia, and at the Oakland Art Gallery's Exhibition of Sculpture, where the work receives an honorable mention.

1937–39 Jalanivich teaches pottery at the San Francisco Art Institute.

1938   San Francisco studio closes.

1939   Jalan exhibits pottery in the Decorative Arts Exhibition of the Golden Gate International Exposition, San Francisco.

early 1940s Relocates to Belmont, California. With the entry of the United States into the war, Jalan puts aside artware production for defense work. Jalanivich and Olsen give pottery classes to wounded soldiers at Letterman Hospital, San Francisco.

1944 June—Jalanivich dies in Belmont.

1948 Olsen exhibits his collaborations with Charles Nye at the Pacific Coast Ceramic Exhibition, Rotunda Gallery, San Francisco.

1959 July 9—Olsen dies.

J. JESSOP AND SONS, JEWELERS, SAN DIEGO
JOSEPH JESSOP (1851–1932)

1851 April 11—Joseph Jessop born in Kirkburton, England.

1860s Learns watchmaking from George Jessop, his uncle.

c. 1870 Marries Mary Carter.

1870 Opens jewelry store in Kirkburton.

1882 Moves to Lytham, England, where he opens a jewelry store.

1890 The Jessops move to California for health reasons and purchase a ranch at Miramar, near San Diego.

1893 Opens jewelry store at 1317 F Street, San Diego.

1896 Store moves to 910 Fifth Street.

1906 Store moves to 952 Fifth Street.

1907 The display of the main clockworks for the elaborate Jessop street clock receives a gold medal at the California State Fair, Sacramento.

1908 Designs and manufactures a silver presentation box for Rear Admiral Robley D. Evans of the Great White Fleet of the United States Navy.

1927 Store moves to 1041 Fifth Street.

1932 April 16—Joseph dies in Coronado, California, from injuries after being struck by an automobile.

1949 Jessop's opens its first branch store—in La Jolla, California— and eventually grows to eight branches, becoming the largest family-owned jewelry business in the United States.

1970 Dayton Hudson Corporation of Minneapolis buys the company and later sells it to Henry Birks International of Canada.

RALPH HELM JOHONNOT (1880–1940)
SALOME L. JOHONNOT (1883–1962)

1880 July 28—Ralph Helm Johonnot born in Syracuse, New York.

1883 December 20—Salome L. (maiden name unknown) born in Maryland.

1909 Ralph teaches art at Pratt Institute, Brooklyn. At some point, he is made head of the Department of Design.

1912 The Johonnots move to Pacific Grove, California.

c. 1913 Ralph gives private lessons in design and color to RUDOLPH SCHAEFFER.

1913 January—the Johonnots lecture and exhibit arts and crafts at the San Francisco Institute of Art. The objects displayed include Salome's Hindu-style embroidery and Ralph's hand-wrought jewelry, made from designs by his brother Carl.

1914 February–March—Ralph teaches a course in interior decoration in Pasadena. March–April—Ralph teaches the same course in Los Angeles.

1915 The Johonnots exhibit textiles, embroideries, and design in the Southern California Exhibition of Applied Arts by Southern California Craftsmen at the Panama-California Exposition, San Diego. July–August—the Johonnots teach wood-block printing on textiles, embroidery, and landscape interpretation at their Summer School of Design and Hand Work in Pacific Grove (again in 1916).

1916 April—three dyed and stenciled scarves by the Johonnots are shown at the Boston Society of Arts and Crafts gallery.

1917 July—the Johonnots are in Chicago. August—Ralph teaches landscape interpretation at the summer school in Pacific Grove.

1919 July–August—the Johonnots teach design, landscape, and embroidery at their newly established summer school in Carmel Highlands, California.

1921 July–August—the Johonnots and Emma Waldvogel teach design, landscape, and embroidery at the Johonnot-Waldvogel Summer School in Monterey, California.

1922 November—the Johonnots, now living in New York, exhibit landscapes there at the Artists' Cooperative Galleries.

1926 February–April—the Johonnots teach design and landscape painting in San Francisco.

1930s Ralph runs artists' supply shop in Carmel and gives private lessons in art.

1940 November 19—Ralph dies in Los Gatos, California.

1962 April 11—Salome dies in Monterey County.

RUFUS B. KEELER (1885–1934)

1885 October 2—Rufus Bradley Keeler born in Bellingham, Washington.

1887 Family moves to the San Francisco Bay Area.

c. 1905 Rufus is employed by the Carnegie Brick and Pottery Company in Tesla, California, where he meets his future

277

wife, Mary Leary.

1908–9 Takes courses at the University of Illinois, Champaign-Urbana, in ceramic engineering.

1909 Joins the American Ceramic Society. Works briefly as a draftsman at Gladding, McBean & Company in Lincoln, California.

1910–11 Superintendent at Carnegie Brick and Pottery Company.

1911–16 Returns to work at Gladding, McBean & Company.

1917 Becomes president and manager of his own Southern California Clay Products on East Fifty-second Street, Vernon, California.

1923 Firm is renamed California Clay Products Company and relocates to Liberty and Otis streets, South Gate, California.

1924 Keeler builds a house on Victoria Avenue in South Gate, which is heavily and imaginatively decorated with his tiles.

1926 Named manager of MALIBU POTTERIES.

1932 Malibu Potteries closes.

1934 Keeler begins work at Emsco Refactories Company, South Gate. October 30—dies in South Gate of heart failure two weeks after exposure to cyanide in an industrial accident.

ALICE KLAUBER (1871–1951)

1871 May 19—Alice Ellen Klauber born in San Diego.

1885 The Klaubers move to San Francisco for their children's education. While there, Alice studies painting at the Art Students League.

1892 The Klaubers return to San Diego.

1902 Alice is a charter member of the Bookbinders' Guild of California.

1907 Studies with William Merritt Chase in Italy.

1910 Assists HAZEL WOOD WATERMAN with interior designs for the Wednesday Club, San Diego. Opens Torii Shop with Robert G. Nichols to sell interior furnishings. Shop closes in 1913.

1912 Studies with the painter Robert Henri in Spain.

1915 Serves as chairman of the Art Department at the Panama-California Exposition, San Diego. With Henri and Dr. Edgar Hewett, she is curator of San Diego's first exhibition of contemporary American art; she also designs the interior of the Women's Headquarters Persimmon Room—both at the exposition.

1916 Exhibits at the Panama-California International Exposition, San Diego.

1926 Founding member of the San Diego Fine Arts Society.

1928 Her book, *Poems,* is published by Denrich Press, Chula Vista, California.

1931 Studies with Hans Hofmann at the Chouinard School of Art in Los Angeles.

1935 Exhibits at the California-Pacific International Exposition, San Diego.

1940 Named honorary curator of oriental art at the Fine Arts Gallery of San Diego.

1951 July 5—dies in Lemon Grove, California.

PEDRO J. LEMOS (1882–1954)

1882 May 25—Pedro Joseph Lemos born in Austin, Nevada, the son of Portuguese immigrants. He is raised in Oakland.

1899 *Employed by the Pacific Press Publishing Company, Oakland.*

c. 1900 Studies under ARTHUR F. MATHEWS at the Mark Hopkins Institute of Art, San Francisco (later the San Francisco Institute of Art).

1901 *Employed as an artist at Pacific Press.*

1905 *In San Francisco, Pedro and John Lemoses' engraving firm, Lemos Bros., is at 140 Geary Street.*

1906 April 18—San Francisco studio destroyed in earthquake and fire.

1907 *Lemos Illustrating Co., artists and illustrators—run by Pedro, John, and Frank Lemos—is at 824 Athens Avenue, Oakland.* August 20—Pedro marries Reta A. Bailey in Oakland.

1909 *Firm again listed as Lemos Bros.*

1910 *Firm listed as engravers.*

1911 While FRANK INGERSON travels in Europe, Lemos fills Ingerson's position of instructor of decorative design at the California School of Design, San Francisco Institute of Art. *Lemos Bros. is closed.*

1912 July—visits Cathedral Oaks, Alma, California.

1913 Summer—studies under Arthur Wesley Dow at the Art Students League in New York.

1914 Summer—appointed director of San Francisco Institute of Art. Begins several years as illustrator and typographical supervisor on the University of California yearbook.

1915 Exhibits five works at the Panama-Pacific International Exposition in San Francisco, winning a bronze medal.

1917 Named director of the Stanford University Museum of Art, Stanford, California, a post he holds through 1945.

1927 Appointed first president of the Carmel Art Association, Carmel, California.

1928   Family travels to Europe; while there, Lemos arranges an exhibition of contemporary European arts and crafts for the Stanford University Museum of Art.

1929   Designs building for the Allied Arts Guild in Menlo Park, California.

1930   Summer—travels to New Mexico and Arizona, where he collects Hopi and Najavo arts and crafts.

1931   Summer—travels to Mexico and the southwestern United States to study and collect Mexican and Native American arts and crafts.

1945   Resigns directorship of Stanford University Museum of Art.

1954   December 5—dies.

GRACE LIVERMORE. *See* O'HARA & LIVERMORE

PAUL LOHMAN (1861–1928)

1861   July 20—Frederick Paul Lohman born in Germany.

1870s   Studies art and china decorating in Dresden.

c. 1883 Immigrates to the United States; marries Maria Meisner.

1894   Employed as a sign painter in San Francisco.

1904   Possibly attends Louisiana Purchase Exposition, St. Louis.

1905–7 Lives in Chicago, where he works as a commercial artist.

c. 1911 Moves to San Diego for health reasons.

1915   Establishes his home and studio at 3509 Cabrillo Street, East San Diego.

1915–17 As a decorator for Alfred Stahel & Sons crockery store in San Diego, develops Persimmon Red, a line of decorated china.

1922   Moves his home and studio to 1322 C Street, San Diego.

1928   September 4—dies in San Diego.

REGINALD MACHELL (1854–1927)

1854   June 20—Reginald Willoughby Machell born in Crackenthorpe, England.

c. 1870s Studies at Uppingham and Owens College, where he excels in drawing and classics.

1875   Marries Ada Mary Simpson. Goes to London to study art.

1876   Studies in Paris at the Académie Julian.

1880   Returns to London. Exhibits a portrait at the Royal Academy.

1887   Becomes a Theosophist.

1890   Does interior decoration for the Theosophical Society's London headquarters, under the direction of the society's founder, Madame Helena P. Blavatsky.

1891   After Blavatsky's death, designs the urn in which her ashes are kept.

1893   Elected to the Royal Society of British Artists.

1895   Illustrates Irene Osgood's book *An Idol's Passion.*

1897   Illustrates Osgood's *Chant of the Lonely Soul.*

1900   December 28—moves to Lomaland, the Theosophical community at Point Loma near San Diego.

c. 1900s Works on the decoration of Lomaland. Makes architectural elements, paintings, and furnishings.

1914   Illustrates Kenneth Morris's *Fates of the Princes of Dyfed.*

1927   October 8—dies in San Diego.

MALIBU POTTERIES
MAY K. RINDGE (1864–1941)

c. 1857 Frederick Hastings Rindge born in Cambridge, Massachusetts.

1864   May 9—Rhoda May Knight born in Trenton, Michigan.

1887   May 17—Knight marries Frederick Rindge and becomes known as May K. Rindge; they move to California.

1892   Frederick Rindge purchases the thirteen-thousand-acre Rancho Malibu for use as a weekend and summer retreat.

1905   August 29—Frederick dies in Yreka, California.

1921   Marblehead Land Company, with May K. Rindge as president, becomes the official owner of Rancho Malibu.

1926   Malibu Potteries opens on the Rindge ranch under the management of RUFUS B. KEELER.

1927   In its second year of operation, Malibu Potteries employs 127 people. Designer J. Donald Prouty begins work on the commission for twenty-three decorative tile panels for the Los Angeles city hall.

1929   Rindge begins construction of her fifty-room dream house on Laudamus Hill, Malibu. Work begins on the Adamson House (for Rhoda Adamson, Rindge's daughter), which is extensively decorated with Malibu tile.

1931   November 11–12—a night fire destroys half the tile factory and thousands of tiles.

1932   Malibu Potteries ceases operation.

1936   Rindge's mansion, still unfinished, is sold to Marblehead Land Company.

1940   Marblehead sells Malibu Potteries equipment as junk.

1941   February 8—Rindge dies.

1942   The house, its grounds, and the complete inventory of unsold tiles are bought by the Franciscan Friars of California for use as a retreat. Franciscan Brother Benedict Schlickum and tile setter Michael Braun begin work completing the tiling of the mansion. Braun will work on this project for twenty-three years.

1970   The retreat is destroyed by fire, but much of the tile is salvaged and integrated into ceramic collages in the rebuilding.

HERMAN MARKHAM (1849–1922)

1849   August 13—Herman Markham born in Ann Arbor, Michigan.

1884   *Works as a farmer and apiarist in Ann Arbor.*

1898   *Marries Ione Sprague.*

1899   *Works as a traveling salesman.*

1903   *Works as general manager for the Twentieth-Century Home Delivery Library.*

c. 1904 Begins making vases at home, because commercially available pots cause his roses to wilt.

1904   *Again works as a traveling salesman.*

1905   Is joined by his son Kenneth Sprague (1877–1952) in the pottery, which has become a commercial venture.

1907   Markham pottery is displayed in the Fifteenth Annual Exhibition of the New York Society of Keramic Arts.

1913   After visiting CALIFORNIA CHINA PRODUCTS COMPANY in National City, California, the Markhams move their pottery there. They set up shop at 1212 Seventh Avenue and make use of the CCPCo kilns.

1915   Markham pottery is shown in the Varied Industries Building at the Panama-California Exposition, San Diego; it receives a gold medal.

1917   Markham Pottery moves to 1123 B Avenue when CCPCo closes.

1921   February—the pottery is incorporated. Late in the year—the pottery closes. Kenneth moves to Los Angeles.

1922   November 18—Herman dies in San Diego.

ARTHUR F. MATHEWS (1860–1945)
LUCIA K. MATHEWS (1870–1955)

1860   October 1—Arthur Francis Mathews born in Markesan, Wisconsin.

1867   Family settles in Oakland.

204. Furniture Shop (Arthur F. and Lucia K. Mathews). *Sheet-Music Cabinet,* c. 1915–20. Painted wood, 36¼ x 29¼ x 19⅝ in. The Oakland Museum; Gift of the estate of Marjorie Eaton.

1870   August 29—Lucia Kleinhans born in San Francisco.

1875   Arthur is apprenticed to his architect father.

1885–89 Arthur studies in Paris under Gustave Boulanger and Jules Lefebvre. Receives Grand Gold Medal, Académie Julian, in 1886. Exhibits in the Paris Salons, 1887–89.

1889   Arthur returns to San Francisco. He teaches at the Art Students League and the California School of Design.

1890   Arthur appointed director of the California School of Design (after 1893 known as the Mark Hopkins Institute of Art).

1892   Lucia enrolls at Mills College, Oakland, but withdraws before graduation.

1893   Lucia enrolls at the Mark Hopkins Institute of Art.

1894   June—Arthur and Lucia, his student, marry.

1906   April—Mathews studio at Hopkins Institute destroyed in the fire following the earthquake. Arthur resigns his directorship of the institute. June—Beach-Robinson Company incorporated as a furniture manufactory and retailer of furniture and furnishings. John Zeile is principal investor of Beach-Robinson Company The company is located at 1717 California Street, San Francisco, sharing space with the Furniture Shop. October—Arthur and Lucia begin publication of monthly magazine *Philopolis* and establish Philopolis Press.

1907   Lucia helps reestablish the Sketch Club, which had been disrupted by the 1906 earthquake.

1908–9 Lucia serves as president of the Sketch Club.

1913   The Furniture Shop provides interior designs and furnishings for the Masonic Temple at 25 North Van Ness Avenue.

1914   Philopolis Press closes.

1915   Lucia's watercolor *Monterey Pine* awarded a silver medal at the Panama-Pacific International Exposition, San Francisco.

1916   September—last issue of *Philopolis* published.

1920   The Furniture Shop ceases production.

1922   American Institute of Architects awards Arthur its Fine Arts Gold Medal for his murals.

1945   February 19—Arthur dies in San Francisco.

1955   July 14—Lucia dies in Los Angeles.

BERNARD MAYBECK (1862–1957)

1862   February 7—Bernard Ralph Maybeck born in New York.

c. 1880 Briefly attends the College of the City of New York. Joins his father working at Pottier and Stymus, an architectural carving and furniture shop.

1881   Studies design in the Paris studio of Pottier and Stymus.

1882   March—enters the Ecole des Beaux-Arts, where he studies architecture.

1886   Returns to New York and enters the firm of Carrère and Hastings.

1889   Attempts to establish his own firm in Kansas City, Missouri, but is hindered by the economic depression. Meets Annie White.

1890   Employed by Wright and Saunders of San Francisco. October 29—marries Annie White in Kansas City; they settle in Oakland. Employed as a designer of furniture and interiors for the Charles M. Plum Company, San Francisco.

1892   Employed by A. Page Brown's architectural firm. Oversees construction of the California Building at the Chicago World's Columbian Exposition. The Maybecks move to Berkeley.

1894   With A. C. Schweinfurth, designs the Swedenborgian Church of the New Jerusalem, San Francisco. Fall—appointed instructor in drawing at the University of California, Berkeley.

1895   Appointed director of the Architectural Section of the Mark Hopkins Institute of Art, San Francisco. Designs Charles Keeler House, Ridge Road and Highland Place, Berkeley.

1898   Made instructor of instrumental drawing and engineering design at the university.

1899   Designs Hearst Hall, Channing Way near College Avenue, Berkeley.

1902   Opens architectural office at 307 Sansome Street, San Francisco. With Charles Keeler, forms the Berkeley Hillside Club. Work begins on Wyntoon, Phoebe Hearst's Siskiyou County, California, estate, with furniture designed by Maybeck and FREDERICK H. MEYER. Designs Charles Keeler studio, 1736 Highland Place, Berkeley. August—designs Faculty Club at the university.

1903   Spring—resigns from the university. April—designs Grove Clubhouse in Bohemian Grove, on the Russian River, Sonoma County, California.

1906   April 18—Maybeck's office is destroyed in the earthquake and fire. Maybeck and his assistant, Mark White, take temporary business quarters at 821 Eddy Street, San Francisco.

1907   Maybeck and White move to 35 Montgomery Street, San Francisco.

1908   November—work begins on his bookshop for PAUL ELDER, 239 Grant Avenue, San Francisco.

1909   Designs own home, 2701 Buena Vista Way, Berkeley.

1910   August—work begins on First Church of Christ, Scientist, at Dwight Way and Bowditch Street, Berkeley.

1912   November—work begins on Temple of the Wings, a residence for the Charles C. Boynton family at 2800 Buena Vista Way, Berkeley (completed by A. Randolph Monro). December—planting of the Rose Walk garden at Rose Path and Euclid Avenue, Berkeley.

1913   Designs Palace of Fine Arts for the Panama-Pacific International Exposition, San Francisco.

1918   December—designs general plan of Mills College in Oakland for Phoebe Apperson Hearst.

1923   September—fire destroys Maybeck's home.

1956   Annie Maybeck dies in Alameda County, California.

1957   October 3—dies in Alameda County.

MEAD AND REQUA
FRANK MEAD (1865–1940)
RICHARD S. REQUA (1881–1941)

281

1865   Frank Mead born in Camden, New Jersey.

1881   March 27—Richard S. Requa born in Rock Island, Illinois.

1885   The Requa family moves to Norfolk, Nebraska; he attends Norfolk College.

c. 1900 Mead establishes an architectural office in Philadelphia with Bart Keane; travels to North Africa to photograph the indigenous architecture.

1900   Requa moves to San Diego and is employed as an electrical engineer by Hartwell Electrical Company.

1903   Mead moves to San Diego and is employed by IRVING GILL.

1907   Mead serves as Gill's partner for about seven months, then leaves San Diego.

1908   Mead, concerned about the plight of the Mojave Apache people, visits President Theodore Roosevelt and is given authority to purchase land for them in the Verde River valley of Arizona.

1908–10 Requa employed as Irving Gill's superintendent.

1909   Mead serves as superintendent for the Lame Deer Reservation, Montana.

1910   Mead relocates to the Pala Reservation in San Diego County.

1912   Mead and Requa form an architectural partnership in San Diego.

1913   Edward Drummond Libbey commissions Mead and Requa to rebuild the town of Nordhoff, California, after a disastrous fire. They continue working in Nordhoff (which from 1917 is called Ojai) through 1919.

1914   Requa tours Cuba, Panama, and South America, where he photographs Spanish Colonial architecture.

1918   Requa obtains a patent for an improved hollow building tile.

1920   Mead and Requa dissolve their partnership. Mead leaves San Diego. Requa forms a partnership with Herbert Jackson. Requa and Jackson are hired by the Santa Fe Railway to design a civic center for Rancho Santa Fe, California.

1926   Requa writes and illustrates with his own photographs *Architectural Details: Spain and the Mediterranean*.

1929   Requa writes and illustrates with his own photographs *Old World Inspirations for American Architecture*.

1940   December 10—Mead dies in Santa Monica from injuries sustained in an automobile accident.

1941   June 10—Requa dies in San Diego.

FREDERICK H. MEYER (1872–1961)

1872   November 6—Friedrich Heinrich Wilhelm Meyer born in Grossen Berkel, Germany. As a boy he is apprenticed to his two uncles, one a furniture designer, the other a blacksmith.

1888   Moves to Fresno, California, to live with his uncle William Meyer, a vineyardist. Through German friends he is hired by a Fresno nursery. Contracts malaria. After his recovery works at his friends' nursery in Niles, California.

c. 1890 Studies art at San Jose State Normal School.

c. 1893–94 Spends eighteen months at an unidentified technical university in Cincinnati. Stricken with typhoid. Spends six months at the Pennsylvania Museum School of Industrial Art (now University of the Arts), Philadelphia.

c. 1894–96 While visiting parents in Germany, takes private lessons from a graduate of the Royal Art School in Berlin and attends that school for two years. Graduates in 1896.

1896–97 Returns to Philadelphia and completes his Pennsylvania Museum studies. Graduates in 1897.

1897–98 Works in an architect's office in San Jose. Teaches at San Jose Normal School. Works at the Lick School in San Francisco and makes illustrations for the *San Francisco Chronicle*.

1898   Hired as drawing supervisor for the Stockton, California, public schools.

1902   June—marries Laetitia Summerville, a teacher. Leaves Stockton when offered post teaching drawing at the University of California, Berkeley. Concurrently is professor of applied arts at the San Francisco Institute of Art. Opens the Craftsman's Shop, where he designs furniture made by Stanley Kopersky. With BERNARD MAYBECK, designs furnishings for Phoebe Apperson Hearst's Siskiyou County, California, estate, Wyntoon.

205. Frederick H. Meyer, wall cabinet, portfolio stand, baby's crib, and settle, photographed c. 1904.

1904 Designs furnishings for the San Francisco Room in the California Building at the Louisiana Purchase Exposition, St. Louis. Becomes the main furniture designer for United Crafts and Arts of California. December—serves on the Exhibition Committee for the second annual exhibition of the San Francisco Guild of Arts and Crafts.

1905 October—elected president of the San Francisco Guild of Arts and Crafts.

1906 April—Meyer's cabinet shop and home are destroyed in the earthquake and fire. He resigns his teaching posts. Takes position as designer for either the Furniture Shop of ARTHUR F. AND LUCIA K. MATHEWS or its sponsor, Beach-Robinson Company. Travels to Europe to buy equipment for the shop and to see modern furniture in Norway and Sweden. An impromptu speech to the San Francisco Guild of Arts and Crafts on his dream of founding a practical arts-and-crafts school is published in the *San Francisco Call,* resulting in a wave of prospective students.

1907 Founds the CALIFORNIA SCHOOL OF ARTS AND CRAFTS at Shattuck Avenue and Addison Street, Berkeley, with Laetitia, Perham W. Nahl, and Isabelle Percy West.

1908 Appointed head of the Art and Drawing Department of the Berkeley public schools. Delivers two rooms of furnishings to the James Adam Barr family of Stockton. The painter Xavier Martinez builds a studio at 324 Scenic Avenue, Piedmont, California, to Meyer's design.

1911 CSAC moves to 2119 Allston Way, the site of the old Berkeley High School.

1913–19 Is director of art for the Oakland public schools, a part-time post.

1915 Awarded gold medal at the Panama-Pacific International Exposition, San Francisco, presumably for the CSAC Alumni group's model of an artist's studio in the Palace of Education.

1936 CSAC is renamed California College of Arts and Crafts.

1944 Retires from directorship of CCAC and is given title of president emeritus.

1961 January 6—dies in Oakland.

CHARLES B. AND WALTER H. NORDHOFF. *See* CALIFORNIA CHINA PRODUCTS COMPANY

O'HARA & LIVERMORE
LILLIAN O'HARA (1861–1959)
GRACE LIVERMORE (1867–1927)

1861 April 8—Lillian Ada O'Hara born in Bowmanville, Canada.

1867 August 3—Grace G. Livermore born in Wisconsin.

late 1870s O'Hara studies in a Canadian art school.

1885 September 18—O'Hara goes to California with her mother, settling on the Wildasin ranch in Independence, Inyo County.

1889 April 26—O'Hara signs a declaration of intention to become a United States citizen.

1892 Lillian O'Hara, Grace Livermore, and Marea van Vleck open an interior decoration shop and artists' studio at 120 Sutter Street, room 70, in San Francisco. Van Vleck leaves to become a teacher.

1893 O'Hara & Livermore executes the interior designs for the San Francisco Women's Committee Room in the California Building at the World's Columbian Exposition, Chicago.

1904 *Pasadena branch of O'Hara & Livermore opens at 38 South Raymond Street.* San Francisco shop moves to 356 Sutter Street, with the factory in an adjacent building. They employ more than a dozen artisans working in applied arts, burnt-leather goods, bronze lamps, and curios. The shop deals in these items, as well as imported handmade bronze objects. O'Hara and Livermore visit London, Dublin, Bruges, and Munich.

1905 *Boston branch of O'Hara & Livermore opens at 2 Arlington Street.* O'Hara designs and builds Klah-ha-ne, a redwood house in San Anselmo, California.

c. 1906 O'Hara & Livermore leatherwork with brocade inlay is sold through PAUL ELDER & Co.

1906 April—San Francisco shop is destroyed in the fire following the earthquake.

1907 *Boston shop moves to 16 Arlington Street. San Francisco shop reopens at 1611 Franklin Street.* June 6—O'Hara and Livermore attend the Irish International Exhibition in Dublin. They also visit London.

1908 August—San Francisco shop moves to 1366 Sutter Street. September 30—O'Hara goes to Boston to close the shop there.

1909 O'Hara & Livermore exhibits six objects at the Alaska-Yukon-Pacific Exposition in Seattle, including leatherwork and transparent watercolor screens. The firm receives a silver medal for the screens and a bronze medal for bookbinding.

1912 *San Francisco shop moves to 522 Sutter Street.*

1913 April–October—O'Hara travels in Italy, Germany, France, England, and Scotland.

1915 O'Hara & Livermore receives a medal of award for its display at the Panama-Pacific International Exposition, San Francisco.

1922 Livermore retires. January—O'Hara goes on a year-long

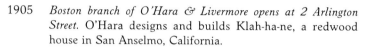

sightseeing and buying trip to France, North Africa, Sicily, Spain, Italy, Ireland, England, Scotland, and Switzerland.

1924   *Interior decorator Arthur Baken joins O'Hara & Livermore as a partner.*

1925   January 16—O'Hara and Livermore sign an agreement with Baken that gives him possession of the business in exchange for a monthly payment of $100 to each woman every month for life. January 17—O'Hara leaves San Francisco for a trip to Spain, North Africa, Italy, France, Belgium, Switzerland, Austria, Hungary, England, and Ireland.

1927   July 16—Livermore dies in San Anselmo.

1935   *O'Hara, Livermore & Arthur Baken closes its San Francisco shop.*

1938   *The Pasadena shop is renamed Arthur Baken.*

c. 1950 O'Hara decorates a group of apartments on Broadway, Russian Hill, San Francisco.

1959   November 28—O'Hara dies in San Anselmo.

INGVARDT OLSEN. *See* JALAN

DR. ORLOF N. ORLOW. *See* UNITED CRAFTS AND ARTS OF CALIFORNIA

LILLIAN PALMER (1872–1961)
EMILY WILLIAMS (1869–1942)

1869   Emily Williams born.

1872   Lillian McNeill Palmer born in Stonington, Connecticut, a cousin of the painter James McNeill Whistler. Her father, employed in the mining industry, travels widely and becomes acquainted with the craft of blacksmithing in the mining camps.

c. 1880s The Palmers settle in St. Louis, where Lillian attends private school.

c. 1890 The Palmers move to California.

1898   After her father's death, Emily Williams lives with the Palmer family in San Jose. She and Palmer forge a friendship based on their shared interest in women's rights and begin a personal and professional partnership that lasts forty-two years.

1901   *Palmer employed by the Mercury Publishing Company, publisher of the* San Jose Mercury. *Her position is probably editorial.*

early 1900s Williams studies architecture at the Lick School in San Francisco. She is unable to find a position in a male-dominated firm, so she and Palmer independently build a house in Pacific Grove, California. After establishing a professional reputation with this venture, Williams has a successful career as an architect.

1907   Palmer does copperwork in the basement of her home at 66 South Priest Street, San Jose, with her assistant, D'ARCY GAW.

c. 1908–9 Palmer travels to Vienna to study metalwork, returning to the United States by way of the Orient. Studies electrical engineering in Chicago.

1910   *Opens an art-metal shop at 1026 Polk Street, San Francisco. The shop operates on a profit-sharing basis, with women employees paid as much as men.*

c. 1911 HARRY DIXON is hired as foreman of the shop.

1911   *The shop moves to 1345 Sutter Street, San Francisco.*

1913   *The shop is incorporated as the Palmer Shop.*

1915   The Palmer Shop exhibits its work in the Varied Industries Building at the Panama-Pacific International Exposition, San Francisco.

1917   February—Palmer founds the Business and Professional Women's Club, San Francisco, and serves as its president through December 1919.

1918   Entry of the United States into World War I leads the government to request that metal be conserved; the Palmer Shop closes.

1920   *Palmer is listed as a metalworker working out of her home at 1039a Broadway, San Francisco.*

1921   Named honorary president of the Business and Professional Women's Club, a post she holds until her death.

1922   Teaches course at her home in basic household repair for women.

c. 1933 Retires to Los Gatos, California.

1933   After inheriting the Whistler homestead, drives cross-country to Connecticut to dispose of the estate. Returns with family journals, which provide material for several lectures on the character of Anna Whistler, Whistler's mother.

1942   June 3—Williams dies.

1961   February 4—Palmer dies in Los Gatos.

REDLANDS POTTERY. *See* WESLEY H. TRIPPETT

RICHARD S. REQUA. *See* MEAD AND REQUA

FREDERICK HÜRTEN RHEAD (1880–1942)

1880   August 29—Frederick Hürten Rhead born in Hanley, England.

c. 1895 Studies at Wedgwood Institute, Burslem, and the Stoke-on-Trent Government Art School.

1899   Becomes art director of the Wardle Art Pottery, Hanley.

1901   Marries Agnes (b. 1877; maiden name unknown) in England.

1902   Employed by the Vance/Avon Faience Company in Tiltonville, Ohio.

1904   Works at Weller Pottery in Zanesville, Ohio, early in the year; then as art director of the Roseville Pottery in Zanesville.

1908   Goes to Long Island, New York, to work at the Jervis Pottery.

1909   Named instructor in pottery at the University City pottery in University City, Missouri, near St. Louis.

1911   November—with Agnes, implements the pottery program at the AREQUIPA Sanatorium in Fairfax, California.

c. 1912 Dr. Philip King Brown of Arequipa sends Rhead to assist pottery instructor Isabel Morton with her first firing at the Santa Barbara Normal School of Manual Arts and Home Economics.

1913   Takes over the financial management of the pottery but does not perform to the directors' satisfaction. May—resigns. Works briefly for Steiger Pottery in San Francisco. Moves to Santa Barbara and founds Rhead Pottery there, in Mission Canyon. Begins periodic teaching of ceramics at the Santa Barbara Normal School, a course sponsored by Brown.

1914   January—Rhead Pottery is incorporated by its directors, Rhead, Christoph Tornoe, and Ralph Radcliffe Whitehead. March—Rhead pottery is shown in the Santa Barbara Art Committee art exhibition at the State Normal School of Manual Arts (formerly the Santa Barbara Normal School).

1915   Exhibits pottery in the Southern California Exhibition of Applied Arts by Southern California Craftsmen at the Panama-California Exposition, San Diego; receives a gold medal.

1916   March—the Rheads divorce. Frederick Hürten Rhead may have spent several months at the utopian Llano colony near Riverside, California. April—a group of "Chinese black" (probably mirror black) pottery is shown at the Boston Society of Arts and Crafts gallery. December—Rhead begins publication of his periodical, the *Potter*.

1917   The *Potter* folds after the third monthly issue. September 16—Rhead marries Lois Whitcomb, a decorator at his pottery. The pottery proves financially unfeasible. The Rheads move to Zanesville, Ohio, where Rhead is employed as director of research by the American Encaustic Tiling Company.

1918   July—Rhead Pottery stock is auctioned in Santa Barbara. Rhead becomes a naturalized American citizen.

1920–25 Serves as chairman of the Art Division of the American Ceramic Society.

1927   Becomes art director of the Homer Laughlin China Company in Newell, West Virginia.

1929   The Rheads divorce.

1934   The American Ceramic Society awards Rhead its Charles Fergus Binns Medal for his contributions to the advancement of ceramic art.

1935   August 31—marries Winifred Pardell.

1942   November 2—dies in New York.

MAY K. RINDGE. *See* MALIBU POTTERIES

ALEXANDER W. ROBERTSON (1840–1925)

1840   December 15—Alexander William Robertson born in England.

1853   Immigrates to the United States.

1860   Marries Helen Barteaux.

1865   Establishes pottery for brownware manufacture in Chelsea, Massachusetts.

1868   Brownware discontinued in favor of plain-and-fancy flowerpots.

1872   Robertson's father, James, and brothers, George and Hugh, join the operation, which is named the Chelsea Keramic Art Works.

206. Alberhill Pottery (Alexander W. Robertson). *Vase,* 1914. Earthenware with green matte glaze, 9⅝ x 2¹³⁄₁₆ in. Gary Keith.

1873	Robertson visits California and, on his return to Chelsea, makes an experimental series of pots from California clays.
1880	James dies.
1884	Alexander leaves Chelsea for California.
1885	Settles in Oakland.
1891	July—visits Stockton Terra-Cotta Company in hopes of overseeing an art pottery there. Although Robertson makes a small pitcher at Stockton, nothing immediately comes of the artware plan. Meets LINNA VOGEL IRELAN, wife of the California state mineralogist and a tireless promoter of California clays; they make several attempts over the next seven years to found a pottery.
1898	Robertson and Irelan establish the Roblin Art Pottery in San Francisco. The ware is thrown and glazed by Robertson, decorated by Irelan.
1900	Roblin pottery is exhibited at the Universal Exposition, Paris, where it receives a special mention and award.
1903	Robertson's son Fred joins him in San Francisco. Roblin is awarded the gold medal at the California State Fair in Sacramento, where Robertson has been demonstrating throwing techniques.
1906	April—Roblin Art Pottery is destroyed by the earthquake and fire. Alexander and Fred move to Southern California, where they work for Los Angeles Pressed Brick Company.
1910	Alexander establishes an art pottery and school at the utopian community of Halcyon, near Pismo Beach, California.
1912	Employed by ALBERHILL Coal and Clay Company near Riverside, California, to experiment with local clays.
1913	Financial problems lead to the closing of Halcyon Art Pottery.
1914	Leaves Alberhill when it becomes clear that an art pottery will not be established.
1915	Exhibits pottery in the Southern California Exhibition of Applied Arts by Southern California Craftsmen at the Panama-California Exposition, San Diego; receives a gold medal for his Alberhill experiments. Retires from active pottery work.
1925	October 10—dies in Glendale, California.

FRED H. ROBERTSON (1869–1952)

1869	September 6—Fred H. Robertson born in Massachusetts.
1903	Joins his father, Alexander, at Roblin Art Pottery in San Francisco. Marries Laura V. (maiden name unknown).
1906	April—Roblin Art Pottery is destroyed by the earthquake and fire. Fred and Alexander move to Southern California,

where they work for Los Angeles Pressed Brick Company. Fred begins firing artware in his employer's kilns.

207. Robertson Pottery (Fred H. Robertson). *Three Vases*, c. 1913–16. Glazed stoneware. Left: 7⁹⁄₁₆ x 4⁵⁄₁₆ in., Gary Keith. Center: 5⁷⁄₁₆ x 3¼ in., Gary Keith. Right: 5¼ x 2¾ in., Stephanie Lynn and David Mills.

1915	Fred's crystalline-glaze pottery wins a gold medal at the Panama-Pacific International Exposition, San Francisco.
1916	Fred's pottery wins two gold medals at the Panama-California International Exposition, San Diego.
1921	Fred moves to the newly opened Claycraft Potteries in Los Angeles.
1925	His son George B. joins him at Claycraft.
1934	Fred and George establish Robertson Pottery in Los Angeles. It will move several times over the years to different locations within the city.
1952	Robertson Pottery closes. December 23—Fred dies.

RUDOLPH SCHAEFFER (1886–1988)

1886	June 26—Rudolph Schaeffer born in Clare, Michigan.
1904–6	Attends Michigan Central State Normal School, Mount Pleasant.
1906–7	Attends Thomas Normal Training School, Detroit. Graduates. Teaches manual arts at the Evening Mission Schools (location unknown).
1907–8	Teaches art metalwork and jewelry making at the William Morris School for Arts and Crafts in Columbus, Ohio. Teaches manual training to grades five through nine, first briefly in Toledo, Ohio, then through 1910 in Columbus.

Summer 1908—travels in France and England.

1909 In Columbus takes Ohio State University course in artistic lettering. Summer—takes courses in graphic design and composition under ERNEST A. BATCHELDER at the Handicraft Guild, Minneapolis.

1910 Moves to Pasadena with the encouragement of Batchelder. Teaches art metalwork and manual training at the Polytechnic Elementary School of the Throop Polytechnic Institute through 1914.

1911 Summer—takes courses in art metalwork, design, and jewelry making under DOUGLAS DONALDSON at the Institute of Mechanic Arts at Mount Hermon, Santa Cruz, California.

1912 Takes private design classes from Batchelder in Pasadena.

c. 1913 Takes private design and color classes with RALPH HELM JOHONNOT.

1913 Teaches art metalwork and jewelry making at the Los Angeles Polytechnic Evening High School. Summer—teaches art metal, jewelry, and design at the Institute of Mechanic Arts.

1914 Chosen as one of a commission of twenty-five manual training and industrial-art teachers to study industrial education in Munich, Germany. Studies at Royal School for Applied Art, Munich, with courses in decorative art, lithography, and gold- and silversmithing. Meets Josef Hoffmann in Vienna and becomes acquainted with the work of the Wiener Werkstätte.

1915 Teaches design and metalwork for one term at Fremont High School in Oakland. Gives private classes in design and handicraft, Berkeley and Piedmont, California. Exhibits metalwork and graphic design in the Southern California Exhibition of Applied Arts by Southern California Craftsmen at the Panama-California Exposition, San Diego. Spring—teaches at the CALIFORNIA SCHOOL OF ARTS AND CRAFTS. Summer—gives private classes in Berkeley in interior, fabric, and metal design; jewelry making; and silversmithing.

1916 Founds the Rudolph Schaeffer Summer School of Design and Handicrafts, Piedmont. Teaches design, jewelry making, and wood-block printing. April—shows his metalwork at the Boston Society of Arts and Crafts gallery; receives the society's first prize in decorative design.

1917 July–August—operates his summer school in Piedmont.

1917–23 Professor of design and handicrafts, California School of Fine Arts, San Francisco Institute of Art.

1918 Visiting professor, Stanford University, Stanford, California.

1921 Designs sets for a Sam Hume production of the Detroit Symphony Society Drama Season. Spring—shows work as part of series of exhibitions of modern art in the Architecture Building, University of California, Berkeley.

1922–24 As art director for the Greek Theater on the Berkeley campus, designs stage sets and costumes for productions directed by Hume.

1923 Professor, California School of Fine Arts.

1924 Designs sets for a Hume production of the Detroit Symphony Society Drama Season. Gives classes in color for teachers at the Detroit Art Museum. Exhibits stage designs at the International Exhibition of Theatre Arts, Amsterdam.

1925 Travels in Europe and the Near East. Sees the Paris *Exposition internationale des arts décoratifs et industriels modernes.*

1926 Founds the Rudolph Schaeffer School of Design on Grant Avenue, San Francisco.

1927 The school moves to St. Anne Street.

1988 March 5—dies in San Francisco.

MORGAN SHEPARD (1865–1947)

1865 Morgan van Roorbach Shepard born in Brooklyn.

1881 After his mother's death, travels to South America and allegedly becomes involved in a Central American revolution.

1888 Employed as a Bank of America clerk in San Francisco.

1889 While still a bank clerk, attempts to cofound a printing and engraving firm, Reed, Shepard, and Tyler. The venture folds within a year.

1897 Meets PAUL ELDER.

1898 March—Elder and Shepard open the Book and Art Shop at 238 Post Street, San Francisco. They publish books under the Elder & Shepard imprint. Shepard's contributions include the design of books, bindings, and graphics as well as the redwood furniture for the shop.

1900 Marries Mary Elliot Putnam.

1902–3 President and charter member of the Bookbinders' Guild of California. Elder is secretary-treasurer.

1903 May—Shepard leaves the firm.

1904 Travels in Europe, where he studies book printing, bookbinding, and jewelry design.

1906 Returns to San Francisco, opening a design firm. April 18—the office is destroyed in the earthquake, and Shepard's legs are seriously injured. Moves to New York and establishes the Morgan Shepard publishing firm, which produces material similar to Elder & Shepard's.

c. 1911 Becomes a writer and publisher of children's books under the pen name John Martin.

1942 Mary Shepard dies.

1947 May 16—dies in New York.

SHREVE & CO.

1822 George Coates Shreve born in Massachusetts.

1852 George Shreve and his half-brother Samuel S. Shreve, recently arrived from New York, open a retail jewelry business at 139 Montgomery Street, San Francisco.

1859 September 12—Samuel drowns when the *Central America* sinks en route from Havana to New York. Lucius Thompson joins George as a partner, and at about this time the shop moves to 525 Montgomery Street.

1870 The shop moves to 110 Montgomery Street.

1881 Albert J. Lewis joins the firm as a partner.

1883 The firm begins manufacturing its own silver.

1885 October 8—fire destroys the Shreve factory.

1886 April—a new factory opens.

1892 The firm moves its shop to the corner of Post and Market streets.

1893 October 13—George Shreve dies in Mountain View, California. His son, George Rodman Shreve, becomes president.

1894 January—the firm is incorporated as Shreve & Co.

1895 September 17—Albert J. Lewis commits suicide.

1905 A new factory opens at 539 Bryant Street.

1906 March—the shop moves to the new Shreve Building at Post Street and Grant Avenue. April 18—the shop and factory are destroyed in the fire following the earthquake, but Shreve's losses are covered by insurers. The firm's offices move briefly to Oakland, then to two temporary structures in San Francisco at 2429 Jackson Street and 1701 Van Ness Avenue.

1908 November 28—Shreve & Co. absorbs the old San Francisco firm of W. K. Vanderslice, which was bankrupted by the earthquake and fire.

1909 The retail shop reopens on Post Street. The firm begins producing original lines of flatware and holloware—including Dolores, Norman, and XIV Century—designed by Joseph E. Birmingham.

1912 George R. Shreve sells his shares in the company to the J. E. Hickingbotham family.

1913 A new factory opens at 539 Bryant Street, on the site of the factory that was destroyed in 1906 (remains in constant use by the firm until 1968).

1914 August 4—George R. Shreve dies in San Mateo, California.

1925 PORTER BLANCHARD designs the Flemish line of flatware for the firm.

1929 Blanchard designs the Old English line of flatware.

1967 The firm is sold to Dayton Hudson Corporation of Minneapolis and ceases to operate as a manufacturing concern. The retail shop remains open.

ALBERT L. SOLON (1887–1949)

1887 December 27—Albert Louis Solon born in Stoke-on-Trent, England, the son of Louis Marc Solon, a ceramist and writer.

early 1900s Trains as a ceramic engineer at the Victoria Institute in Stoke. Apprentices at the Minton china factory, where his father is employed.

1912 Immigrates to California. Works as a chemist at several brick and terra-cotta companies. Makes a survey of clays in Southern California.

1913 July—takes over from FREDERICK HÜRTEN RHEAD as manager of AREQUIPA POTTERY in Fairfax, California.

1916 May—leaves Arequipa to take a position at San Jose State Normal School, where he teaches physics and ceramics.

1920 Leaves the school and begins manufacturing tile with Frank P. Schemmel at Fourth and Carrie streets, San Jose.

1923 Solon & Schemmel commissioned to provide tiles for the San Jose State Normal School's new Home Economics

208. Solon & Schemmel. *Four Tiles in a Square,* c. 1925. Machine-pressed fired clay with multicolored glaze, 11¾ x 11¾ in. The Oakland Museum; Art Acquisition Fund.

Building. Solon & Schemmel tiles are used for the Steinhart Aquarium alligator pool in Golden Gate Park, San Francisco.

1925 Solon & Schemmel moves its operations to 1881 South First Street, San Jose.

c. 1926 Marries Emma Ness (maiden name uncertain).

1932 Hires George Poxon to develop Sainte Claire ware, a line of unbreakable pottery for restaurants.

1936 Schemmel retires. April—Paul Gifford Larkin becomes Solon's new partner. Larkin manages the plant, Solon handles sales.

1947 Solon & Larkin becomes the Larkin Tile Company and moves to 1651 Pomona Avenue, San Jose. *Solon continues to be listed as a tile maker on South First Street.*

1949 August 2—dies in Santa Barbara.

JULIUS STARKE (1837–1918)

1837 February 15—Julius Starke born in Dresden, Germany.

c. 1850s Studies botany and does research at the Jardin des Plantes, Paris.

1863 Immigrates to the United States.

c. 1870s Ill and suffering from business problems, goes to California on horseback and settles in the Sierra Nevada, where he lives reclusively and studies local plants until his health returns.

1883 Opens wood-carving studio on Chapala Street, Santa Barbara.

1900 Exhibits paintings and an inlaid table at the Universal Exposition in Paris to great acclaim.

1902 Winter—marries in Santa Barbara.

1903 June 12—Mrs. Starke dies in Yosemite after drinking wood alcohol—accidentally, Starke says.

1905 Publishes his pamphlet *California Woods.*

1914 March—exhibits in the Santa Barbara Art Committee art exhibition at the State Normal School of Manual Arts.

1918 March 7—dies in Santa Barbara.

STOCKTON ART POTTERY

1890 December—Stockton Terra-Cotta Company, Stockton, California, is incorporated as a manufacturer of firebrick, sewer pipe, and stove pipe.

1891 July—production begins under the supervision of E. T. Mapel. July—Charles Bailey, from Excelsior Pottery Works

of Trenton, New Jersey, visits Stockton Terra-Cotta Company and suggests that an art pottery be established there. Bailey's companion, ALEXANDER W. ROBERTSON, demonstrates the possibilities by making a small pitcher. Nothing immediately comes of the artware plan.

1892 July—Mapel leaves Stockton Terra-Cotta Company. Thomas W. Blakey, a Scottish-trained potter, comes from the East Coast to manage the pottery.

1893 December—Blakey and his son John begin producing art pottery.

1894 Stockton Terra-Cotta Company receives a gold medal at the California Midwinter Fair, San Francisco; it is not known if this was for their art pottery. Late in the year—the company first produces Reckston ware.

1895 Summer—Stockton Terra-Cotta Company becomes insolvent. Funds are raised locally by the new manager, Arthur C. Hopkinson, to allow the art pottery to continue.

1896 October 21—Stockton Art Pottery is incorporated. Reckston ware becomes known as Rekston.

1897 Nathan-Dohrmann & Co. of San Francisco and New York begins distributing for Stockton Art Pottery. The operation of the pottery is suspended briefly to allow for reorganization and clearance of old stock. December 18—Thomas W. Blakey dies.

1898 February—John Blakey succeeds his father as superintendent of Stockton Art Pottery. A decorative line similar to Rekston is marketed as Mariposa Pottery, no doubt to appeal to Eastern retailers.

1900 Poor financial conditions force the pottery to close.

1901 August—Stockton Brick and Pottery Company is formed to make sewer pipe and brick from local clay deposits. The firm has plans to make a full line of functional and decorative Rekston ware under John Blakey.

1902 November 17—the Stockton Brick and Pottery Company plant is destroyed by fire. Although the company continues, the production of art pottery ceases.

CHAUNCEY R. THOMAS. *See* CALIFORNIA FAIENCE

LILLIAN TOBEY (c. 1880–c. 1925)

c. 1880 Lillian West Tobey born in Chicago.

c. 1900 Moves to San Francisco and establishes a design studio at 414 Pine Street, next door to the painters William Keith and Maynard Dixon.

1904 Serves as president of the San Francisco Guild of Arts and Crafts. Sells leatherwork through the UNITED CRAFTS AND ARTS OF CALIFORNIA shop.

1905 Marries Maynard Dixon. Serves as second vice president of the San Francisco Guild of Arts and Crafts. At about this time, her leatherwork and furniture collaborations with FREDERICK H. MEYER are retailed through the shops of PAUL ELDER.

1906 After the earthquake and fire the Dixons move to Sausalito, California. They live there for a year; later travel to New York and Tucson.

1912 The Dixons return to San Francisco.

1917 The Dixons divorce.

1918 After studying at the CALIFORNIA SCHOOL OF ARTS AND CRAFTS, Tobey joins the Art Department at the University of California, Berkeley.

1920s Maintains a studio on Union Street, Russian Hill, San Francisco. Moves to Salt Lake City.

c. 1925 Dies in Salt Lake City.

290

WESLEY H. TRIPPETT (1862–1913)

1862 January 23—Wesley H. Trippett born in New York.

c. 1880s Educated in New York art schools. Works as a metal designer for such firms as Tiffany, Mott Bronze and Iron Works, John Williams, and Mercereau and Company. Modeler for architectural and decorative metal. Works in Ohio. Marries Mary G. (maiden name unknown).

c. 1895 Moves to California. Unable to find work as a metal designer, he uses his familiarity with clay modeling to become a potter.

1899 Lives in Redlands, California *(city directories list him only after 1902).*

c. 1902 Establishes Redlands Pottery.

1905 Redlands pottery is retailed through the shops of PAUL ELDER.

1909 Redlands Pottery closes.

1911 November—hired by CALIFORNIA CHINA PRODUCTS COMPANY of National City, California, to manage their art department.

1912 January—begins working at CCPCo.

1913 January 11—dies in San Ysidro, California.

UNITED CRAFTS AND ARTS OF CALIFORNIA
DR. ORLOF N. ORLOW (1860?–1924)

1902 Dr. Orlof N. Orlow first appears in the San Francisco newspapers, a mysterious character known for his mystical lectures and philanthropic acts. He had most recently taught Hindu philosophy in Chicago's office in Steinway Hall.

c. 1903 Opens a shop and workshop, United Crafts and Arts of California, at 2203 Presidio Avenue, San Francisco.

1903 September 10—United Crafts and Arts of California is incorporated by Orlow and William Kuehulein, along with three minor shareholders.

1904 The shop moves to 147 Presidio Avenue and becomes known as a full-service Arts and Crafts salon, supplying furnishings and interior designs. FREDERICK H. MEYER is the main furniture designer. Among the other artists represented by the shop is LILLIAN TOBEY, who shows leatherwork.

1906 March—seriously in debt, Orlow mortgages 147 Presidio Avenue to his attorney, L. M. Hoefler. November 30—when no license tax is received for 1907, the incorporation lapses.

1907 June—Hoefler discovers that Orlow has stopped paying rent and sues him for the missing funds. The court finds that Orlow and United Crafts and Arts must vacate 147 Presidio Avenue. The shop does not relocate, and Orlow leaves San Francisco.

1924 April—Orlow dies in New York, where he has been living under the name John Orth. His death is followed by a flurry of speculation that he was actually the exiled Austrian archduke Johann Nepomuk Salvator, a claim Orlow encouraged while alive.

1927 Articles published in the *New York Times* prove that Orlow was not the missing archduke.

UNITED GLASS WORKS

1868 Harry Pyle Hopps born in San Francisco.

1873 July 3—Bert Wallace Hopps born in San Francisco.

1897 *United Glass Works is opened at 62 Eighth Street, San Francisco, by Hugo Schmitz and William F. Taylor.*

1900 *Taylor leaves the firm.* United receives a medal at the Universal Exposition, Paris.

1902 *Harry P. Hopps joins United as a partner.*

1905 *United moves to 1323 Market Street.*

1907 *Schmitz leaves the firm. United moves to 115 Turk Street.* The firm is incorporated by the Hoppses and Fabius T. Finch, an attorney.

1909 United designs dome for Hibernia Bank, San Francisco, and art glass for the Palace Court of the Palace Hotel, San Francisco.

c. 1918 Designs and executes a peacock window for 243 O'Farrell Street, San Francisco (currently Bardelli's Restaurant).

1919 *Final listing in San Francisco city directory.*

1939   Harry Hopps dies in Los Angeles.

1942   March 29—Bert Hopps dies in Berkeley.

ALBERT VALENTIEN (1862–1925)
ANNA VALENTIEN (1862–1947)

1862   February 27—Anna Marie Bookprinter born in Cincinnati. May 11—Albert Robert Valentine born in Cincinnati.

1875–80 Valentine attends the University of Cincinnati School of Design.

1881   September—Valentine hired as first full-time decorator by Rookwood Pottery, Cincinnati.

before 1882 Bookprinter attends University of Cincinnati School of Design.

1882   Bookprinter trains as a wood-carver with Benn Pitman in Cincinnati; attends evening classes in drawing and modeling at the Art Academy of Cincinnati.

1882–83 Valentine changes surname to Valentien.

1884   October—Bookprinter hired by Rookwood.

1887   June 1—Bookprinter and Valentien marry.

1893   Anna's life-size sculpture *Ariadne* is exhibited at the World's Columbian Exposition, Chicago.

1895   Anna's life-size sculpture *Hero Waiting for Leander* wins a gold medal at the Atlanta Cotton States and International Exposition.

1899   The Valentiens travel to Europe, where Anna studies sculpture with Auguste Rodin.

1900   Albert's watercolor *Winter* and Anna's bronze portrait medallion of Albert are exhibited at the Paris Salon. He receives a collaborative gold medal at the Universal Exposition, Paris, for his work with Rookwood. Both Valentiens visit the Exposition.

1905   The Valentiens leave Rookwood.

1908   They settle in San Diego. Albert commissioned by local philanthropist Ellen Scripps to paint the wildflowers of California.

1911   Valentien Pottery Company founded with the backing of Joseph W. Sefton, Jr., and the technical assistance of Arthur Dovey.

1913   Valentien Pottery Company closes.

1914   Anna teaches numerous crafts at the San Diego State Normal School (through 1916).

1915   Anna receives a collaborative gold medal for crafts at the Panama-California Exposition, San Diego. Albert receives a silver medal, presumably for painting.

1916   At the Panama-California International Exposition, San Diego, Anna receives two gold medals.

1917   Anna begins teaching sculpture and pottery at the San Diego Evening High School.

1925   August 5—Albert dies in San Diego.

1926   Anna studies bronze casting at the Santa Barbara School of the Arts under Archibald Dawson.

1938   Anna retires from teaching.

1947   August 25—Anna dies in San Diego.

DIRK VAN ERP (1860–1933)

1860   January 1—Dirk Koperslager van Erp born into a family of coppersmiths in Leeuwarden, the Netherlands.

1886   Immigrates to the United States, settling in Merced, California.

1890   Moves to San Francisco, where he is employed by Union Iron Works.

1892   Marries Mary Richardson Marino. The van Erps move to Benicia, California.

1895   Agatha van Erp born.

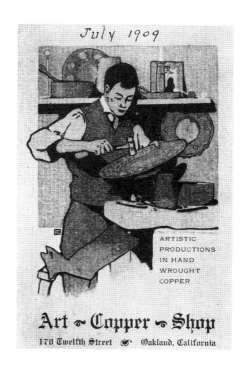

209. Advertisement for the Art Copper Shop, July 1909. The Oakland Museum; Van Erp Family Archive, Archives of California Art.

1896   Van Erps move to San Francisco.

1898   February–November—van Erp is in the Yukon in a failed attempt to make his fortune.

1899   Again employed by Union Iron Works.

1900   Moves to Vallejo, California. Working as a marine copper-smith on Mare Island, makes vases from brass shell-casings in his leisure time. William Henry van Erp born.

c. 1902–6 Van Erp consigns art-metal pieces at the shop of Vickery, Atkins, and Torrey in San Francisco.

1908   Opens a copper shop at 170 Twelfth Street in Oakland. October—participates in the Idora Park Arts and Crafts Exposition, Oakland.

1909   Alexander J. Robertson joins van Erp as a partner. Van Erp takes HARRY DIXON as an apprentice. The firm exhibits twenty-five copper and two brass objects at the Alaska-Yukon-Pacific Exposition in Seattle, for which they receive a gold medal.

1910   The shop moves to 1104 Sutter Street, San Francisco. Robertson leaves. March 1—D'ARCY GAW joins the firm as partner and designer. PEDRO J. LEMOS does some designing. A Gaw-designed lamp is shown at the Ninth Annual Exhibition of Original Designs and Decorations and Examples of Art Crafts Having Distinct Artistic Merit, Art Institute of Chicago.

1911   January 30—the Gaw–van Erp partnership is dissolved. Van Erp's nephew August Tiesselinck arrives from the Netherlands, already a master metalsmith at age twenty.

210. Dirk van Erp Studio (William van Erp?). *Covered Bowl,* c. 1930–40. Hammered and pierced silver with ivory, 4⅞ x 5⅛ in. The Van Erp Family.

1914   Agatha van Erp begins teaching metalwork at the San Francisco Institute of Art, where she will remain through 1918.

1915   Dirk exhibits at Panama-Pacific International Exposition, San Francisco.

1916   Returns to Union Iron Works to do war-related work; his shop scales down production.

1926   Tiesselinck teaches metalcraft at Mission High School, San Francisco.

1929   Dirk van Erp retires.

1933   July 18—dies in Fairfax, California. Mary van Erp dies four hours later. William van Erp continues to operate the shop until his death in 1977.

WALRICH POTTERY
GERTRUDE RUPEL WALL (1881–1971)
JAMES WALL (1877–1952)

1877   April 11—James Alfred Wall born in Burslem, Stoke-on-Trent, England.

1881   Gertrude Rupel born in Greenville, Ohio.

c. 1890s? Wall employed for several years at Royal Doulton pottery works in Burslem.

c. 1898–1902 Rupel attends Denison University, Granville, Ohio, sporadically; drops out owing to poor health. Teaches school in Xenia, Ohio, to finance return to college.

1905   Attends Oberlin College, Oberlin, Ohio; does not graduate. Begins teaching career.

1908–12 Briefly attends Chicago Academy of Fine Arts. Teaches art in Kokomo, Indiana, public schools. Attends Herron Art Institute, Indianapolis, for one and a half years on a part-time basis while working as supervisor of art for the Kokomo schools.

c. 1910 Wall and Rupel meet in Kokomo.

1912   November 17—Wall and Rupel marry.

1912–22 The Walls move to California, settling in Berkeley. James is employed by the Standard Sanitary Manufacturing Company in Richmond, California, and later by West Coast Porcelain Manufacturers in Millbrae, California. Gertrude teaches pottery at the University of California, Berkeley, summer school. Gertrude studies painting under Xavier Martinez and PEDRO J. LEMOS.

c. 1914 Son, Richard, born.

1914   Gertrude attends William Merritt Chase's summer painting classes in Carmel, California.

1922   The couple open their Walrich Pottery (named for their

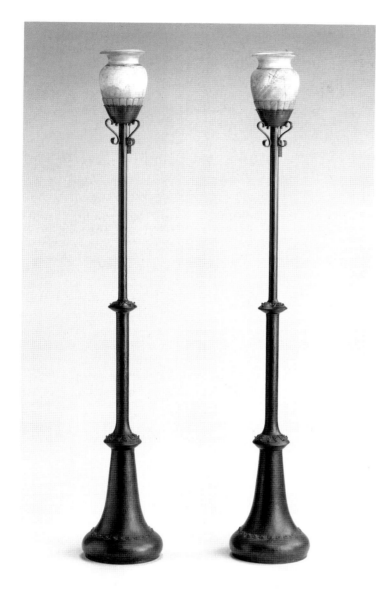

211. August Tiesselinck. *Pair of Torchères,* c. 1926. Copper with
alabaster shades, 60½ x 9⅝ in., each. Isak Lindenauer.

son) at 2330 Browning Boulevard, Berkeley. James keeps
his job for financial security.

1922–24 Gertrude teaches herself to throw pots. The Walls develop
their own clay bodies and glaze formulas.

1924   Walrich Pottery moves to 1285 Hearst Avenue, Berkeley.

1927   Exhibition of Walrich pots held at the Oakland Art Gallery.

1930   Gertrude gives classes in ceramics and basket weaving to
female inmates at San Quentin State Prison in Marin
County, California.

c. 1930s James works for the San Francisco Schools District.

1952   March 31—James dies in San Francisco.

1971   March 28—Richard dies in Saigon, Vietnam. July 3—
Gertrude dies in San Mateo County, California.

HAZEL WOOD WATERMAN (1865–1948)

1865   May 5—Hazel Wood born in Tuskegee, Alabama.

1868   Family moves to California.

1886   Graduates from the University of California, Berkeley,
where she studied art and design.

1889   April 11—marries Waldo Sprague Waterman, the son of the
governor of California. The Watermans move to Julian,
California, in San Diego County, where Waldo manages his
father's Stonewall Mine. Hazel paints landscapes.

1893   The Watermans move to San Diego.

c. 1900 The Watermans commission IRVING GILL to design their
house.

1902   Hazel's illustrated article on her Gill-designed house, "A
Granite Cottage in California," appears in the March issue
of *House Beautiful.*

1903   February 24—Waldo dies. Waterman begins her architec-
tural training through International Correspondence
Schools. Employed as a tracer by the architectural firm of
Hebbard and Gill.

1904–5 Works as a drafter for Hebbard and Gill on three houses
designed for Alice Lee and Katherine Teats on Seventh
Avenue, San Diego.

1908   Restores the 1827–29 Estudillo House in Old Town, San
Diego.

1910   Designs the Wednesday Club at Sixth Avenue and Ivy Lane,
San Diego. ALICE KLAUBER assists with the interior designs.

c. 1910s Designs Julius Wangenheim garden, San Diego.

1911   Designs Ackerman House at 3170 Curlew Street, San
Diego. Designs the Baby Building for the Children's Home
Association in Balboa Park, San Diego.

1926   Designs the Children's Home Association Administration
Building, San Diego.

1933   Awarded American Institute of Architects' Certificate of
Honor for Wangenheim garden.

1948   January 22—dies in Berkeley.

MARGERY WHEELOCK (c. 1890–c. 1967)

c. 1890 Margery Wheelock born in Riverside County, California.

191?–14 Attends CALIFORNIA SCHOOL OF ARTS AND CRAFTS in

212. California School of Arts and Crafts (Margery Wheelock, designer and carver). Top: *Wall Cabinet,* 1915. Oak carved and rubbed with pigment, hammered-copper hinges, 20 x 74 x 10½ in. Bottom: *Print Cabinet,* 1915. Oak carved and rubbed with pigment, hammered-copper hinges and pulls, 35¼ x 39½ x 12½ in. California College of Arts and Crafts, Oakland.

> Berkeley, studying furniture and interior design under FREDERICK H. MEYER.

1914   May—graduates. Employed as a designer for CSAC. Designs the CSAC Alumni group's model of an artist's studio for the Panama-Pacific International Exposition, San Francisco, which receives a gold medal.

1916   March—marries HARRY DIXON. Works with him in his metal shop as designer and bookkeeper.

1918   March 21—son, Dudley Newhall Dixon, born.

c. 1932 The Dixons divorce.

c. 1967 Margery dies, possibly in Southern California.

FRED H. WILDE (1856–1943)

1856   August 27—Frederick Harry Wilde born in Brosley, Stoke-on-Trent, England.

late 1870s–early 1880s Employed by Maw and Company, a tile firm in Jackfield, England. Marries Ellen S. Wilcox.

1885   January 4—son, John, born. The family immigrates to the United States.

1886   Hired as ceramist by International Tile and Trim Company, Brooklyn, New York.

1891   Employed by Maywood Tile Company, Maywood, New Jersey.

1892   March 25—daughter, Dorothy, born.

1899   October—leaves Maywood.

1900   Works briefly at Providential Tile Company, Trenton, New Jersey. Hired by Robertson Art Tile Company, Morrisville, Pennsylvania.

1903   Summer—leaves Robertson. Employed as superintendent of the Pacific Art Tile Company, Tropico, California (renamed Western Art Tile Company in 1904).

1911   Employed by CALIFORNIA CHINA PRODUCTS COMPANY, National City, California. While employed by CCPCo, oversees the firm's tile commission for the Panama-California Exposition, San Diego.

1916   September—leaves CCPCo. Becomes manager of AREQUIPA POTTERY in Fairfax, California. Introduces tile into production.

1918   November—because of the war, Arequipa ceases production as a pottery. Wilde settles in Glendale, California.

1923   Employed by Pomona Tile Manufacturing Company, Pomona, California. His son, John, also employed by Pomona.

1937   Ellen Wilde dies.

1940   Retires from active work.

1943   November 24—dies in Glendale.

EMILY WILLIAMS. *See* LILLIAN PALMER

BIBLIOGRAPHY

Kenneth R. Trapp
Kim Cooper

BOOKS AND CATALOGS

Andersen, Timothy J., Eudorah M. Moore, and Robert W. Winter, eds. *California Design, 1910*. Pasadena, Calif.: California Design Publications, 1974. Reprint. Salt Lake City: Peregrine Smith, 1989.

Bowman, Leslie Greene. *American Arts and Crafts: Virtue in Design*. Los Angeles: Los Angeles County Museum of Art; Boston: Little, Brown and Company, 1990.

Bray, Hazel V. *The Potter's Art in California, 1885–1955*. Oakland, Calif.: Oakland Museum Art Department, 1978.

Cardwell, Kenneth H. *Bernard Maybeck: Artisan, Architect, Artist*. Salt Lake City: Peregrine Smith, 1977.

Clark, Robert Judson, ed. *The Arts and Crafts Movement in America, 1876–1916*. Princeton, N.J.: Princeton University Press, 1972. Revised, with new preface and updated bibliography, 1992.

Current, William R., and Karen Current. *Greene and Greene: Architects in the Residential Style*. Fort Worth: Amon Carter Museum of Western Art, 1974.

Dale, Sharon. *Frederick Hürten Rhead: An English Potter in America*. Erie, Pa.: Erie Art Museum, 1986.

Evans, Paul. *Art Pottery of the United States: An Encyclopedia of Producers and Their Marks*. New York: Scribner's, 1974.

Freudenheim, Leslie Mandelson, and Elisabeth Sacks Sussman. *Building with Nature: Roots of the San Francisco Bay Region Tradition*. Santa Barbara, Calif., and Salt Lake City: Peregrine Smith, 1974.

Herr, Jeffrey. *California Art Pottery, 1895–1920*. Northridge: California State University, 1988.

Jones, Harvey L. *Mathews: Masterpieces of the California Decorative Style*. Oakland, Calif.: Oakland Museum Art Department, 1972.

Kaplan, Wendy, et al. *"The Art that is Life": The Arts and Crafts Movement in America, 1875–1920*. Boston: Museum of Fine Arts; New York Graphic Society, 1987.

Lamoureux, Dorothy. *The Arts and Crafts Studio of Dirk van Erp*. San Francisco: San Francisco Crafts & Folk Art Museum, 1989.

Lindenauer, Isak. *August Tiesselinck: A Lifetime in Metal, 1890–1972*. San Francisco: Isak Lindenauer, 1989.

Longstreth, Richard. *On the Edge of the World: Four Architects at the Turn of the Century*. New York: Architectural History Foundation; Cambridge, Mass.: MIT Press, 1983.

McCoy, Esther. *Five California Architects*. New York: Reinhold Publishing Corp., 1960.

Makinson, Randell L. *Greene and Greene: Architecture as a Fine Art*. Salt Lake City: Peregrine Smith, 1977.

———. *Greene and Greene: Furniture and Related Designs*. Salt Lake City: Peregrine Smith, 1979.

Morse, Edgar W., ed. *Silver in the Golden State: Images and Essays Celebrating the History and Art of Silver in California*. Oakland, Calif.: Oakland Museum History Department, 1986.

Page, Marcia, ed. *Ceramic Art of the Malibu Potteries, 1926–1932*. Malibu, Calif.: Malibu Lagoon Museum, 1988.

Thornton, Sally Bullard. *Daring to Dream: The Life of Hazel Wood Waterman*. San Diego: San Diego Historical Society, 1987.

Weitze, Karen J. *California's Mission Revival*. Los Angeles: Hennessey & Ingalls, 1984.

Winter, Robert W. *The California Bungalow*. Los Angeles: Hennessey & Ingalls, 1980.

ARTS AND CRAFTS PERIODICALS

Architectural Record (New York; 1891–).

Arroyo Craftsman (Pasadena, Calif.; 1909).

Arts and Architecture (San Francisco and Los Angeles; 1911–May 1915, published as *Pacific Coast Architect;* June 1915–March 1919, published as *Architect;* April 1919–December 1923, published as *Building Review;* January 1924–January 1929, published as *Pacific Coast Architect and Building Review;* February 1929–January 1944, published as *California Arts and Architecture;* thereafter *Arts and Architecture*).

Bungalow Magazine (Los Angeles; March 1909–February 1910; and Seattle; August 1912–March 1918).

California Garden (San Diego; 1909–).

California Southland (Pasadena, Calif.; August 1918–January 1929; February 1929, absorbed by *Arts and Architecture*).

Clay-Worker (Indianapolis; 1884–December 1933).

Club Life (San Francisco; May 1902–April 1906).

Craftsman (Eastwood, N.Y.; October 1901–December 1916).

Crockery and Glass Journal (New York; 1874–).

House and Garden (New York and Philadelphia; 1901–).

House Beautiful (Chicago and Boston; December 1896–).

Impressions Quarterly (San Francisco; March 1900–December 1905; March–August 1900, published as *Personal Impressions;* September 1900–December 1901, published as *Impressions*).

Keramic Studio (Syracuse, N.Y., and Columbus, Ohio; 1899–April 1924; May 1924–April 1930, published as *Design and Keramic Studio*).

Mark Hopkins Institute Review (San Francisco; December 1899–Summer 1904).

Out West (Los Angeles; June 1894–April 1923; 1894–December 1901, published as *Land of Sunshine;* 1902, merged into *Overland Monthly,* San Francisco, vols. 33–40).

Overland Monthly (San Francisco; July 1868–December 1875 and 1883–July 1935; 1876–1882, suspended publication).

Pacific Coast Architect and Builder (Seattle; 1902–).

Philopolis (San Francisco; October 1910–September 1916).

Potter (Santa Barbara, Calif.; December 1916–February 1917).

Southwest Builder and Contractor (Los Angeles; 1893–).

Sunset (San Francisco; May 1898–).

Temple Artisan (Halcyon, Calif.; 1900–).

West Coast (Los Angeles; September 1906–January 1914).

ARCHIVES

Archives of American Art, Smithsonian Institution, Washington, D.C. Of special interest are the materials on Porter Blanchard, Rudolph Schaeffer (as yet uncataloged), and Charles Frederick Eaton (in the Louisiana Purchase Exposition Records, Department of Art Papers).

Atascadero Historical Society, Atascadero, California. Photography collection.

Bancroft Library, University of California, Berkeley. Extensive collections of manuscripts and books on the West. Arequipa Sanatorium annual reports—accounts of each year's activity at the Marin County sanatorium; the years 1911–17 include discussion of the pottery. The Regional Oral History Office is also located at the library.

California Historical Society, San Francisco.

California State Library, Sacramento, California Room. Biographical card files on California artists, writers, and musicians, c. 1906–20.

California State Library, Sutro Library, San Francisco. United States and California censuses, 1900 and 1910; historical collection of national and statewide city directories.

The Greene and Greene Center for the Study of the Arts and Crafts Movement in America, the University of Southern California and the Huntington Library, Art Collections, and Botanical Gardens, San Marino, California, plus assorted papers and ephemera.

Mission Inn Collection, Riverside, California.

The Oakland Museum, Archives of California Art. Biographical files; the Paul Evans California Art Pottery Research Collection, Archives of California Art; and The Elliott Evans–The Paul Evans California Silver Research Collection.

Oakland Public Library, Oakland History Room.

Riverside Municipal Museum Archives, Riverside, California. Frank Miller Scrapbook; Sherman Institute Scrapbook.

Riverside Public Library, Riverside, California. Vertical files.

San Diego Historical Society. Biographical files; Oral History Collection.

San Francisco Public Library, San Francisco Room. Biographical card index.

Santa Barbara Historical Society, Santa Barbara, California. Biographical card index; scrapbooks.

A. K. Smiley Library Archives, Redlands, California. Historical information on the growth of Redlands; Redlands Indian Association, Minute Book 1, March 1894–December 1903; Minute Book 2, April 1904–November 1928.

Swedenborgian Church, San Francisco.

Tile Heritage Foundation, Healdsburg, California.

University of California, Santa Barbara, Architectural Records Collection.

MISCELLANEOUS SOURCES

Archibald, Allene. "William Alexander Sharp: Artist of the Mission Inn." Master's thesis, University of California, Riverside, 1989.

Dunn, Catherine Cressey. "A Study of Redlands, California, as Characterized by Its Novelists." Master's thesis, University of Redlands, 1957.

Gordon, Ruth I. *Paul Elder: Bookseller-Publisher, 1897–1917: A Bay Area Reflection.* Ann Arbor, Mich.: University Microfilms International, 1978.

Hailey, Gene, ed. *Arthur Mathews . . . Biography and Works.* California Art Research Monographs, vol. 7. San Francisco: Works Progress Administration, 1937.

Hanley, Theresa E. "'Tourists and Art Lovers': The Mission Inn as Museum, 1903–25." Manuscript, 1991, Mission Inn Foundation, Riverside, California.

Irelan, Linna. "Pottery." In *Ninth Annual Report of the State Mineralogist for the Year Ending December 1, 1889.* Sacramento: California State Mining Bureau, 1890.

Miller, Grace Louise. "The San Diego Progressive Movement, 1900–20." Master's thesis, University of California, Santa Barbara, 1976.

Rich, Ednah Anne. "An Account of the Santa Barbara State Normal School of Manual Arts and Home Economics from the Date of Its Establishment, March 27, 1909, until June 30, 1916, during the Period When Miss Ednah Anne Rich Was President." Manuscript, Special Collections, University of California, Santa Barbara.

Rounds, Michael. "A Booster in Paradise: Frank Augustus Miller's Early Career, 1874–1902." Master's thesis, University of California, Riverside, 1988.

ACKNOWLEDGMENTS

In bringing this book and its exhibition into being over the past seven years, I have been helped by many people, and it is my pleasure to thank them here.

In 1986 I received a Benno Forman Fellowship from the Winterthur Museum, Gardens, and Library in Winterthur, Delaware, to research the Arts and Crafts movement in California. I am grateful to Winterthur for this financial support, which provided me with a period of uninterrupted research. I am deeply grateful to those foundations and agencies who expressed faith in this project through their generous financial support. Major support for this exhibition and book came from the Lila Wallace–Reader's Digest Fund. The Henry Luce Foundation, Inc., provided initial support for the project. The National Endowment for the Arts and the National Endowment for the Humanities, both federal agencies, awarded the museum grants. The Oakland Museum Women's Board has generously assisted with this project by providing matching funds for the National Endowment for the Humanities grant and by purchasing or supporting the purchase of works of art for the museum's permanent collection. The first grants that the museum received for this project came from the Kahn Foundation and from the L. J. Skaggs and Mary C. Skaggs Foundation. Without the generous help of the lenders, who are listed separately, this exhibition and book would have remained a dream. I am especially grateful to those lenders who permitted me to study their collections and who willingly parted with works of art months in advance so that they could be photographed in Oakland.

I thank the administrative staff of The Oakland Museum for their support: Kay Winer, former director; Phil Mumma, associate director for public programs; Mark Medeiros, chief financial officer; Lynn Upchurch, development director; Philip E. Linhares, chief curator of art; and Barbara Henry, chief curator of education. Colleagues in other museum departments freely offered their assistance: Inez Brooks-Myers, Carey Caldwell, Deborah Cooper, Marcia Eymann, L. Tom Frye, Mickey Karpas, and Cheri Newell in History and Christopher Richards and Tom Steller in Natural Sciences.

Within the Art Department I work with colleagues who form a cooperative team. Harvey L. Jones, senior curator, has supported this project from its beginning. Christine Droll coordinated the earliest photography and handled many details in preparing grants. Arthur Monroe, registrar, arranged the shipment of pieces to the museum. Head preparator Denis Yasukawa, Ginny Bowen, Catherine Buchanan, and David Ruddell arranged for the delivery and return of many objects that had to be photographed and conserved. Karen Nelson, interpretive specialist, prepared the video program that accompanies the exhibition and the splendid educational programs for young students and adults. Janice Capecci, registrar/researcher, answered calls for help.

Lisa L. Lock began to work on this project as a volunteer intern from the University of California, Berkeley, in 1988. Although she had never before worked in a museum, she became an excellent assistant who shirked no task and was an indispensable ally. I am deeply indebted to Kathy L. Borgogno, curatorial aide, who undertook the monumental task of typing all essays and other materials for the book. Kim Cooper, researcher, and Victoria Carlson, project coordinator, joined this project in January and in June 1991, respectively. Kim carried out extensive research in archives, libraries, historical societies, and any other resource that could help us in compiling the artists' biographies and company histories. To this end, she organized a team of volunteer researchers to help with this major effort: Sidney Bernstein, Toby Bielawski, Peter Monsour, John Murphey, Heidi Oline Pruett, Sarah Shen, Holly Simonton, and Lorie Sugarman. Victoria coordinated the seemingly endless details that engulf a project of this scope. I am particularly indebted to her for arranging to ship works of art to Oakland, for keeping track of conservation records and photography, and for securing photographs and pertinent information for the essays.

John Burke, the museum's conservator, administered the National Endowment for the Arts grant to conserve carved, polychromed, and gilded wood objects from the museum's collection of works by Arthur F. and Lucia K. Mathews. This grant concided with the organization of *The Arts and Crafts Movement in California: Living the Good Life.* I am especially grateful to Douglas Lawler, conservation technician, who coordinated the many details pertaining to the conservation of objects in the show from the museum's permanent collection as well as from lenders. He—along with Thérèse O'Gorman, assistant conservator, who worked with metals, leather, and parchment; and Krassimer Gatev, technical specialist—performed miracles. Mark Harpainter and Peter Eastman deserve a bow for the exceptional work they did with badly damaged furniture. I thank James Bernstein, independent conservator, and Elisabeth Cornu, conservator at the Fine Arts Museums of San Francisco, for their conscientious and careful attention to the treatments they made. M. Lee Fatherree and his assistant, Nick Cedar, coped with a difficult schedule in photographing several hundred works of art over some nine months.

I am deeply grateful to the seven authors, whose indefatigable research, intel-

ligent scholarship, and fine writing have made this book such a valuable contribu-
tion to the field of Arts and Crafts study: Leslie Greene Bowman, Los Angeles
County Museum of Art; Cheryl Robertson, formerly with Sotheby's, New York;
David C. Streatfield, University of Washington, Seattle; Joseph A. Taylor, Tile
Heritage Foundation, Healdsburg, California; Karen J. Weitze, Dames & Moore,
Austin, Texas; and Richard Guy Wilson, University of Virginia. They also offered
welcome guidance in the selection of objects for the exhibition. Clifford E. Clark,
Jr., M. A. and A. D. Hulings Professor of American Studies at Carleton College,
Northfield, Minnesota, joined the project in early 1991 as a consultant and
reader. His insightful reading of the essays was very helpful. Fronia W. Simpson
edited the essays with much-appreciated attention to detail and grace under pres-
sure. The book for *The Arts and Crafts Movement in California: Living the Good Life*
is the The Oakland Museum's first publishing venture with Abbeville Press. It
has been our good fortune to have worked closely and harmoniously with Nancy
Grubb, senior editor, who expedited the production of the book long distance and
against often demanding deadlines. In his design of the book, Joel Avirom has
captured the spirit of the Arts and Crafts movement in California with imagination and sensitivity.

Without the help of many individuals and colleagues in museums, libraries,
historical societies, universities, and other cultural agencies across the country this
project would never have materialized. The authors and I are grateful to those
who contributed to the fruition of this book: Brandon Allen; Mr. and Mrs.
Reggie Allen; American Ceramic Society, Columbus, Ohio—Thomas Shreves;
American Craft Museum, New York—Nina Stritzler; American Decorative Arts
Forum of Northern California; American Silver Museum, Meriden,
Connecticut—W. Scott Braznell; Timothy J. Andersen; Mrs. Charles Anderson;
Eleanor Anderson; Judy Anderson; Allene Archibald; Archives of American Art,
Southern California branch at the Huntington Library, Art Collections, and
Botanical Gardens, San Marino, California—Barbara Wilson; Connie and George
Beardsley; Arizona State University, Tempe—Beverly K. Brandt; Art Institute of
Chicago—Milo M. Naeve; Atascadero Historical Museum, Atascadero,
California—Kent Kenny, William Lewis, and Marjorie Mackey; Dianne Ayers;
Bryce Bannatyne, Jr.; Dr. and Mrs. James Adam Barr; Joan Barriga; Denise
Barry; Leonora Harris Bedolla; June and Robert Berliner; Harriete Estel Berman;
David Bertrand; Sherri Birdsong; John Blaisdell; Boston Public Library—Janice
H. Chadbourne; Bothin-Arequipa Collection, Fairfax, California; Gary
Breitweiser; Brooklyn Museum—Kevin Stayton; Marilyn J. and Anthony P.
Brown; Gerald E. Buck; Bernard Bumpus; Mr. and Mrs. Edward Bunting;
Frances Butler; California College of Arts and Crafts, Oakland—Neil Hoffmann;
California Department of Transportation, Sacramento—John W. Snyder;
California Institute of Technology, Pasadena—Shelley Erwin and Bonnie Ludt;
California State Library, Sacramento—Gary Kurutz, Richard Terry, and Sibyl
Zemitis; Ceramic Tile Institute, Los Angeles; Cincinnati Art Museum—Anita J.

299

Ellis, Anne El-Omami, Mary Ellen Goeke, and Gretchen A. Mehring; Lyn Clark; Carol and Barrie Coate; Steve Coffman; Shaun Collins; Alana Coons; Dr. Harold Copp; Cranbrook Academy of Art Museum, Bloomfield Hills, Michigan—Gregory M. Wittkopp; Nicholas Crevecoeur; Dallas Museum of Art—Charles L. Venable; Nancy Daly; Florence Dixon; Helen Hyde Dorra; Mary T. Dorra; Carol Doty; Riley Doty; Jack Douglas; Lynn Downey; Mike Duff; Eastern Washington State Historical Society, Cheney Cowles Museum, Spokane—Glenn Mason; Burton Peek Edwards; the late Scott Elder and Mrs. Madeline Elder; Paul Evans; Inger Feeley; Stuart Feld; Dawn Ferry; Fine Arts Museums of San Francisco—Lee Hunt Miller; Fresno County Library, Fresno, California—Linda Sitterding; Denis Gallion; John Gallo; Gamble House–University of Southern California, Pasadena—Edward R. Bosley III and Randell L. Makinson; Shelby M. and Frederick Gans; Mrs. Alice Goodkind; Stephen Gray; Carolyn and John Grew-Sheridan; Gerald M. Halweg; Greene and Greene Library, Gamble House–University of Southern California—Doris Gertmenian and Doris Whitney; Haggin Museum, Stockton, California—Joanne Avant and Tod Ruhstaller; Annette Handy; Gladys Hansen; Tim Hansen; Emily and Mike Henderson; High Museum of Art, Atlanta—Jody Cohen and Donald Pierce; Historical Society of Delaware, Wilmington—Thomas Beckman; Barbara Curtis Horton; Grace Hudson Museum, Sun House, Ukiah, California—Sandra J. Metzler; Pamela Hudson; Huntington Library, Art Collections, and Botanical Gardens, San Marino, California—Brita Mack, Jenny Watts, and Linda Kay Zoeckler; Linda and Jim Jaffe; Mr. and Mrs. Albert A. Jaussaud; Joseph E. Jessop; Carrie Johnson; Brian Kaiser; Norman and Shannon Karlson; Audrey and Philip Keeler; Gary Keith; Christy and Scott Kendrick; Caroline and Gary Kent; Jon King; Sharon and Robert Kinney; Steven Kleiff; Ernest and Irene Knops; Dorothy Lamoureux; Neil Lane and Bob Rehnert; Charlotte Laubach; Isak Lindenauer; Dr. Craig Lindhurst; Dr. Jovin Lombardo; Tazio N. Lombardo; Los Angeles County Museum of Art—Ann Diederick and Elliot Shirwo; Los Angeles Municipal Art Gallery—Jeffrey Herr; Los Angeles Public Library, Central Library—Bettye Ellison, Caroly Kozo, Mary Van Orsdol, Tom Owens, and Mel Rosenberg; Alexa Luberski; Stephanie Lynn and David Mills; Nancy McClelland; Lynn McDaniel and Simon Miles; Mavina McFeron; Jeanne McGirk; Caro Macpherson; Tamsin McVickar; Robert Maddox; Kim and John Maeder; Janeen Marrin; Vonn Marie May; Memorial Libraries, Deerfield, Massachusetts—David R. Proper; Phyllis Menefee; Sheila A. Menzies; Forrest L. Merrill; Marilee Boyd Meyer; Pauline Meyer; Bill Meyers; Minneapolis Institute of Arts—Tran Turner; Mission Hills First Congregational–United Church of Christ, San Diego—Barbara Wiggins; Mission Inn Foundation, Riverside, California—Michael Rounds and Nancy Wenzel; Susan Montgomery; Jack Moore; Edgar W. Morse; Daniel Morris; Roger and Jean Moss; Nancy Moure; Museum of Fine Arts, Boston—Edward S. Cooke, Jr.; Museum of Fine Arts, Houston, Bayou Bend Collection—Katherine S. Howe; Museum of History and Art, Ontario, California—Therese E. Hanley; David F.

Myrick; Natural History Museum of Los Angeles—David Debs; Kathleen Neeley; Elizabeth Nesbitt; William Noonan; Alva Norman; North Dakota State University, Fargo—Ronald L. M. Ramsay; Norton Simon Museum, Pasadena—Kristin Brock; Norwest Corporation, Minneapolis—David Ryan; Oakland Public Library—William Sturm; Occidental College, Los Angeles—Robert W. Winter; Oregon Historical Society, Portland—Jack Cleaver; Pasadena Historical Society—Susan Coffman; Ruth Penka; Julia Perry; Ann Phillips; Joan Ploetz; Portland Art Museum, Portland, Oregon—Dan Lucas; Clare Porter; John Edward Powell; Princeton University—Robert Judson Clark; D. J. Puffert; Dave Rago; David Reneric; Renwick Gallery of the National Museum of American Art, Smithsonian Institution, Washington, D.C.—Michael Monroe; Mrs. Sim Bruce Richards; Ronald Rindge; Don Ritchie; Riverside Municipal Museum, Riverside, California—Chris Moser and H. Vincent Moses; Riverside Public Library, Riverside, California—Ron Barker; Charles B. Roblin; Michelle Rottner; Stella Haverland Rouse; Robert Rust; Saint Louis Art Museum—Norma Sindelar and Laurie A. Stein; San Anselmo Historical Commission, San Anselmo, California—Bill Davis; San Diego Central Library—Mary Allely; San Diego Historical Society—Thomas Adema, Mac Griswold, Susan Painter, Barbara Pope, Betty Quayles, and Stephanie Tanaka; San Francisco Art Institute—Jeff Gunderson; San Francisco Craft and Folk Art Museum—Carole Austin; *San Francisco Examiner*, Library—Judy Canter; San Luis Obispo County Historical Society Museum, San Luis Obispo, California—Mark P. Hall-Patton; San Luis Obispo County Library, San Luis Obispo, California—Virginia M. Crook; San Mateo Public Library, San Mateo, California—Thomas S. Fowler; Santa Barbara Historical Society—David Bisol and Michael Redmon; Santa Catalina Island Company, Santa Catalina, California—Donna Harrison; Pat Schaelchlin; Dorothy Shephard; Dorothy and Richard Sherwood; A. K. Smiley Public Library, Redlands, California—Larry E. Burgess and Christie Hammond; Catherine Smith; Barbara Snelling; Robert Soares; Gonnard Solberg; Sonoma County Museum, Santa Rosa, California—J. Eric Nelson; Southwest Museum, Los Angeles—Richard Buchen and Craig Klyver; William Stout; Vanessa Swarovski; Swedenborgian Church, San Francisco—Dr. James F. Lawrence; Temple of the People, Halcyon, California—Barbara Green Baker and Eleanor Shumway; Theosophical Society Library, Pasadena, California—John Van Mater and Kirby Van Mater; Tile Heritage Foundation, Healdsburg, California—Lee Rosenthal; Don Treadway; Kitty Turgeon; University of California, Berkeley, College of Environmental Design, Documents Collection—Lisabeth Chester and Stephen Torbriner; University of California, Berkeley, College of Environmental Design, Library—Elizabeth D. Byrne and Susan Synder; University of California, Berkeley, University Art Museum—Stephanie Cannizzo; University of California, Davis, University Library—Donald Kunitz; University of California, Santa Barbara—David Gebhard; University City, Missouri, Public Library—Linda Ballard; University of Oregon, Eugene, Museum of Art—Claudia Fischer;

301

University of Southern California, School of Cinema-Television—Jae Carmichael; University of Virginia, Charlottesville—Margaret Kelley, Loria Lagua, Thaisa Way, and Ellie Wilson; University of Washington, Seattle—John Medlin and Carla Rickerson; William van Erp; Ventura County Museum, Ventura, California— Charles Johnson; Virginia Museum of Fine Arts, Richmond—Frederick Brandt and David Park Curry; Mary F. Ward; George Washington University, Washington, D.C.—Richard Longstreth; Isabel Weil; Michael Weller; Winterthur Museum, Gardens and Library, Winterthur, Delaware—Jill Hobgood and Neville Thompson; Sandra G. and Steven Wolfe; Wolfsonian Foundation, Miami Beach—Anita Gross; B. U. Wulf; and Evans and John Wyro.

I thank my friend Don F. Mahan, who has sympathetically followed the evolution of this book and exhibition from the start. I thank him for his experienced editorial pen and for all that cannot be explained.

Kenneth R. Trapp

302

ABOUT THE AUTHORS

Leslie Greene Bowman is head curator of the Decorative Arts Department at the Los Angeles County Museum of Art.

Bruce Kamerling has served as curator of collections for the San Diego Historical Society since 1980.

Cheryl Robertson is the former assistant director for Sotheby's American Arts Course, New York, and former assistant professor for the master's program at the Winterthur Museum in Wilmington, Delaware.

David C. Streatfield is chair of the Department of Landscape Architecture, professor of landscape architecture and of urban design and planning, and adjunct professor of architecture at the University of Washington, Seattle.

Joseph A. Taylor is cofounder and president of the Tile Heritage Foundation, Healdsburg, California.

Kenneth R. Trapp is curator of decorative arts at The Oakland Museum and project director for *The Arts and Crafts Movement in California: Living the Good Life.*

Karen J. Weitze is senior architectural historian for the international environmental-engineering firm of Dames & Moore and manages architectural projects in the western United States and in Mexico.

Richard Guy Wilson is professor and chair of the Department of Architectural History, School of Architecture, at the University of Virginia.

LIST OF LENDERS

Brandon Allen
Brandon Allen and Al Nobel
Eleanor Anderson
Dr. and Mrs. James A. Barr
Connie and George Beardsley
June and Robert Berliner
Bothin-Arequipa Collection, Fairfax,
    California
Gary Breitweiser
The Buck Collection
Mr. and Mrs. Edward Bunting
Frances Butler
California College of Arts and Crafts,
    Oakland
Ceramic Tile Institute, Los Angeles
Lyn Clark
Carol and Barrie Coate
Cranbrook Academy of Art Museum,
    Bloomfield Hills, Michigan
Nicholas Crevecoeur
Nancy Daly
Helen Hyde Dorra
The Gamble House, USC, Pasadena
Carolyn and John Grew-Sheridan
President and Fellows of Harvard
    College
High Museum of Art, Atlanta
Barbara Curtis Horton

Jim and Linda Jaffe
Mr. and Mrs. Albert A. Jaussaud
Norman and Shannon Karlson
Gary Keith
Christy and Scott Kendrick
Caroline and Gary Kent
Irene and Ernest Knops
Neil Lane and Bob Rehnert
Isak Lindenauer
Tazio N. Lombardo
Los Angeles County Museum of Art
Stephanie Lynn and David Mills
Kim and John Maeder
Randell L. Makinson
Forrest L. Merrill
Mission Hills First Congregational
    Church—United Church of Christ,
    San Diego
Jack Moore
Roger and Jean Moss
William Noonan
The Norwest Corporation,
    Minneapolis
The Oakland Museum
Private collectors
D. J. Puffert
David Reneric
Mrs. Sim Bruce Richards

Don Ritchie
San Diego Historical Society
Santa Barbara Historical Society
Dorothy and Richard Sherwood
William Stout
Swedenborgian Church, San Francisco
Archives, Theosophical Society
    Library, Pasadena

Tile Heritage Foundation, Healdsburg,
    California
The Van Erp Family
The Mitchell Wolfson, Jr., Collection;
    Courtesy of The Wolfsonian
    Foundation, Miami

213. Robertson Pottery (Fred H. Robertson). *Electrical Lamp,* c. 1913–16. Stoneware with crystalline glaze and leaded-glass inserts, 17¼ x 12³⁄₁₆ in. The Oakland Museum; Gift of the William F. and Helen S. Reichell Trust and the Collectors Gallery.

Alberhill Pottery
Alexander W. Robertson
Triangular Vase, 1913
Biscuit-fired buff earthenware with modeled lizard
6 x 3¼ x 3½ in.
The Oakland Museum; Bequest of the estate of Helen Hathaway White (75.75.1)
See plate 154

Alberhill Pottery
Alexander W. Robertson
Double-Handled Vase, 1914
Biscuit-fired buff earthenware
11¼ x 6¼ in.
Private collection
See plate 196

Alberhill Pottery
Alexander W. Robertson
Vase, 1914
Earthenware with green matte glaze
9⅝ x 2¹³⁄₁₆ in.
Gary Keith

Charles Anderson. *See* DIRK VAN ERP STUDIO

Arequipa Pottery
Bowl, c. 1911–12
Earthenware with dark green semimatte glaze
2³⁄₁₆ x 9⅛ in.
David Reneric

Arequipa Pottery
Frederick Hürten Rhead (?)
Bowl, c. 1912

Earthenware with deep blue matte glaze
5 x 9⅜ in.
The Oakland Museum; Gift of the estate of Phoebe H. Brown (91.9.3)
See plate 106

Flower Holder, possibly Italian in origin, 19th century (?)
Carved white marble
6 x 10⅞ in.
The Oakland Museum; Gift of the estate of Phoebe H. Brown (91.9.2)
See plate 106
This piece was the inspiration for the Arequipa bowl above.

Arequipa Pottery
Frederick Hürten Rhead (?)
Plate, 1912
Earthenware with multicolored glaze and traces of luster
Diameter: 10½ in.
The Oakland Museum; Gift of the estate of Phoebe H. Brown (91.9.35)
See plate 6

Arequipa Pottery
Frederick Hürten Rhead (?)
Vase, 1912
Earthenware with slip-trailed leaf design and multicolored matte glaze
10 x 5⅛ in.
William Noonan
See plate 104

Arequipa Pottery
Frederick Hürten Rhead (?)
Garden Urn, c. 1912–13
Earthenware with press-molded design and
white glaze
11⅛ x 8⅝ x 7¼ in.
The Oakland Museum; Gift of the estate of
Phoebe H. Brown (91.9.10)

Arequipa Pottery
Frederick Hürten Rhead (?)
Vase, c. 1912–13
Earthenware with carved leaf design and
black semimatte glaze
5¼ x 2¹¹⁄₁₆ in.
Gary Keith
See plate 107

Arequipa Pottery
Frederick Hürten Rhead (?)
Vase, c. 1912–13
Earthenware with sgraffito floral design and
multicolored glaze
13 x 10⅜ in.
The Oakland Museum; Gift of the estate of
Phoebe H. Brown (91.9.1)
See plate 108

Arequipa Pottery
Patio Tile (oak), c. 1917
Fired clay with glazed sgraffito design
18⅛ x 18⅜ in.
Bothin-Arequipa Collection, Fairfax,
California
Oakland only

Arequipa Pottery
Patio Tile (redwood), c. 1917
Fired clay with glazed sgraffito design
24½ x 20 in.
Bothin-Arequipa Collection, Fairfax,
California
Oakland only
See plate 73

Ernest A. Batchelder
Firescreen, 1904
Painted repoussé tin in oak frame
36 x 29⁵⁄₁₆ x 8¾ in.
Christy and Scott Kendrick
See plate 1

Ernest A. Batchelder
Tile (Mission San Gabriel), 1911
Hand-pressed fired clay colored with
pigmented slip

8 x 8 in.
Ceramic Tile Institute, Los Angeles

Batchelder & Brown
Tile (castle), 1912
Press-molded fired clay colored with
pigmented slip; oil finish
18½ x 12¼ in.
Ceramic Tile Institute, Los Angeles

Batchelder & Brown
Tile (redwoods), c. 1916
Press-molded fired clay colored with
pigmented slip
18¼ x 12 in.
Ceramic Tile Institute, Los Angeles
See plate 76

Batchelder & Brown
Tile (Viking ship), c. 1916
Press-molded fired clay colored with
pigmented slip; oil finish
17¼ x 17¼ in.
Ceramic Tile Institute, Los Angeles

Ernest A. Batchelder and Douglas Donaldson
Electrical Lamp, c. 1908–10
Earthenware base colored with pigment, with
opalescent glass in copper frame
21 x 23⅝ x 20⅝ in.
Jack Moore
See plate 128

Batchelder-Wilson
Tile (stylized peacock in circle), c. 1920
Press-molded fired clay colored with
pigmented slip
5¾ x 5¾ in.
The Oakland Museum; Gift of Hazel V. Bray
(71.24.8)

Batchelder-Wilson
Sample Fireplace, c. 1923
Fired clay colored with pigmented slip
20 x 29¼ x 11 in.
Jack Moore

Batchelder-Wilson
Tile (boy standing between the stone pillars
of a gate), c. 1923
Press-molded fired clay colored with
pigmented slip
11¾ x 12 in.
Gary Breitweiser

Batchelder-Wilson
Tile (trees with winding road and castle in
distance), c. 1924

Press-molded fired clay colored with pigmented slip
7⅝ x 7¹¹⁄₁₆ in.
Norman and Shannon Karlson

Batchelder-Wilson
Tile (two peacocks standing on grapevine),
c. 1925
Press-molded fired clay colored with
pigmented slip
10 x 10 in.
Stephanie Lynn and David Mills

Porter Blanchard
Cocktail Shaker, c. 1930
Silver
12⅛ x 3½ in.
The Oakland Museum; Gift of Judy and
Austin Olson and the Chevron Corporation
matching fund, Betty and Raymond Barnett,
and Marcia Chamberlain in memory of Hazel
V. Bray (91.46)

Porter Blanchard
Coffee Server, c. 1930
Silver with ebony handle
7½ x 9¼ in.
The Oakland Museum; Gift of the
Architectural Council (92.2)
See plate 135

Porter Blanchard
Four Matching Cordials, c. 1930
Silver with gilt
4³⁄₁₆ x 1¹⁵⁄₁₆ in., each
The Oakland Museum; Gift of the Art Guild
(91.41.1–4)
See plate 199

Porter Blanchard
Tea Server, c. 1930
Silver with ebony handle
4¾ x 10⅜ in.
The Oakland Museum; Gift of the Collectors
Gallery, Sandra G. and Steven Wolfe, and
Kenneth R. Trapp (92.3)
See plate 135

Harry Brawner. *See* WILLIAM TEMPLETON
JOHNSON

Digby S. Brooks
Monumental Tray, 1918–23
Hammered and patinated copper with pierced
handles
Diameter: 30¼ in.
The Mitchell Wolfson, Jr., Collection;

Courtesy of The Wolfsonian Foundation, Miami (XX1990.59)
See plate 85

Fred Brosi. *See* OLD MISSION KOPPERKRAFT, YE OLDE COPPER SHOP

A. Page Brown, designer
Alexander J. Forbes, maker
Chair, c. 1894, for the Swedenborgian Church of the New Jerusalem, San Francisco
Maple with rush seat
36½ x 20⅞ x 19¾ in.
Swedenborgian Church; Courtesy of Dr. James F. Lawrence
Oakland only
See plate 4

Elizabeth Eaton Burton
Electrical Lamp, c. 1905–10
Hammered copper and copper tubing with black abalone–shell shades
15½ x 15⅝ x 20⅝ in.
Isak Lindenauer
See plate 5

Elizabeth Eaton Burton
Electrical Lamp, c. 1910
Hammered and pierced copper, painted black
19½ x 22 in.
Tazio N. Lombardo
See plate 145

Elizabeth Eaton Burton
Hanging Electrical Lamp, c. 1910
Hammered, cut, and pierced copper, with Gumboot chiton shells and mantles, mica, and chain link
10⅞ x 25¾ in.
D. J. Puffert
See plate 144

California Art Tile Company
Tile—End of the Trail, c. 1925
Press-molded fired clay with multicolored glaze
5⅝ x 5⅝ in.
The Oakland Museum; Gift of Kenneth R. Dane (72.14)

California Art Tile Company
Tile—End of the Trail, c. 1925
Press-molded fired clay with multicolored glaze
5¹¹⁄₁₆ x 5½ in.
Norman and Shannon Karlson

California Art Tile Company
Tile (English cottage with stone bridge), c. 1925
Press-molded fired clay colored with pigmented slip
5¾ x 11½ in.
Norman and Shannon Karlson

California Art Tile Company
Tile (oak, one of a pair), c. 1925
Press-molded fired clay colored with pigmented slip
15⅝ x 3⅝ in.
Gary Breitweiser

California Art Tile Company
Tile (redwood, one of a pair), c. 1925
Press-molded fired clay colored with pigmented slip
15⅝ x 3⅝ in.
Gary Breitweiser

California China Products Company
Tile (landscape with two poplars), c. 1912
Machine-pressed fired clay with slip-trailed design and multicolored glaze
5¹⁵⁄₁₆ x 5¹⁵⁄₁₆ in.
Gary Breitweiser

California China Products Company
Four-Tile Mural (Torrey pines), c. 1913
Machine-pressed fired clay with slip-trailed design and multicolored glaze
6 x 24 in.
San Diego Historical Society; Gift of Kathleen Suros (SDH 87.63 A–D)
See plate 3

California China Products Company
Four Tiles in Square (fleur-de-lys in radiating design), c. 1914
Machine-pressed fired clay with raised-line design and multicolored glaze
11¹⁵⁄₁₆ x 11¹⁵⁄₁₆ in.
Norman and Shannon Karlson

California Clay Products Company
Tile (two peacocks standing on potted tree), c. 1925
Press-molded fired clay with multicolored glaze
5½ x 11⅜ in.
The Oakland Museum; Gift of Stephen L. Champlin (82.78.1)

California Clay Products Company
Tile (profile of Mayan with glyph), c. 1925
Press-molded fired clay with glaze

3⅜ x 11½ in.
The Oakland Museum; Gift of Stephen L. Champlin (82.78.2)

California Faience
Roundel (mission), 1920
Slip-cast fired clay with raised-line design and multicolored glaze
Diameter: 5¼ in.
Gary Breitweiser

California Faience
Stella Loveland Towne
Tile (ship in full sail), c. 1924
Slip-cast fired clay with slip-trailed design and multicolored glaze
6 x 6 in.
The Oakland Museum; Gift of Mrs. D. W. Towne (69.34.1)

California Faience
Tile (Iznik-style radiating floral design), c. 1925
Machine-pressed fired clay with raised-line design and multicolored glaze
8 x 8 in.
Gary Breitweiser

California Faience
Tile (stylized lotus blossom), c. 1925
Machine-pressed fired clay with multicolored glaze
4½ x 6⅛ in.
Gary Breitweiser

California Faience
Pair of Covered Jars, c. 1925–30
Slip-cast earthenware with turquoise glaze
10 x 4⅞ in., each
The Oakland Museum; Timken Fund (92.6.2 a, b and 92.6.3 a, b)

California Faience
Vase, c. 1925–30
Slip-cast earthenware with dark green matte glaze
6¼ x 3⅞ in.
The Buck Collection
See plate 112

California Faience
Vase, c. 1925–30
Slip-cast earthenware with in-mold design and red and blue matte glaze
6⁷⁄₁₆ x 4 in.
Brandon Allen
See plate 113

California Faience
Vase, c. 1925–30
Earthenware with slip-trailed design and
multicolored glaze
8³⁄₁₆ x 4 in.
Stephanie Lynn and David Mills
See plate 113

California Faience and West Coast Porcelain
Manufacturers
Lemonade Set, c. 1925
Porcelain with mottled green-gray glaze
Pitcher, 6¾ x 8½ in.
Six tumblers, 4½ x 2¾ in., each
The Oakland Museum; Gift of Museum
Donors Acquisition Fund (77.173.1–6, 9)
See plate 111

California School of Arts and Crafts
Margery Wheelock, designer
Armchair, 1915
Oak rubbed with pigment
48½ x 22 x 22 in.
California College of Arts and Crafts,
Oakland

California School of Arts and Crafts
Margery Wheelock, designer and carver
Print Cabinet, 1915
Oak carved and rubbed with pigment,
hammered-copper hinges and pulls
35¼ x 39½ x 12½ in.
California College of Arts and Crafts,
Oakland
See plate 212

California School of Arts and Crafts
Margery Wheelock, designer and carver
Trestle Table, 1915
Oak carved and rubbed with pigment,
hammered-copper pulls
29 x 48½ x 30 in.
California College of Arts and Crafts,
Oakland

California School of Arts and Crafts
Margery Wheelock, designer and carver
Wall Cabinet, 1915
Oak carved and rubbed with pigment,
hammered-copper hinges
20 x 74 x 10½ in.
California College of Arts and Crafts, Oakland
See plate 212

Cathedral Oaks
Tile (close-up of redwoods), c. 1915
Hand-pressed fired clay with glaze

9³⁄₁₆ x 9⅛ in.
Carol and Barrie Coate

Cathedral Oaks
Tile (close-up of redwoods, with trail in
foreground), c. 1915
Hand-pressed fired clay with glaze
6⅜ x 6⅜ in.
Carol and Barrie Coate

Claycraft Potteries
Four Tiles in a Square (señorita playing guitar
in front of courtyard), c. 1926
Press-molded fired clay colored with
pigmented slip
17⅝ x 17¹¹⁄₁₆ in.
Gary Breitweiser
See plate 18

Claycraft Potteries
Tile (English cottage with castle in background), c. 1926
Press-molded fired clay colored with
pigmented slip
12 x 15¾ in.
The Oakland Museum; Timken Fund
(92.6.5)
See plate 56

Claycraft Potteries
Tile—Bridal Veil Falls, Yosemite, c. 1926
Press-molded fired clay colored with
pigmented slip
11⅞ x 7⅞ in.
Tile Heritage Foundation; Gift of Bart
Huffman, Healdsburg, California
See plate 62

Claycraft Potteries
Tile—El Capitan, Yosemite, c. 1926
Press-molded fired clay colored with
pigmented slip
11⅝ x 11½ in.
Tile Heritage Foundation; Gift of Bart
Huffman, Healdsburg, California
See plate 61

Claycraft Potteries
Tile—Vernal Falls, Yosemite, c. 1926
Press-molded fired clay colored with
pigmented slip
11⅞ x 7¹¹⁄₁₆ in.
Tile Heritage Foundation; Gift of Bart
Huffman, Healdsburg, California

Claycraft Potteries
Wall Sconce, c. 1926

Press-molded fired clay colored with
pigmented slip
12¾ x 9 x 3 in.
The Oakland Museum; Gift of Bob Jessup
(87.51.7)
See plate 186

Copper Shop
Dirk van Erp and Alexander J. Robertson (?)
Pair of Bookends, c. 1908–10
Hammered and cut copper
4⅝ x 6³⁄₁₆ x 4⅛ in., each
Private collection

Copper Shop (?)
Dirk van Erp
Vase, c. 1908–10
Hammered and patinated copper
15¾ x 8¾ in.
The Oakland Museum; Gift of Mr. and Mrs.
William van Erp (69.16.2)
See plate 11

Harry Dixon
Box with Hinged Lid, c. 1921–30
Hammered copper with wood lining
3¼ x 7¼ x 4¼ in.
Don Ritchie

Harry Dixon
Desk Set, c. 1921–30
Hammered, patinated, and enameled copper
Pair of bookends, 5¹¹⁄₁₆ x 5⅛ x 4½ in., each
Pen tray, 13¼ x 3¹³⁄₁₆ in.
Letter opener, 8¹⁄₁₆ x 1⁹⁄₁₆ in.
The Oakland Museum; Gift of the William F.
and Helen S. Reichell Trust (91.34.1–4)
See plate 200

Harry Dixon
Double Mailbox, c. 1921–30
Hammered copper with glass windows
17⅞ x 15⅝ x 3¾ in.
Jack Moore

Harry Dixon
Electrical Floor Lamp, c. 1921–30
Copper and iron
63¾ x 23 x 23 in.
The Oakland Museum; Gift of Dr. and Mrs.
John J. Sampson (80.40)
See plate 117

Harry Dixon
Vase, 1929
Hammered copper
6¾ x 3 x 3 in.

The Oakland Museum; Art Curators Fund (89.49)

Douglas Donaldson
Covered Chalice (also known as *Freshman Singing Cup)*, 1914
Silver, parcel gilt, champlevé enamels, opal, moonstones, turquoise, emeralds, and peridots
8⅜ x 3⁵⁄₁₆ in.
President and Fellows of Harvard College, Cambridge, Massachusetts (587.1928)
See plate 132

Douglas Donaldson
Tea Caddy, c. 1915
Silver, enamels, and carnelian
6¼ x 2⅝ in.
Cranbrook Academy of Art Museum; Gift of George G. Booth (1944.115)
See plate 133

Douglas Donaldson
Covered Bowl, 1945
Silver and carnelian
4½ x 6½ in.
Nancy Daly
See plate 134

Douglas Donaldson. *See also* ERNEST A. BATCHELDER AND DOUGLAS DONALDSON

Harold L. Doolittle
Chest, 1907
Carved and varnished oak with hammered-and-pierced-brass hinges and hammered-brass handles
22½ x 45½ x 25 in.
Mr. and Mrs. Edward Bunting
See plate 126

Louis B. Easton
Bench, 1906
Redwood
15⁹⁄₁₆ x 37¼ x 15½ in.
Barbara Curtis Horton
See plate 125

Charles Frederick Eaton
Tea Screen, c. 1901–4
Patinated repoussé tin and windowpane oyster
8 x 15½ in.
The Buck Collection
See plate 143

Charles Frederick Eaton and Robert Wilson Hyde
Wedding Album, 1903, with marriage certifi-
cate of Robb de Peyster Tytus to Grace Selley Henop, May 19, 1903
Hinged brass covers with mother-of-pearl, windowpane oyster, natural suede, and ink and paint on vellum
12¾ x 9¼ in.
The Mitchell Wolfson, Jr., Collection; Courtesy of The Wolfsonian Foundation, Miami (TD1990.194.65)
See plates 141, 142

Charles Frederick Eaton and Robert Wilson Hyde
Child's Record Book, c. 1904
Hinged covers with natural suede (oiled) overlaid with cut copper, shell, and ink and paint on vellum
13⅛ x 9¾ in.
Helen Hyde Dorra
Oakland only

Charles Frederick Eaton and Robert Wilson Hyde
Guest Book, c. 1904
Hinged covers with natural suede overlaid with cut and hammered copper, ink and paint on vellum, and paper
18¼ x 12½ in.
The Oakland Museum; Timken Fund (92.6.4)
See plate 118

Clemens Friedell
Coffee Service, c. 1910
Hammered silver with chased orange blossoms, gilt, and ivory
Coffee server, 10½ x 8 in.
Covered sugar bowl, 5½ x 6¾ in.
Creamer, 4¾ x 4 in.
June and Robert Berliner
See plate 130

Clemens Friedell
Coffee Service, c. 1910
Hammered silver, gilt, and ivory
Tray, diameter: 11¹⁄₁₆ in.
Coffee server, 6⅞ x 7³⁄₁₆ in.
Sugar bowl, 2¼ x 4⅛ in.
Creamer, 3 x 3⅝ in.
Dorothy and Richard Sherwood
See plate 131

Clemens Friedell
Plate, c. 1910
Silver with chased orange blossoms
Diameter: 11⁵⁄₁₆ in.

The Oakland Museum; Art Acquisition Fund (89.26)

Clemens Friedell
Trophy Vase, c. 1915
Presented to Anita Baldwin at the Panama-Pacific International Exposition, San Francisco, 1915
Hammered and engraved silver with chased peacock design
18 x 9 in.
Neil Lane and Bob Rehnert
See plate 129

Furniture Shop
Arthur F. Mathews and Lucia K. Mathews
Candlestick, c. 1910–15
Turned, carved, and painted maple (?)
63¾ x 10 in.
The Oakland Museum; Gift of Concours d'Antiques, Art Guild (66.196.40)

Furniture Shop
Lucia K. Mathews
Covered Jar, c. 1910–15
Carved, painted, gilded, and shellacked maple (?)
11½ x 11½ in.
The Oakland Museum; Gift of Concours d'Antiques, Art Guild (66.196.38 a, b)
See plate 93

Furniture Shop
Arthur F. Mathews and Lucia K. Mathews
Desk, c. 1910–15
Carved and painted maple (?), oak, tooled leather, and (replaced) hardware
59 x 48 x 20 in.
The Oakland Museum; Gift of Mrs. Margaret R. Kleinhans (72.15)
See plates 91, 92

Furniture Shop
Lucia K. Mathews
Folding Screen, c. 1910–15
Framed plywood panels with oil, gilding, and oil-resin glaze
72 x 80 in.
The Oakland Museum; Gift of Concours d'Antiques, Art Guild (66.196.35)
See plate 2

Furniture Shop
Arthur F. Mathews and Lucia K. Mathews
Masonic Lodge Throne Chair, 1913
Mahogany (?) veneer; roundel of carved magnolia blossoms painted and gilded; (replaced)

upholstery
56⅝ x 32¼ x 31 in.
D. J. Puffert
Oakland only

Furniture Shop
Arthur F. Mathews and Lucia K. Mathews
Sheet-Music Cabinet, c. 1915–20
Painted wood
36¼ x 29¼ x 19⅝ in.
The Oakland Museum; Gift of the estate of
Marjorie Eaton (87.24.10)
See plate 204

Furniture Shop
Arthur F. Mathews
Youth, c. 1917
Oil on canvas in carved, painted, and gilded
wood frame made by the Furniture Shop
59½ x 67¾ in., framed
The Oakland Museum; Gift of Concours
d'Antiques, Art Guild (66.196.24)
See plate 90

D'Arcy Gaw. *See* DIRK VAN ERP STUDIO

Irving Gill and Frank Mead
Chair, 1907, from the Wheeler J. Bailey
House, La Jolla
Redwood and (replaced) cowhide
38⅛ x 19⅞ x 19½ in.
Mrs. Sim Bruce Richards
See plate 179

Irving Gill and Frank Mead
Desk, 1907, from the Wheeler J. Bailey
House, La Jolla
Redwood with wrought-iron pull
28¾ x 41¼ x 27¹⁵⁄₁₆ in.
Mrs. Sim Bruce Richards
See plate 177

Louis J. Gill
Altar Chair, 1920, one of a pair, from the
Mission Hills Congregational Church, San
Diego
Mahogany veneer
53⅛ x 25⅛ x 21¾ in.
Mission Hills First Congregational
Church–United Church of Christ, San Diego
See plate 181

Gladding, McBean & Company
Tile Mural—A Child's Storybook World, 1927
Fired clay with multicolored glaze
24 x 60 in.
The Mitchell Wolfson, Jr., Collection;

Courtesy of The Wolfsonian Foundation,
Miami (84.7.108)
See plate 80

Benjamin Gordon
Theosophical Society, Point Loma
Untitled (Moonlight Landscape), c. 1910
Oil on board in carved and gilded wood
frame
25¼ x 31½ in., framed
San Diego Historical Society; Gift of Mrs.
Iverson Harris in memory of her husband
(SDH 79.17.17)
See plate 162

Grand Feu Pottery
Pair of Escargot Servers, c. 1913–16
Stoneware with brown glaze
1⁷⁄₁₆ x 5½ in., each
The Oakland Museum; Gift of Nicholas
Crevecoeur (91.17.1–2)
Oakland only

Grand Feu Pottery
Vase, c. 1913–16
Stoneware with dark green semimatte glaze
7 x 3½ in.
Stephanie Lynn and David Mills
See plate 139

Grand Feu Pottery
Vase, c. 1913–16
Stoneware with deep green gloss glaze
10 x 4⅛ in.
Gary Keith

Grand Feu Pottery
Vase, c. 1913–16
Stoneware with brown semimatte glaze
7⅜ x 2⅞ in.
The Oakland Museum; Bequest of the estate
of Helen Hathaway White (75.75.7)

Grand Feu Pottery
Vase, c. 1913–16
Stoneware with green-blue snowflake
crystalline glaze
11½ x 5 in.
Gary Keith

Grand Feu Pottery
Vase, c. 1913–16
Stoneware with copper-colored transmutation
glaze
10¾ x 4⅝ in.
Gary Keith
See plate 138

Grand Feu Pottery
Vase, c. 1913–16
Stoneware with copper-colored transmutation
glaze
6⁵⁄₁₆ x 9⅛ in.
Stephanie Lynn and David Mills
See plate 138

Grand Feu Pottery
Vase, c. 1913–16
Stoneware with brown transmutation glaze
8⅝ x 4³⁄₁₆ in.
Stephanie Lynn and David Mills
See plate 138

Charles Sumner Greene and Henry Mather
Greene
Desk, 1904, from the Adelaide M. Tichenor
House, Long Beach
Ash
50 x 31 x 16 in.
Randell L. Makinson
Oakland only
See plate 119

Charles Sumner Greene and Henry Mather
Greene
Peter Hall Manufacturing Company,
Pasadena, maker
Breakfast Table, 1907, from the Robert R.
Blacker House, Pasadena
Mahogany, ebony, and inlay of mother-of-
pearl and silver
30 x 36 x 22¼ in.
The Oakland Museum; Gift of the Women's
Board, Donors Acquisition Fund, and
Marjorie Eaton, Elizabeth Elston, and Mr.
and Mrs. Harold E. Sherman, by exchange
(87.10.9)
See plate 121

Charles Sumner Greene and Henry Mather
Greene
Peter Hall Manufacturing Company,
Pasadena, maker
Hall Armchair, 1907, from the Robert R.
Blacker House, Pasadena
Teak, oak, and (replaced) leather
40¼ x 24 x 23⅞ in.
Los Angeles County Museum of Art; Museum
Acquisition Fund (81.3.3)
See plate 120

Charles Sumner Greene and Henry Mather
Greene
Peter Hall Manufacturing Company,

Pasadena, maker
Dining-Room Sideboard, 1909, from the Charles
M. Pratt House, Nordhoff (now Ojai),
California
Walnut and ebony
36 x 64½ x 21¼ in.
High Museum of Art, Atlanta; Virginia
Carroll Crawford Collection (1986.194)
See plate 123

Charles Sumner Greene and Henry Mather
Greene
Peter Hall Manufacturing Company,
Pasadena, maker
Dining-Room Sideboard, 1909, from the
William R. Thorsen House, Berkeley
Fruitwoods, ebony, and mother-of-pearl
40 x 80 x 24 in.
The Gamble House, USC, Pasadena
See plate 124

Halcyon Art Pottery
Signed with unidentified initials of SRL
Vase, 1911
Biscuit-fired earthenware
2⅞ x 3¼ in.
The Oakland Museum; Bequest of the estate
of Helen Hathaway White (75.75.19)

Halcyon Art Pottery
Alexander W. Robertson
Covered Incense Burner, 1912
Biscuit-fired earthenware
2½ x 1¾ in.
The Oakland Museum; Bequest of the estate
of Helen Hathaway White
(75.75.17 a, b)

Halcyon Art Pottery
Alexander W. Robertson
Low Bowl, 1912
Biscuit-fired earthenware
2⅝ x 4 in.
The Oakland Museum; Bequest of the estate
of Helen Hathaway White (75.75.18)

Halcyon Art Pottery (?)
Alexander W. Robertson
Triangular Vase, 1912
Earthenware with gloss glaze and green-glazed
modeled lizard
5⅞ x 3⅜ x 3½ in.
Caroline and Gary Kent

Robert Wilson Hyde
Illumination, c. 1904
Gold leaf, ink, and paint on vellum

16¾ x 20¾ in.
Gary Breitweiser
See plate 146

Robert Wilson Hyde. *See also* CHARLES FREDERICK
EATON AND ROBERT WILSON HYDE

Linna Vogel Irelan. *See* ROBLIN ART POTTERY

Jalan
Manuel Jalanivich and Ingvardt Olsen
Vase, c. 1920–30
Earthenware with red and white crackle glaze
5⅛ x 8¼ in.
The Oakland Museum; Gift of Mr. and Mrs.
Elliott Peterson (69.43.1)
See plate 114

Jalan
Manuel Jalanivich and Ingvardt Olsen
Pair of Vases, 1938
Earthenware with yellow crackle glaze
16 x 8⅜ in., each
The Oakland Museum; Gift of Paul Evans
(69.18.1–2)

Hans Jauchen. *See* YE OLDE COPPER SHOP

J. Jessop and Sons, Jewelers
Covered Box, 1908
Presented to Rear Admiral Robley D. Evans,
commander of the Great White Fleet, by the
citizens of San Diego in 1908
Silver, olive wood, and cabochon turquoise
7½ x 7¼ x 4½ in.
The Oakland Museum; Gift of Florence
Dixon in honor of Hazel V. Bray, the Tribute
Fund, and Martha and William Steen (89.30)
(The gold brooch in the shape of a key,
encrusted with pearls and tourmalines, that
originally accompanied this piece has been
lost.)
See plate 173

William Templeton Johnson, designer
Attributed to Harry Brawner, maker
Chest, 1926–28
Carved redwood with hammered-iron hinges
and handles
22 x 52 x 24¾ in.
Connie and George Beardsley
See plate 183

William Templeton Johnson, designer
Attributed to Harry Brawner, maker
Desk, 1926–28
Carved redwood
51 x 38 x 14⅝ in.

Connie and George Beardsley
See plate 184

Marian Plummer Lester
Theosophical Society, Point Loma
Batik of Landscape with Trees, c. 1910–20
Batik dye on pongee silk
14 x 9 in.
San Diego Historical Society; Gift of the
artist (SDH 80.18.2)
See plate 165

Marian Plummer Lester
Batik of Landscape with Eucalyptus Trees,
c. 1931–40
Batik dye on silk
15 x 10½ in.
San Diego Historical Society; Gift of Jim
Stelluti (SDH 82.27.8)

Frederick H. W. Leuders
Electrical Lamp, c. 1910
Hammered, cut, and patinated copper with
windowpane oyster
26½ x 25⅝ in.
Santa Barbara Historical Society
See plate 20

Paul Lohman, decorator
Vase, c. 1915–20
Austrian-porcelain blank painted overglaze in
persimmon red and black
9¾ x 4¼ in.
San Diego Historical Society; Gift of Florence
D. Hord (SDH 87.48.1)
See plate 176

Reginald Machell, designer and carver
Theosophical Society, Point Loma
Chair (one of a pair), c. 1905–10
Carved and painted wood
37¾ x 16 x 16 in.
San Diego Historical Society; Gift of the
Theosophical Society, Pasadena
(SDH 82.37.1B)
See plate 164

Reginald Machell, designer and carver
Theosophical Society, Point Loma
Chair (one of a pair), c. 1905–10
Carved and painted wood
37 x 17½ x 17¼ in.
San Diego Historical Society; Gift of the
Theosophical Society, Pasadena
(SDH 82.37.2B)
See plate 164

Reginald Machell, designer and carver
Theosophical Society, Point Loma
Folding Screen, c. 1905–10
Carved and painted wood
78¼ x 81⅛ in.
Archives, Theosophical Society Library, Pasadena
See plate 157

Reginald Machell, designer and carver
Theosophical Society, Point Loma
Katherine Tingley's Throne Chair, c. 1905–10
Carved and painted wood
52½ x 29½ x 25 in.
Archives, Theosophical Society Library, Pasadena
See plate 164

Malibu Potteries
Pair of Interlocking Faux-Mosaic Tiles, c. 1926–28
Press-molded fired clay with multicolored glaze
6½ x 6½ in., each
Jim and Linda Jaffe

Malibu Potteries
Tile (padre), c. 1926–28
Fired clay with blue glaze inlaid design
11½ x 11½ in.
Jim and Linda Jaffe

Malibu Potteries
Tile (profile of Mayan chieftain), c. 1926–28
Press-molded fired clay with glaze
5¾ x 7¾ in.
Jim and Linda Jaffe

Malibu Potteries
Tile (seated Mayan death figure with crossed legs), c. 1926–28
Press-molded fired clay with glaze
12 x 12 in.
Jim and Linda Jaffe

Malibu Potteries
Tile (floral design with red blossoms), c. 1927–29
Fired clay with dry-line arabesque design and multicolored glaze
5$\frac{13}{16}$ x 5$\frac{13}{16}$ in.
Jim and Linda Jaffe

Malibu Potteries
Tile (four-pointed geometric star), 1929
Press-molded fired clay with multicolored glaze
5⅞ x 5⅞ in.
Jim and Linda Jaffe

Markham Pottery
Vase, c. 1913–21
Earthenware with pigmented dull finish
5⅛ x 3¼ in.
Stephanie Lynn and David Mills
See plate 172

Markham Pottery
Vase, c. 1913–21
Earthenware with pigmented dull finish
6¾ x 5⅜ in.
Stephanie Lynn and David Mills
See plate 172

Markham Pottery
Vase, c. 1913–21
Earthenware with pigmented dull finish
9⅞ x 9 in.
Stephanie Lynn and David Mills
See plate 172

Markham Pottery
Vase, c. 1913–21
Earthenware with dark brown glaze
5 x 3 in.
The Oakland Museum; Gift of the estate of Helen Hathaway White (75.75.20)
See plate 171

Arthur F. Mathews. *See* FURNITURE SHOP

Lucia K. Mathews
Covered Box, 1929
Painted wood and gilt
5 x 16 x 12 in.
The Oakland Museum; Gift of Concours d'Antiques, Art Guild (66.196.42c)

Lucia K. Mathews. *See also* FURNITURE SHOP

Frank Mead. *See also* IRVING GILL AND FRANK MEAD

Frank Mead and Richard S. Requa
Chest of Drawers, 1915, from the Wheeler J. Bailey "Hopi" House, La Jolla
Redwood with (replaced) leather pulls
31 x 41⅞ x 19½ in.
San Diego Historical Society; Gift of Wheeler G. North (SDH 90.31)
See plate 180

Frederick H. Meyer
Chair, 1908, from the James Adam Barr House, Stockton
Genizero wood and (replaced) upholstery of cotton, wool, and nylon
32⅜ x 19 x 19½ in.
Dr. and Mrs. James A. Barr
Oakland only

Frederick H. Meyer
Settle, 1908, from the James Adam Barr House, Stockton
Genizero wood, glass, hammered-copper fittings, and (replaced) upholstery of cotton, wool, and nylon
65$\frac{1}{16}$ x 91½ x 27 in.
The Oakland Museum; Gift of Laetitia Meyer (71.17.1)
See plate 94

Mills & Burnley
Bowl, c. 1920–30
Hammered and patinated copper
3⅜ x 9¼ in.
Don Ritchie
Oakland only

Muresque Tiles, Inc.
Three-Tile Mural (knights and ladies on horseback riding into redwood forest with castle in distance), c. 1927
Press-molded fired clay colored with pigmented slip
12⅜ x 36¾ in.
Irene and Ernest Knops
Oakland only

Muresque Tiles, Inc.
Tile (English cottages with stone bridge), c. 1927
Press-molded fired clay colored with pigmented slip
8⅛ x 12 in.
The Oakland Museum; Gift of Clyde L. Evans (71.27.1)

Muresque Tiles, Inc.
Tile (Pacific coast cypress), c. 1927
Press-molded fired clay colored with pigmented slip
16½ x 4⅛ in.
Norman and Shannon Karlson

Muresque Tiles, Inc.
Tile (Pacific coast landscape with cypress and mission in distance), c. 1927
Press-molded fired clay colored with pigmented slip
8 x 16$\frac{1}{16}$ in.
The Oakland Museum; Gift of Kenneth R. Dane (72.12)
See plate 21

Muresque Tiles, Inc.
Tile (ship in full sail), c. 1927
Press-molded fired clay colored with
pigmented slip
15¹⁵/₁₆ x 4¾ in.
Norman and Shannon Karlson

Muresque Tiles, Inc.
Two-Tile Mural (hacienda), c. 1927
Press-molded fired clay colored with pig-
mented slip
8¼ x 16⅛ in.
Frances Butler
See plate 22

Attributed to Old Mission Kopperkraft
Fred Brosi (?)
Bud Vase, c. 1922–26
Hammered copper and glass vial holder
8¼ x 4¾ x 5 in.
Private collection

Old Mission Kopperkraft
Fred Brosi (?)
Candlestick, c. 1922–26
Copper
16¼ x 6⁷/₁₆ in.
D. J. Puffert

Old Mission Kopperkraft
Fred Brosi (?)
Firestarter, c. 1922–26
Spun, hammered, and patinated copper;
dipper with wrought-iron handle and pumice
end
Kerosene container, 8½ x 8¼ in.
Dipper, 13⅜ x 2 in.
The Oakland Museum; Art Acquisition Fund
(88.71)
See plate 116

Ye Olde Copper Shop
Fred Brosi
Bowl, c. 1923–24
Spun, hammered, painted, and lacquered
copper
5⅝ x 9½ in.
The Oakland Museum; Timken Fund
(92.6.1)

Ye Olde Copper Shop
Hans Jauchen
Desk Set, c. 1923–24
Hammered and patinated copper with cast
green-pigmented eucalyptus leaf
Double inkwells and tray, 3¹/₁₆ x 16¾ x 5 in.
Letter holder, 5³/₁₆ x 6¼ x 2½ in.

Letter opener, 9¾ x 1½ in.
Blotter, 2¼ x 5⅛ x 2½ in.
The Oakland Museum; Kahn Collection
(87.45.3.1 a–e; 87.45.3.2–4)
See plate 8

Ingvardt Olsen. *See* JALAN

Attributed to Lillian Palmer Studio
Electrical Lamp, c. 1925–30
Bronze base with enamels; shade with copper
frame, mica, and Japanese stencils
22⅝ x 18¼ in.
Isak Lindenauer
Oakland only

Redlands Pottery
Wesley H. Trippett
Covered Bowl, 1902–9
Carved and burnished earthenware with green
finish
3¼ x 5¾ in.
The Oakland Museum; Art Acquisition Fund
and Gift of the American Decorative Arts
Forum of Northern California (87.53)
See plate 156

Redlands Pottery
Wesley H. Trippett
Vase, 1902–9
Carved and burnished earthenware with green
finish
6½ x 3⁷/₁₆ in.
The Buck Collection
See plate 155

Redlands Pottery
Wesley H. Trippett
Vase, 1902–9
Carved and burnished earthenware
6⅞ x 3½ in.
The Oakland Museum; Art Acquisition Fund
and Gift of D. J. Puffert (88.2)
See plate 155

Redlands Pottery
Wesley H. Trippett
Bonbon Box, c. 1905
Burnished earthenware with modeled lizard
2 x 3¼ in.
Gary Keith

Richard S. Requa. *See* FRANK MEAD AND RICHARD S.
REQUA

Frederick Hürten Rhead. *See also*
AREQUIPA POTTERY

Rhead Pottery
Lois [Loiz] Whitcomb, decorator
Low Bowl, 1913–17
Earthenware with sgraffito design and
multicolored glaze
1⅛ x 8¾ in.
The Oakland Museum; Bequest of the estate
of Helen Hathaway White (75.75.4)
See plate 148

Rhead Pottery
Frederick Hürten Rhead
Vase, 1913–17
Earthenware with mirror black glaze
12 x 9½ in.
The Oakland Museum; Bequest of the estate
of Helen Hathaway White (75.75.22)
See plate 149

Rhead Pottery
Frederick Hürten Rhead
Vase, 1913–17
Earthenware with sgraffito design and
colorless glaze
15⁵/₁₆ x 7⅜ in.
The Oakland Museum; Gift of Rod and Lynn
Holt (91.37)
See plate 150

Rhead Pottery
Frederick Hürten Rhead
Vase, 1913–17
Earthenware with sgraffito design and
multicolored glaze
7¾ x 4¼ in.
The Oakland Museum; Kahn Collection
(87.45.2)
See plate 148

Rhead Pottery
Frederick Hürten Rhead
Vase, 1913–17
Glazed earthenware
8¾ x 5¼ in.
Carolyn and John Grew-Sheridan
See plate 151

Rhead Pottery
Frederick Hürten Rhead
Vase, 1913–17
Glazed earthenware
7⅛ x 5½ in.
Nicholas Crevecoeur
Oakland only

Rhead Pottery
Frederick Hürten Rhead

Vase, 1913–17
Earthenware with incised design and inlaid multicolored glaze
$11\frac{1}{2}$ x $6\frac{1}{4}$ in.
Isak Lindenauer
See plate 152

Alexander J. Robertson. *See* COPPER SHOP

Alexander W. Robertson. *See* ALBERHILL POTTERY, HALCYON ART POTTERY, ROBLIN ART POTTERY

Robertson Pottery
Fred H. Robertson
Vase, 1913
Stoneware with green matte glaze
$6\frac{3}{16}$ x 4 in.
The Oakland Museum; Bequest of the estate of Helen Hathaway White (75.75.14)

Robertson Pottery
Fred H. Robertson
Bud Vase, c. 1913–16
Stoneware with purple matte glaze
$5\frac{1}{4}$ x $2\frac{3}{4}$ in.
Stephanie Lynn and David Mills
See plate 207

Robertson Pottery
Fred H. Robertson
Bud Vase, c. 1913–16
Stoneware with metallic crystalline glaze
$4\frac{1}{4}$ x $2\frac{5}{8}$ in.
The Oakland Museum; Bequest of the estate of Helen Hathaway White (75.75.24)
See plate 137

Robertson Pottery
Fred H. Robertson
Electrical Lamp, c. 1913–16
Stoneware with crystalline glaze and leaded-glass inserts
$17\frac{1}{4}$ x $12\frac{3}{16}$ in.
The Oakland Museum; Gift of the William F. and Helen S. Reichell Trust and the Collectors Gallery (91.36 a, b)
See plate 213

Robertson Pottery
Fred H. Robertson
Low Bowl, c. 1913–16
Stoneware with metallic crystalline glaze
$3\frac{3}{16}$ x $5\frac{9}{16}$ in.
Stephanie Lynn and David Mills

Robertson Pottery
Fred H. Robertson
Vase, c. 1913–16
Stoneware with green crystalline glaze
$7\frac{5}{8}$ x $5\frac{3}{4}$ in.
David Reneric
See plate 136

Robertson Pottery
Fred H. Robertson
Vase, c. 1913–16
Stoneware with green crystalline glaze
$4\frac{1}{2}$ x $4\frac{5}{8}$ in.
The Oakland Museum; Bequest of the estate of Helen Hathaway White (75.75.23)

Robertson Pottery
Fred H. Robertson
Vase, c. 1913–16
Stoneware with purple crystalline glaze
$7\frac{9}{16}$ x $4\frac{5}{16}$ in.
Gary Keith
See plate 207

Robertson Pottery
Fred H. Robertson
Vase, c. 1913–16
Stoneware with purple-green matte glaze
$5\frac{7}{16}$ x $3\frac{1}{4}$ in.
Gary Keith
See plate 207

Robertson Pottery
Fred H. Robertson
Vase, c. 1913–16
Stoneware with brown metallic crystalline glaze
$6\frac{5}{16}$ x $3\frac{3}{8}$ in.
Caroline and Gary Kent
See plate 137

Robertson Pottery
Fred H. Robertson
Vase, c. 1913–16
Stoneware with brown metallic crystalline glaze
6 x $2\frac{1}{2}$ in.
Stephanie Lynn and David Mills
See plate 137

Roblin Art Pottery
Linna Vogel Irelan, decorator
Vase, 1898
Red earthenware painted with blossoms in white slip
$3\frac{5}{8}$ x 3 in.
The Oakland Museum; Bequest of the estate of Helen Hathaway White (75.75.25)
See plate 87

Roblin Art Pottery
Alexander W. Robertson
Miniature Vase, 1898–1906
Earthenware with semimatte black glaze
$3\frac{7}{16}$ x $2\frac{5}{16}$ in.
Caroline and Gary Kent

Roblin Art Pottery
Alexander W. Robertson
Miniature Vase, 1898–1906
Earthenware with semimatte black glaze
$2\frac{5}{16}$ x $1\frac{5}{8}$ in.
Private collection
Oakland only

Roblin Art Pottery
Alexander W. Robertson (?)
Miniature Vase, 1898–1906
Earthenware with semimatte black glaze
$2\frac{5}{8}$ x $1\frac{1}{2}$ in.
Private collection
Oakland only

Roblin Art Pottery
Alexander W. Robertson
Miniature Vase, 1898–1906
Biscuit-fired earthenware with charcoal matte finish
$3\frac{1}{4}$ x $2\frac{1}{4}$ in.
Private collection
Oakland only

Roblin Art Pottery
Alexander W. Robertson (?)
Vase, 1898–1906
Earthenware with speckled green-brown glaze
$3\frac{5}{8}$ x $3\frac{1}{2}$ in.
Stephanie Lynn and David Mills
See plate 88

Roblin Art Pottery
Alexander W. Robertson (?)
Vase, 1898–1906
Orange-colored earthenware with colorless glaze
$4\frac{11}{16}$ x $3\frac{1}{16}$ in.
Stephanie Lynn and David Mills
See plate 88

Roblin Art Pottery
Vase, c. 1900
Biscuit-fired orange-colored earthenware
$3\frac{9}{16}$ x $2\frac{1}{2}$ in.
The Oakland Museum; Gift of Paul Evans (75.74.3)
See plate 87

Roblin Art Pottery
Alexander W. Robertson
Vase, c. 1900–1906
Earthenware with green semimatte glaze
5⅞ x 3³⁄₁₆ in.
Caroline and Gary Kent

Roblin Art Pottery
Alexander W. Robertson (?)
Vase, 1905
Earthenware with multicolored glaze
3 x 2¾ in.
Private collection

Roblin Art Pottery
Alexander W. Robertson
Vase, 1905
Earthenware with mottled olive-brown glaze
2¹³⁄₁₆ x 4⅞ in.
The Oakland Museum; Bequest of the estate
of Helen Hathaway White (75.75.27)
See plate 88

Roblin Art Pottery
Alexander W. Robertson
Vase, 1905–6
White earthenware with carved leaf design
4⁵⁄₁₆ x 4¹⁄₁₆ in.
Stephanie Lynn and David Mills

Roblin Art Pottery
Alexander W. Robertson
Footed Vase, 1906
Biscuit-fired buff earthenware with carved feet
3¼ x 4¼ in.
The Oakland Museum; Bequest of the estate
of Helen Hathaway White (75.75.26)
See plate 87

Roblin Art Pottery
Linna Vogel Irelan, decorator
Vase, 1906
Biscuit-fired buff earthenware with modeled
lizard
3⅛ x 3½ in.
Caroline and Gary Kent
See plate 87

Roblin Art Pottery
Alexander W. Robertson
Vase, 1906
Earthenware with mottled deep brown and
green glaze
3⅜ x 3⅞ in.
The Oakland Museum; Gift of Paul Evans
(75.74.5)
See plate 88

Shreve & Co.
Pair of Compotes, c. 1895–1900
Silver with chased chrysanthemums
5 x 12⁵⁄₁₆ in., each
The Oakland Museum; Gift of the Collectors
Gallery (92.8.1–2)
Oakland only

Shreve & Co.
Eight Spoons, c. 1900
Silver
7 x 1⅞ in., each (approximately)
The Oakland Museum; Gift of the Collectors
Gallery (92.9.2.1–8)

Shreve & Co.
Coffee Server, c. 1900–1910
18-karat-gold-plated brass and ivory
7 x 8⅜ in.
The Oakland Museum; Gift of the Women's
Board (92.1)
See plate 95

Shreve & Co.
Compote, c. 1900–1905
Japanese Satsuma earthenware bowl mounted
on silver stem with pierced foot
6⁵⁄₁₆ x 4⅞ in.
The Oakland Museum; Gift of Judy and
Austin Olson and the Chevron Corporation
matching fund (88.54)
See plate 97

Shreve & Co.
Water Kettle on Stand, c. 1900–1910
Hammered silver and ivory
10 x 7½ in.
The Norwest Corporation, Minneapolis
See plate 96

Shreve & Co.
Carving Platter, 1905
Silver
2⅜ x 22¼ x 16³⁄₁₆ in.
The Oakland Museum; Gift of the Collectors
Gallery (92.9.1)

Attributed to Shreve & Co.
Plate, c. 1910
Silver with chased nasturtium leaves
Diameter: 11¼ in.
Nicholas Crevecoeur
Oakland only

Shreve & Co.
Smoking Set, c. 1910
Hammered copper with silver trim and

attached projectile points
Tray, 15 x 12¼ in.
The Oakland Museum; Gift in memory of
Karl E. Schevill (88.3)
Pipe tray, 6⁹⁄₁₆ x 3³⁄₁₆ in.
Ashtray and matchholder, 2¹¹⁄₁₆ x 5⅝ in.
Don Ritchie
See plate 7

Shreve & Co.
Bowl and Pair of Candlesticks, 1917
Silver with chased nasturtium leaves
Bowl, 4½ x 13¾ in.
Candlesticks, 13½ x 5½ in., each
Lyn Clark
Oakland only

Solon & Schemmel
Tile (stylized floral design), 1920
Hand-pressed fired clay with raised-line design
and multicolored glaze
6 x 5⅞ in.
Gary Breitweiser

Solon & Schemmel
Four Tiles in a Square (radiating geometric
design), c. 1925
Machine-pressed fired clay with multicolored
glaze
11¾ x 11¾ in.
The Oakland Museum; Art Acquisition Fund
(89.27.1–4)
See plate 208

Stockton Art Pottery
Pitcher, 1896–1902
Earthenware painted with underglaze slip
12½ x 5½ in.
The Oakland Museum; Gift of Mr. and Mrs.
Kenneth R. Dane (80.47)
See plate 86

Stockton Art Pottery
Pitcher, 1896–1902
Earthenware painted with underglaze slip
7 x 5½ in.
The Oakland Museum; Gift of Mr. and Mrs.
Kenneth R. Dane (70.65.1)
See plate 86

Stockton Art Pottery
Three-Handled Cup, 1896–1902
Earthenware painted with underglaze slip
4½ x 3¾ in.
The Oakland Museum; Bequest of the estate
of Helen Hathaway White (75.75.11)
See plate 86

August Tiesselinck
Pair of Torchères, c. 1926
Copper with alabaster shades
60½ x 9⅝ in., each
Isak Lindenauer
Oakland only
See plate 211

Stella Loveland Towne. *See* CALIFORNIA FAIENCE

Wesley H. Trippett. *See* REDLANDS POTTERY

Anna Valentien
Bowl, c. 1910–20
Hammered and etched copper
2 x 9¼ in.
San Diego Historical Society; Gift of Mavina
McFeron (SDH 80.45.12)

Anna Valentien
Pair of Bookends, c. 1910–20
Etched copper
6½ x 3¼ x 3 in., each
San Diego Historical Society; Gift of Mavina
McFeron (SDH 80.45.10 A–B)

Anna Valentien
Tray, c. 1910–20
Etched copper
Diameter: 11⅜ in.
San Diego Historical Society; Gift of Mavina
McFeron (SDH 80.45.15)

Anna Valentien
Wall Mirror with Sconces, c. 1910–20
Patinated copper with cutout overlay design
and mirror
18 x 10 x 3 in.
San Diego Historical Society; Gift of Mavina
McFeron (SDH 80.45.19)
See plate 175

Valentien Pottery Company
Albert Valentien, decorator
Vase, 1911–13
Earthenware with low-relief interlace design;
dull finish
10 x 4¼ in.
San Diego Historical Society; Purchase from
the Mrs. William A. Edwards Curatorial
Fund (SDH 91.19)
See plate 170

Valentien Pottery Company
Albert Valentien, decorator
Vase, 1911–13
Earthenware slip-painted with red tulips; dull
finish

12 x 5³⁄₁₆ in.
William Stout

Valentien Pottery Company
Albert Valentien, decorator
Vase, 1911–13
Earthenware slip-painted with golden poppies;
dull finish
15 x 5⅜ in.
Kim and John Maeder

Valentien Pottery Company
Albert Valentien, decorator
Vase, 1911–13
Earthenware slip-painted with yellow tulips;
dull finish
10⅞ x 7½ in.
Brandon Allen and Al Nobel

Valentien Pottery Company
Anna Valentien, decorator
Vase, 1911–13
Earthenware with three modeled figures; dull
finish
16¾ x 16½ in.
Mr. and Mrs. Albert A. Jaussaud
See plate 169

Valentien Pottery Company
Vase, 1911–13
Slip-cast earthenware with relief decoration
and brown matte glaze
8¼ x 3 in.
The Oakland Museum; Gift of the estate of
Helen Hathaway White (75.75.6)

Valentien Pottery Company
Vase, 1911–13
Slip-cast earthenware with relief decoration
and green matte glaze
8⅞ x 3⅜ in.
Brandon Allen

Valentien Pottery Company
Vase, 1911–13
Slip-cast earthenware with relief decoration
and green glaze
9 x 3½ in.
The Oakland Museum; Gift of Josephine and
Elmer Morse (91.41)

Dirk van Erp
Vase, c. 1900–1906
Hammered and patinated brass shell casing
8 x 3¹⁵⁄₁₆ in.
Private collection

Dirk van Erp. *See also* COPPER SHOP

Dirk van Erp Studio
Dirk van Erp and D'Arcy Gaw, designer
Electrical Lamp, 1910
Hammered and patinated copper with mica
27³⁄₁₆ x 26¹⁄₁₆ in.
Roger and Jean Moss
See plate 101

Dirk van Erp Studio
Dirk van Erp and D'Arcy Gaw, designer
Kerosene Lamp, 1911
Hammered and patinated copper with mica
and glass chimney
21½ x 22⅝ in.
Roger and Jean Moss

Dirk van Erp Studio
Dirk van Erp and D'Arcy Gaw, designer
Monumental Jardiniere, 1910
Hammered copper patinated deep red
10½ x 16¾ in.
Don Ritchie
See plate 12

Dirk van Erp Studio
Dirk van Erp
Jardiniere, c. 1910–25
Hammered copper patinated deep red
5¾ x 7 in.
Roger and Jean Moss
See plate 103

Dirk van Erp Studio
Dirk van Erp
Pair of Bookends, c. 1910–25
Hammered and pierced copper
5⅛ x 6⅛ x 4⅛ in., each
Isak Lindenauer

Dirk van Erp Studio
Dirk van Erp
Pair of Electrical Wall Lamps, c. 1910–25
Hammered copper with frosted-glass shades
11 x 5 x 7⁹⁄₁₆ in.; 11 x 5 x 8¼ in.
David Reneric
See plate 100

Dirk van Erp Studio
Dirk van Erp
Vase, c. 1910–25
Hammered copper patinated deep red
11⅞ x 7¾ in.
Roger and Jean Moss
See plate 103

Dirk van Erp Studio
Dirk van Erp

Vase, c. 1910–25
Hammered copper patinated deep red
10⅞ x 7³⁄₁₆ in.
Roger and Jean Moss
See plate 103

Dirk van Erp Studio
William van Erp (?)
Covered Bowl, c. 1930–40
Hammered and pierced silver with ivory
4⅞ x 5⅛ in.
The Van Erp Family
See plate 210

Dirk van Erp Studio
Charles Anderson
Lidded Box, 1932
Hammered and patinated copper with wood

lining
2⅝ x 6⅛ x 5⅜ in.
Eleanor Anderson
Oakland only

Walrich Pottery
Roundel (mission), c. 1925
Slip-cast porcelain with yellow, green, and
blue glaze
Diameter: 6⁹⁄₁₆ in.
Norman and Shannon Karlson

Walrich Pottery
Tile (oak with sunset), c. 1925
Slip-cast porcelain with yellow and green
glaze
5⁷⁄₁₆ x 5⅜ in.
Norman and Shannon Karlson

Walrich Pottery
Covered Bowl, c. 1925–30
Slip-cast earthenware with relief decoration
and lavender matte glaze
4¾ x 6 in.
The Oakland Museum; Gift of the Collectors
Gallery (66.30.3)
See plate 115

Margery Wheelock. *See* CALIFORNIA SCHOOL OF
ARTS AND CRAFTS

Lois Whitcomb. *See* RHEAD POTTERY

INDEX

321

Photography Credits

The photographers and the sources of photographs other than those indicated in the captions are as follows. Courtesy Atascadero Historical Museum, Atascadero, California: plates 54, 55; Benjamin Blackwell: plate 9; Jim Blades: plate 188; John Blaisdell: plate 35; courtesy Leslie Greene Bowman: plate 147; courtesy Marilyn J. Brown and Anthony P. Brown: plates 105, 197, 198; courtesy Lynn Daniels and Simon Miles: plate 127; courtesy Florence Dixon: plate 203; M. Lee Fatherree Photography, Oakland: plates 1–8, 11, 12, 14, 18, 20–22, 34, 56, 61, 62, 73, 76, 86–95, 97, 100, 101, 103, 104, 106–9, 111–18, 121, 125, 126, 128, 129, 131, 134–39, 141–46, 148–52, 154–57, 162, 164, 165, 169–73, 175–77, 179–81, 183, 184, 186, 194, 196, 199, 200, 202, 204–8, 210–13; courtesy Gamble House, USC, Pasadena: plate 17 (Marvin Rand), 26 (Leroy Hulbert); courtesy David Gebhard: plate 195; courtesy Huntington Library, Art Collection, and Botanical Gardens, San Marino, California: plates 31, 58, 63, 65; Tim McAfee/City Light Studio, Inc.: plates 80, 85; Michael McKelvey: plate 123; courtesy Malibu Lagoon Museum, Malibu, California: plate 81; courtesy Mission Inn Foundation, Riverside, California: plates 50, 51; Gary Mortensen: plate 96; courtesy Oakland Museum: plates 77, 99, 102, 110, 153, 201, 209; Steven Oliver: plate 122; courtesy D. J. Puffert: plate 60; Stephen Rahn: plate 130; Marvin Rand: plates 119, 124; Cleota Reed: plates 72, 74; courtesy Riverside Municipal Museum, Riverside, California: plate 52; courtesy Saint Louis Art Museum: plate 84; courtesy San Diego Historical Society: plates 25, 27, 45, 47, 158–61, 163, 166–68, 174, 178, 182, 185, 189; courtesy San Francisco Public Library: plate 98; courtesy Dorothy Shepard: plate 190; courtesy A. K. Smiley Public Library, Redlands, California: plates 48, 49, 53; Joseph A. Taylor: plates 82, 83; courtesy Tile Heritage Foundation, Healdsburg, California: plates 69, 70, 75, 79; courtesy University of California, Santa Barbara: plates 23, 36, 38, 40–42, 120, 191–93; Karen J. Weitze: plate 37.